Also by Bill Sloan

GIVEN UP FOR DEAD: AMERICA'S HEROIC
STAND AT WAKE ISLAND

JFK: BREAKING THE SILENCE

JFK: THE LAST DISSENTING WITNESS

ELVIS, HANK, AND ME: MAKING MUSICAL HISTORY
ON THE LOUISIANA HAYRIDE (WITH HORACE LOGAN)

THE OTHER ASSASSIN (FICTION)

THE MAFIA CANDIDATE (FICTION)

Brotherhood of Heroes

THE MARINES AT PELELIU, 1944—
THE BLOODIEST BATTLE
OF THE PACIFIC WAR

Bill Sloan

SIMON & SCHUSTER

NEW YORK   LONDON   TORONTO   SYDNEY

SIMON & SCHUSTER
Rockefeller Center
1230 Avenue of the Americas
New York, NY 10020

Copyright © 2005 by Bill Sloan
All rights reserved, including the right of reproduction
in whole or in part in any form.

SIMON & SCHUSTER and colophon
are registered trademarks of Simon & Schuster, Inc.

For information about special discounts for bulk purchases,
please contact Simon & Schuster Special Sales:
1-800-456-6798 or business@simonandschuster.com

Designed by Jeanette Olender
Maps designed by Jeffrey L. Ward
Insert designed by Leslie Phillips
Manufactured in the United States of America

1   3   5   7   9   10   8   6   4   2

Library of Congress Cataloging-in-Publication Data
Sloan, Bill.
Brotherhood of heroes : the Marines at Peleliu, 1944 :
the bloodiest battle of the Pacific War / Bill Sloan.
p. cm.
Includes bibliographical references and index.
1. Peleliu, Battle of, Palau, 1944. 2. United States.
Marine Corps—History—World War, 1939–1945. I. Title.
D767.99.P4S66 2005   940.54'266—dc22   2004065316
ISBN 0-7432-6009-0

Photographs used in the picture insert were supplied as follows: 1, 7, courtesy Fred Miller; 2, courtesy Marlyn Jones; 3, courtesy Sterling Mace; 4, courtesy Charles Womack; 5, 6, 8–11, 18–20, 25, National Museum of the Pacific War; 12, 13a, courtesy Fred Fox; 13b, 14, photos by Lana Sloan; 15, courtesy Ray Stramel; 16, 26, Marine Corps Historical Center; 17, courtesy Arthur Jackson; 21, courtesy William J. Leyden; 22, courtesy R. V. Burgin; 23, 24, courtesy Vincent Santos; 27–30, courtesy Jim McEnery

To all the "invisible" heroes

still among us

CONTENTS

PROLOGUE

His heart pounding in his throat, Private First Class William J. Leyden raised his head above the side of the amphibious tractor and got his first glimpse of the beach ahead. It was anything but reassuring.

Enemy mortar shells and high-explosive artillery rounds were blasting the shoreline as far as Leyden could see in both directions, sending up huge water spouts in the surf. Further inland, the big guns of Navy ships, firing since dawn from several miles out to sea, raised towering clouds of coral and rock, fire and smoke, as they hammered at Japanese targets still invisible behind walls of flame. Carrier-based Hellcat fighter planes roared low over the beach, their wing guns spitting .50-caliber tracers at enemy pillboxes and gun pits.

All of it was dead ahead and alarmingly close now—only a couple of minutes away, Leyden figured. He shuddered and tried to steady himself on rubbery knees, feeling as if the jaws of hell were opening to swallow the amphibious tractor and everyone in it.

Leyden was in the first wave of Marines about to storm ashore on an obscure speck of an island called Peleliu 600 miles west of Mindanao in the Philippines. Until a few days ago, he and his comrades had never heard of the place, but the brass said it had to be taken to protect the flank of Army General Douglas MacArthur's forces when MacArthur made good on his promise to liberate the Philippines from two and a half years of brutal Japanese occupation.

Leyden was supposed to be the first of a dozen men to exit the right side of the amtrack while another dozen went out the left side. But the skinny rifleman-scout from New York was only eighteen, untested in combat, and jittery as hell. The thought of leaving the protective confines of the tractor and exposing himself to hostile fire for the first time filled him with anticipation and dread. This was the moment he'd been training for, and anticipating with a mixture of excitement and forboding, ever since he'd joined the Marines on his seventeenth birthday. Still, he couldn't shake the thought that maybe he didn't have what it took to get through the next few minutes.

Would he live up to his own—and his buddies'—high expectations, or would he freeze up? Even worse, would he turn and run?

Leyden squeezed his eyes shut and called on his faith for strength. He pictured his devout Irish Catholic mother saying a novena for him at this very moment.

Hail Mary, full of grace, the Lord is with thee . . .

Opening his eyes, Leyden found Corporal Leonard Ahner, his friend and fire team leader, staring at him from inches away. Ahner, a lanky Hoosier from Huntington, Indiana, had been through the landing at New Britain the year before, so he had a good idea of what to expect.

"You scared, Bill?" Ahner asked. There was no condemnation in the veteran's question.

"Nah, I'm okay," Leyden said, fighting the butterflies in his stomach. He could hardly hear his own voice for the explosive roar around him.

"Well, if you ain't scared, you're the only guy here who ain't," Ahner said with a crooked grin. "I'll go out first if you want me to."

Leyden shook his head. "No, I'm ready. I'm okay."

He glanced at the faces of his squad mates lined up behind him, a grim-visaged cross section of young America: PFC Marion Vermeer from Washington state, PFC Roy Baumann from Upper Wisconsin, PFC Ray Rottinghaus from Iowa, Corporal Ted Barrow from Texas. Leyden couldn't imagine a greater disgrace than letting these guys down. He'd rather die than let somebody else do his job for him. Yet he knew that Ahner was right—that every man around him was gripped by the same conflicting feelings. Each was lost in his own thoughts, imagining the best and worst of himself and what the Japanese would throw at them. Each knew what was expected of him. Each wanted to do his job, but nobody wanted to die doing it.

Just relax, a voice in his head whispered. *Hell, this probably isn't even the most dangerous thing you've ever done.*

Actually, that was true. The craziest, riskiest, most foolhardy thing he'd ever done was when he was twelve years old, and he and his best friend, Donald Muñoz, had decided to take a ride across Brooklyn on top of a subway car. They'd been okay in the first three tunnels, where the clearance between the roof of the coach and the tunnel was about a foot and a half. But in the fourth tunnel, they'd come to a place where the clearance was much less—no more than eight or nine inches. Donald had been killed instantly, and Leyden himself had spent weeks in the hospital with a fractured skull.

That was something he'd never, ever wanted to think about, and usually he'd been able to keep it firmly locked away in the back of his mind. But now, with the panoramic hell of Orange Beach 2 spread out ahead of him, the memory of the horror in the subway tunnel was somehow reassuring. Almost comforting.

If I could live through that, he thought, *I can live through anything.*

A few dozen yards behind Leyden, the amtrack carrying Corporal R. V. Burgin's mortar squad was coming under increasingly heavy fire. But the nervous tension that had kept Burgin awake much of the night was gone now, replaced by a feeling of calm fatalism. His worries about the trip to shore had eased the moment he'd noticed the sign with the big "13" posted on the side of his amtrack.

Lots of people might have interpreted the number as a bad omen, but it was a kind of good-luck charm as far as Burgin was concerned. The wiry young Texan had celebrated his twentieth birthday just over a month ago on August 13. His father had been born on May 13, and two of his brothers had birthdays on November 13. He considered the number lucky enough that he'd even chosen to join the Marines on November 13, and so far, everything had worked out pretty well. He'd seen men die all around him on New Britain, but up to now he'd come through without a scratch. He took his favorite number on the amtrack as a sign that his good luck was still holding.

Burgin and his squad were still several hundred yards from the beach, and the naval shelling from behind them had dwindled to almost nothing. For a few moments, there was an eerie, almost total silence broken only by the low rumble of the amtrack's engine and the water lapping against its hull.

Then enemy shells began to burst along the beach and in the waves ahead. Seconds later, Burgin felt the tractor bump the reef and stall, twisting helplessly as the driver tried to wrench it free. A few yards away, a Japanese mortar shell slammed into the water. Then another. And another.

On the opposite side of the amtrack, Burgin saw Platoon Sergeant John Marmet grabbing at his .45 and screaming at the driver: "Get this damned thing moving, or I'll kill your ass!"

The driver did his best to comply, gunning the engine hard as the tractor's treads clawed at the reef. Ever so slowly, the treads caught and the amtrack eased forward. Just as it did, a 75-millimeter enemy shell exploded thirty yards dead ahead.

Burgin's throat felt powder-dry. If the driver hadn't gotten the amtrack hung up on the reef, he realized, the shell could easily have landed right in his lap.

He closed his eyes and thanked God for good old lucky 13.

The flamethrower and its twin fuel tanks on Corporal Charles "Red" Womack's back felt more like 700 pounds than just seventy. The tanks were brim-full of napalm and diesel, and each time the amtrack carrying Womack's weapons section topped a wave, he could feel the weight crushing down against his neck and shoulders.

It would be worse when he hit the beach in three or four minutes and had to haul his weapon through the surf and sand to find cover.

It was a good thing that his high school football coach had made him spend lots of time working out with weights and blocking sleds, Womack thought. He hadn't enjoyed those workouts at the time, but they'd made him one of the best defensive tackles in the state of Mississippi at 180 pounds. They'd helped make him a damn good flamethrower operator, too.

In his last battle at Cape Gloucester on New Britain, Womack had manned a .30-caliber machine gun similar to the one his father had fired in France in 1918. But for reasons he still didn't fully understand, he'd volunteered as a gunner in a new flamethrower section after the Cape. It wasn't a very good job, Womack admitted, but he was strong enough to handle it as well as any of the other five gunners assigned to the Third Battalion of the Fifth Marine Regiment. He was a little uneasy because he'd never used his new weapon in combat.

Just think about it like it was a football game, he told himself. *You'll do all right.*

He glanced over at his best buddies, PFCs John W. Louder and Don "Chick" Meyer. Somber-faced, jaws tight, they stared straight ahead, but Womack drew comfort from the sight. The three of them had stood on the deck of their LST early that morning, watching the Navy shells streaking overhead and kidding each other nervously. Like most of the other guys in the outfit, Louder and Meyer both called Womack "Red" because of his carrot-colored hair and beard.

"Hey, Red," Meyer had joked. "When we get ashore, don't forget you're supposed to barbecue those Nips, not tackle 'em."

With only a minute or so to go until the amtrack clattered onto the beach, Womack groped in the pocket of his dungaree shirt and took one last look at the photo of Hilda Hughes, the girl he'd married back in McComb, Mississippi, a few weeks before he shipped out for overseas.

For several seconds, Womack stared intently at the smiling face in the picture, then slipped it hurriedly back into his pocket. He closed his eyes and saw a neat house with a tree-shaded yard, where Hilda was planting flowers and children were laughing and playing. It was an imaginary scene, not yet real, but if he lived through the next few minutes, maybe it would be someday.

Then the amtrack bumped the shore as enemy machine gun and small-arms rounds rattled off its gunwales. The rear exit ramp dropped open. It was time to go.

It was a battle the First Marine Division was expected to win in seventy-two hours or less. Instead, the battle for Peleliu would stretch into thirty days of continuous, no-quarter combat against enemy defenders burrowed into more than 600 fortified caves, bunkers, and pillboxes on a tiny chunk of coral and limestone half a world away from home. It would be among the bloodiest, most costly battles the Marines ever fought, before or since.

Survivors recall the struggle for Peleliu as the toughest, most savage fight of the Pacific war, yet the vast majority of twenty-first-century Americans have never heard of it. As an added irony, many post–World War II military historians have described the battle as strategically pointless—one they maintain should never have happened. Even while Marines were dying there, it became clear that Peleliu posed no offensive threat to MacArthur's Philippine invasion and could easily have been bypassed by U.S. forces. Because of this, Peleliu not only ranks as the least-known major battle of World War II but is often dismissed as unnecessary. Yet the hard lessons learned there helped prepare the Marines for larger battles to follow, especially on Okinawa.

Less than a third of the way through the Peleliu fight, one of the First Marine Division's three infantry regiments was cut to pieces and forced out of action with nearly six out of every ten men in its ranks either killed or wounded. Before the issue was finally settled, almost half the enlisted men and officers in the other two regiments became casualties as well.

This is the story of what happened to these Marines during thirty terrible days from September 15 to October 15, 1944, as they faced an insidious new kind of defensive warfare in some of the most excruciating conditions ever endured by American fighting men.

Much of the following narrative focuses on the hour-by-hour struggles of a dozen or so courageous young individuals, but it also captures the broader story of 16,000 Marines—all members of an incredible brotherhood.

CHAPTER ONE

OLD BREED, NEW BLOOD

The saga of the Americans who endured the agony of Peleliu—and eventually prevailed—began long before the first landing craft reached shore on the island. Its origins can be traced to the trenches of World War I and beyond. They lead through Guantánamo, Cuba, and a string of Caribbean islands, where Marines of the 1930s learned the art of amphibious warfare at a time when nobody else cared. They spread from Guadalcanal, where the United States first took the offensive against Japan, to New Britain, where the offensive continued, to Australia, where tens of thousands of teenage boys were transformed into Marines.

They extend to a hated island called Pavuvu, where shared miseries and hardships forged a bond between recruits and veterans that even Peleliu couldn't break. It could kill and maim them by the thousands—and it did. But it never dented the spirit of mutual devotion that welded them together.

When a gangly country boy named R. V. Burgin left home in November 1942 to enlist in the Marine Corps, his main concern was volunteering before an impending date with the draft. He was sworn in a couple of days later in San Antonio, not knowing that he was about to become an apprentice in a mystical military fraternity dating to Revolutionary War times. Among the inner circle of veterans who had paid their dues in blood, sweat, and misery in its ranks, it was known simply as the "Old Breed." Before any newcomer could claim full membership, he had to prove himself worthy of its standards and traditions.

Burgin had never heard of the Old Breed. Few outsiders had.

At the time, thousands of young men were volunteering each month for service in the Corps, and in many ways Burgin typified the kind of recruit the Marines were looking for.

He was strong and lean, toughened by eighteen years of life on a hardscrabble southeast Texas farm, where his family grew almost everything it ate, and Burgin and his six brothers and sisters helped wrest a living from the earth. He'd excelled in competitive sports in high school, learned to shoot rabbits and squirrels by the time he was ten years old, and was endowed with enough confidence to think he could hold his own with any man.

"But when it came to hard work and tough goin'," Burgin recalled, "I hadn't seen nothin' till I landed in the First Marine Division."

Nothing came easy, and there were no free rides during a recruit's initiation to the Old Breed, Burgin learned. But once you achieved full membership, it would be yours for life.

Ever since its creation in 1941 as the first division-size unit in the history of the Corps, the First Marine Division has, rather than the Corps itself, been synonymous with the Old Breed. Yet the sobriquet itself is much older than the division, and the concept underlying it dates back nearly 230 years, to the first man who ever called himself a Marine. According to legend, that happened at a tavern in Philadelphia in November 1775, shortly after the Continental Congress authorized the raising of two battalions of Marines to serve as a landing force with the fledgling American fleet.

When this first Marine recruit reported for duty aboard a ship in the Philadelphia naval yard, the story continues, the officer of the deck didn't know what to do with him, so he sent the Marine aft until he could find out. A few minutes later, a second Marine showed up and was also sent aft, where he received this disparaging greeting from the first Marine: "Listen boy, you should've been in the *old* Corps!"

Since then, the Marines have fought in every war in American his-

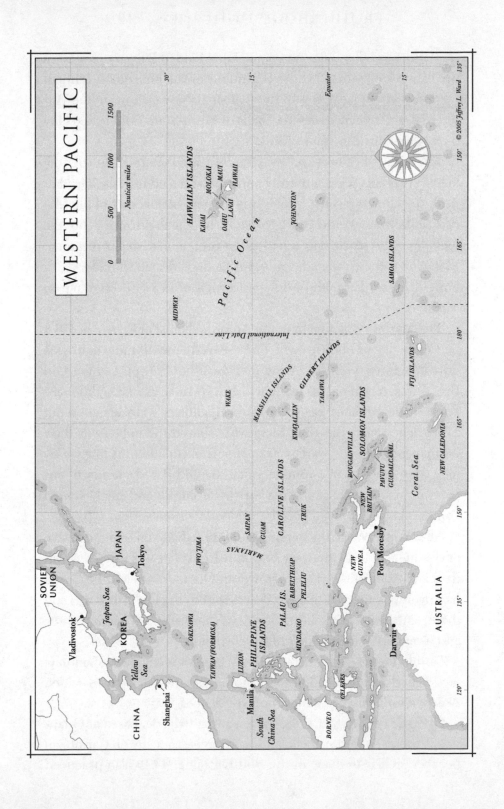

tory and more than a few nonwars. They battled Barbary pirates on the "shores of Tripoli" at the beginning of the nineteenth century, helped Andrew Jackson rout the British at New Orleans in the War of 1812, and marched into the "halls of Montezuma" in Mexico City during the Mexican War of 1848.

The term "Leatherneck" was coined around 1800 to identify members of this select fraternity and can be traced to a black leather neck stock, or stiff collar, which was then an official part of the Marine uniform. By World War I, the stock had been discarded, but the nickname had stuck, and it had taken on a much deeper meaning. Men who earned it were described as having "drilled shoulders . . . a bone-deep sunburn, and a tolerant scorn of nearly everything on earth."

The Marines who fought in the Argonne Forest of France in 1918 had no divisions of their own. They served in small units that were fully integrated with U.S. Army divisions, but the spirit of the Old Breed was very much in evidence. In an American Expeditionary Force made up almost entirely of citizen-soldiers, Marines stood out as hardened professional fighters who viewed the military as their permanent home and warfare as their sole occupation. As thirty-year men were replaced by young recruits, the Old Breed's legacy of uncompromising cynicism, fierce esprit de corps, and finely honed combat skills perpetuated itself.

After World War I, the nation's military fell into an ominous cycle of decline. By 1933, the year Franklin Roosevelt was elected president and Adolf Hitler came to power in Germany, the Marine Corps had dwindled to fewer than 20,000 men. But the Old Breed was still there, embedded in the heart of a newly formed Fleet Marine Force and its tactical unit, the First Marine Brigade.

During the rest of the 1930s, the Marines quietly developed new tactics and techniques in amphibious warfare—an area in which America's military had almost no experience.

Over the next six years, the First Marine Brigade, based at Quantico, Virginia, staged six fleet landing exercises, mostly on Caribbean beaches similar to those in the South Pacific. They also practiced amphibious assaults in the heat and dust of Guantánamo, Cuba, where they took to calling themselves the "Raggedy-Ass Marines." The Corps' only other brigade at the time, the San Diego–based Second, was known as the "Hollywood Marines" because it sometimes loaned personnel to the big movie studios.

Among the innovations perfected by the "Raggedy Asses" were the amphibious tractor and the Higgins landing boat. Both would become mainstays of the island-hopping campaign that formed the basis of U.S. Pacific strategy in World War II. When their training was complete, they would be rated by their Corps as the best amphibious fighters in the world.

On February 1, 1941, when the First Marine Division was officially formed, with Major General Philip Torrey as its first commanding officer, the First Brigade served as its nucleus. Fittingly, the brigade was aboard ship at the time, bound for its seventh—and largest—fleet landing exercise on the Caribbean island of Culebra. At its birth, the unit was a division on paper only, with less than half its authorized manpower, but it grew quickly in weeks to come, nourished by the call-up the previous fall of all organized Marine reserves across the country.

The new division became the modern embodiment of the Old Breed, and, like R. V. Burgin, many other young men across the nation were drawn to test their mettle in its ranks. One of them was Bill Leyden, who got into so many scrapes as a teenager on Long Island that his parents gladly signed for him to become a Marine on the day he turned seventeen. For Leyden, it was the fulfillment of a long-standing dream.

"The happiest day of my life was May 27, 1943, when I was sworn into the Marine Corps," he said. "The second happiest day of my life was when I was assigned to the First Marine Division. The veterans gave recruits like me a fish-eyed stare at first, but I had the feeling the men and officers I was serving with were the best anywhere. I wanted to prove myself to them more than I'd ever wanted anything in my life."

Leyden started proving himself in boot camp. He was the

youngest guy in his platoon, but he was among just five out of a class of eighty recruits who qualified as expert marksmen on the rifle range.

"I'm proud of you, Leyden," his drill instructor told him. "I won't call you 'Gertrude' anymore."

Eugene B. Sledge, a young Alabaman who arrived in the South Pacific in 1944 with the same replacement battalion as Leyden, had similar feelings about the division. As Sledge later wrote: "If I had had an option—and there was none, of course—as to which of the five Marine divisions I served with, it would have been the First Marine Division."

To Sledge, his new outfit was unique among the six Marine divisions that would fight with distinction in the Pacific between 1942 and 1945. It possessed a heritage, he said, that forged "a link through time" with his forebears in the Corps.

Such is the stuff of which the Old Breed's legends are made. They stretch from the halls of Montezuma to the jungles of Vietnam and the deserts of Iraq. But in all the annals of the U.S. Marine Corps, the Old Breed never fought a costlier, more vicious battle than the one that began in the late summer of 1944 on a little-known Pacific island named Peleliu.

Burgin, Leyden, and Sledge, along with 16,000 of their buddies, witnessed that battle at close range. More than 6,500 Marines left their blood there.

Three infantry regiments formed the cornerstone of the First Marine Division at the time of its creation: the First Marines, the Fifth Marines, and the Seventh Marines. (These designations are often confusing to outsiders, but within the Corps, regiments are routinely referred to simply as "Marines." Divisions, however, are identified by their full, official names: First Marine Division, Second Marine Division, and so on. In keeping with this practice, regiments within the First Marine Division are identified throughout this book as "First Marines," "Fifth Marines," "Seventh Marines," and so on.)

The Fifth Marines was the division's first regiment to become functional, and most men from the old First Brigade were initially assigned there. Soon, however, the Fifth was split in half to form the Seventh Marines. Then the First Marines was organized out of segments of both the Fifth and Seventh.

By the time the division returned from the Caribbean in May 1941, it had outgrown its base at Quantico, and half its men had to be quartered at Parris Island, South Carolina. Within a few days, all were hustled aboard ship again and reunited at New River, North Carolina, where the Corps had just purchased more than 111,000 acres of land, water, and swamp, and where the brick buildings of Camp Lejeune would soon rise.

At the moment, the area was only an insect-infested wilderness, and the new home of the First Marine Division was a crude tent city, much of which the men had to build themselves. Here, on a barren stretch of sand dunes called Onslow Beach, they would undergo their most intense amphibious assault training yet in the stifling heat of that last prewar summer.

The grueling practice landings of those two months were designed to prepare the division for the First Joint Training Force Exercise, the largest amphibious training operation ever held in the United States. The exercise kicked off on August 11, 1941, with forty-two naval vessels, four squadrons of Marine aircraft, and 16,000 men taking part. Phases of the operation included an assault landing, establishment of a beachhead, hauling 2,200 tons of supplies ashore, advancing inland for about nine miles, and, finally, a three-day simulated forced withdrawal.

On August 7, 1942—just four days less than a year later—the men of the First Marine Division would land on another beach and seize another beachhead. This time, though, it was no training exercise. This time, it would take every skill and tactic mastered during all those months in the Caribbean and North Carolina—plus a lot of new ones learned under extreme duress—to sustain them.

The beach was halfway around the world on an enemy stronghold in the heart of Japan's Pacific empire. It was eight months to the day after Pearl Harbor when the Old Breed landed there to launch the first offensive action by American ground forces in the Pacific.

The name of the place was Guadalcanal.

The Japanese defended Guadalcanal with vastly superior numbers and fanatical determination. Although the Marines slaughtered them in droves, the outcome of the battle remained in doubt for weeks while the enemy sent in daily waves of reinforcements and relentlessly attacked U.S. ships and aircraft supporting the invasion.

"One thing I can say about war is that it separates the men from the boys," wrote twenty-five-year-old Second Lieutenant Andrew A. Haldane in a letter to Adam Walsh, his old football coach at Bowdoin College in faraway Maine. "I've got examples of it in my platoon."

A native of Lawrence, Massachusetts, who had been a star fullback and captain on Bowdoin's state championship team of 1940, Haldane signed his letters "Andy," and many of them still had a youthful tone about them. But as his Marines would soon learn, there was no better example of a boy turning into a man—and a natural leader—than Haldane himself.

"I'd like to tell you just what is happening, but I can't," Haldane wrote. "I can tell you that the Marines are still holding their own in the Solomons regardless of what Japanese propagandists say." He mentioned nothing to Walsh about an incident a few days earlier on Guadalcanal, one that would lead to a quick promotion to first lieutenant for Haldane and earn him lasting respect and admiration from men in the ranks.

In the South Pacific, almost every commissioned officer in the Marine Corps was given a nickname as a matter of brutal necessity: If the enemy overheard an officer addressed by his rank or as "sir," he instantly became a higher priority target. But there was a larger reason for the nickname bestowed on Andy Haldane by the men who served with him.

Haldane's platoon had been laying wire from the beach to forward positions a few hundred yards inland when Japanese snipers opened up from the trees above. It was hard to tell how many there were.

"Hit the deck!" Haldane yelled, throwing himself to the ground. He scrambled behind a clump of undergrowth with several other Marines as rifle bullets smacked the sand inches away.

"Where the hell are the sons of bitches?" panted one of the men beside him. "I can't see a thing."

"Everybody just stay down and keep still," Haldane said. He studied the canopy of trees overhead for any flicker of movement, but he didn't see anything either. He noticed that the PFC next to him was carrying a Browning automatic rifle. There was one designated BAR man in every four-man fire team.

Haldane nudged the guy. "Let me borrow your weapon for a minute," he whispered.

Haldane rolled onto his back, propped the BAR firmly against his shoulder, and fired a series of long bursts into the trees, spraying rounds into as many of them as he could reach. When he stopped firing, there was total silence for a moment. Then a body plummeted down from one of the trees and hit the ground with a dull thud. It was followed by another. Then another.

The men stood up warily, staring at the three dead Japanese, then at their lieutenant.

Haldane calmly handed the BAR back to its owner. "Okay, guys, vacation's over," he said. "Let's get back to work."

A few feet away, a crusty sergeant laughed as he picked up a roll of wire. "Way to go, Ack-Ack," he said. From that day on, Lieutenant Andrew Allison Haldane was affectionately referred to as Ack-Ack by every Marine in his command.

When the division was finally relieved on Guadalcanal in mid-November 1942, after three and a half months of fighting, its 16,000 men had faced a total of more than 40,000 Japanese, and three-fourths of the enemy troops had died there.

Marine battle casualties, by contrast, were almost incredibly light—621 killed and 1,517 wounded. It was disease, not combat, that left the division unfit for action well before it was finally evacuated. More than 5,600 division personnel were hospitalized with malaria—Ack-Ack Haldane among them—and scores of others were felled by dysentery, heat exhaustion, and battle fatigue.

Guadalcanal was one of the most highly celebrated and widely publicized victories of the war—and rightly so. It marked the first time that U.S. forces had expelled Japanese troops from enemy-held territory, effectively ending the threat of a Japanese invasion of Australia, and inflicting damage to Japan's mighty military machine from which it never recovered. Enemy losses in ships, planes, and other vital matériel, as well as in men, left Japan permanently weakened.

The Japanese navy limped away from Guadalcanal on November 15, 1942, after an all-out attempt to regain control of the island failed, and it would never again pose a serious offensive threat to U.S. operations in the Pacific. Final victory was still nearly three years away, but the resounding nature of the Japanese defeat moved Vice Admiral William F. "Bull" Halsey to exult: "We've got the bastards licked."

Guadalcanal was an important morale booster, both to the folks at home and to the Marines themselves. The Old Breed had taken the best punches the Japanese could throw and still came out on top. It was undeniably one of the turning points of the war, and no battle was harder fought by the Marines. Yet the First Marine Division's losses at Guadalcanal represented only a small fraction of the carnage to come at Peleliu.

Brooklyn-born Sergeant Jim McEnery of Company K, Third Battalion, Fifth Marines (K/3/5), who fought in both battles and earned his three stripes at Guadalcanal, witnessed a sharp contrast between the enemy's tactics in the two battles.

"At Guadalcanal, the Japs thought they could wear us down by running at our lines with bayonets, but they changed the way they fought at Peleliu, and it led to the dirtiest kind of constant combat," said McEnery. "When the Japs pulled one of their so-called banzai charges, we'd just sit there and mow 'em down. That was how the

First Marines killed about a thousand Japs and only lost twenty-five of their own men at the Tenaru River on Guadalcanal. On Peleliu, the Japs hid in caves and made us come and get 'em. We were always in their gun sights, and their only goal was to kill as many of us as they could."

With victory secure at Guadalcanal, the men of the First Marine Division turned the island over to the Army and Navy and went back to Camp Balcomb near Melbourne, Australia, where they'd been stationed for several months before hitting the 'Canal. Fresh replacements were waiting there to fill the gaps in their ranks, and the veterans got a chance to rest up and get well. There was time to enjoy some liberties, meet girls, have fun, and relax. In the opinion of many of the Marines stationed at Balcomb, there was no better place to do these things than Melbourne.

When PFC R. V. Burgin arrived in Melbourne in late March 1943, the bustling city of about a million people was one of the most beautiful places he'd ever seen. Like most other new replacements, Burgin was only about three months out of boot camp in San Diego, and he still had plenty of work to do to become a full-fledged member of the Old Breed. But that didn't keep him from exploring the wonders of Melbourne to the fullest—and finding a steady girlfriend there.

"The people of Melbourne treated us like royalty," Burgin recalled. "They knew the American victory at Guadalcanal had eliminated the threat of a Japanese invasion, and they called the guys who fought there 'the Saviors of Australia.' Basically, the Aussies and Americans just liked each other, anyway."

Burgin and his best buddy, PFC Jimmy Burke, had met aboard the luxury-liner-turned-troopship USS *Mount Vernon* as they crossed the Pacific in March 1943 with the Ninth Replacement Battalion, and they almost always pulled weekend liberties together. Sometimes, they'd hop a "cattle car" bus for the trip to the city. Other times, they'd catch a train and ride the forty miles past neat farms and quiet suburbs to crowded Flinder Street Station in the heart of downtown Melbourne. Across the street was Young & Jackson's Pub, a famed local watering hole, where they often made their first stop.

Burke, a gregarious Irishman from the Mississippi River town of Clinton, Iowa, could drink more beer than any man Burgin had ever known. "There were lots of pubs in Melbourne, and sometimes Jimmy would stay in one of them constantly from the time it opened until it closed in the evening," Burgin recalled. "But I never once saw him act drunk. His brother owned a bar back in the States, and I guess he was just used to drinking lots of beer."

Another friend and frequenter of the pubs was PFC Merriel Shelton, an excitable, small-statured youngster from south Louisiana who had arrived with the same group of replacements as Burgin and Burke. Shelton was a whiz at poker, but otherwise his primary talents involved getting confused, lost, in trouble, and generally fouled up. He would argue about anything at the slightest opportunity, and when he was agitated or inebriated, all these tendencies grew more pronounced. They were also magnified by Shelton's inability to speak understandable English at such times.

"How much money you got?" someone asked one day as the cattle car bounced along toward Melbourne.

Shelton laboriously counted his Australian currency for several minutes, then announced: "I t'ink I got maybe aroun' two pounds and ten ounces—plenty much for some drinks an' poker, eh?"

"You know what you are, Shelton?" Burgin said. "You're just one big snafu lookin' for a place to happen."

Everybody laughed, and the nickname stuck. Nobody in his mortar section ever called Merriel Shelton by his first name again. He was Snafu from that moment on.

Burgin himself usually left the pubs behind after the first pint or two and went in search of other diversions. As a civilian, the longest trip he'd ever taken from his hometown of Jewett, Texas, population

600, was to Houston or Dallas, and his family vacations usually consisted of loading up a farm wagon when the crops were in and riding ten miles to the Navasota River for a few days of trotline fishing. Now he was eager to see the sights of the biggest, most sophisticated city he'd ever been in. Melbourne had miles of glistening beaches, seaside amusement parks, boat rides on the river, horse-drawn carriages available for hire, big department stores and fancy restaurants, movie houses and soda fountains, tennis courts and golf courses, and scores of parks and flower gardens.

During the weeks at Camp Balcomb, everything Burgin saw constantly reminded him that he was in the midst of the biggest war in history, but in Melbourne he found a comforting sense of peace and normalcy. To him and other homesick young Americans, it was what one chaplain described as a "symbolic civilian environment" that endeared the city to the Marines like none other in the Pacific.

In the course of his wanderings, Burgin met a girl named Florence Riseley at an ice cream parlor. He asked her out on a double date with Jimmy Burke and Florence's friend, Doris, and almost immediately, he sensed something special about her. After that, he spent less and less time with Jimmy in the pubs, where women usually weren't allowed, and more and more time on long walks with Florence.

The idyll lasted for about four months. Then, suddenly, it was ending. In the late spring of 1943, word came that the division would soon ship out, first to New Guinea, some 2,800 miles due north of Melbourne, then to someplace else. As yet, nobody knew where the "someplace else" was.

By this time, Burgin and Florence were unofficially engaged, and saying goodbye to her was the most difficult task he'd ever faced. Harder than leaving home. Harder than boot camp. Harder than anything.

"I'll be back," he told her firmly on their last evening together. "No matter what happens, I'll be back."

For as long as he could remember, Burgin had always been tough-minded, physically strong, and thoroughly at home with any type of work. As a kid, he'd picked cotton for thirty cents per 100 pounds and gathered wild berries to sell in town for a dime a gallon to pay for his school clothes. As a 140-pound defensive end and blocking back on his high school football team, he'd earned enough respect from his teammates to be elected captain his senior year.

After being assigned to a mortar squad, Burgin had learned to set up his 60-millimeter gun faster than anybody else in the section—a feat that got him promoted to PFC the very next week. He was the kind of guy who followed his own instincts but was also a good team player. He had a low tolerance for bullshit, and he made no secret of it. He also exuded Texas bravado, and he didn't care who knew that, either.

On that final evening in Melbourne, though, he could only wish that he felt half as confident as he sounded.

In July 1943, the reinforced, rejuvenated First Marine Division shipped out for New Guinea and more training. On the day after Christmas of that year, they landed on the western coast of New Britain, a small island across a narrow strait from eastern New Guinea, in what has been called the most nearly perfect amphibious assault operation of the war. To the Old Breed veterans, however, such landings had become routine by now: Another island. Another beach. Another bunch of fanatical Japanese. But climate-wise, New Britain was worse than the others. It was so wet that men's socks rotted in their boots, and their dungarees fell apart in a matter of weeks.

Once the division got ashore, its mission was to seize and hold an enemy airfield at Cape Gloucester, but the Japanese had other ideas. One night in early January 1944, R. V. Burgin, Jimmy Burke, Snafu Shelton, and the other men of Company K, Third Battalion, Fifth Marines, fought off no fewer than five frenzied banzai charges in the space of a single hour. The recently appointed company commander of K/3/5 was now-Captain Ack-Ack Haldane, who was in the thick of the hand-to-hand struggle. Haldane won a Silver Star for leading the fight that night, but he credited the tenacity and courage of the dozens of undecorated enlisted men who fought beside him for the victory. He never forgot what they'd done to save their own lives—and his.

Among them was Fred Miller, a youngster with a shock of blond hair and an infectious grin who was one of the company's newest replacements. Miller was admittedly obsessed by a "hero complex" when he'd dropped out of Christian Brothers High School in St. Joseph, Missouri, after his sophomore year to join the Marines in June 1942. But after boot camp, he found himself assigned to cooks and bakers school, and a rule that new recruits be sent to the specialty school with the greatest need of manpower at the time left him no way out of it. "I was really ticked off," Miller recalled. "What I craved most was front-line action and lots of medals and parades. I didn't want to be no damn cook."

After completing the school, Miller worked in the mess hall at Camp Elliott near San Diego for a couple of months. Then he landed a spot in a replacement battalion headed for duty with the First Marine Division in the Pacific. When he reached Australia in the spring of 1943, he was assigned to the headquarters platoon of Haldane's K/3/5.

Miller felt as if he'd been reborn. He knew there were no cooks in an infantry company in combat because the only food available was canned rations, and he hoped to wangle his way into a rifle squad. With Haldane's support, that's exactly what he did at Cape Gloucester on New Britain.

As a cook with no cooking to do, Miller served as a runner for Haldane, and his high proficiency ratings and eagerness to please quickly caught the CO's attention. Miller had made corporal in November 1942 before leaving the States, and on July 1, 1943, he became one of the youngest buck sergeants in the First Marine Division. He wasn't quite eighteen years old.

Soon after the landing on New Britain, Miller further endeared himself to his captain. When Haldane asked him to do a routine check of an ostensibly abandoned enemy bunker that the CO wanted to use as a command post, Miller found three Japanese huddled together in the bunker. He killed all three with a single burst of fire from his M-1. But as he stepped around the bodies, a booby trap exploded, and a half-dozen bits of shrapnel hit Miller in the nose, lip, and leg. He was quickly patched up at an aid station and rejoined his platoon.

On December 30, 1943, the day the Marines took control of the airfield at Cape Gloucester, the captain summoned the teenage sergeant to his command post.

"You're too good a fighter to spend this war in a mess hall," Haldane said. "I'm picking twelve men from headquarters platoon to form a new rifle section. How'd you like to be a squad leader in that section?"

Miller grinned from ear to ear. "That'd be great, sir."

A short time later, Miller was crouching just to Haldane's right when the Japanese hurled their post-midnight bayonet charges against K Company's lines, catching the Marines in a vulnerable position on the side of a hill. It was a little after one o'clock in the morning.

The enemy soldiers crept to within a few yards of the Marine positions, then rushed screaming out of the darkness with fixed bayonets. K Company's veterans had faced the same tactics again and again on Guadalcanal, and they were ready. Some of the replacements were stunned and scared, but they also met the attack head-on with M-1s, BARs, carbines, pistols, Ka-Bar knives, and whatever else they could lay hands on.

Miller emptied the clip of his rifle, then used its butt as a club, feeling the impact as he slammed one Japanese in the head and smashed him to the ground. As he turned to swing at another, he heard Haldane blazing away with his .45 just to Miller's left.

Then a second enemy soldier was on him, and Miller dropped the rifle and grappled hand-to-hand with his attacker's shadowy form, grunting, cursing, and trying to avoid the bayonet he knew was there. He felt no sensation of pain at first when the blade ripped across his right wrist and jabbed into his left hand, but then he saw the blood and realized it was his own. He pulled free and rolled away from the bayonet as another Marine shot the attacker at point-blank range.

When the last of the charges was repelled, Miller went back to the aid station to get his wounds stitched up. Grateful to be alive, he knew the terror of the previous night was something he'd never forget. In one sense, maybe it was just another night's work, but it forged a lasting bond between Haldane and the men who served under him. "It was a hell of a scrap," Haldane wrote to a friend a few days later, "but again we came out on top."

Once Cape Gloucester was securely in American hands, Miller hitched a ride one night aboard a Navy PT boat on a raid against the Japanese base at Rabaul about a hundred miles away. It was a dangerous lark, and it earned Miller a rare chewing-out when his captain found out about it.

Haldane was known for never raising his voice to an enlisted man, but he left no doubt that he was seriously peeved. "I'd like to see you get home alive, son," he said, "but if you have to die, I'd rather you do it right here with K Company and not the Navy. In the future, just stay away from PT boats, okay?"

Miller nodded and stared at the ground.

"And by the way, when's the last time you wrote your mother?"

Miller frowned. "I'm, uh, not sure, sir. Maybe three, four weeks ago."

"Well, you make certain you write her at least once a week from now on. And no excuses, Sergeant. Understood?"

Miller never went on another Navy raid. He never forgot the promise he made that day, either. His mother was pleasantly surprised at how many more letters she received from that point on.

In late April 1944, Army troops arrived on New Britain to relieve the First Marine Division. By the middle of the first week in May, the last of the battle-weary Marines had loaded up their gear, boarded ships, and sailed for an unknown destination.

Scuttlebutt had been rampant for several weeks that the division was going back to Melbourne. Supposedly, this information came from the lips of Major General William H. Rupertus, the division commander, himself. Virtually to a man, the troops were excited to hear it, especially those like now-Corporal R. V. Burgin, who had a special person waiting there.

It wasn't to be, however. The military powers who controlled their fate had a far less desirable destination picked out for the Marines.

CHAPTER TWO

A REST CAMP FROM HELL

Several dozen men lounged topside aboard the troopship, their voices rising in raspy unison above the sound of Lieutenant "Hillbilly" Jones's guitar:

"Waltzing Matilda, waltzing Matilda . . . You'll come a-waltzing Matilda with me . . ."

The old Australian folk tune had become the First Marine Division's unofficial theme song during its two long stays at Camp Balcomb outside Melbourne. Now, with word circulating that the division was headed back to the land down under, the men's spirits were higher than they'd been in months.

The weather was warm and pleasant as the ship steamed southwest through calm seas. The stifling heat, unyielding wetness, and fierce fighting of New Britain were now just bad memories that could almost be erased by a few weekends in Melbourne. As yet, there was no official confirmation that the division was Australia-bound, but if the rumors were true, they were a cause for celebration, even for men with feet and armpits infected by jungle rot or bowels wracked with diarrhea.

A pair of Texans, Corporal R. V. Burgin and PFC George Sarrett, were among the singers and kibitzers on deck as Jones struck a final chord and the strains of "Waltzing Matilda" faded away.

"Hey, Hillbilly," somebody yelled, "How about a little 'San Antonio Rose'?"

Burgin and Sarrett grinned. The hit tune by Bob Wills and his Texas Playboys was one of their favorites. It always brought a chorus of appreciative "Awww-hawww's!" from the guys from Texas. Jones

27

smiled as he lightly brushed the guitar strings, and the music swelled up again on the sea breeze.

"Deep within my heart lies a mel-o-dy . . ."

First Lieutenant Edward A. Jones had just turned twenty-seven years old, but he was already a legendary figure among the men who served with him. He could pick out a song on his guitar after hearing it just once or twice, and his willingness to share his talent made him vastly popular with ordinary troops. But there was more to Jones than a gifted ear for music and an engaging grin. Next to Captain Haldane, the company CO, Hillbilly was probably the best liked and most respected officer in K/3/5. He was easy to talk to, easy to trust, and a damned good listener.

Jones was fond of recalling boyhood weekends on his grandfather's farm near his birthplace of Whiteford, Maryland, a stone's throw from the Pennsylvania border. His neighbors had known him as a popular, polite, fun-loving youngster who sang in the choir at Whiteford's small Methodist church and whose rich tenor earned him occasional paid singing engagements in the area. When his father was disabled in the early 1930s, Ed, as the eldest son in a family of ten children, took on the role of "second daddy" to his younger brothers and sisters. He'd joined the Civilian Conservation Corps fresh out of high school and sent most of his salary home to keep food on the family's table during the depths of the Depression.

Every veteran in the outfit knew that Hillbilly had enlisted in the Corps as a private in 1936 and served five years as a seagoing Marine before the war. His bravery under fire at Guadalcanal, where he singlehandedly wiped out a Japanese machine gun nest, had earned him a Bronze Star and a set of lieutenant's bars. He reportedly turned down the commission the first time it was offered, however, because it was in the reserves, not the regular Marines. Now he was in charge of the company's machine gun section, but he still had the soul of a wandering minstrel. His idea of a good time was to drift among the men's tents singing, strumming his guitar, and welcoming anybody who wanted to join in.

"He didn't have what you'd call a really great voice," Burgin recalled, "but it was a soothing, pleasant voice—and, man, he could make that guitar talk!"

Jones, Burgin, Sarrett, and other participants in the sing-along on the deck of the troopship that mellow afternoon in May 1944 would soon realize that their celebration was premature. There would be no return to Australia.

When the announcement came a short time later, bitter disappointment settled over the men aboard all the transports. At first, some clung to a faint hope that the news was wrong and they'd end up back at Balcomb after all. But the last flicker of hope died when the ships dropped anchor in Macquitti Bay and the men stared out at Pavuvu, a desolate chunk of mud, coral, swamp, and jungle in the Russell Islands about sixty miles west of Guadalcanal.

Pavuvu had made a highly favorable impression on a group of Army staff officers who flew over it while searching for a rest camp site. From the air, it seemed a pleasant, picturesque place with a gentle surf, pristine white beaches, a graceful shoreline, and neatly spaced groves of coconut palms.

In reality, it was far from the tropical paradise it appeared to be from an altitude of several hundred feet. If the officers had bothered to set foot on the island—much less seen the armies of land crabs that marched over it, smelled the thick mat of rotted coconuts that covered much of it, or watched their boots disappear into the gooey muck that lurked just below its surface—they would've known better.

Ironically, however, Pavuvu's unlovely surroundings and harsh conditions were to have a strangely positive impact on the men sent there in the spring of 1943. Today, aging veterans of the First Marine Division still talk about Pavuvu in much the same way they talk about the actual battles they fought in the Pacific. In certain respects, Pavuvu *was* more like a battle than a rest camp, and it endowed those who came through it with an intangible asset that few recognized until later.

"As the months passed, something wonderful happened to the division on Pavuvu," said PFC Bill Leyden, who reached the island as a new recruit fresh from the States. "It happened without us knowing it, and I'm sure it was never anticipated, even in the upper command echelons."

The very wretchedness of Pavuvu created a peculiar, positive chemistry between the battle-hardened veterans and raw recruits who came there. Men who arrived on the island with little in common found unity in its misery. They drew strength and purpose from its adversities. Almost imperceptibly, they came to share a spirit of kinship that helped fuse the First Marine Division into one of the finest fighting forces in modern military history.

The interlude on Pavuvu was a pivotal time for the division. What happened during those four months would affect every Marine who fought at Peleliu.

After New Britain, high-ranking Marine brass had pressed for a new R&R area away from Guadalcanal, which had developed by this time into one of the largest rear-area U.S. military complexes in the Pacific. Because it bustled with so much constant activity, exhausted Marines were likely to encounter more work than recuperation there. When the Third Marine Division had been sent to the 'Canal following its Bougainville campaign, it was ordered to provide 1,000 men each day for work parties. This not only kept the veterans from getting rest but also denied the replacements adequate time to train for the division's next landing at Guam.

In the spring of 1944, the First Marine Division was in no condition for this kind of daily grind. It had lost 1,347 killed and wounded on New Britain, a casualty rate that was actually lower than originally anticipated. But the division had left Cape Gloucester with thousands more men who were too sick with malaria, dysentery, and jungle rot, or too weak from malnutrition to do much more than drag themselves along. The last thing they needed was long, arduous days on work details. Besides, there was concern among the brass that returning to Guadalcanal, where so many veterans had lost buddies in 1942, could be a demoralizing experience.

There was another reason for seeking out a new locale more conducive to rest and recuperation. Top military planners wanted a site much nearer than Melbourne to the First Marine Division's next objective—already penciled in as Peleliu, although no one in the division knew it yet. Melbourne was an extra 1,000 miles or more away, and at this point in the war, there was no shortage of convenient Allied-held Pacific islands to choose from.

Pavuvu was well located from a strategic and logistical standpoint. Its proximity to Guadalcanal, where the division's baptism of fire had taken place almost two years earlier, undoubtedly figured in its selection. Beyond that, the choice of Pavuvu was based almost entirely on the false face it presented to the search committee that flew over it.

Officers of the Second Marine Raider Battalion, the only American unit that had spent any time on the island, could surely have warned the brass about Pavuvu's myriad pitfalls. Major General Roy S. Geiger, commander of the III Marine Amphibious Corps, made the final decision without bothering to consult anyone who had actually been there.

Even to the Marines who would quickly come to despise it, Pavuvu had a deceptively attractive appearance at first glance. "It looked like a paradise from the ship we were on," said PFC Joe Dariano, a rifleman in K Company, Third Battalion, First Marines (K/3/1). "The palm trees were swaying in the breeze, and the lagoon was beautiful. Then we went ashore and discovered what it was really like."

Pavuvu is the largest of the Russell Islands, a string of small dots of land that runs along the southeastern edge of the Solomon group. It measures about ten miles from east to west and about six miles from north to south. In its interior, a cone-shaped hill rises to around 1,500 feet, but beyond the beach, just about everything else is dense jungle or impassable swamp. Until the battle-weary veterans of the

First Marine Division arrived there in early May 1944, and the green recruits of the Forty-sixth Replacement Battalion followed about a month later, nothing of any great note had ever happened on Pavuvu.

The Raiders had landed there in the spring of 1943 and searched the island for Japanese. They found only a few score natives, who had worked as copra harvesters until their British employers fled at the beginning of the war. Now, a year later, the only structures on the island were several empty copra sheds, a couple of vacant plantation houses, and the rusty remnants of barbed wire beach defenses left by the Raiders. Except for General Rupertus and his staff, nobody in the division had ever heard of the place until the loudspeakers aboard their transports told the Marines to get ready to disembark on Pavuvu.

Expecting to find at least a crude preliminary camp site when they landed, the men from New Britain were sorely disappointed. By the time the division reached Pavuvu, roads were supposed to be in, water wells drilled, a dock constructed, and "most other difficulties" eliminated, according to General Geiger, and a full battalion of Seabees would be ready to assist the Marines "in every way possible."

In reality, only a handful of Seabees were on the island when the Marine veterans arrived. No roads had been built, no drill or bivouac areas prepared, no buildings or tents erected. There was no electricity and no fresh water until wells could be dug. The Seabees were awaiting rotation back to the States and in no mood to bust their butts in the meantime. The Marines would have to build every facet of their rest camp themselves—from scratch.

From the palm groves on the island rose the overpowering smell of unharvested coconuts left to ruin. They formed a stinking mat of decay covering hundreds of acres to depths of up to several feet. One of the Marines' jobs that started earliest and lasted longest was cleaning up this decomposing mess.

Then there was the sea of mud and quicksand that lay just beneath a thin crust of solid soil. By the time the ground was traversed a few times by hundreds of human feet and scores of pieces of equipment, the crust had become an oozy, knee-deep morass. Inhabited areas had to be paved foot by foot with crushed coral before men or machines could move without bogging down. It took countless man-hours to move coral from pits scattered around the island, in containers ranging from dump trucks to helmets, to create a reliable surface.

Tens of thousands of land crabs and hordes of hungry rats ran rampant over the island every night. The crabs scuttled into the tents and hid in every available nook and cranny. They particularly enjoyed making themselves at home in men's boots. Meanwhile, the rats screeched, darted across the faces of sleeping Marines, and tried to eat anything that got in their path.

It seemed fitting that a steady rain was falling as the division's veterans tromped ashore to claim their new home. The rainy season was supposed to be over on Pavuvu by this time, but the elements had failed to get the word.

"We'd been told that rainfall in the Russell Islands averaged six feet, three inches per year," said Corporal Wilfred "Swede" Hanson, a skinny eighteen-year-old Cape Gloucester veteran from Duluth, Minnesota, now assigned as an intelligence scout with the Third Battalion, First Marines. "I think it rained six feet and three inches the first damned day we were there."

In a sense, it was fortunate that the rain lasted longer than usual that spring. For the next several weeks, brief afternoon showers would offer the only chance most of the Marines had to take baths or wash their filthy sweatshirts and dungarees.

On that first day, mounds of moldy, castoff Army tents, most of them full of holes, were piled haphazardly on the beach. Mildewed, half-rotted canvas cots were heaped nearby. Designated bivouac areas stood in several inches of water. Marines stood somberly in the mud, looking at one another and shaking their heads as they confronted the ultimate example of the term "boondocks." Some managed a bitter laugh. Others yelled, swore, and kicked things. Many asked the same question again and again: "Who the hell's bright idea was this?"

Then they started digging holes in the muck for tent poles, sewing up tears in the six-man pyramidal tents, covering larger holes with their ponchos, and searching for scraps of wood to provide a bit of dry footing beside their cots. More than a few of the cots fell to pieces when weary men tried to lie down on them. Some improvised by stringing jungle hammocks over the wooden frames of the cots. Others abandoned their tents and strung their hammocks in the rain between two palm trees.

When the sun set, darkness engulfed the island. Loneliness and a need for companionship were intensified by the absence of electrical power. Even the division command post had no lights for the first few days, and company bivouac areas were without electricity for the entire stay on Pavuvu.

To compensate, a handful of old-timers taught others a trick learned in France during World War I. They fashioned crude lamps by partially filling empty cans or other metal containers with sand, adding a few ounces of gasoline, and using a piece of tent rope as a wick. The lamps cast enough light for writing letters, playing cards, and other simple tasks, but they were smoky, smelly—and unsafe. When seventeen-year-old PFC Seymour Levy unwittingly used a Coke bottle to construct his lamp, instead of a wide-mouthed metal container, it turned into a Molotov cocktail that set his tent on fire.

"Sy Levy was a bright kid, but he just didn't have much common sense," said his buddy, PFC Sterling Mace. "Other guys were a little wary of bunking with him after that."

For weeks, removing spoiled coconuts and dumping them in a swamp was a daily chore for hundreds of Marines. It was nauseating duty, made worse by rotten nuts that broke apart when they were picked up, spattering anyone nearby with the putrid milk inside.

The smell permeated everything. Men claimed they could even taste it in their drinking water.

The most backbreaking labor was hauling the tons of crushed coral required to pave roads, company streets, and bivouac areas. Division engineers excavated thick veins of coral, but the need was so pressing that many Marines carried material for their tent decks one helmetful at a time. It was common to see whole platoons lugging coral coolie-style in whatever containers they could find.

Until the paving progressed enough to allow normal functions on relatively dry surfaces, many men put their boots aside and waded barefoot through the loblolly. Meanwhile, drainage ditches had to be dug around the company areas, along with collection pools for runoff, to keep them from flooding during the daily downpours.

Marine regulations called for tents in rest camps to be decked with wood, but the lumber shortage made this impossible on Pavuvu. Every man was desperate to find a few scraps of board or an old packing crate to keep his personal possessions out of the muck. The small stocks of wood available had to be kept under guard to keep scroungers from making off with them.

If anything, the food available on Pavuvu, and the circumstances in which it was eaten, were just as bad—maybe worse—than at Cape Gloucester. It took weeks to get screened-in mess halls erected and functioning. In the interim, men lined up for chow outdoors in the mud and rain, where they were served from large pots heated over blazing coconut logs and propped on stumps.

No advance arrangements had been made for adequate provisions, and since there was virtually no refrigeration on the island, the menu was devoid of fresh meat, vegetables, eggs, and other perishables. The overall quality of the food was abysmal, and at times even the powdered and dehydrated varieties were next to nonexistent. PFC Gene Sledge, a new replacement who joined Corporal Burgin's mortar squad on Pavuvu and was promptly nicknamed "Sledgehammer," recalled one four-day period when K/3/5 was served nothing but oatmeal—three times a day.

Usually, there was a little more variety, but not much. Day-to-day fare consisted mainly of powdered eggs, dehydrated potatoes and vegetables, several types of canned meats (all identified as "Spam" by the men), heated C rations, and a pale yellow, lemon-flavored drink known as "battery acid."

The only bread available was baked on the island out of flour heavily infested with weevils and other insects. It was so heavy, according to Sledgehammer, that when a slice was held by its side, the rest of it broke away of its own weight. Buried within each slice were more bugs "than there are seeds in a slice of rye bread," he added.

Most of the men were hungry enough to eat it anyway. Some even managed to joke about it. "Hey, the bugs are good for you," they said. "They put more protein in your diet."

Others simply preferred to go hungry. "After a few weeks of Pavuvu food," wrote George McMillan in *The Old Breed,* his classic 1949 history of the First Marine Division, "many men came to breakfast with only a canteen cup, satisfied to begin their day on coffee alone."

Loneliness could be more intense on Pavuvu than in an actual combat zone because men had more time to dwell on their feelings than when their minds were focused on sheer survival. Having a buddy to confide in helped a lot, and when a Marine chose to spend his nights in silence and solitude, it was considered a danger sign.

Conditions were miserable enough to affect even men in good physical and mental health. For those with battle fatigue and threadbare nerves, Pavuvu could be a veritable hell on earth. Survivors disagree on the number of Marines who cracked up there, but according to eyewitnesses, mental breakdowns were widespread, and even suicides weren't uncommon.

"I knew one guy who blew his brains out with his own rifle while he was on guard duty one night," said PFC Ray Rottinghaus, a twenty-three-year-old BAR man with a K/3/5 rifle squad. "Other guys just went crazy and started screaming all of a sudden. They'd yell stuff like, 'They're killing me! They're killing me!' and they'd get taken to the Navy hospital for psychiatric treatment. It was really the after-effects of the battles they'd been through, but conditions on Pavuvu didn't help any."

PFC Bill Leyden was even more outspoken about the suicide rate. "Hardly a night would pass without the sound of a rifle shot," Leyden said. "It was usually a suicide caused by a Dear John letter, or just somebody who couldn't take it any longer."

The Marines on Pavuvu did seem to receive an inordinate number of Dear John letters, and the island's conditions put unusual strain on personal relationships back home. Pavuvu's chaplains reported a sharp increase in the number of Marines they counseled about marital discord and estranged wives.

Others took long-distance breakups in stride. When eighteen-year-old PFC Vincent Santos got a letter from his high school sweetheart telling him that she was marrying an "Air Force guy," he laughed the whole thing off. "Congratulations," the easygoing mortar man from San Antonio wrote in reply. "If you have any kids, name one for me."

Men with faithful wives or girlfriends at home drew great comfort from their mail. First Lieutenant Everett P. Pope of the Third Battalion, First Marines, who received his captain's bars on Pavuvu, spent several hours each week composing letters to his wife, Eleanor, in North Quincy, Massachusetts. Hard as he tried, he never managed to squeeze as many words as he wanted into the cramped space on a V-Mail letter.

Corporal Charles "Red" Womack, a husky machine gunner from McComb, Mississippi, who switched to flamethrowers on Pavuvu, also wrote often to his bride, Hilda. He found another constructive way to combat loneliness and boredom by combing the beach for an unusual type of black seashell, eventually collecting enough to have a buddy make a necklace from them for Hilda. Womack sent her the finished product as a gift just before embarking for Peleliu.

. . .

Some in the division grew so hardened to comrades committing suicide that they used the grimmest sort of black humor as a defense mechanism. When one teenage sentry came in from four hours of slogging through the mud, put his M-1 in his mouth, and blew the top of his head off, a noncom in the next tent was alleged to have complained: "Jeez, now I got to find the padre. It's getting so they won't even let a guy out of here *that* way without a pass."

For every suicide or severe psychiatric disorder, there were dozens of milder cases of mental upset or erratic behavior, especially during the division's first couple of months on the island. The Marines called it "going Asiatic," a term originally used to describe personality quirks developed by men serving long hitches in the Far East.

The Pavuvu strain of going Asiatic reached epidemic proportions, as illustrated by the oft-told story of a Marine who ran out of his tent one evening and threw himself at the base of a coconut tree. He beat the tree savagely with his bare fists and wept uncontrollably.

"I hate you, goddamn it!" he screamed. "I hate you! I hate you!"

"Hit the son of a bitch once for me," shouted somebody from a nearby tent. Otherwise, none of the dozens of men within earshot offered the slightest reaction to the outburst. On Pavuvu, it was just another part of the nightly routine.

Attacked far more often than palm trees were the island's two principal varieties of "wildlife"—rats and land crabs—both of which the Marines hated with an unbridled passion. But these attacks were usually the outgrowth of normal anger and frustration, rather than going Asiatic.

Some of the more enterprising men built elaborate snares to capture the rats, then doused the pests with gasoline and set them on fire. Others killed rats with booby traps made from percussion caps inserted in packages of crackers. On one occasion, a company commander led an attack with flamethrowers that destroyed more than 400 rats in a single night. But by the next evening it was obvious that

Pavuvu's rat population was as large and active as ever, and the discouraged attackers called off their offensive.

One night after movies had reached the island, PFC Bill Leyden was engrossed in the film on the outdoor screen when a giant rat jumped out of a coconut tree straight into his shirt pocket. "He was after some lemon drops I had in there, and I thought for sure he was going to bite me," Leyden recalled. "I ripped off my shirt with the rat trapped inside, and with the help of the guy next to me, I did my best to beat it to death, but somehow it got away."

The land crabs were considerably more docile than the rats but just as infuriating. "Those rotten coconuts had been a haven for the land crabs," said Corporal Red Womack. "When we moved the coconuts, the crabs got more active, and no man on Pavuvu would dare put on his boots in the morning without shaking the crabs out of them first. Sometimes two or three would fall out of one boot."

The larger land crabs were about the size of a man's hand and incredibly slimy. Like the rats, they always appeared at night, slithering sideways in all directions. Even the live ones had an awful odor about them, and when they were killed with sticks, rifle butts, bayonets, or other handy objects, the smell was even more revolting.

In one all-out assault, 128 of the creatures were killed overnight in a single tent, whose occupants made the mistake of shoveling the smashed crabs into empty gasoline drums and setting them on fire. The stench was so severe that the men were forced to vacate the tent for an entire day.

As the weeks on Pavuvu dragged by, there were no more happy renditions of "Waltzing Matilda." Melbourne might as well have been on some other planet, and the associations the song brought to mind were too painful. Hillbilly Jones and his musical cohorts concentrated instead on mournful ballads about wasted lives, hard times, and lost loves.

"Oh, if I had the wings of an angel, over these prison walls I would fly . . ."

. . .

If Pavuvu was a nightmare, the neighboring island of Banika represented the sweetest of dreams—dreams made more tantalizing by the tales of forbidden pleasures that drifted back to Pavuvu.

Except for the few lucky veterans who were rotated home that summer, Banika was as close to utopia as any member of the First Marine Division could hope to get in mid-1944. For men who would've given a month's wages for a glimpse of a real American woman, a couple of ice-cold beers, or a Hershey bar, it was the ultimate isle of desire.

Banika was home to the Fourth Naval Base Depot, where acres of foodstuffs and consumer goods were stockpiled. There were miles of asphalt roads; scores of permanent buildings, some of them air-conditioned; three outdoor amphitheaters with nightly first-run movies; a recreation hall where enlisted men could buy up to six beers per week; officers clubs where cocktails flowed freely every afternoon; and several well-stocked post exchanges that sold all kinds of stateside merchandise.

More than 100 females—most of them young Navy nurses or Red Cross canteen workers—were also stationed on Banika. They were housed behind barbed wire fences and guarded around the clock, but to denizens of Pavuvu, the mere sight of an attractive woman was a red-letter occasion.

Banika was separated from Pavuvu by only a narrow channel, but between the channel and the Marines' camp lay ten miles of impassable swamp and jungle, which, for all practical purposes, put Banika in another world. The only regular contact between the two islands was the daily mail boat, and while it was docked at Pavuvu, sentries stood watch, checking out anyone trying to board. Few stowaways avoided apprehension.

Most of the First Division Marines who made it to Banika did so as patients at its Navy hospital, one of the island's four large medical facilities. Others were lucky enough to be sent there on brief errands. They rarely stayed longer than overnight but invariably brought back tales of luxury and largesse that made their buddies' jaws drop in envy.

Thus, when Captain Haldane called in about ten of his Guadalcanal and Cape Gloucester veterans and told them they'd been selected for a two-week assignment on Banika, they almost fainted. And that was before they found out the nature of the duty.

"Your orders are to work eight hours a day guarding a supply dump at the Navy depot," Ack-Ack said. "Lieutenant Jones and Sergeant Day will be in charge of the detail. Enjoy yourselves and stay out of trouble."

"What're we guarding in this supply dump, sir?" Hillbilly Jones inquired.

Haldane grinned. "Several thousand cases of beer and soft drinks, I understand."

One of the chosen was ex-farmboy R. V. Burgin, who compared the assignment to "sending a bunch of hogs to watch over a well-loaded corncrib." Jones and Sergeant Jim Day weren't strict disciplinarians, anyway, and they pretty much gave the rest of the men a free rein. "We served about four hours on duty and ninety-six hours off," Burgin said. "It was like one big party."

Actually, the living conditions on Banika might have seemed fairly ordinary to men stationed there but not to a band of refugees from Pavuvu. The K/3/5 detail was housed in new six-man tents with electric lights, sturdy wooden decks, and flaps that opened to let in the breeze. They took many of their meals on a Navy ship anchored in the harbor, where they were handed menus and asked what they wanted to order. The food was uniformly excellent—fresh eggs, meat, fruits, and vegetables, fresh-baked bread (minus the bugs), rich desserts, even ice cream—all served on real dishes.

The beer in the supply dump was, of course, basically free for the taking, and they all consumed plenty of it. For the most part, they had to drink it warm, or barely cool at best, but to men who hadn't tasted the stuff in eight or nine months, beer was beer.

Especially during the first weeks on Pavuvu, Marines debated among themselves whether the abominable conditions were part of a calculated plan to make them meaner, madder, and more likely to take out their bitterness on the Japanese in their next battle. Opinions on the subject remain divided to this day, but whether it resulted from an intentional scheme or a simple foul-up, the agony paid dividends that weren't readily apparent at the time.

PFC Gene Sledge felt that most of his comrades took the hardships and frustrations in stride for two main reasons—stern discipline and esprit de corps. "Well-disciplined young men can put up with a lot even though they don't like it," he said, "and we were a bunch of high-spirited boys proud of our unit."

Many of the men eventually came to recognize the benefits that grew out of the Pavuvu ordeal. More than six decades later, some still embrace it, both as a badge of honor and a wellspring of the comradeship that grew among them.

"Through all the misery, a bond developed among the men," said Bill Leyden. "Each got to know the very soul of his comrades, and we became like blood brothers. This bonding gave us a closeness that lasted the rest of our lives. It made our division one of a kind and enabled us to face things at Peleliu that might have defeated the average American combat division."

For replacements like Sledge and Leyden, the Pavuvu experience represented final initiation to full membership in the First Marine Division. It fostered an "us against the world" mind-set that drew together newcomers and veterans alike, melding them into one cohesive, resilient, mutually supportive union—in the best traditions of the Old Breed.

Ever so gradually, and thanks primarily to the labors of the Marines themselves, Pavuvu began to take on more and more characteristics of civilization as the summer of 1944 wore on.

Mess halls, a sparsely stocked PX, and other semipermanent structures had been erected. Bivouac areas were fast and firm for the most part, now that the rains were less frequent, and it was finally possible for men and vehicles to move around the island without bogging down to their knees or axles. A swimming hole had been set up along the beach, where men had a chance to cool off from the heat. Outdoor movies were offered several times a week, and some outdoor recreation areas were dry enough to allow games of basketball and softball. On the Fourth of July 1944, the division held a field day with relay races and other competitive sports events. PFC Vincent Santos picked up the nickname "Speedy" that day for coming in dead-last in one of the races.

But by far the most wondrous event to take place on Pavuvu that summer was a surprise visit by comedian Bob Hope and his USO troupe. The open-air show staged by Hope, Frances Langford, Jerry Colonna, and Patty Thomas is still remembered as the best morale-booster that the Marines encountered there.

"In addition to the great show they put on, the fact that they'd come to a godforsaken place like Pavuvu really lifted our spirits," said Bill Leyden. "It made us feel like we weren't totally forgotten after all."

Close to three-fourths of the division turned out for the show, and Hope himself later described flying into Pavuvu in a small plane and circling over the thousands of cheering Marines below as one of the high points of his Pacific tour. Hope even managed to draw a laugh about the despised land crabs during one of his patented digs at the string of perennially losing racehorses owned by his friend, crooner Bing Crosby.

"I noticed your land crabs," Hope said. "They reminded me of Crosby's horses because they all run sideways."

Much of July and August 1944 was devoted to landing exercises on inlets and beaches away from the main camp. Lack of space made all maneuvers difficult, and some had to be held on company streets because other areas were too swampy or choked with jungle growth. The exercises placed heavy emphasis on landings from amtracks, amphibious vehicles designed to carry assault troops. This was something the division had never done in combat.

As July wound down, a quiet, almost imperceptible change came over the division. The last of the rotten coconuts had finally been cleaned up, and the mud was mostly gone. The men complained less about the food, the rats, the crabs, and the isolation. They paid more attention to cleaning their weapons, making sure their gear was in order, and other routine chores—all more willingly than before.

An inner instinct began to warn the Marines that their next battle wasn't far away—and that it would likely make the hardships of Pavuvu seem mild by comparison.

Captain Andy Haldane described his feelings at about this time in a letter to Paul Nixon, dean of students at Bowdoin College, Haldane's alma mater. One of Haldane's former classmates and fellow athletes at Bowdoin was Captain Everett Pope, now commanding a rifle company in the First Marines, and he often mentioned Pope in his letters.

"More of our officers have gone home, but Ev and I are still around," Haldane noted in late July 1944. "But I'm sure if we get through the next one, we'll be home to get a few days rest. [Meanwhile] all we can do is carry on. This next one is going to be a peach. Woe is me!"

Plenty of others in the company shared Haldane's foreboding. Like him, they'd served constantly in the Pacific war zone without a stateside furlough for well over two years, and each had gone through at least two major battles. In addition to Haldane and Pope, they included such K/3/5 veterans as Lieutenants Hillbilly Jones and John E. "Moose" Barrett, and Sergeants Jim McEnery, Jim Day, and John Marmet.

Under the so-called twenty-four-month rule, nearly a third of the division's officers and enlisted men were eligible for rotation back to the States. But word filtered down from III Corps headquarters that the rule was being set aside. Only a small fraction of the twenty-four-monthers would actually be granted leave because, without them, there simply weren't enough Marines to handle the job ahead. General Rupertus and Colonel John Selden, his chief of staff, were told bluntly: "Your people will have to stick it out, at least for the next operation."

Just over a month after Haldane wrote his letter, he and the rest of the First Marine Division broke camp and headed for combat. Their exile on Pavuvu was over.

CHAPTER THREE

THE ROAD TO PELELIU

During the last days of August 1944, the 16,459 combat troops of the reinforced First Marine Division loaded their gear and themselves aboard thirty LSTs—shallow-draft landing ships with huge clamshell doors designed to disembark tanks and amtracks as well as men—and bade farewell to Pavuvu.

Their initial destination was Guadalcanal, where they held a final week-long series of landing maneuvers. The beaches there bore little resemblance to the ones the Marines would storm on Peleliu, but they were at least spacious enough to accommodate such a large number of troops. Some division veterans hoped to visit the military cemetery on Guadalcanal, where many of their fallen comrades were buried, but no one was allowed to leave the training area.

On the morning of September 4, the LSTs weighed anchor for the 2,100-mile voyage to Peleliu. Skies were clear, and the sea was as smooth as glass. The men of K/3/5 and other rifle companies passed the time by lounging on deck, playing cards, smoking, and talking quietly about the great unknown that lay ahead. Once again, a crowd gathered around Hillbilly Jones and his guitar, but the tunes were mostly plaintive, sentimental, and verging on melancholy.

"From this val-leee they say you are leavin'... We will miss your bright eyes and sweet smile..."

"There's a long, long trail a-winding... into the land of my dreams..."

The men on the LSTs could see in the distance part of the vast armada of firepower accompanying them. A line of warships stretched along the horizon, their batteries of heavy guns outlined against the pale blue sky.

In briefings before leaving Pavuvu, the Marines had been told that their assignment was vital for protecting General MacArthur's right flank during the coming Philippines campaign. After securing a beachhead, the division's primary objective would be to take and hold a large enemy airfield a few hundred yards inland.

They were also informed that the First Marine Division had been increased in strength to 28,000 for the Peleliu mission, making it the largest division ever to mount an amphibious assault. The problem was, nobody seemed to know who—or where—all these additional people were.

PFC Gene Sledge recalled hearing a cynical NCO warn an exuberant young replacement not to be overly impressed by such numbers. "Use your head, buddy," the veteran snapped. "Sure we got the First Marines, the Fifth Marines, and the Seventh Marines; them's infantry. The Eleventh Marines is our division artillery. Where the hell's all them people who's supposed to 'reinforce' the division? Have you seen 'em?"

The young replacement had not. Nobody else had, either. Clearly, they hadn't been on Pavuvu, and they weren't in this convoy.

The truth was that most of these "extra" troops were rear-echelon specialists of one type or another, none of whom would ever get anywhere near the actual fighting. In reality, the coming battle would be won or lost by the Marines now aboard the LSTs—mainly the 9,000 men in the three infantry regiments, the 3,000 in the artillery regiment, plus a few hundred more in amphibious tank and amtrack battalions. The rest of the 16,000-plus combat troops included regimental and battalion headquarters staffs, as well as engineering, supply, maintenance, and communications units.

The accepted manpower formula for a U.S. amphibious assault called for invaders to outnumber defenders by at least three to one. But if only front-line combat troops were counted, the Marines would have nowhere near that margin when they landed on Peleliu.

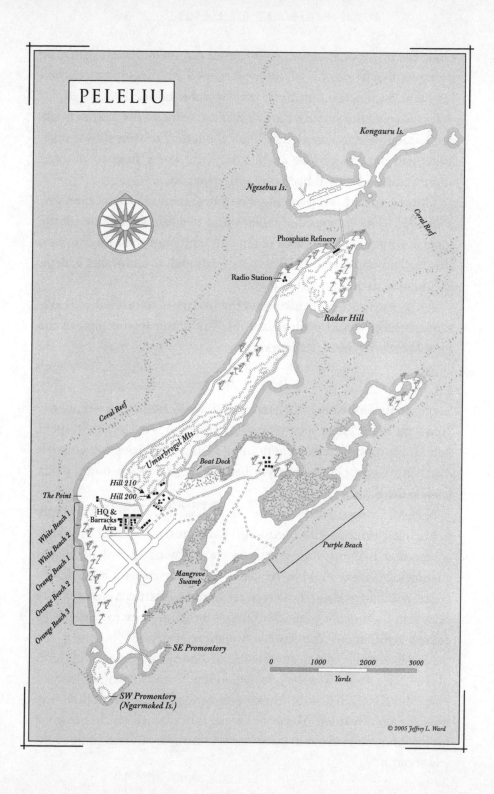

PELELIU

Kongauru Is.

Ngesebus Is.

Coral Reef

Phosphate Refinery

Radio Station

Radar Hill

Umurbrogol Mts.

Boat Dock

Hill 210

Hill 200

The Point

HQ &
Barracks
Area

White Beach 1

White Beach 2

Orange Beach 1

Orange Beach 2

Orange Beach 3

Purple Beach

Mangrove
Swamp

SE Promontory

SW Promontory
(Ngarmoked Is.)

Coral Reef

0   1000   2000   3000

Yards

© 2005 Jeffrey L. Ward

Once the battle was joined, 9,000 American infantrymen would be trying to dislodge some 10,900 well-trained and deeply entrenched Japanese. So much for formulas and favorable odds.

It was only after leaving Pavuvu that the name of the Marines' target became general knowledge. Since then, they'd been shown relief maps and models of Peleliu, but they still knew next to nothing about the island they'd been ordered to invade.

They practiced pronouncing the strange name to each other. *Pel-le-loo. Pel-le-loo.* It sounded mellow and melodic as it came off the tongue, conjuring up images of fanciful nights on moonlit beaches, although no one on the LSTs was naive enough to think that a tropical paradise actually awaited them.

While the origin of its name and the history of the island were obscure, Peleliu would soon mean only one thing to the men of the First Marine Division: hell on earth.

Sergeant Jim McEnery, a platoon guide who ranked as one of the "old guys" in K/3/5 at age twenty-four, sometimes felt as if he'd spent half his life in the Pacific. But nothing he'd gone through at Guadalcanal and Cape Gloucester had been enough to earn him a ticket back to the States.

Now McEnery stared over the rail of *LST 661,* listening absently to Hillbilly Jones and his cornpone chorus and pondering the twists of fate that had put him where he was. Having grown up in the shadow of Ebbets Field in Brooklyn, McEnery wasn't a big fan of country music. Although he'd never known a better Marine of any rank than Lieutenant Jones, McEnery's taste ran more to "Sidewalks of New York" than "You Are My Sunshine."

He felt a twinge of bitterness along with the steady, powerful throb of the LST's engines as they propelled him toward Peleliu. Plenty of guys who'd logged less time in the war zone were either on their way home or already there. McEnery, on the other hand, was heading for his third major invasion in three years. Outwardly he was philosophical about it.

"I got no particular bad feelings about Peleliu," he reassured PFC Sterling Mace, a young fellow New Yorker who was heading into his first action. "Based on what they're telling us, maybe it won't be too tough. At least it shouldn't last as long as the Cape or the 'Canal."

McEnery could only hope that he was right. But echoing in his mind above the sounds of Jones's guitar and the LST's engines were the shouts of the jeering noncoms at Parris Island when he'd arrived there for boot camp in September 1940:

You'll be sor-reee! You'll be sor-reee!

McEnery would've been even sorrier had he known about the high-level command decisions made behind the scenes over the past several months—decisions that were sending the First Marine Division into what many would later consider a pointless battle and an unnecessary bloodbath.

Prior to Japan's pre–World War II military buildup in the Pacific, Peleliu was one of the least-known points on the globe—and seemingly one of the least important. But the island's status changed dramatically in the late 1930s, when the Japanese launched an exhaustive base-building project that would turn the obscure mass of coral limestone into one of the most heavily fortified islands in Tokyo's Pacific empire.

Peleliu is the second-largest island in the Palaus chain, a 110-mile-long archipelago lying west of the Carolines and east of the Philippines. It consists of about 350 islands, most of them uninhabited and many too small to show up on even detailed maps. Located just north of the equator, Peleliu measures some six miles long from north to south and about two miles wide from east to west at its widest point. The exact amount of land area—usually estimated at five-plus square miles—has proved difficult to determine because roughly a quarter of the island is impenetrable mangrove swamp. Its shape has frequently been compared to a lobster's claw, with the swamp lying between an elongated top pincer and a shorter bottom one.

From earliest times, Peleliu and the rest of the Palaus have been shrouded by a veil of cultural, linguistic, and geographical peculiarities. The first recorded contact between Europeans and Palauan natives was in 1564, when Spanish explorers reached the islands and claimed them for Spain. But nearly a century and a half would pass before the first recorded visit by Spanish missionaries in 1712. Sustained contact with the outside world began when an ill-fated English vessel, the *Antelope,* ran aground in 1783 on the coral reef that surrounds nine of the ten major Palau Islands.

More than 300 years of Spanish control did little to influence native customs. The people continued to speak a unique, tongue-twisting Malayo-Polynesian language distantly related to Indonesian. They lived in small, isolated villages and followed practices and rituals that dated back for centuries. Except to itinerant fishermen and whalers, the islands had little apparent value and drew scant attention in a Spanish colonial empire that then circled the globe.

In 1899, following Spain's crushing defeat in the Spanish-American War, Peleliu and the rest of the Palaus were sold to Germany, which was eager to establish a strong colonial foothold in the Pacific. Berlin businessmen foresaw vast opportunities for trade in the Pacific and Asia, and militarists envisioned fueling stations and naval bases, with the Palaus playing a key role. But with conflict looming in Europe and Germany's attention focused on the crisis there, the visions went unfulfilled.

Fifteen years later, at the outbreak of World War I, the Palaus and other German holdings in the region were occupied by the Japanese. After the war, a League of Nations mandate gave Japan long-term control of the islands, yet for the better part of two decades the Japanese did no more to develop them than had the Spanish or Germans.

But toward the end of the 1930s, the thinking of Japan's aggressive war planners abruptly changed. The Palaus, lying some 2,000 miles south of Tokyo, now seemed ideally suited for furthering the militarists' plan to turn the western Pacific into a veritable Japanese lake.

By spring 1939, a 3,000-man naval force had been dispatched to the Palaus, along with several shiploads of heavy equipment and 500 Korean laborers. A massive construction project was launched on Peleliu, although Japan's administrative and military headquarters for the Palaus remained on Koror Island, about twenty-five miles north. Significant steps were also taken to fortify Babelthuap, the largest of the Palaus, with roughly twenty times the land area of Peleliu, but Peleliu itself became the main focal point of the military buildup. Some of the 600 or so natives were conscripted to work for the Japanese, but most of the population continued to live much as it had for hundreds of years. It is unclear how many natives remained on Peleliu at the time of the battle, but most had apparently left.

In six months of intensive work, a large, first-class airfield was completed on Peleliu. Its pair of crisscrossing runways of hard-packed coral, one measuring 6,000 feet in length and the other 3,500 feet, could handle the largest available military aircraft and allowed for simultaneous landings and takeoffs. The field was equipped with excellent taxiways, paved turning circles, protective revetments for planes, hangars and barracks, a communications center, an electric generating plant, machine shops, and a two-story headquarters structure of reinforced concrete.

Other improvements included a network of cisterns designed to catch and store rainwater—a resource vital for survival on Peleliu because the island has no fresh water. An auxiliary airstrip for fighter planes was built on the neighboring islet of Ngesebus, and a causeway was constructed across the 500 yards of shallow water between Ngesebus and Peleliu.

A six-mile north–south road of crushed coral along Peleliu's western coast linked the main airfield with the causeway to Ngesebus and a phosphate-crushing plant at the native village of Akalokul on the extreme northern tip of the island. Above the road for approximately two-thirds of its length loomed a series of densely wooded ridges, most between 100 and 250 feet high but with a maximum altitude of about 550 feet and known collectively as Umurbrogol Mountain.

By early December 1941, Tokyo had assigned a major role to the

Palaus in the massive offensive strike it was preparing to launch in the Pacific. Almost 12,000 well-trained Japanese ground troops were garrisoned on Peleliu. Its airfield was a principal refueling stop for a steady stream of Betty bombers and Zero fighters bound for deployment around the Pacific. A carrier-led naval task force was positioned a dozen miles north of Peleliu in the harbor of the Malakal Atoll.

When the first bombs fell on Pearl Harbor on December 7, enemy forces in the Palaus were poised to join the broader attack. In another surprise strike roughly ten hours later, naval aircraft from the carrier task force and land-based planes from Peleliu joined other Japanese planes based on Formosa to decimate U.S. airpower in the Philippines. The raiders destroyed many of General MacArthur's B-17 bombers and fighter planes before they got off the ground. Meanwhile, ships from the task force attacked the southern Philippines, and seasoned Japanese troops based in the Palaus helped spearhead the ground assault that overwhelmed American and Filipino defenders.

Over the next two years, however, the complexion of the war changed dramatically. By late 1943, American-led forces were on the offensive all over the Pacific, driving the enemy back and punching gaping holes in the ring of steel erected by Japan to protect its sphere of influence.

In mid-February 1944, a U.S. Navy task force virtually obliterated the giant Japanese naval base at Truk, 1,000 miles east of the Philippines in the Carolines, leaving its supposedly impregnable harbor in ruins. More than 250 Japanese planes and almost three dozen Japanese ships were destroyed, but the consequences of the enemy defeat were much more far-reaching.

Destruction of communications facilities and other ground installations was so complete that Admiral Mineichi Koga, commander of Japan's Combined Fleet, was forced to move his headquarters to the Palaus. U.S. air- and sea-power had proved conclusively that even a base as formidable as Truk could be neutralized without committing ground troops. In other words, Truk could be safely bypassed, isolated, and left to atrophy as American forces drove on toward Japan.

With the Japanese fleet on the run and in need of a short-term haven until a new permanent base could be completed in the Philippines, a plan was devised to move the fleet temporarily to the Palaus. But less than two weeks after the Truk debacle, the plan went up in smoke—along with 160 more Japanese planes. On March 2, 1944, scores of Hellcat fighters and Dauntless dive-bombers from the carriers *Hornet, Lexington,* and *Bunker Hill* ravaged Peleliu's airstrip in relentless day-long raids. Low-flying Avenger torpedo planes sowed hundreds of magnetic mines across the entrances to Malakal harbor, trapping some thirty enemy ships inside, then returned to sink or disable all of them.

When the attack was over, the airfield was a shambles of bomb craters, twisted steel, and piles of rubble. Every surrounding structure was demolished except for the outer walls of the blockhouse-type headquarters building. Of the scores of Zeroes and other attack aircraft based on Peleliu, fewer than a dozen planes survived the day in flyable condition.

Simply put, Peleliu's offensive capabilities had been obliterated nearly six and a half months before the First Marine Division was scheduled to go ashore there. As of mid-September 1944, it was out of the question that the remaining Japanese forces on Peleliu could pose the slightest offensive threat to MacArthur's impending return to the Philippines.

Yet for an assortment of reasons—some strategic, some political, some emotional, and some, perhaps, merely vainglorious—plans for the invasion of Peleliu moved forward inexorably.

As supreme commander of Allied forces in the Pacific, MacArthur undoubtedly knew that Peleliu's offensive teeth had been pulled, but he continued to insist that the island be invaded to protect his right flank. MacArthur thought of the First Marine Division as "his" Marines, and he wanted to hold on to them as long as possible. Admiral Chester W. Nimitz, commander in chief of the Pacific Fleet, had other priorities. Nimitz had originally supported the assault on Peleliu, but he began to have serious second thoughts as D-Day approached. One likely reason was his desire to see the First Marine Division returned to Navy control.

The Japanese high command, meanwhile, had no illusions about Peleliu's offensive capabilities and declared the island's garrison expendable. Even the Japanese commander on Peleliu, Colonel Kunio Nakagawa, knew that his troops' only remaining mission was to mount as tenacious a defense as possible if and when an American landing came. He and his 10,900 men had spent more than half a year getting ready to do just that.

Of all the principal players in this drama, only the men of the First Marine Division remained in the dark concerning what they were about to face on Peleliu—and why.

Jim McEnery and his comrades had no way of knowing that their assault on Peleliu was part of a broader plan for the Pacific war agreed upon a year earlier at the highest levels. At a secret conference in Quebec, Canada, in August 1943, the plan had been tacitly approved by President Franklin D. Roosevelt, British Prime Minister Winston Churchill, and members of the Allied Combined Chiefs of Staff.

Dominating the Quebec conference were decisions about the planned invasion of France the following spring and the choice of a supreme commander to direct the liberation of Europe. But FDR and Churchill also settled on a list of key objectives in the Pacific and approved a flexible, long-range plan for achieving them.

Basically, the plan was a reaffirmation of the island-hopping strategy that had started at Guadalcanal a year earlier. It emphasized retaking the Philippines, and, as an adjunct to the Philippines campaign, it endorsed the capture or neutralization of enemy strongholds in the Caroline and Palau Islands. At the time, Peleliu was among the most formidable of these fortress-islands, and Admiral Nimitz had been eyeing it for months as an advance base for attacking Truk. Nimitz's reasons differed from MacArthur's, but both saw the taking of Peleliu as a top priority.

These decisions were made before the neutralization of Truk and the crippling air attacks on Peleliu, however. Now everything had changed, but neither Nimitz nor his superiors seemed to notice—at least not at first.

On March 26, 1944, while the First Marine Division was still engaged at Cape Gloucester, but well after the attacks on Truk and Peleliu, Nimitz dispatched a "warning order" to General William Rupertus, the division commander. The order, approved by the U.S. Joint Chiefs of Staff, directed the division to prepare to invade Peleliu no later than September 15, 1944.

Four months later, at a meeting at Pearl Harbor with Roosevelt and MacArthur, Nimitz revealed a striking change of heart. He argued not only against the assault on Peleliu but also against the invasion of the Philippines that it was intended to support. What caused this about-face remains a matter of speculation, but it may have stemmed in part from objections voiced by Nimitz's Navy colleagues, and in particular by Admiral Bull Halsey, who outspokenly opposed the Palaus operation.

But an emotional appeal from MacArthur, in which he warned of "breaking a promise to the Filipino people" and the "slaughter of women and children" by the Japanese if the Philippines weren't retaken, ultimately convinced FDR to overrule Nimitz. On July 26, 1944, the president give final approval to both the Philippines and the Peleliu invasions.

From all indications, Rupertus was almost as much in the dark about the controversy surrounding the invasion of Peleliu as were the rank-and-file Marines of his division. He'd been in the States while most of the planning for the invasion was taking place, and had only recently returned to the Pacific to assume command. But while critiquing his troops' dress rehearsals on Guadalcanal just four days before the invasion fleet sailed, Rupertus issued a prediction that fairly rang with confidence.

"We're going to have some casualties, but let me assure you this is going to be a short one, a quickie," he announced to his unit commanders. "Rough but fast. We'll be through in three days. It might take only two."

The code name selected for the Palaus campaign would prove highly appropriate—and bitterly ironic—to those who lived through it. No one can say with any certainty how or why the name was chosen, but it flew squarely in the face of Rupertus's upbeat prediction about what lay ahead.

The name was Operation Stalemate.

Tension and boredom had settled over the Marines after a few days at sea. As the LSTs and transports steamed toward Peleliu, each man found his own ways of passing the time and dealing with the stressful monotony.

PFCs Sterling Mace and Seymour Levy had grown up a few miles apart in New York City but otherwise had little in common. Mace, a nominal Protestant from Queens, was an outgoing, athletic eighteen-year-old who pitched on the K Company softball team. Levy was a scholarly, slightly built Jewish kid from Brooklyn whose domineering mother had practically disowned him for lying about his age to join the Marines. Although his sharp wit sometimes made him seem older, Levy was still barely seventeen.

They had met as replacements aboard a decrepit freighter crossing the Pacific, then became best friends on Pavuvu. Now the two young riflemen in K/3/5 shared a billet on the deck of *LST 661*, sheltered from the elements by only the davit-supported hull of a small landing craft. Here they spent hours playing an improvised board game called Battleships while Levy rattled off endless recitations of Rudyard Kipling poems. He seemed to have memorized everything Kipling ever wrote, but "Gunga Din"—complete with Cockney accent—was clearly his favorite.

"It was Din! Din! Din! You 'eathen, where the mischief 'ave you been," Levy would intone. "Now you put some *juldee* in it, or I'll marrow you this minute, if you don't fill up my helmet, Gunga Din . . ."

"Better pay attention to the game, Sy," Mace would warn. "I'm about to sink all your ships."

"Don't bank on it," Levy would pause to say, then plunge right back into the poem, louder than before. "We shouted, 'Harry By!' till our throats were bricky-dry. Then we wopped 'im 'cause 'e couldn't serve us all . . ."

Some of the other boredom-killing diversions they found were a lot more dangerous.

"One day we climbed down a steel ladder into the bottom of the ship's hold," Mace recalled much later. "There was an opening down below the clamshell doors on the bow of the LST, and we noticed that every time a wave broke over the bow, water rushed in through that opening. So we decided it might be fun to take a dip."

By hanging on to the very end of the ladder, Mace and Levy could immerse themselves for a few seconds in about eight feet of cool, refreshing seawater. Then the bow would rise again, and all the water would drain out through the opening.

"We did it five or six times before we started thinking about it and getting nervous," Mace continued. "The tug of the water was fierce, and if we'd lost our grip on that ladder for even a second, we'd have been washed out to sea, and nobody would ever have seen us again."

In the waters off Peleliu, meanwhile, the Navy was playing a much more deadly game of Battleships. Five dreadnought-class behemoths—the *Pennsylvania, Idaho, Maryland, Mississippi,* and *Tennessee*—were training their sixteen- and fourteen-inch guns on the island. Other players in Rear Admiral Jesse Oldendorf's Peleliu Fire Support Group included eight cruisers, twelve destroyers, seven minesweepers, fifteen landing craft converted to rocket launchers, and a half-dozen submarines. Three heavy aircraft carriers and five escort carriers were also in attendance, giving the Peleliu force a for-midable amount of aerial firepower.

Nimitz and others at CinCPac (Commander in Chief, Pacific Fleet) headquarters at Pearl Harbor have been criticized for sending a "second team" of ships and commanders to handle the pre-invasion softening up of Peleliu. Nevertheless, the Fire Support Group was a powerful armada, and Oldendorf was an experienced battle commander who had handled similar assignments in three previous Marine landings. In addition to the armada of warships, a total of nearly 400 Hellcat fighters, Dauntless dive-bombers, and other attack aircraft provided blanket air cover virtually unchal-lenged by enemy planes.

At 5:30 A.M. on September 12, 1944—D-Day-minus-3—Olden-dorf issued the order to commence firing. In the next instant, every big gun in the armada began hurling high-explosive shells at Peleliu as fast as its crew could fire and reload. Supposedly, there was no such thing as random firing. Each gun crew was assigned specific tar-gets, and each had been briefed well in advance on the number of rounds needed to achieve the desired results.

For precisely half an hour, the shelling continued in one huge, un-broken roar. Then, at 6:00 A.M., the batteries abruptly fell silent as the ships took a break and waves of carrier planes blistered the island with 500-pound fragmentation bombs and napalm.

The coordinated bombardment continued in the same pattern—thirty minutes of constant naval gunfire, followed by thirty minutes of intensive aerial assaults—until the sun was about to set that eve-ning. Then several reconnaissance planes zoomed low over the smoldering island, taking hundreds of photographs of the Navy's handiwork. The photos indicated that close to 300 of the assigned targets had been destroyed or severely damaged by the all-day bom-bardment. Virtually every aboveground structure and fortification had been wiped out. The airport and its few usable planes were re-duced to rubble and wreckage.

But as Oldendorf studied the pictures and compared them to reconnaissance photos made several weeks earlier, there was ample cause for uneasiness. Throughout the furious bombardment of the past twelve hours, no return fire had been detected from the concentrations of enemy heavy artillery clearly shown in the earlier photos, and the big guns were nowhere to be seen in the latest photos. This almost certainly meant that the Japanese had moved these weapons underground, where they could have survived the bombing and shelling with little or no damage.

At dawn the next morning, September 13, Oldendorf peered at Peleliu through powerful binoculars from the bridge of his flagship, the *Pennsylvania,* and what he saw gave further reason for concern.

In the earlier reconnaissance photos, the Umurbrogol, the broad wedge of high ground stretching from north to south along the western side of the island, appeared as a single, relatively flat plateau. But now, with its cover of dense foliage blasted and burned away by the tons of napalm and high-explosives rained on it the day before, the terrain looked strikingly different.

Oldendorf could see a profusion of steep cliffs, tortuous coral outcroppings, and yawning ravines that hadn't been visible twenty-four hours earlier. The nearest of them jutted up no more than 600 yards inland, and others stretched away in ragged, sawtooth lines almost to the far end of the island.

At 6:30 A.M., Oldendorf ordered the second day of coordinated air and sea bombardment to begin. By shortly after midday, every specified target on a master list in the *Pennsylvania's* combat center had been struck repeatedly, but the shelling and air attacks continued for the rest of the afternoon.

Early that evening, Oldendorf conferred with his staff, then radioed his superiors at Pearl Harbor. His fleet had "run out of targets," his message said, and he'd made the decision to call off the bombardment, despite a pre-arranged schedule for Operation Stalemate that called for a third full day of attacks. No record exists of any objections from Nimitz or anyone else at CinCPac.

One who undoubtedly would have objected—if anybody had

bothered to ask him—was Lieutenant Colonel Lewis B. "Chesty" Puller, commander of the First Marines, who watched from one of the LSTs in the invasion convoy. While studying detailed maps and reconnaissance photos of the beach area, Puller had noticed a gnarled coral outcropping that stood alone and rose sharply some thirty feet above the north end of White Beach 1.

It was designated simply as "the Point," and in Puller's view, its potential as a defensive strongpoint was too obvious for the Japanese to overlook. He was worried enough about it that he sent a message to Oldendorf's staff specifically asking that it be targeted in the Navy's bombardment. Puller was assured that the Point would be "taken care of," yet it was left virtually untouched.

Meanwhile, the two Marine officers in charge of the Peleliu operation—General Roy Geiger, commander of the III Marine Amphibious Corps, and General Rupertus, the division commander—knew nothing of Oldendorf's decision. They couldn't have objected, anyway, since both were sailing toward Peleliu under a strict communications blackout.

It remains unclear why Oldendorf chose to abandon the bombardment when he did, especially after confiding to aides that he thought the Japanese had moved their heavy weapons underground. Perhaps he believed his mission had been accomplished, or that, if the first two days of attacks hadn't produced the desired results, a third day of bombing and shelling would be equally pointless. During the two days of air and sea attacks, Navy ships had fired a total of 519 sixteen-inch rounds and 1,845 fourteen-inch rounds at Peleliu, and U.S. carrier planes had dropped nearly 1,800 500-pound bombs on the island.

After the war, in a rare comment on the situation, Oldendorf seemed inclined to accept some of the blame for the ineffectiveness of his bombardment even as he spread the rest of it around.

"If military leaders—and that includes Navy brass—were gifted with the same accuracy of foresight that they are with hindsight," he said, "then the assault on Peleliu should never have been attempted."

. . .

On September 14—D-minus-1—a mood of quiet intensity settled over the Marines on their LSTs. Men checked and rechecked their combat packs to make sure nothing essential had been left out. They gave their weapons a last careful cleaning, drew allotments of rations and ammo, and made other last-minute preparations for the landing.

It was imperative for amphibious assault troops to move inland quickly, and the Corps had made a concerted effort to minimize the weight each Marine had to carry in a landing, but the poundage was still considerable. Typical contents of a combat pack included a folded poncho, a dungaree cap, an extra pair of socks, two packages of K rations, salt tablets, twenty or thirty extra rounds of rifle or carbine ammo, two hand grenades, a toothbrush, and toothpaste. Most men also packed such personal items as writing paper, a pen or pencil, some photos, and a few prized letters. Hooked on to the back of the pack was an entrenching tool in a canvas cover—one item that would prove almost useless on Peleliu because the coral was too hard to dent with it. As a holdover precaution from World War I, a gas mask was also required equipment.

Much more weight was attached to the web belt around each Marine's waist. This invariably included a first-aid pouch containing dressings, packets of sulfa power, and a hypodermic tube of morphine; another pouch with several clips of ammo; and a Ka-Bar knife in a leather sheath. With high heat expected and no natural source of fresh water on Peleliu, each man also had a full half-gallon of water in two quart canteens hooked to his belt.

In addition, each man carried at least one type of firearm, and many carried two. Most riflemen were armed with nine-pound semi-automatic M-1 rifles, but in each four-man fire team, one designated AR man carried a nineteen-pound Browning automatic rifle. Members of an eight-man mortar squad were equipped with .30-caliber carbines instead of M-1s, because the carbines were four pounds lighter. Some also carried .45 automatic pistols. Gunners were responsible for lugging their own forty-five-pound mortars, and other squad members hauled heavy bags of mortar ammo. One man in each mortar squad carried the shoulder-held rocket launcher known as a bazooka.

When men weren't engrossed in last-minute preparations, they talked quietly among themselves, mostly in groups of twos and threes. They tried hard not to sound too nervous or give away their worries about what the next day might hold in store.

That evening, PFC Sterling Mace stood on the deck of *LST 661* and thought back to his last night on Pavuvu, when he and a couple of old friends—PFC Larry Mahan and Private George McNevin— had gotten together to share a serious moment.

Mace and Mahan had met at the Brooklyn Navy Yard on their first full day as Marines. They'd found themselves next to each other when the new recruits lined up in alphabetical order, but they were split up soon after when the recruits got their permanent company assignments. Mace became the last of the Ms assigned to K Company, and Mahan the first assigned to L Company. Still, they were both in the Third Battalion, Fifth Marines, and they had lived in adjoining bivouac areas, so they remained friends. Mace and McNevin, meanwhile, had gone to high school together, and they'd run into each other again at Pavuvu, where McNevin was a veteran in E Company, Second Battalion, First Marines.

Mace remembered how the three of them had joined hands, wished each other well, and made a solemn vow. "We're gonna get through this and meet again when it's all over," they said, facing each other over their clasped hands. "Lots of luck, and see you later!"

Now Mace could only wonder what the odds were that their reunion would ever happen.

Not far away on the deck of the same LST, PFC Gene Sledge and a buddy leaned against the rail and watched the daylight fade. Sledgehammer later remembered marveling at the beauty of the Pacific sunset, then recoiling with apprehension as he contemplated the next day.

"Suddenly a thought hit me like a thunderbolt," he recalled. "Would I live to see the sunset tomorrow? My knees nearly buckled as panic swept over me."

As darkness descended, Mace's reverie and Sledge's fretful musings were interrupted by a strident voice from the ship's loudspeaker: "Now hear this. Now hear this. All troops lay below to quarters. All troops lay below to quarters."

Back in their compartment, Sledge and the rest of his mortar section received a terse assessment of what they could expect the next morning from their platoon commander, Second Lieutenant Charles "Duke" Ellington.

"General Rupertus says the fighting will be extremely tough but short," Ellington told them. "It'll be over in three or four days— a fight like Tarawa. Rough but fast. Then we can go back to a rest area.

"Remember what you've been taught. Keep your heads down going in on the amtrack. Get off the beach fast. The Japs'll plaster it with everything they've got, and if we get pinned down on the beach, their artillery and mortars will ruin us. Come out of the amtracks ready for anything. Have a round in the chamber of your small arms and your mortar rounds ready for immediate use as soon as we're called on to fire. Reveille will be before daylight, and H-hour will be at 0830. Hit the sack early. You'll need the rest. Good luck and carry on."

After the briefings were over, Hillbilly Jones went back to his quarters, sat down on his bunk, and picked up his guitar. He'd hauled the well-worn instrument the equivalent of three or four times around the world, and as he cradled it in his arms, his mind drifted back to the first time he'd tried to pick out a tune at the age of twelve. His childish fingers had found the right chords effortlessly—almost like a miracle—and he'd been playing by ear ever since. Over the years, the guitar had often come to feel like a physical extension of himself— but he knew he couldn't take it where he was about to go. He'd long ago accepted the necessity of leaving treasured possessions behind. As he'd observed in a recent letter to Mildred Glasgow, a onetime childhood playmate back in Whiteford for whom he'd come to feel something deeper than mere friendship: "I've dropped many of my personal possessions along jungle trails that I valued much more than the combined wealth of Japan."

God willing, Jones told himself, he could reclaim the guitar when the battle ahead was over. In the meantime, it was his machine gun section that would be making the music.

He sat down on the bunk, hugged the guitar against his chest as tenderly as he might have embraced a woman, and brushed his fingers lightly across the strings. For a moment, he considered taking it topside for one last round of songs before the landing, but then he decided he wasn't in the mood.

"So long, old girl," he murmured. "We'll have ourselves a real hoedown when I get back."

He shoved the guitar under the bunk and turned out the light.

Out on the fantail of *LST 661,* Captain Andy Haldane stared down at the ship's white wake in the dark water as his thoughts drifted to the other side of the globe and the tree-shaded campus of Bowdoin College. The trees would be turning, now that it was mid-September, and the Maine woods would soon be one blazing mass of color.

Despite the war, these were still festive times at Bowdoin. The college was celebrating its 150th anniversary, and it would've been fun to be there, he thought. It was also football season. It came as a shock to realize that he'd almost forgotten about football during the past few weeks, and there was undoubtedly a big game on tap for the coming weekend. He wondered who the Polar Bears would be playing on Saturday, and who would be carrying the ball for them. He hoped that at least a few people in the stands would remember old Number 26.

God, it would be so good to go home, he thought. And if this thing on Peleliu went as quickly as it was supposed to, there was a chance that he *could* get home before the end of autumn. Maybe he could actually be there in time to see the leaves in full color, cheer the Polar Bears to victory, and join the Bowdoin anniversary celebration. At least it was something to hope for. But in the meantime, there was another sort of game to be won. The kickoff was set for Orange Beach 1 at 0830 the next day, and Haldane had the feeling it was going to be a tough one.

Corporal Matthew Rousseau hadn't been home to Mineola on Long Island since January 1942—more than two and a half years ago. Since then, he'd fought at Guadalcanal and Cape Gloucester, and now he was the leader of a rifle squad in B Company, First Battalion, Fifth Marines. The details of his battles often ran together in his mind, but he remembered much more clearly the chilly day his father had driven him to the end of the subway line for the trip down to the recruiting station on Whitehall Street.

"You can still change your mind, you know," his dad had said as Matt opened the car door.

"Yeah, but I'd just get drafted in a few weeks if I did," Matt replied. "It's better this way."

And maybe it *was* better. Maybe. But as he lay on his bunk and scribbled a few lines in his diary on the evening of September 14, Rousseau wondered for the thousandth time if he should have taken his dad's suggestion. If he had, he wouldn't be where he was now, and maybe the same insidious thought wouldn't be running through his head every few seconds. It was like a line from a song that you never wanted to hear again—only you couldn't stop humming it over and over to yourself.

Matt had been fairly lucky up to now. A case of malaria on Guadalcanal and an appendectomy at sea had been the worst things to happen to him so far in the war. But he knew that every time he went into battle, his odds of getting out in one piece went down a notch. At least that's what they said. Maybe that was why the inner voice kept dogging him. It was a drumbeat in his brain that refused to go away. It had been there ever since the ship left Pavuvu, and that night it was louder and more ominous than ever:

Oh shit, I'm gonna get it. This time I know I'm gonna get my ass shot off!

CHAPTER FOUR

SEA OF CHAOS; ISLE OF FIRE

Sometime in the small hours after midnight, the LSTs and transports in the invasion fleet slowed to a crawl, then to an almost imperceptible halt. The sound of their engines faded, and they lay still in the calm waters under an overcast sky. The sea breeze died as well, until the air scarcely stirred. The Pacific seemed to be holding its breath. It was Friday morning, September 15, 1944—D-Day at Peleliu.

H-hour was still several hours away, but in the galleys belowdecks, mess crews labored over heavy metal pans of steaming scrambled eggs, and chunks of beef sizzled on large grills. The Navy was preparing the First Marine Division's traditional before-battle "warrior's meal" of steak and eggs, although few of the men would feel like eating when it was served.

Corporal R. V. Burgin hadn't had much luck sleeping during the night, and since he'd grown up on a farm, he was an early riser anyway. He'd already been awake for quite a while when the first notes of reveille sounded at 5:30 A.M., and he was already sitting on the edge of his bunk pulling on his boondocker shoes when Sergeant John Marmet, his platoon leader, came into the compartment.

"Okay, let's get 'em up, Burgy," Marmet said. "Come on, you guys. Hit the deck."

Burgin nudged PFC Gene Sledge, then reached down to shake Corporal Merriel Shelton. "Rise and shine, Sledgehammer. Time to snap to, Snafu. Don't want to keep the Japs waitin'."

The other men in Burgin's mortar squad were soon out of their bunks. They were silent for the most part, and what words were spoken came in hoarse, subdued whispers. Burgin watched his squad mates collect their gear and move toward the showers, noting a total absence of the usual morning horseplay. He could feel the tension in the air.

One of the few men who seemed unperturbed as the squad headed down to chow was PFC Vincent Santos, the young gunner from San Antonio who took pride in his ability to get off up to ten rounds from his 60-millimeter weapon before the first round hit. While other guys sipped coffee and either ignored their food or merely picked at it, Santos downed his steak and eggs with gusto.

His friend and assistant gunner, PFC John Redifer, looked at Santos and shook his head. Redifer was a pretty easygoing guy himself, and he usually didn't let anything bother him, but he had no appetite this morning.

"How can you eat all that?" Redifer asked.

Santos grinned. "Hey, man, how often do you get real steak—or real eggs, either—in this outfit? I'd invade a Jap island again tomorrow for another breakfast like this."

Burgin ate part of his steak and drank some coffee. Across the table, Gene Sledge, looking slightly green, his stomach tied in knots, turned away from his plate.

Everything about the amphibious assault on Peleliu was neatly diagrammed on the planners' maps and charts, making the D-Day maneuver look simple enough on paper.

The three infantry regiments of the First Marine Division would land abreast on beaches extending up the west side of the island from near its southern tip to just below the point where the upper pincer of Peleliu's lobster-claw curves back to the east. Squarely at the center of this 2,500-yard stretch of beach and about 300 yards inland lay the airfield, whose seizure was the invasion's primary early objective.

White Beaches 1 and 2 at the left, or north, end of the landing area were the responsibility of the First Marines, commanded by Colonel Chesty Puller. After securing its section of the beach, the First's next objective was to seize some of the high ground to the north.

The Fifth Marines under Colonel Harold D. "Bucky" Harris were to land on Orange Beaches 1 and 2 at the center of the beachhead and move immediately on the airport, fighting their way across it on the first day if possible.

The Seventh Marines, commanded by Colonel Herman H. Hanneken, a Medal of Honor winner in Haiti in 1920, were to land on Orange Beach 3 to support the right flank of the Fifth Marines, then drive across the narrow southern tip of the island and seize two large promontories extending out into the ocean. One of the Seventh's three battalions was to be held in reserve. In a coordinated assault, elements of the Army's Eighty-first Division were to land on Angaur, an island about seven miles south of Peleliu.

U.S. planes had kept Peleliu under intense aerial surveillance for more than six months, and the U.S. submarine *Seawolf* had photographed all the potential landing sites in late June. Planners had determined well in advance that the only feasible places for a landing in force were the beaches on the southwestern section of the island. All other beaches were ruled out for being too narrow to support a secure beachhead, too close to impenetrable swamps, too dominated by high ground presumably held by the enemy, or too far from the airfield.

The beaches selected had several distinct liabilities, however. For one, the five battalions of infantry in the initial assault—about 5,000 men—would have to cross a shallow coral reef up to 700 yards wide before they reached the shore. For another, the landing areas were within easy range of any Japanese artillery and heavy mortars that had survived the naval and air bombardments and were still concealed in the high ground that began to rise just a few hundred yards from the water's edge.

To avoid a repeat of the heavy casualties inflicted on the Marines while crossing a similar reef at Tarawa, all assault troops at Peleliu were to come ashore in amphibious tractors. The amtracks were less likely than the smaller Higgins boats to get hung up on the reef, and they could also carry the troops onto dry land.

To the men who had to go ashore in them, another appealing feature of the amtracks was their exit ramp, which opened to the rear for greater protection. "It was a damned site better than having to go over the gunwales of a Higgins boat into five or six feet of water while you were taking heavy fire," said Sergeant Jim McEnery, who had done just that at Guadalcanal.

Unfortunately, some of the amtracks were older types without the tailgate ramps, and on the newer models the ramps had a tendency to stick and refuse to open at the critical moment. Old or new, the amtracks were slow and cumbersome, with a maximum speed of just 4.5 knots, compared to the brisk 12-knot top speed of a Higgins boat. Moreover, many of the amtrack drivers had little, if any, experience guiding the vehicles under enemy fire.

The planners' goal was to place the first eight waves of assault troops, about 4,500 men, ashore on Peleliu within nineteen minutes of H-hour, and 2,500 more within another sixty-one minutes—a total of 7,000 men in one and a third hours. Achieving this objective would require precise timing, near-perfect coordination, minimal resistance from the enemy, and exceptional good fortune with the amtracks—none of which the Marines would get.

In retrospect, the goal was utterly unrealistic, but it reflected the heady optimism shared by U.S. military strategists, who had grossly miscalculated both the resolve and intentions of the Japanese on Peleliu.

Well before first light, the Navy guns had opened up again, and the noise on the decks of the LSTs was so loud that Marines had to shout directly into each other's ears to make themselves heard as they boarded their assigned amtracks. Across the three and a half miles of ocean now separating them from Peleliu, the shoreline was obscured by a pall of smoke. To the future author and historian

Robert Leckie, who was aboard one of the LSTs as a young Marine, the island seemed like one giant "holocaust."

The battleships several miles further out fired one thunderous salvo after another. Closer in to shore, destroyers pummeled the beach and the rising ground beyond with their five-inch guns while rows of missiles spurted like giant Roman candles from infantry landing craft converted into rocket ships. Navy carrier planes roared low over the island, peppering it with bombs and tracer bullets.

To PFC Bill Leyden, who nervously watched the fireworks with other members of his rifle squad while waiting to board an amtrack for his first taste of combat, the sound and fury were like music in his ears. He could hear the five-foot-long shells from the battleships hissing directly overhead, followed seconds later by blasts that shook the sea beneath him and sent towering clouds of smoke, dust, and flame skyward.

"I didn't see how the hell anything could live through that kind of punishment," Leyden recalled. "I told myself that maybe all the Japs would already be dead by the time we went ashore. It looked like the whole island was on fire."

What Leyden didn't know was that at least three-fourths of the 10,900-man Japanese garrison—along with its artillery, tanks, heavy mortars, and machine guns—was holed up in deep caves and concrete bunkers, and practically untouched by this last-minute pyrotechnics display. Only the more exposed pillboxes and gun emplacements near the beaches were vulnerable to the Navy's bombardment, and even many of them survived intact. Soon, Leyden and his mates would discover just how misleading appearances could be.

Meanwhile, a complex panorama of pre-invasion maneuvers was unfolding at sea. It began more than ten miles from shore, and viewed from high above, it might have resembled an intricate ballet of ships, landing craft, and small boats as they took their positions in five designated lines or areas. To those caught up in it at sea level, however, it looked like utter chaos.

Furthest out was the transport line, where the big supply ships were anchored. Then came the LST unloading line, where the landing ships were to pause long enough to discharge wave commanders into small boats to lead the LSTs to the launching line 6,000 yards from the beach. At this point, the LSTs would open their clamshell bow doors and launch the amtracks loaded with Marines. Then the amtracks would proceed to the line of departure, a rendezvous point 4,000 yards from Peleliu, where the amtracks would be grouped and dispatched toward their specified landing sites, still a half-hour away. Finally, 2,000 yards beyond the reef was the transfer control line, the point to which the amtracks would return after taking their initial assault waves ashore, to pick up more men or supplies transferred from small boats.

A system of flags hoisted by a landing force control officer aboard the destroyer *Hazelwood* was to tell each wave when to head for shore. Leading the amtracks in would be five patrol boats—one for each section of beach—which would peel off at the transfer control line. Here, wave commanders in Higgins boats would take over and lead the amtracks to within 1,000 yards of the beach.

From there, they would be on their own.

As the amtracks slid into the sea and started plowing shoreward, the big warships on the horizon began lifting their barrage of the beach, and the attacking carrier planes flew their final sorties. Some of the men on the LSTs watched a Navy Hellcat fighter coughing smoke as it made a final pass over the island. Then the plane crashed in a fireball on the beach.

It was a sobering sight—clear evidence that at least some of the Japanese on Peleliu were still alive and firing back.

"Don't stop now—keep it up," PFC Sterling Mace urged the Navy gunners under his breath. It bothered him when the rate of fire from the battlewagons started tailing off. Mace figured that every sixteen-inch round the big ships slammed into the island meant fewer live Japanese waiting to greet him when he hit the beach.

The tank deck on *LST 661* was filled with diesel fumes and the roar of engines. Huge exhaust fans whirred overhead, working to clear the smoky air as the first wave of amtracks, each loaded with about two dozen Marines and a driver, jerked forward and clattered down the ramp into daylight and the ocean.

Mace, huddled between Sergeant Jim McEnery and PFC Seymour Levy, felt his own amtrack settle heavily into the water. Rifle barrels stuck out like porcupine quills in every direction, and as if the tractor wasn't crowded enough already, some jokers had crammed a 37-millimeter field piece aboard just before it went down the ramp. Now there was hardly room to breathe. Mace sagged under his nineteen-pound BAR, a bag of ammo that weighed about the same, nearly ten pounds of water in his canteens, and assorted other gear.

As his amtrack pulled away from the LST, Mace looked up at a group of sailors standing on the bow. They were laughing, drinking coffee, and waving towels.

"Go get 'em, Marines!" he heard them holler.

Mace frowned and didn't acknowledge the sendoff. Tonight, he thought, the sailors would be enjoying a hot meal, maybe watching a movie, and sleeping in comfortable bunks a world away from the blazing island where the amtracks were headed.

He stole a peek over the gunwale at the distant white beach of Peleliu and the curtain of black smoke hanging over it.

"Christ," he muttered, "sometimes I think I joined the wrong outfit."

To Gene Sledge, his own amphibious tractor looked like a big duck as it floated away from the LST moments behind Mace and his rifle squad.

"Want a cigarette, Sledgehammer?" yelled Snafu Shelton, holding out a pack of smokes.

"You know I don't smoke, Snafu," Sledge shouted back. "I've told you a million times."

Snafu laughed. "Yeah, well, I'm makin' you a bet. 'Fore today's over, you'll be smokin' ever' cigarette you can get your hands on."

"Knock it off," said R. V. Burgin, squatting next to them against the gunwale of the amtrack. "Just hang on and stick close to me and Snafu, Sledgehammer. You'll be okay."

An eternity seemed to pass before a Navy officer in a Higgins boat gave the signal for the amtrack carrying Burgin's mortar squad to head for shore, but the waiting brought Sledge no relief. Cold sweat broke out on his face, and he found it impossible to swallow around the lump in his throat. The driver revved his engine, and the amtrack wallowed forward.

"This is it, boys!" shouted Lieutenant Duke Ellington, leader of the K/3/5 mortar section, waving a half-pint bottle of whiskey. "Anybody want a drink?"

After taking a healthy swig from the bottle himself, Ellington passed it to a couple of other Marines who followed suit. But when the bottle was held out toward Sledge, he shrank away, certain that even one whiff of the whiskey would make him pass out.

A huge enemy shell burst a few yards to the right front of the amtrack, hurling seawater skyward, as Sledge clung to the rail. The amtrack rocked drunkenly in the wake of the blast, as if a big snort of Lieutenant Ellington's booze had gotten into its fuel tanks by mistake.

Sledge was gripped by nausea and almost certain that he was about to either throw up or wet his pants—maybe both. He almost felt better when he glanced to the other side of the amtrack and saw his squad mate, PFC Vincent Santos, leaning over the side and losing his steak-and-egg breakfast into the blue Pacific.

At least, Sledge thought, he wasn't the only sick, scared Marine in this invasion.

On White Beach 1, several hundred yards north of where Sledge's amtrack was heading, PFC Edgar Brown, a seventeen-year-old gunner from Knoxville, Tennessee, squatted behind his snub-nosed

75-millimeter howitzer and peered out the open turret of his tank at a scene of utter bedlam.

Brown and the rest of the Third Armored Amphibious Tank Battalion were the first Marines to reach the beach, and he would've given his soul to be anywhere else on earth at that moment. The island seemed to be blowing up around him as Japanese artillery and mortar rounds rained down on all sides.

The battalion's seventy-two amphibian tanks had rolled out of the LSTs and headed shoreward in zero wave, just a couple of minutes ahead of the amtracks carrying the first waves of infantrymen. The tanks and their six-man crews were assigned to engage whatever Japanese positions might still be firing from a slight rise 200 yards inland and provide a protective screen for the rifle platoons coming in hard on their heels. The tanks were only lightly armored, but their hulls could stop machine gun bullets and small-arms fire, and each mounted a .30- and .50-caliber machine gun in addition to the howitzer.

It had been a rough ride in—the first time the First Marine Division had used amphibious tanks in a landing—and nothing had worked right. The entire first platoon of five tanks had already been knocked out or sunk by enemy fire. Now Brown could see others behind him being hit by Japanese pillboxes on both sides of him before they could reach dry land.

Brown glanced toward the tank to his left, thinking of a buddy from Memphis who was somewhere down in its steel bowels. Then, before he could blink, the tank was blown to pieces by a 75-millimeter enemy shell. Shards of its metal hide flew past Brown's head and clanged off the side of his own tank.

Looking the other way, Brown saw one of the amtracks already beached, its riflemen clambering down the rear ramp. Some of them threw themselves into the surf, dodging the debris from the ruined tank.

Brown felt his assistant gunner tap him on the back to signal that the howitzer was loaded and set to fire.

"Ready!" he heard the guy say.

Brown sighted in on one of the enemy pillboxes and slammed his fist against the firing button, but nothing happened. He tried two or three more times with the same result.

"Gun's jammed," he said. "It won't fire."

His words were lost as an armor-piercing shell ripped through the center of the tank just below his seat. It tore a hole big enough for a man to crawl through and blew apart two infantrymen just outside, but no one in the tank was seriously hurt.

"Everybody outta here!" the tank commander shouted. "That son of a bitch has got our range."

Brown hauled himself out of the turret, jumped to the ground, and ran like a jackrabbit for the nearest shell hole. There were plenty of those, so he didn't have far to go.

PFC Bill Leyden's amtrack slammed against Orange Beach 2 with a sudden jolt, sending men tumbling as the rear ramp fell open. Leyden stumbled down the ramp, almost falling in the wet sand, then ran around the tractor and charged across the beach, dimly aware of other members of his squad running behind and beside him.

Thirty yards to his left, an enemy shell exploded, but the firing in the immediate vicinity had eased off. It seemed to be much heavier further to the left, where the remains of burning and disabled amtracks dotted the beach and the reef beyond. Green-clad lumps at the edge of the surf and further inland marked the spots where Marines were dead or down.

He pounded forward about a dozen steps. The rattle of small-arms fire came from just ahead, and he heard occasional bullets buzzing like bees around him, but there was no sign of enemy soldiers. He threw himself flat against the sand, hugging his rifle and wishing he could dig a hole right there. Then the distant but well-remembered voice of Leyden's drill instructor at Parris Island echoed in his mind, warning him:

A beach is not a good place to be. When you're on a beach, the first thing you want to do is get the hell off of it as fast as you can.

"Let's go!" shouted Corporal Leonard Ahner, Leyden's fire team leader. "Let's keep moving!"

About sixty yards directly in front of him, Leyden could see the edge of the airfield and a line of green foliage that marked the point where the beach ended. In the distance, a long series of misty, green ridges rose against the sky, reminding him of the mysterious island in the movie *King Kong.*

Leyden scrambled to his feet and started running again. A few moments later, he was on the fringe of the airfield, and he silently congratulated himself for moving inland so quickly. Then he realized he was all alone. He couldn't see anyone from his platoon in front of him or beside him, and when he looked back, there were no Marines behind him, either. Taking cover behind a partially defoliated palm tree, he lay there panting and sweating. The climbing sun radiating off the sand and coral was already murderously hot, and he felt it getting hotter by the second.

Leyden thought about the long-ago Saturday, just a couple of months before the subway train disaster that killed his best friend, Donald Muñoz, when he'd decided to walk all the way from Yonkers to Vermont just for the hell of it. He'd ended up hungry, shivering, and disoriented, spending the night in a cave somewhere well south of White Plains. He felt even more confused and forlorn now than he had then.

The next two or three minutes seemed like half an hour, but there was still no sign of the rest of his platoon. Leyden was about to head back toward the beach when he saw a uniformed figure running toward him from the right. He raised his rifle and almost fired before he realized it was another Marine.

Leyden didn't recognize the guy who plopped down beside him, but he knew he wasn't from K/3/5. The other Marine's face was covered with black and green camouflage paint with rivulets of perspiration running through it.

"Damn, I almost shot you," Leyden said. "What's your outfit?"

"Seventh Marines," the guy panted.

"Then what the hell are you doing on my left? I'm Fifth Marines, and you guys are supposed to be off to the right of us."

The guy shook his head. "All I know," he said, "is this is where they parked my ass."

Leyden shrugged. "It's good to know I'm not the only one that's lost," he said. They both ducked as a Japanese mortar shell exploded a dozen yards away.

On Orange Beach 1, a short distance north of Leyden's position, Corporal Red Womack and other members of the flamethrower section of Weapons Company, Third Battalion, Fifth Marines, found themselves in a hornet's nest.

Mortar and small arms fire were kicking up sand all around them as the six two-man flamethrower squads ran onto the beach. The husky, red-bearded Womack braced himself under the seventy pounds of weapon and fuel on his back and tried not to break stride. His assistant gunner, PFC William Lewis, trailed close behind.

As he bolted around the side of the amtrack and turned inland, Womack recognized a fallen Marine writhing on a patch of bloody sand almost under the front end of the tractor. The guy had been just ahead of him and Lewis as they came down the landing ramp. Now he looked to be badly hurt, maybe dying. Womack thought the guy's name was Beeson, and he wanted to stop and try to help him, but he didn't. Behind him as he ran on, he heard someone call for a corpsman.

Minutes later and approximately a football field's length from the water's edge, Womack heard another yell:

"Hey, Corporal. We need your blowtorch over here!"

Keeping low, Womack moved as quickly as he could toward the voice until he spotted a four-man Marine fire team pinned down in a hole. Just over a slight rise, he caught sight of a Japanese soldier with a light machine gun firing from behind piled-up chunks of coral.

With Lewis and several other Marines providing covering fire,

Womack moved to within about fifty feet of the enemy gunner. Lewis scrambled up behind him and tapped his knuckles on Womack's helmet.

"You're set, Red," he said.

Womack clenched his teeth and moved cautiously forward, trying to keep his mind fixed on the task at hand. He wanted it to be automatic, and he did everything in his power to blank out the consequences.

Just do it the way you've been trained to do—the way you've done it a hundred times before. There's no difference today. It's the same as it's always been.

Only it wasn't. Always before, the target had been a dummy foxhole or empty bunker. Now, for the first time, he was about to unleash the awesome power in his hands against a living human being.

Womack jerked the trigger and held it. From the flamethrower's nozzle, a cloud of bright orange fire and black smoke spewed, obscuring everything in its path. A four- or five-second burst would have been plenty to do the job, but in his nervousness, Womack expended his full fifteen seconds' worth of fuel and released the trigger only when his tank was empty.

As the inferno abated slightly, he caught a glimpse of the enemy soldier, a blazing figure trying to run but shriveling like a wad of burning paper. Then it disappeared in a hail of Marine rifle bullets.

The blowback from Womack's weapon was almost hot enough to singe his beard, and the odor it flung into his face was the worst he'd ever smelled. He staggered backward, fighting the choking sensation in his throat.

The first thing Sergeant Jim McEnery saw as his rifle platoon ran onto Orange Beach 2 was a large cur dog watching the Marines from near the edge of the surf. The dog was wagging its tail, and its body was shaking from its hips to its shoulders. It seemed addled by the gunfire, but unhurt. It stared at McEnery for a few seconds, then trotted away down the beach, leaving the sergeant to wonder:

*If that dog can come through such a massive pre-invasion bom-
bardment without a scratch, what about the Japanese?*

The answer came soon enough. The platoon hadn't gone far before McEnery spotted a group of enemy soldiers behind a pile of
rocks. They were moving a 75-millimeter field piece into position to
fire toward the beach.

"Take cover, you guys," he said. "Let's see if we can get some big
stuff in here."

As platoon guide and third in command of K/3/5's Third Platoon,
McEnery was carrying a two-way "Spam can" walkie-talkie. But
when he tried to call for artillery support to knock out the Japanese
gun, he found the radio was useless. He could hear a jumble of
voices competing with each other on various frequencies, but when
he yelled into the thing, he got no response.

"There's a tank coming, Mack," he heard one of the men yell.

McEnery turned to see an amphibious tank rumbling toward
them with its own 75-millimeter cannon.

Apparently, the tank was having no luck with its radio, either.
"We're looking for the Seventh Marines," the tank commander
shouted from the open turret.

"They're not in this sector," McEnery called back, "but come on
with us. We can use your help." He gestured toward the Japanese artillery emplacement.

"Can you take out that thing?"

"Consider it done," the tank commander said.

The tank's turret turned, and a second later its howitzer opened
fire. The first round hit the target dead-center, hurling the smashed
field piece onto its side and sending chunks of coral flying. Some of
the enemy gunners and ammo handlers tried to run, but the Marine
riflemen picked them off before they could take more than a few
steps.

When McEnery and his men reached the wrecked gun, all the
Japanese were dead.

． ． ．

About 200 yards inland, near the invisible line dividing Orange Beach 2 from Orange Beach 3, Sergeant Fred Miller was crouching in the sand at the bottom of a three-foot-deep shell crater. Although he was in no great pain, Miller could tell he was seriously hurt. The blood saturating his dungaree pants from just below his cartridge belt to near his left knee told him his wound was bad. He also had no sensation in his left leg.

Miller had had a bad feeling about this day ever since the previous afternoon when he'd learned that his best buddy, PFC Howard Mahaney, was in sick bay with a throat infection and was going to miss the invasion. The feeling had turned out to be right. Everything had been screwed up from the start. Then it had gone from bad to worse.

Less than half an hour earlier, Miller had come ashore in the same amtrack with Captain Ack-Ack Haldane and most of the rest of the K/3/5 headquarters platoon. They'd encountered no major problems most of the way in, but the enemy shelling grew heavier as they approached their assigned destination near the center of the beachhead. By the time they exited the amtrack, the platoon was under intense artillery, mortar, and machine gun fire. Dozens of wrecked and burning amtracks and amphibious trucks littered the beach or wallowed helplessly in the surf, especially off to the left, where the First Marines were taking a terrific pounding.

Seconds after landing, Miller had glanced seaward in time to see the amtrack right behind his own—the one carrying the company's radio man and all its communications equipment—take a direct hit and explode. As debris fell around him, Miller remembered Haldane shouting, "Let's get moving! We're in a crossfire, and we've got to get off this beach."

Miller had run past several fallen Marines. He'd tried not to look at them, but one in particular caught his eye. The man was dragging himself along in the sand with one of his feet turned the wrong way and attached to his leg only by a single exposed tendon.

The platoon pushed inland, running a dozen or so steps at a time, then hitting the deck. The nearest cover, except for the shell holes and bomb craters pocking the beach, looked to be some scrubby brush in the distance. But about halfway to the brush, a tank trap ditch yawned in front of them. Haldane motioned the others into it, then jumped in after them.

The firing from in front was still fierce—most of it from unseen machine guns that had set up interlacing fields of fire, making every move by a Marine a gamble with death. But the platoon was also beginning to take fire on its right flank, from the direction where the Seventh Marines should have been. Confusion, chaos, and death seemed to be everywhere.

"I need a runner, Sergeant," Haldane told Miller. "All our communications equipment was on that amtrack that got hit, so we've got no contact with the Seventh Marines. They're supposed to form a line even with us on our right, but they don't know where we are and vice versa. We may end up shooting each other unless we hook up soon."

"What do you want me to do?" Miller asked.

"Fall back about fifty yards toward the beach where the firing's not so heavy," the captain said. "Then try to work your way to the right, and see if you can locate anybody from the Seventh. Tell them our position, and let's see if we can get ourselves coordinated."

It was about five minutes later when Miller ran afoul of the machine gun in the Japanese pillbox. It had loomed up suddenly some twenty yards ahead as he darted from behind a patch of brush. He'd dived headlong for the crater just as the machine gun opened fire. He'd been a split second too late.

At first he thought he'd merely stumbled at the edge of the hole, and that was what had caused his fall. Then, when he saw the blood and realized he was hit, he was afraid the bullet had pierced his stomach. The fear left his throat dry and made the rising heat of the day feel even more intense. He reached instinctively for one of his canteens, but a warning thought stopped him.

You can't drink water, damn it. If you're gut-shot, they say drinking water can kill you quicker than the wound itself.

A strange calmness descended on him. He took out his Ka-Bar knife and slit open his upper pants leg. Blood pulsed out of his left thigh through a red-black hole the size of his little finger. He held a compress from his first-aid kit tightly against the hole until the bleeding slowed to an ooze. He shook sulfa powder onto the wound and gave himself a shot of morphine, although he felt little pain.

Then he noticed that a second bullet had punched through his left hand. The hand was numb and bleeding slightly, but he could still move his fingers a little. Compared to a bullet in the belly, the damage to his hand and thigh seemed almost inconsequential. He treated himself to a long gulp of water.

Using his right hand, Miller picked up his M-1, wondering if he could put a round or two through the narrow gun port in the front of the pillbox. He had 300 rounds of ammo for the rifle, so he could keep up a steady rate of fire for a long time if he dared try. At least, it might keep the Japanese from rushing him for a while. Common sense told him that other Marines had to be close by—maybe within a few yards—but he'd never felt so isolated.

For a while, he lost track of time. He was growing woozy from the heat and the loss of blood, but every couple of minutes, he'd stick the muzzle of the M-1 over the edge of the crater and squeeze off a few shots at the pillbox. Each time, the Japanese gunner would respond with a burst of fire that kicked up sand and sent it cascading down on Miller as he ducked. But the enemy soldiers made no attempt to move toward him. Now and then, to fight the stifling heat, he took a swig of water. There was no shade in the crater, and the sun was scorching and blindingly bright.

When he pushed himself up to fire at the pillbox again, he caught sight of two Marines. They weren't more than 100 feet away, and when he waved at them, they saw him and started working their way toward him. Miller tossed a pair of smoke grenades out in front of the pillbox to give them cover, and, seconds later, they jumped into the hole with him.

Miller managed a wide grin. He'd never been so elated to see anybody in his life. The presence of the two Marines made him feel as secure as if a whole battalion had just showed up.

Just try something now, you damned Japs, he thought. *Come on, I dare you!*

"Seventh Marines?" he asked groggily.

"Yeah," one of them replied. "You hit bad?"

"I'll make it. My leg's just not working too good."

He drifted into unconsciousness for a few minutes, and when he came to, the pillbox had been silenced and a Navy corpsman was working on him. Soon two stretcher-bearers were carrying him through sporadic fire to an aid station. Just over an hour after Miller had landed on Peleliu, he was on his way to a hospital ship offshore.

It would be seventeen months before he recovered enough to walk unaided. But, as Miller and most of the 9,000 infantrymen of the First Marine Division who remained behind would readily agree, he was one of the lucky ones.

CHAPTER FIVE

THE WHITE BEACHES TURN RED

While the Fifth Marines battled confusion and chaos on the Orange Beaches, Colonel Chesty Puller's First Marines were running into a wall of fierce Japanese resistance on the northernmost portion of the beachhead, designated as White Beaches 1 and 2. Even before the first wave of assault troops landed, their amtracks had come under heavy fire, and once ashore they found themselves caught in the jaws of what amounted to a giant meat grinder.

Sixty yards off White Beach 1, mortar shells were dropping all around the amtrack carrying the headquarters platoon of K/3/1, commanded by Captain George Hunt. Seconds later, Hunt, who had left a job as a staff writer for *Life* magazine to lead a rifle company, also heard the whine of enemy machine gun fire.

"Damn, those are bullets," shouted the tractor's commander from behind his .50-caliber weapon. "Heads up! I'm gonna spray the trees."

"Son of a bitch," Hunt muttered to himself. "The beach is lousy with the bastards." Most of the heavier fire seemed to be coming from slightly above and to his left. As Hunt glanced that way, he immediately recognized the sheer walls of a promontory called the Point, which jutted about twenty-five yards into the ocean.

There were Japanese on the beach, all right, but Hunt knew that the Point was the biggest hotbed of enemy firepower in the vicinity. He'd stared many times at aerial photos of the craggy formation, showing at least two pillboxes carved into it and a network of concrete fortifications around its base. Taking the Point was his company's number one objective, and if the Japanese guns embedded in it were still operational, it meant a mess of trouble for this whole section of beach. The hollowed-out coral mass, resembling a giant worm-eaten chocolate drop, harbored enough mortars, machine guns, and small-bore artillery to menace every man and object for several hundred yards to the south.

As the amphibious tractor—one of too many with no rear ramp—bounded ashore, its nose tilted sharply upward, then leveled out again. Hunt looked over the gunwale to see shattered coconut trees and splintered stumps. Then the amtrack commander nodded in Hunt's direction.

"Everybody out!" the captain said as he jumped over the side. The impact of the eight-foot drop to the ground jarred Hunt's legs and threw him off-balance, but he recovered quickly. He ran inland as fast as he could for about seventy-five yards, until he spotted a good-sized shell hole and slid into it.

The air was full of black smoke and the acrid smell of gunpowder. Hunt's mouth and throat were dry, and sweat was dripping off the end of his nose. As he took a swig of water from his canteen, a bullet smacked the sand inches away.

Along with Hunt in the shell hole were his headquarters platoon leader, Second Lieutenant Ray Stramel; two of his runners, PFCs Coleman Blackburn and Patrick J. Kelly; a radio operator; and several other Marines. First Sergeant Schmittou was crouching behind a bush just beyond the rim of the hole.

"Corpsman, up here," Schmittou called out. "We got a man hit."

Hunt had no idea where the rest of his company was. He couldn't see any of his three rifle platoons or any of his machine guns, but he thought he heard some of them firing to his right and left.

Heavy enemy mortar rounds shook the ground in an ominous pattern. The blasts straddled the crater where Hunt and the others huddled. As they drew closer, some of the shells burst within a few feet of the hole, but none hit it directly.

To Hunt's amazement, Lieutenant Colonel R. P. Ross, the regiment's executive officer, suddenly jumped into the hole. Ross seemed as stunned and confused as everyone else. He and the rest of the regimental command staff were supposed to be well to the right on White Beach 2, and Hunt couldn't imagine what Colonel Puller's second in command was doing in the midst of all this mayhem. Hunt offered a cigarette, but Ross declined.

"I've got to keep moving." The colonel's voice was a breathless wheeze. "Take care of my radio operator. He's been hit."

A corpsman clambered over to where the radio man lay. "He's dead, Colonel," the medic said.

"Oh. Well, good luck," Ross said. He ran on down the beach just as the voice of Lieutenant William "Bull" Sellers, Hunt's own second in command, crackled over the radio. Sellers was supposed to be about fifty yards away. Hunt hoped he was no further.

"Send up stretchers," Hunt snapped. "We're getting casualties."

Moments later, Hunt heard a scuffling sound behind him and turned to see Blackburn, one of his runners, writhing in pain with an arm wound. After Blackburn was tended to, there was still no sign of any stretcher-bearers, so Hunt got Sellers on the radio again.

"Where in hell are the stretchers?"

"They should be there by now," Sellers said. "There's Japs all around us back here."

The first wave of amtracks crawled onto White Beach 1 at 0832 —barely two minutes behind the planners' schedule—and other waves crowded in only seconds behind them. Each of the amphibious tractor drivers was trying desperately to dump his contingent of two dozen men ashore and get out of the danger zone as fast as possible.

The resulting congestion gave the Japanese a tempting array of closely packed targets along the length of the White Beaches, and they were taking maximum advantage of it. Instead of strengthening the beachhead, the arrival of more amtracks thrusting more Marines onto the crowded shore only made the situation more deadly.

As Captain Everett Pope led C Company, First Battalion, First

Marines (C/1/1) across the beach, he counted at least fifteen or six-teen burning amtracks to his left and right. There was no time for a more accurate tally. Marines were being hit all around him.

The beach was very shallow, and Pope saw that the Japanese had it rigged like a shooting gallery. Every enemy gun barrel on the island seemed to be aimed squarely at his 235 men.

"Don't bunch up!" Pope yelled. "Spread out and get down!" Then he took his own advice and threw himself onto the sand.

The same interlacing fields of enemy fire that Pope's friend, Andy Haldane, had experienced on the Orange Beaches with the Fifth Marines were far more deadly in the First Marines' sector. Close to half the regiment's amtracks looked to have been blasted crossing the reef, or just as they touched shore, and men were falling by the dozens as they tried to escape the blazing hulks. At some points, the surf was red with American blood.

The situation was desperate from the outset and aggravated by a near-total communications breakdown. All five of the LVT amphibian tanks carrying the regiment's communications equipment suffered direct hits before they got across the reef. Rifle platoons, and even whole companies, were left pinned down, isolated, and at the mercy of concentrated enemy fire originating from a slight embankment about 100 yards inland.

Meanwhile, fire from the Point, the knob of rock jutting up from the north end of the beach, was gnawing away at the exposed left flank of the entire Third Battalion. Further south, on White Beach 2, the Second Battalion was also within range of the Point's heavy mortars and artillery.

In addition to the relentless fire from these positions, Marines also came under attack from a network of "spider holes" along the beach, each harboring at least one Japanese rifleman. On White Beach 2, Lieutenant Colonel Russell Honsowetz, commanding the Second Battalion, saw his adjutant killed by an enemy soldier who jumped from a small hole and shot the officer at point-blank range.

. . .

Despite the fact that he was getting his first taste of combat, PFC Fred K. Fox had volunteered to man the .30-caliber machine gun on the right side of his amtrack on the way in. Fox, an eighteen-year-old from Houston, was a flamethrower operator attached to K/3/1, but he'd also trained on machine guns. Now, 100 or so yards from shore, his tractor was receiving intense mortar and anti-boat gunfire. So far, none of the enemy shells had hit home, but Fox was soaking wet from seawater flung up by near-misses.

Lacking any discernible targets, Fox fired into the coconut trees as the tractor approached the beach. Then, some fifty yards to his left, he spotted a camouflaged gun embrasure and a Japanese soldier trying to push the brush aside to see out. Fox turned loose the machine gun, grabbed his flamethrower, and buckled it on.

Lieutenant Ralph "Black Jack" Estey, leader of the Third Platoon, was the first man down the rear ramp of the amtrack. Fox was close behind, followed by his assistant gunner and fellow Texan, PFC Thomas "Whitey" Hudson. While Estey moved in another direction, Fox and Hudson ran straight for the Japanese gun emplacement. They paused as Hudson fired several blasts toward the embrasure from his 12-gauge military shotgun and Fox readied the flamethrower for action.

They were within about twenty yards of the embrasure when Fox squeezed on the valve of the flamethrower and pressed the igniting trigger. Nothing happened.

Fox ran closer and tried again. Still nothing. Roughly half his fuel squirted out, splattering the embrasure and the brush around it, but the firing mechanism still refused to work.

"It's no good," Fox yelled to Hudson. "Let's get out of here!"

They ran back toward the beach, but there was no cover there. Their amtrack was already in the water again, heading out to pick up another load. They made for the nearest protection—a gaping, four-foot-deep shell hole. Three Marine demolition engineers were already in the hole, staring nervously at a bright orange aerial bomb standing nose up in the sand, where it had been buried by the Japanese as an anti-tank mine.

"I don't think this is a good place to be," one of the engineers said.

Fox agreed. He dumped his flamethrower pack, gas mask, and life belt at the bottom of the hole, and the five of them jumped up and ran toward a tangle of burned trees and brush some twenty yards away.

Behind him, Fox heard someone shout, "Gas! Gas!"

He hesitated for an instant, thinking of going back for his gas mask. Then he changed his mind and ran on.

As Fox reached the undergrowth, the first thing he saw was Lieutenant Estey, sitting in a clump of brush and bleeding from a deep gash in his left arm above the elbow. While Fox was trying to cut away the lieutenant's sleeve and get a bandage on the wound, a stream of machine gun bullets spattered the sand beside them. Fox rolled away and Estey fell to the ground, but the bullets missed them both.

"I can't handle this tommy gun," Estey said, indicating the Thompson submachine gun beside him. "I'll trade you for your pistol."

They'd just made the exchange when PFC Kelly, one of Captain Hunt's runners, dropped down beside them.

"Looks like we lost all our damned machine guns out in the water," Kelly said, "and the company's taking heavy casualties. The captain wants to know how the Third Platoon's making out."

"Tell him I've been hit, and we're shot up pretty bad," Estey said, "but I'm sending the rest of the platoon on to the Point. If we don't root the Japs out of there, we're all dead."

Corporal Swede Hanson was Norwegian by birth, rather than Swedish, but that hadn't mattered to his buddies in boot camp, who quickly dubbed him with the nickname he'd been known by ever since. Hanson had connived his way into the Marines in early 1943 by chasing down a truck filled with new recruits and stowing away on it after he'd been told there was no room for him. As an extra man without proper papers, he'd been cursed, berated, and threatened for three days before a lieutenant colonel finally relented and swore him into the Corps.

Now, as Hanson charged through the chaos and carnage on White Beach 1, he could only wonder why he'd gone to so damned much trouble to get himself in a mess like this.

A veteran S-2 intelligence scout attached to Captain Hunt's K/3/1, Hanson had known going in that he'd have to move fast or die. Out of the corner of his eye, he could see amtracks circling in the surf and tanks plowing toward shore. The beach was being inundated with men, and many of them were never going to live to get off.

With bullets clanging off the steel hull of his amtrack, and Marines getting cut down as they piled out on its north side, Hanson climbed over the opposite gunwale instead. If not for that, plus the fact that he was as skinny as a fence post—over six feet tall and only about 130 pounds—he figured he would've been hit already.

He stayed on the heels of Lieutenant Sellers, the burly ex–Alabama farmboy and company exec who commanded his platoon, until they came to a thick concrete pillar in the sand a few yards inland. It was part of a Japanese tank trap and the only concealment in sight. As Hanson and Sellers hurled themselves behind it, a burst of enemy machine gun bullets slammed the concrete, sending chips of it flying.

Several tank crewmen, lugging a .30-caliber machine gun and identifiable by their insignia and goggles, tumbled down beside Hanson and crouched there, panting. One of them was wearing a gorgeous string of black pearls around his neck.

"I thought you guys were supposed to be out ahead of us," Hanson said.

The tanker grinned. "We were, but our tank got hit. You got a Jap machine gun right on your fanny, so don't move till we can take care of it."

Despite the warning, Sellers risked a look around the edge of the pillar. "There's also two 47-millimeter anti-boat guns in the pillbox

right in front of us," he said, ducking quickly as more slugs ricocheted off the concrete. "My God, we're getting small-arms fire, too.
The damned Japs are everywhere."

At that instant, one of the anti-boat guns opened fire, and a shell
hissed directly over Sellers's head. From the sound, it didn't miss
the lieutenant by more than a few inches. He flattened himself
against the ground, shaking and swearing, while the machine gunners next to him got busy with their own weapon.

"Son of a bitch, that was close!" Sellers said.

Hanson felt strangely giddy. He stared at Sellers for a moment,
then laughed uncontrollably. He had no idea why he did it, but he
couldn't stop himself. Maybe it was panic or pure hysteria. He didn't
know. All he knew was that he kept laughing until Sellers yelled at
him.

"Damn it, Swede, if you don't shut up, I'm gonna slug you."

Hanson fell silent. He felt the heat radiating off the concrete
pillar. It wasn't even nine o'clock yet, but it was already unmerci-
fully hot—hotter than it had ever been back in Duluth, he thought.
(The Marines had been told to expect D-Day temperatures in the
upper nineties; in reality, the mercury would soar past 115 by mid-
afternoon.) Streams of sweat ran down Swede's face, and he didn't
feel like laughing anymore. He felt more like screaming. Beside him,
the tankers were blazing away with their .30-caliber weapon at one
of the Japanese positions.

"Haven't you got that bastard yet?" Hanson asked.

"We're working on our third one right now," one of the gunners
said. "When we tell you guys to get going, you better run like hell."
There was another long burst from the machine gun. "Now!" the
gunner shouted. "Go!"

Hanson did as he was told, running at a crouch past a wrecked
amtrack. But he'd gone only a few steps further when he spotted a
wounded Marine lying right at the water's edge. The guy's face was
fish-belly white, and Hanson could tell he was seriously hurt. No
wounds were visible on the upper part of his body, but his lower ex-

tremities were underwater, and swirls of blood darkened the surf around him.

Hanson's training told him to keep moving, but the fallen Marine looked up as he ran past, and when their eyes met, he knew he had to stop. The firing had slacked off as Swede dropped to the wet sand and crawled up to the wounded man's side.

"Keep going, man," the guy said, trying to wave Hanson away. "Please, there's nothing you can do for me."

"I can't leave you here like this," Swede said. He reached down and lifted the man's head. "I'll get a corpsman."

"No use, I tell you. Just go on and save yourself."

Despite the man's protests, Hanson took him by the shoulders and tugged, trying to pull him out of the water. Only then did he realize, to his horror, that the man's body had been virtually severed in half. His head, arms, and torso were in one piece, the rest of him in another.

"See what I mean?" the Marine said calmly. "There's no hope for me. Forget it, and find yourself some cover."

A shudder passed through Hanson as he relaxed his grip and eased the man back onto the sand. But instead of leaving, he flattened himself beside the dying Marine. By rights, he knew the man should be dead already, but sometimes the human body could play weird tricks. Swede recalled a train accident when he was a boy in northern Minnesota. A hobo had suffered the same type of fatal injuries when he was run over by a locomotive, yet he was still conscious and talking when would-be rescuers reached him. The pressure of the wheels had sealed the victim's wounds tightly enough to keep him from bleeding to death for a while. It had to be the same way with the Marine.

"I'll go pretty soon," Swede said. "What happened?"

"Got in the way of one of our tanks. Wasn't his fault. The driver never saw me."

Hanson stayed with the man for about ten minutes, talking quietly to him over the incessant sound of gunfire and whining bullets. He said whatever popped into his mind while the Marine grew steadily weaker and less responsive.

"I got to go now," Swede said finally. "The Lord be with you, buddy."

"Stay low," the man whispered. "Be sure you stay low."

Those were the last words Hanson heard him say.

Colonel Chesty Puller confronted the slaughter engulfing his regiment on the beach with the brashness and bravado for which he was either famous or notorious, depending on the point of view.

In days to come, Puller would be faulted bitterly and often for either failing, or refusing, to recognize the plight of his First Marines on Peleliu, or even to acknowledge the terrible losses they suffered during the first few days of the fighting there.

Blame for the bloodbath on the White Beaches on September 15 probably rests most heavily on the Navy, given the ineffectiveness of its pre-invasion bombardment, plus the fact that Puller's request for artillery strikes on the Point had been ignored. But in the ensuing struggle to capture and hold the Point, and in the fighting of the next few days in the treacherous ridges of the Umurbrogol, Puller placed his men in what may have been the most untenable—and costly—situations of the Pacific war. According to his detractors, he wasted many lives and did so while minimizing his regiment's casualties or even concealing their extent from his superiors. Although there were plenty of fresh Army troops in reserve, Puller allegedly avoided calling for reinforcements that could have swung the balance of the battle and significantly cut his losses.

But even among his most outspoken critics, few have questioned the personal bravery and courage under fire that made Puller a legend in his own time and a living personification of the Old Breed. Among the descriptive adjectives applied to him were "cocky," "jut-jawed," "rip-roaring," "totally fearless," and "bigger than life" (although he stood a mere five feet, eight inches).

Puller had distinguished himself in Haiti and China before the war, served as a battalion commander on Guadalcanal and Cape Gloucester, and been given command of his own regiment ahead of numerous more experienced, but less flamboyant, officers. He already had three Navy Crosses, and, word was, he wanted a Congressional Medal of Honor and a brigadier's star to go with them.

He would get neither on Peleliu, but not for lack of valor on the part of his men.

True to form, Puller came ashore during the perilous early moments of the landing, and he was very much in evidence as the First Marines gouged out a fragile toehold in the sand.

In fact, Swede Hanson almost trampled his regimental commander underfoot as he raced along the beach in search of the shell hole where Captain Hunt and his staff were trying to set up a makeshift command post.

"I was running as hard as I could go when I saw Puller sitting cross-legged in the sand like a gook, chewing on his corncob pipe and watching the action," Hanson recalled. "I couldn't believe he was there so close to the front, and the only way I could keep from stepping on him was to jump right over his head. I said, 'Hey, Chesty!' as I went by, and he yelled back, 'Give 'em hell, Marine!' It didn't ruffle him a bit."

About 100 feet further on, Hanson tumbled into what passed for the moment as Hunt's CP. There were only four others there when Hanson arrived, including Hunt, Lieutenants Sellers and Stramel, and Sergeant Schmittou.

Next to reach the CP was a communications man carrying a pack-size radio. He and Hunt were trying, without much success, to contact the rifle platoons when Hunt's runner, PFC Kelly, jumped into the hole.

Kelly grimaced, and Hanson saw blood on his dungaree pants. "I think I've got lead in my leg," Kelly said.

When Hanson tore open the pants leg, he found a neat, round bullet hole above Kelly's knee. "Hold still," he said. "Let me get some sulfa powder and a bandage on it."

"Why don't you just give me your first-aid kit?" Kelly wanted to know.

"To hell with that," said Hanson. "You'll be in sick bay on a hospital ship pretty soon, but I'll be here in this shithole for God knows how long. I may need this first-aid kit worse than you do."

Captain Hunt and the radio man finally managed to reach Lieutenant William Willis, the fast-talking New Yorker who commanded the First Platoon, and the news Willis conveyed wasn't good. The Third Platoon had suffered "a hell of a lot" of casualties, Willis said, and he had no contact at all with the Second Platoon on his right. In the area where the Second was supposed to be, there was "nothing but Japs" as far as Willis could tell.

As soon as Hunt broke contact with Willis, he called Major William McNulty, the battalion exec. "We're pretty well shot up, and there's a gap between my two assault platoons," Hunt said. "I'm throwing the First Platoon in to take the Point. The goddamn naval gunfire didn't faze the Japs. We need stretcher-bearers."

Unless they could break through and capture the Point, Hunt realized, his whole company—maybe the whole battalion—stood to be wiped out. He needed to push in that direction right away to join Willis, but first he crawled over to check on Kelly and see what the wounded runner could tell him.

"Jesus, there's K Company guys lying dead and wounded all around," Kelly panted. "They got shot up going up the beach toward that Point."

The Third Platoon's Lieutenant Estey was wounded, and his second in command, Platoon Sergeant John Koval, was dead. Sergeant Dick Webber, a squad leader, had been running the platoon since fifteen minutes after the landing, Kelly said.

While Kelly was still talking, a bullet clipped off the antenna on the radio.

Hunt had hoped to hold the first platoon in reserve while the other two assaulted the Point. But now he knew he was out of options, and he made the only decision possible. He had no choice but to commit his whole company—all that was left of it—to destroying the Japanese killing machine burrowed into the rocky innards of the Point.

He turned toward the radio operator. "Come on," he said. "We've got to get moving."

There was no answer. The radio man was dead, shot through the head.

In the space of about an hour, Estey's Third Platoon and Willis's First Platoon had lost close to two-thirds of their men, with about sixty either killed or wounded. But the job of dislodging the Japanese from the Point rested squarely on the remaining thin ranks of riflemen—without a single machine gun to cover their advance and only a scattered tank or two in the vicinity to offer artillery support.

Meanwhile, the condition and whereabouts of the Second Platoon remained anybody's guess. Hunt had yet to learn that Second Lieutenant Wayland Woodyard, commander of the Second, had been killed on the beach by a Japanese sniper during the first minutes after the landing.

PFC Joe Dariano, the Second Platoon rifleman from northern Ohio, saw Lieutenant Woodyard fall dead a few feet from him. In the next moment, Corporal Warren Lloyd, the leader of Dariano's four-man fire team, was also killed, and Platoon Sergeant Emil Macek was wounded.

"Our guys were dropping all around me," Dariano recalled later. "We were totally unorganized—without officers or squad leaders, and completely cut off from the rest of the company and battalion. Out of the forty-five guys in my platoon, nineteen were killed and twenty-one were wounded that first day."

Those who lived through the slaughter of the first few minutes finally found cover in a ten-foot-deep tank trap running parallel to the beach. For a moment, Dariano thought he was out of harm's way, but as soon as the platoon's survivors regrouped, they heeded the warnings that had been drummed into their heads to "get off the beach" and started over the other side of the tank trap.

They met an immediate firestorm of rifle and machine gun bullets. Dariano saw a young replacement beside him shot through the head and killed instantly. He fired his own M-1 toward the machine gun nest ahead of him, but he'd gone only about fifteen feet from the tank trap when he was hit, too.

For a few seconds, everything went black. When Dariano came to, blood was running out from under his helmet and streaming down his face. He turned and crawled back toward the tank trap, but before he reached it, he was hit again.

The second bullet tore through Dariano's shoulder and took out a chunk of his collarbone. The first slug had slammed into his helmet, creasing his skull and mangling his left ear.

He rolled to the bottom of the trench and lay there unable to move, wondering if he was dying. He looked up and saw Corporal Douglas Foley, his squad leader, friend, and ex–tent mate back on Pavuvu, leaning over him.

"Jesus, Dariano," Foley exclaimed. "Is that you under all that blood?"

Foley wiped Dariano's face, got a bandage on his shoulder, and lit a cigarette for him. A little later, Pharmacist's Mate Bill Jenkins, a Navy corpsman, dressed the wounds thoroughly and gave Dariano a shot of morphine and some pain pills.

"You'll be okay," Jenkins told him, "so just hang on. We'll get you evacuated as soon as possible, but we've got a lot of dead and wounded guys, and the Japs have us pretty well hemmed in. Looks like we may have to stay in this ditch for a while."

If the Point was to be taken at all, it had to be taken quickly, even without the Second Platoon. Otherwise, Hunt's whole company could be bled to death before it got the job done. The only way to do it was by brutal frontal assault with Willis's platoon leading the attack and Hunt bringing up the rest of his available force on the double. He could only hope he'd have enough men left to break the enemy's hold on the objective once they got to it.

Hurrying north toward the Point, darting from tree to tree through a shell-blasted coconut grove, Hunt and his men ran past an incredible tableau of death and misery. The scenes of "human wreckage" bewildered Hunt at first, then made him burn with anger. As he later recalled: "I saw a ghastly mixture of bandages, bloody and mutilated skin; men gritting their teeth, resigned to their wounds; men groaning and writhing in their agonies; men outstretched or twisted or grotesquely transfixed in the attitudes of death; men with their entrails exposed or whole chunks of body ripped out of them."

Corporal Swede Hanson, who had been sent back down the beach by Hunt to try to find a Sherman tank, worked his way to the top of a rock and stared at the carnage stretched out before him. "I saw more dead Marines than I'd ever seen in one place," he said. "There had to be at least 100 of them in that one bunch."

Hanson heard someone call his name and turned. It was the machine gunner from the tank who had shared a shell hole with Swede earlier. He was sprawled in the sand, his lips black and blood gushing from his belly.

"I'm hit," the machine gunner said. "I'm really hit bad."

"Take it easy, Mac," Swede said. "I'll try to find a doc and send him back for you." It was hopeless, he knew. There were no living corpsmen anywhere near, and the man would be dead within minutes anyway.

Hanson paused again to kneel beside another dying Marine whose intestines had been blown out of his body and lay drying in the sun on top of his stomach.

"Just drag me into the water, and let me die," the man pleaded.

Hanson jerked out his handkerchief, slopped water onto it from his canteen, and laid the wet cloth over the man's intestines. Then he ran on. There was nothing else he could do.

Nearby, Fred Fox also stopped to try to help PFC Russell Mattes, who lay motionless in a widening puddle of blood. Fox opened

Mattes's jacket but couldn't see where the blood was coming from, so he cut his pants open with his knife and ripped them all the way down. There was a hole low in Mattes's abdomen, and purple blood was spurting out of it with each beat of his heart. His eyes were glassy, and more blood was dribbling from his mouth.

"Corpsman! Corpsman!" Fox shouted. There was no response. Fox shook his head, feeling helpless and sick inside, then jumped to his feet and started running again.

To those who stormed the Point and lived, the attack by Hunt's decimated company is remembered as one continuous blur of gunfire, grenade blasts, men's screams, mangled corpses, and ferocious no-quarter struggle.

By the time Hunt's contingent arrived, Lieutenant Willis's Marines had already launched the assault. Their losses had been heavy, but Japanese dead lay all along the base of the rise leading up to the Point. More enemy bodies filled the niches and crannies gouged into the jagged coral mound.

A few dozen yards from the Point itself, Fox, Hudson, and a couple of other Marines stumbled onto an enemy Nambu light machine gun set up in a small clearing. Two dead Japanese in spotless khaki uniforms lay beside it. As a former machine gunner, Fox knew how to operate the gun, so he stuffed about a dozen thirty-round ammo strips into his dungaree jacket, and he and his comrades picked up the gun and hauled it toward the Point.

About fifteen yards further on, a Japanese soldier ran past them and disappeared before they could get a shot off, but they saw that he'd come out of a dugout. On closer inspection, they found a stairway cut into the coral. Fox cradled his tommy gun and pitched a smoke grenade down the steps. When nobody came out, he and his mates tossed in several more. After the smoke thinned out, they ventured inside for a look.

At the bottom of the steps, Fox spotted a Japanese officer staring at him through a pair of black-rimmed glasses with one lens knocked out. The officer's left arm was burned black, but in his right hand he held a Nambu pistol aimed at Fox's face. Fox killed him with a burst from the tommy gun, then moved past him down the steps.

At the foot of the stairway was a twelve-by-fifteen-foot room—some sort of command center for the area, Fox guessed. Another Japanese officer lay dead, the handle of his own samurai sword protruding from his belly. In a corner lay more Japanese bodies, apparently killed by the grenades.

"Any of those Japs got watches on 'em?" asked Hudson when Fox came back up the steps.

Fox shrugged and Hudson went down to check. Seconds later, Fox heard three loud blasts from his assistant's shotgun.

Hudson reemerged souvenir-less, his face white. "Damn, some of those bastards were still alive," he said.

Within fifteen minutes after the assault began, the small band of K/3/1 survivors had taken the Point.

"Good going, Will," Hunt told Willis. "You've done a wonderful job."

"It wasn't me," said Willis softly. "It was these men."

Willis had every right to be proud of his Marines. They'd used M-1s, BARs, and tommy guns to wipe out the protective cordon of Japanese infantry around the base of the Point, then scrambled over rocks and boulders like goats to silence the enemy machine guns. They'd swarmed through the Point's intricate fortifications with a vengeance, using smoke grenades for cover, darting in close enough to hit concrete embrasures with regular grenades, firing rifle grenades through the slits of pillboxes.

Now, for the first time since the landing, it was almost quiet. Men were able to smoke and catch their breath as they took stock of their latest casualties and examined the Point's mazelike interior. The firing had died down to a few sporadic shots.

Hunt found the body of Sergeant David C. McNeel lying directly in front of a 47-millimeter gun in one of the five reinforced concrete pillboxes within the gnarled coral mass. The gun had been blown askew, and the bodies of a half-dozen Japanese were strewn around it. McNeel's eyes were wide open, almost as if they were still admiring his handiwork.

In all, the Marines counted at least 110 enemy bodies in the immediate area. Even more important, the first strategic position on Peleliu was in American hands, at least for the moment.

It was no wonder the Japanese who occupied the Point had inflicted so much damage, Hunt realized. The aerial photos he'd seen hadn't begun to show the true extent of its fortifications and firepower. From its craggy crest, Hunt could see the length of the beachhead. It swarmed with amphibious tractors evacuating wounded, amphibious trucks unloading supplies, hurriedly established aid stations, and thousands of milling men.

"What a target!" he exclaimed to Willis.

Now their challenge was to hold this hard-won knob of limestone and coral—and it would be no easy task. Men were already piling up rocks and fallen logs as breastworks, but by Hunt's tally, fewer than thirty of the surviving Marines with him were fit for combat. The only machine guns they had were a couple taken from dead enemy gunners. The batteries in their radio were fading fast, and there were no phone connections to the Point. Ammunition and grenades were in short supply, and his men were almost out of water.

They were separated from the rest of the battalion on the beach by a no man's-land crawling with Japanese, and Hunt still didn't know where his Second Platoon was—much less if anyone in it was still alive.

The mass confusion that characterized the beaches extended right on up to the First Marine Division's top command level. Brigadier General Oliver P. Smith, executive officer of the division, got his first hint that all wasn't going well on the beachhead about forty-five minutes after H-hour. Smith and his staff boarded the destroyer *Hazelwood* from a Higgins boat, expecting to find an amtrack waiting to take them ashore. But by this time, so many of the tractors were burning, sunk, or wrecked that none was available. They waited for an hour and a half before they were able to hail an LVT, and it picked them up.

On the way in, the inexperienced driver encountered heavy mortar fire and a series of barbed wire entanglements. He took a sharp turn to the north, and Smith had to warn the driver that he was "running out of beach" before he veered back toward the shore. This unexpected detour placed the division staff in the hot spot of White Beach 2 instead of at their intended destination well to the south on relatively calm Orange Beach 2.

Two of Smith's lieutenants found themselves in a firefight with a Japanese in a spider hole before the general even left the amtrack. But once the enemy soldier was killed with a tommy gun, the general was able to set up a command post in an abandoned tank trap. By 11:30 A.M., less than three hours after the first assault troops landed, the CP was in business.

Within the next hour or so, Smith established radio contact with the regimental CPs of both the Fifth and Seventh Marines. Colonel Bucky Harris of the Fifth, anchoring the middle of the beachhead, had a generally encouraging report. He described resistance on Orange Beaches 1 and 2 as "scattered" and not much heavier as the Marines moved inland and took up positions at the edge of the airfield.

Colonel Herman Hanneken's Seventh Marines, however, had run into problems from the outset. The clutter of damaged tanks and tractors on the reef forced the amtracks carrying the Seventh's Third Battalion to go in in single file, dodging mines and underwater obstacles, as well as enemy anti-boat and machine gun fire. When they reached Orange Beach 3, they ran into a maze of barbed wire barricades and land mines, backed by a network of bunkers and pillboxes rivaling those on the White Beaches.

For the first few minutes ashore, enemy fire was relentless. Then, inexplicably, it tailed off, and Hanneken and his staff managed to set up the battalion CP in yet another tank trap. "We've got our hands full," he reported to General Smith. "Right now, we're pretty much pinned down . . . and we need some help from reinforcements and tanks to clear out the south piece of the island." Hanneken described the Seventh's losses as "about what were expected" and "not too heavy."

Meanwhile, from Chesty Puller's First Marines, there was only an ominous silence. Without radio contact, division headquarters had only the vaguest idea of where Puller's command post was and knew nothing of the regiment's condition.

Puller actually may have preferred it this way, at least for the time being. He enjoyed the role of lone wolf and hated having the brass breathing down his neck. Puller's actions that day also suggest that he was trying to deny the harsh reality of the First Marines' situation—not only to his superiors but to himself.

Smith finally had no option but to send a liaison officer out on foot to try to locate Puller. When the winded and badly shaken officer returned early on D-Day afternoon, he'd managed to find the First Marines' CP. It was near the foot of a ridge about 300 yards northeast of Smith's position, he reported, and under relentless fire from Japanese artillery, mortars, and machine guns.

Shortly before 2:00 P.M., a bullet-dodging communications team succeeded in running a phone line to Puller's CP, and Smith got his first authoritative word on what was happening on the White Beaches. But Puller provided little information, and what he did offer was grossly inaccurate.

"How are you coming over there?" Smith asked.

"All right," Puller replied.

"Do you need any help?"

"No, I can manage."

"What about casualties?"

"Maybe as many as forty killed and wounded," Puller said.

The facts that later emerged told a far different story from Puller's. Captain Hunt and the remnants of his company now occupying the Point could have given a much more accurate picture.

In reality, most of the 500-plus men lost on D-Day by the First

Marines—roughly one-sixth of its regimental strength—were already dead or wounded by the time Puller spoke to Smith. More than 100 engineering Marines and other rear-echelon troops from the shore party had already been shanghaied to fill the gaps torn in the First's rifle companies.

Truth was, the entire beachhead was in danger of collapsing. Except for the Point, none of the high ground targeted as first-day objectives had been taken. In all probability, only the enemy's failure to stage a coordinated counterattack in force at this juncture kept the Marines' lines from being rolled up and annihilated.

It was only mid-afternoon. The day was still young, but the men on the White Beaches had aged immeasurably since morning.

CHAPTER SIX

A BLOODY NOSE AT THE AIRFIELD

On Orange Beaches 1 and 2, just over 1,000 yards south of the slaughterhouse on the White Beaches, D-Day had been no picnic for the Fifth Marines. Overall, however, the regiment's two infantry battalions committed that day had sustained far lighter casualties than their cohorts to the north.

As K/3/5 and the rest of the Third Battalion moved inland on Orange Beach 2 toward the airfield, they encountered numerous dead Japanese. Some of the bodies were strewn in pieces near the end of one runway, victims of the early morning shelling and bombing. Others lay peacefully on the coral or in the tangled undergrowth, looking as if they were asleep, their wounds scarcely noticeable.

Japanese artillery rounds hissed overhead every few seconds, punctuated by the constant chatter of enemy machine guns. The scrub between the beach and the airfield was heavily infested with snipers, but the brush in this area gave the Fifth Marines welcome cover that many of their comrades lacked. Enemy positions in this sector were also less heavily dug in and more easily overrun.

PFC Gene Sledge came across the first enemy dead he'd ever seen as his mortar squad paused in an open area. A Japanese medical officer and two riflemen lay close together. As best as Sledge could tell, the medic had been giving first aid to one of the other soldiers when a shell had hit nearby. The force of the blast had torn the officer's abdominal cavity open. His insides, speckled with coral dust, glistened in the sun.

Sledge was still staring at the corpses when two K Company veterans trotted up and expertly began removing souvenirs from the three bodies. One took a Nambu pistol and holster, a pair of horn-rimmed glasses, and a folded Japanese flag from the dead medic, while the other checked the uniforms and packs of the two riflemen. Finally, they disabled the soldiers' rifles by jerking the bolts out and splintering the stocks against the hard coral.

"See you around, Sledgehammer," one of them said casually as they moved on. "Don't take any wooden nickels."

A short time later, Sledge and the rest of Corporal R. V. Burgin's mortar squad were making their way along a slight, brushy embankment that marked the edge of the airstrip when they came under mortar and machine gun fire from their immediate right.

"My God!" Sledge rasped. "The Japs must be right beside us, maybe even behind us."

"I don't think that's Jap fire," Burgin said, flattening himself against the ground. "I think it's the Seventh Marines shooting at us. We've gotten out ahead of them, and they don't know where we are. Just hug the dirt and maybe they'll get tired or figure things out."

Burgin fumbled in his pocket and extracted a crumpled cigarette. As he lit up, he heard Sledge's voice at his elbow:

"Hey, can I have one of those?"

"I didn't think you smoked," Burgin said.

"I never have," Sledge said, "but I'd still like to have one."

Burgin handed him a cigarette, then watched Sledge tear open the paper and stuff the tobacco into his mouth with trembling fingers. Burgin was never sure whether Sledge merely chewed the cigarette's contents or swallowed them whole.

Detroit-born PFC Frank Batchelor, an ammo handler in a .30-caliber machine gun squad attached to one of K/3/5's three rifle platoons, had seen only spasmodic enemy fire on the beach. Ducking and darting, his sixteen-man section was able to move rapidly inland. They'd advanced about 200 yards and were near the edge of the airstrip when the rate of Japanese fire increased sharply, and everybody hit the deck.

The two ammunition boxes that Batchelor was carrying contained nearly 500 rounds of ammo between them. They were heavy as hell, but Batchelor was grateful to have them when the shooting intensified. Without them, he'd have had absolutely nothing to hide behind.

"The other guys in the section were slightly ahead of me, and I was at a right angle to the rest of the file," Batchelor recalled. "They had a little brush around them, but those two five-by-seven-inch boxes were all I had, and they just weren't enough."

Batchelor never saw the Japanese sniper who took him out of the battle, but he caught a flicker of movement and heard the high-pitched pop of an Arisaka rifle. Just as the bullet slammed into his left arm, Batchelor spotted a built-up foxhole of piled stones and cinders covered with some sort of mat, and he knew that was where the shot had come from.

He also knew he was bleeding, but he hugged the dirt and tried not to move. Dimly, he saw Gunnery Sergeant Tom Rigney crawling toward him.

"Corpsman! We got a man down here!" Rigney yelled, then asked Batchelor in a lower tone: "Where are the bastards? Could you tell?"

"There." Batchelor pointed toward the hole with his uninjured right hand.

Rigney scurried away, and Batchelor crawled forward until he met a corpsman coming toward him. As the medic worked on his wounds, Batchelor could hear Rigney talking on his walkie-talkie, giving the location of the enemy position and calling for a rifle squad to take it out. A couple of minutes later, a pair of Marines jerked back the cover on the hole and killed the two Japanese inside.

When the stretcher-bearers showed up to take Batchelor back to an aid station, he assured them that he could walk back on his own.

"Just get on and lie down," one of them said. "We don't want to hang around here any longer than we have to."

They'd gone no more than thirty or forty yards when both stretcher-bearers were hit almost simultaneously by a burst of small-arms fire. The stretcher slammed to the ground as they fell and sent

Batchelor sprawling, but he jumped up immediately and took stock of the situation. One of the bearers was bad off—shot through the spine and unable to move. The other had only an arm wound similar to Batchelor's.

"Let's get your buddy on the stretcher," Batchelor told the man with the injured arm, gritting his teeth. "I think I can handle one end of it if you can get the other."

In that way, the three wounded Marines managed to drag themselves back to the beach. Twenty minutes later, Batchelor and his would-be rescuers were all undergoing treatment at the aid station.

By noon, the mix-up was finally straightened out over the boundaries between the Fifth Marines' section of beachhead and the sector on their immediate right assigned to the Seventh Marines. But there had been no shortage of tragedies and near-disasters during the morning's confusion.

There was still no reliable radio contact with any of the other units, but runners from Captain Haldane's CP brought word up the line that Lieutenant Moose Barrett, K/3/5's popular young executive officer and platoon leader, was dead.

A towering ex–football player from River Forest, Illinois, Barrett had been hit on the beach by a mortar round that took off most of his left leg. He died soon after, and Lieutenant Hillbilly Jones, guitar-strumming commander of the company machine gun section, took over for Barrett as leader of the First Platoon. PFC John W. Steele had also been fatally wounded.

Barrett's loss stunned PFC Bill Leyden when he learned about it a few hours later, but it wasn't the only shock Leyden had to absorb that morning. Corporal Peter Fouts, Leyden's squad mate and one of his best buddies, had taken a machine gun bullet through the arm before he got across the beach.

K/3/5 had been told to halt short of the airfield proper. Some rifle squads, including Leyden's own, had ventured past the edge of the field in the early going, but they'd been ordered back, both to straighten up their lines and to avoid friendly fire from the Seventh Marines. From then on, they'd been told to veer gradually to the right, moving parallel to the airstrip, rather than onto it, to take maximum advantage of the natural embankment and the seared brush along it. Based on past experience, most of the company veterans expected a banzai charge from the Japanese at any time, and they sought out whatever protective cover they could find.

"They'll pull a banzai, and we'll tear their ass up," one veteran assured PFC Gene Sledge. "Then we can get the hell offa this hot rock."

The arrival of a perspiring runner with an urgent message from battalion headquarters for Captain Haldane did little to case the tension. "Battalion says we gotta establish contact with the Seventh Marines," the runner said. "If the Nips counterattack, they'll come right through the gap between us."

The Marines had quickly learned that digging a hole in the coral with a trenching tool was impossible, but for the moment they weren't staying in one place long enough to worry much about it. The routine was to move ahead on the double for a few yards, then pause for extended intervals to take cover however they could.

As they moved to the right, toward the east side of the island, the jungle growth thickened. But they still saw nothing of the Seventh Marines and encountered only occasional live Japanese.

What K/3/5 and the rest of the battalion hadn't yet figured out was that there were two north–south trails—rather than just one—that ran, more or less parallel, through the brush between the beach and the airfield. Inadequate maps, bad visibility, and hordes of enemy snipers made it hard to tell the trails apart. Consequently, when regimental headquarters thought the Third Battalion was lagging behind the Seventh Marines' advance, it was actually on the trail further inland and several hundred yards ahead of where it should've been. Not only was its right flank exposed, but it was also in danger of being isolated and surrounded.

The volume of Japanese mortar and artillery fire increased, and fear grew that the anticipated counterattack was imminent. But most of the shells hit the beach area well to the rear of the Marines' lines, and after a while the firing inexplicably tailed off again.

As the men of the Third Battalion hugged the ground and clung to whatever cover they could find, an unsettling realization began to dawn on them: Many of the enemy shells whistling over their heads and falling close by weren't coming from positions on the flat terrain a short distance ahead of them. Instead, they came from artillery hidden among the ridges on the far side of the airfield—far beyond the reach of a rifle company's machine guns, small arms, and flamethrowers. Even the battalion's tanks and the joint assault signal company, whose job was to direct naval gunfire at enemy gun emplacements, were no help against well-hidden positions in the ridges.

Over the next few days, these southernmost high points of the craggy limestone mass of the Umurbrogol would become known to the Marines on Peleliu by one collective, brutally descriptive name— Bloody Nose Ridge.

It was early afternoon when PFC Sterling Mace and other members of K/3/5's three rifle platoons came up on a Japanese pillbox housing a 75-millimeter field piece. They were less than 200 feet away and practically looking down the gun's barrel by the time they spotted it and dove for cover.

"Stay down," said Sergeant Hank Boyes, a squad leader from Trinidad, California. "There's supposed to be a tank around here somewhere. I'll see if I can find it."

Mace huddled between two of his squad mates, PFCs Seymour Levy and Charlie Allman, and watched Boyes trot back through the undergrowth and disappear. A few minutes later, they heard a rumble and turned to see a Sherman tank approaching with Boyes riding beside its turret.

"There's the Jap gun," Boyes yelled down the open hatch. "Can you get a clear shot from here?"

"We got a bead on it," the tank commander called back. "Cover your ears and hang on."

About 150 feet from the pillbox, the tank stopped. A second later, it opened fire with its 37-millimeter cannon. While the blast still echoed, the tank lumbered slowly forward a few feet, then fired again. A massive cloud of dust rose where the pillbox had been.

With the tank standing by, Boyes jumped to the ground and waved his squad forward. The dust cleared, and the Marine riflemen cautiously approached the target. They found bodies and pieces of bodies draped grotesquely over the remains of the pillbox. The field piece itself had been blown off its base and was leaning to one side.

"Are they all dead?" Levy whispered at Mace's elbow.

"Looks like it," Mace said, stopping a few feet from the wreckage.

"Wait!" Levy hissed. "I saw something move." Nervously, he pointed his rifle at one of the bodies. "I think that Jap's still alive."

"Take it easy, Levy," Mace said. "For Chrissake, can't you see he's got no head?"

They stepped gingerly past the decapitated corpse and moved on.

By mid-afternoon on D-Day, a relative lull had settled over the Fifth Marines' sector. Bill Leyden and the rest of the First Platoon continued to feel their way along the brushy embankment beside the airfield. They were still within a few hundred yards of the beach, but they'd veered steadily south and east of where they'd started encountering increasingly heavy jungle growth. A continuous rumble of gunfire still rolled down from the north, and mortar rounds were still hitting the beach, but in this immediate area, there were only scattered shots from snipers.

Heat waves danced off the coral. Even in the shade, the temperature was approaching 115 degrees. The ground felt as if it were baking in an oven. Leyden had never been so hot in his life, and both his canteens were dry. Despite repeated warnings to conserve water, he'd consumed virtually the whole half-gallon he'd carried ashore within four or five hours after the landing. It had been less than two hours since his last tepid sip, but it felt like a year. He shut his eyes against the sweat running down his face.

For a moment, Leyden almost imagined he could hear PFC Seymour Levy, somewhere off to his left with the Third Platoon, reciting his favorite lines from Kipling:

When the sweatin' troop train lay in a sidin' through the day, where the 'eat would make your bloomin' eyebrows crawl . . .

"You got any water?" Leyden asked Corporal Leonard Ahner, his fire team leader.

Ahner shook his head. "I'm out. Just about everybody else is, too."

Leyden turned away, trying not to think about how parched his lips and throat were and how much the sun burned his skin.

Even with the sun slowly sinking lower in the western sky, there was no letup in the heat. All over the beachhead, men were choking with thirst. Some were too sick with heat exhaustion to move, and there was no water to give them. Many Marines' canteens had been empty for hours, and there was no word when more water would be sent in.

To Leyden, the relentless heat and his own murderous thirst were rapidly becoming even bigger enemies than the Japanese.

To the men of 3/5's rifle companies edging their way inland from Orange Beach 2, the big stuff fired by the enemy seemed less intimidating as the afternoon wore on. Their senses had adjusted somewhat to the continuous hiss and roar of shells, most of which were hitting further away. But it was a different story for the artillerymen of the Eleventh Marines, who were just now coming ashore. To PFC James Mason, the beach area that the infantry had left behind could hardly have presented a more hellish scene as his amtrack approached it shortly after 2:00 P.M.

"I can still close my eyes and see the whole damned thing in front of me," Mason recalled nearly sixty years later. "The first thing I saw was one of those amphibious trucks called ducks take a direct hit from a heavy mortar. Just a couple of seconds later, another amtrack moving along the beach hit a mine and blew sky-high. My impression was that everything was hitting the fan—and that I was about to be in a helluva lot of trouble."

As a veteran of nearly two years in the Pacific, it was clear to Mason that there was nothing random about the Japanese shells hitting the beach. They were well aimed at specific targets, which meant that every moving object on the beach was in constant danger.

Mason was right. The trouble he foresaw persisted long after he landed. The nineteen-year-old native of West Texas, who had grown up near Shreveport, Louisiana, normally served on the crew of a 75-millimeter pack howitzer in the Eleventh's Second Battalion. This afternoon, though, he had a different, and far riskier, job.

The main role of the battalion's three four-gun batteries of 75s was to provide artillery support for the Fifth Marines. But so many amtracks had been damaged or destroyed that day that Mason and three buddies were pressed into service manning Caterpillar tractors. Their assignment was to try to drag ashore several amphibious trailers whose loads of sorely needed equipment and supplies were stranded on the reef.

Working for over an hour under continuous mortar and artillery fire, Mason managed to dislodge one of the trailers and get it to the beach. Then he glanced back toward the reef and noticed that something was wrong with the Cat driven by his best buddy, PFC William "Slim" Vanover. Moments earlier, it had been struggling to free another trailer. Now it was sitting still in the water.

Mason jumped back on his own Cat and went out to see what the problem was. As he drew near, he saw Vanover waiting calmly in the driver's seat of the tractor, despite falling mortar shells.

"What's the trouble?" Mason hollered.

"Engine stalled," Vanover replied in his soft Virginia drawl. "Can't get her started."

"Well, hell," Mason chided, "were you just planning to sit out here all day?"

Vanover grinned. "Aw, Jim, I wasn't worried," he said. "I knew you'd come get me."

As Mason maneuvered close enough to get a towline on the other Cat, he spotted an enemy mortar shell streaking through the air directly at him. The shell missed the two tractors by a few feet and plunged below the surface of the water. An instant later, it exploded, and the subsurface force of the blast flung the heavy Cat into the air and hurled Mason head-first into the ocean twenty feet away.

"It flipped me over like a mud hen," he said, "but I wasn't hurt, and somehow we got the two tractors back to shore."

By about four o'clock on D-Day afternoon, it was apparent to division headquarters that, except for the capture of the Point, virtually none of the Marines' major first-day objectives had been secured. With darkness approaching, there was little choice but to carry over the same objectives to D-plus-1. In the remaining daylight, it was decided, the beleaguered infantry regiments should turn their efforts toward establishing a defensive perimeter to protect what meager ground they held.

General Rupertus, the division CO, was nursing a broken ankle sustained on Pavuvu and had remained—none too agreeably— aboard the troopship *DuPage*. Meanwhile, beachhead operations were being directed by General Oliver Smith, the division executive officer, who had managed to establish contact with the various regimental and battalion command posts.

Smith sent word to his field commanders to form as strong a defensive line as possible along the seaward edge of the airfield and start preparing to dig in for the night. Since the ground beyond the beach was impenetrable rock, "digging in" meant collecting whatever loose stones, chunks of coral, and bits of brush the men could find, then piling them up to form shallow breastworks.

"My 'foxhole' that night was maybe three or four inches deep— just about enough to get my rump in," recalled PFC Jay d'Leau, the bazooka man in Corporal R. V. Burgin's mortar squad. "The rest of me was sticking out in the open."

It was shortly before 5:00 P.M., while hundreds of two-man foxhole teams were taking similar measures and struggling with the same limitations, when the long-anticipated Japanese counterattack finally came.

This time, however, it wasn't the usual banzai bayonet charge predicted by the veterans. This time, the Marines' first warning was a swirling cloud of dust rising abruptly against the low ridges on the north side of the airstrip.

PFC Gene Sledge stared in that direction and saw a line of tracked vehicles racing through the dust. "Hey, what are those amtracks doing all the way across the airfield toward the Jap lines?" he asked a veteran next to him.

"Them ain't amtracks," the man said. "They're Nip tanks."

By this time, General Smith's command post had already been warned of the tanks' approach by a Navy observation plane. Smith quickly alerted the First and Second Battalions of the Fifth Marines, which stood abreast of each other about 500 yards inland from Orange Beach 2, supported by a half-dozen or so Sherman tanks.

Accompanied by some 500 crack Japanese infantrymen, many armed with Nambu automatic rifles, the enemy tanks roared across an open field in an effort to drive a steel wedge between Lieutenant Colonel Robert A. Boyd's First Battalion and Major Gordon Gayle's Second Battalion.

"Very fortunately, I had my tank platoon right at hand, a matter of fifty yards or so from where I was," Gayle said later, "and I was able to send them into the fray at the critical time."

There were other fortuitous circumstances as well. One recently arrived battery of the Eleventh Marines had positioned its four pack howitzers just to the right rear of the First Battalion. The Shermans also drew support from several 37-millimeter anti-tank guns, bazookas, and grenade launchers. Simultaneously, as the attackers turned parallel to the American lines for some distance, Marines targeted the Japanese infantry following in the tanks' path with withering volleys of small-arms and machine gun fire.

South of the enemy's main point of impact, the Third Battalion received orders to deploy on the double. Sledge and PFC Snafu Shelton set up their 60-millimeter mortar in a shallow crater a few yards behind a skirmish line formed by K/3/5's rifle platoons.

"Stand by to repel counterattack!" a platoon sergeant yelled. "Counterattack hitting I Company's front."

Sledge had no idea where I Company was—somewhere to the left, he thought. His sweaty hands grappled with a four-pound, high-explosive mortar shell. Feeling alone and confused, he wondered if all was lost.

"They need ta get some more damned troops up here," Snafu groused beside him as he readied the gun for firing. It was one of Shelton's favorite expressions in times of stress. Sledge had heard it so often that it was almost reassuring.

From all indications, the enemy onslaught was well planned by Colonel Nakagawa, commander of the Japanese garrison on Peleliu. But the Marines' decisive response, plus the Shermans' overwhelming superiority in firepower and armor, rapidly turned the tide of battle. For a finishing touch, a Navy Dauntless dive-bomber showed up and planted a 500-pound bomb in the midst of a cluster of Japanese tanks. In a matter of minutes, the attack was broken. The entire enemy column of about thirteen tanks was left wrecked and burning, and most of the ground troops who had come with them were killed.

As it turned out, the main threat to Shelton, Sledge, and the rest of K/3/5's mortar section that late afternoon didn't come from the counterattacking Japanese but from one of the tanks attached to the Seventh Marines.

The Sherman had moved unnoticed into a small clearing just behind the company. Now its 75-millimeter cannon was engaged in a fiery duel with a Japanese field piece supporting the counterattack, and the tank's machine gunner had mistaken the mortar men for enemy troops. Just as Sledge reached up to drop a round down the tube of the mortar, the .50-caliber gunner opened fire, his tracers coming within inches of Sledge's swiftly withdrawn fingers. Seconds later, Sledge tried to load the mortar again with the same result.

"God, Sledgehammer," rasped PFC John Redifer, an ammo handler crouched in a crater next to Sledge, "don't let him hit that shell, or we'll all be blown to hell."

"Don't worry about it," Sledge snapped. "It's my hand he just about shot off."

"We got bigger worries than that," said Burgin, the squad leader. "As soon as the tanker knocks out the Jap gun, he's gonna swing that 75 over this way. He thinks we're Nips."

Sledge felt a knot of panic in his chest. It was bad enough to be killed by the enemy, he thought, but to be blown away by your own comrades was somehow a hundred times worse.

Moments later, the tank scored a direct hit on the Japanese gun, knocking it off its wheels and killing every member of its crew. But before the Sherman could turn its cannon on the mortar squad's position, someone from K/3/5 managed to get the tankers' attention and wave them off. The machine gun fire from the Sherman abruptly halted, and Sledge's heart rate slowly returned to normal.

For thousands of parched, exhausted men, dusk and the approach of nightfall brought only more fears. As every Marine veteran knew, the Japanese relished the dark and thrived on it. Consequently, this first night ashore would be an even greater test of their nerve and discipline than the day just past. It didn't help when rumors spread through the ranks that the division had suffered unexpectedly heavy casualties. Little hard information was available, but many veterans of Guadalcanal and Cape Gloucester were calling D-Day at Peleliu their worst fight yet.

Twilight also brought a new outburst of Japanese mortar fire. In this case, one of the heaviest concentrations fell on 3/5's battalion command post a few dozen yards behind its thin forward lines. One of its victims was Lieutenant Colonel Austin "Shifty" Shofner, the battalion CO, who had been captured by the Japanese when the Philippines fell, then escaped to fight again.

PFC Bill Leyden was close enough to see the shell burst that hit the CP and showered Shofner with fragments as he was trying to contact his scattered companies with orders for the night. Seconds later, Leyden heard Shofner screaming—more in anger than pain, judging from the tone of it.

"I was maybe thirty or forty yards away, and I could hear him as plain as anything," Leyden said. "He was cussing loud enough to put a platoon sergeant to shame."

Shofner's wounds were sufficiently serious to force his evacuation to a hospital ship at an especially bad moment—before he could reach all his company commanders and get their units into position for the night. Ammunition was short everywhere, and water was almost nonexistent. Now, with full darkness only minutes away, the battalion was suddenly without its top decision-maker, and no replacement for Shofner was readily available at battalion level. Major Robert M. Ash, 3/5's executive officer, had been killed on the beach moments after the landing.

To fill the vacancy, Lieutenant Colonel Lewis W. Walt, executive officer of the Fifth Marines, hurried over from regimental headquarters to take the reins of 3/5. Because radio and phone communications were so sketchy, there was much still to be done when he got there.

In the gathering gloom, Walt—known as "Silent Lew" because of his quiet demeanor—set out through the enemy-infested undergrowth, alone except for a single runner, to contact each unit personally. After locating the command posts for I, K, and L Companies, Walt directed them into their assigned spots in the division's line facing the airfield. Then he had them form a circle of defense against Japanese infiltrators, with 3/5 lined up back to back with 2/5, one battalion facing south and the other north.

Although soaked with sweat from exertion, Gene Sledge felt relieved when he and Snafu Shelton finished constructing a shallow pit for their 60-millimeter mortar and got the gun registered in by firing a couple of test rounds. Sledge dissolved some dextrose tablets in his mouth, swallowed his last few drops of water, and tried to relax a little despite the continuing shriek of American and Japanese artillery shells passing each other overhead. He'd unlaced his right shoe and was about to take it off when he heard Snafu's irritable query: "What the hell you doin'?"

"Taking off my boondockers. My feet hurt."

"And what the hell you gonna do in yo' stockin' feet if the Nips come bustin' outta that jungle?" Shelton demanded. "How you reckon you gonna move around on this coral without no shoes?"

Sledge grimly retightened his shoelaces. He watched Shelton unsheath his Ka-Bar knife and jam the blade into the loose gravel near his right hand. Sledge followed suit with his own knife, then checked to be sure his carbine was fully loaded.

"Get some sleep, Sledgehammer," Snafu said in a milder tone. "I'll take first watch."

His whole body tense, and his senses raw with dread, Sledge closed his eyes and prayed.

Hundreds of similar scenes were unfolding in foxholes and gun pits from the Point on the north all the way down the western beaches to near the southern tip of Peleliu. As the hours of darkness crept by, many a Marine found himself muttering a Hail Mary, repeating the Lord's Prayer, or reciting the Twenty-third Psalm. Men who seldom, if ever, talked to their Maker under ordinary circumstances made exceptions on this seemingly endless night.

"I just said, 'Lord, I'm in your hands; please take care of me,'" recalled the usually hard-nosed Corporal Burgin.

Strict rules were in effect for this first night on hostile ground. They were passed down from regiment to battalion to company commanders, then relayed to each man by platoon and squad leaders: Each foxhole was to be occupied by two Marines, one of whom would be on watch at all times while the other tried to sleep. Each two-man position would be close enough to those on either side that the occupants could reach out and touch each other. No one was to move beyond the confines of his own foxhole. Anyone sensing outside movement was to demand a password and alert his foxhole mate. If he failed to get an immediate and acceptable reply, he was to open fire.

Rules, of course, are made to be broken—especially by men half-mad with thirst.

It was sometime after midnight when Burgin heard a shuffling noise a few feet from the edge of the shallow foxhole he shared with fellow squad leader Jim Burke. Burgin's hand closed instantly over his .45 automatic, and he leveled the weapon at the curtain of darkness in front of him.

"Who's there?" he rasped.

A faint voice mumbled something Burgin couldn't hear, then: "Please, have you got any water? I can't stand it any longer."

Burgin's finger tightened on the trigger. "Password, damn it! Give me the password, or you're dead."

"Bull Run. Bull Run. Oh, God, please . . ."

Burgin's finger went limp on the trigger as he made out the dim shape of a Marine helmet and recognized the voice of PFC Robert Oswalt. Oswalt's face was no more than fifteen inches from the muzzle of the .45.

"You dumb bastard, I almost blew your head off." Burgin was surprised at how calm and steady his voice sounded, since he was shaking so violently that he almost dropped the pistol.

"I . . . I'm sorry. I'm just so thirsty . . ." Oswalt was a quiet, studious eighteen-year-old, who told his best buddies, PFCs Jay d'Leau and Gene Sledge, that he wanted to be a brain surgeon after the war. Right now, he sounded like a lost child who was about to cry.

Burgin sighed and unsnapped the cover on one of his canteens. "There may be a drop or two in there," he said, handing it to Oswalt.

The kid turned up the canteen and drained it. "Thanks," he said.

"Get back where you belong on the double," Burgin growled. "And, hey, if you so much as stick your damned nose out of your foxhole again tonight, I *will* shoot you. I swear to God I will."

By dawn of D-plus-1, most of the men of K/3/5 were so weak and dehydrated that they could hardly walk, much less fight off an enemy attack. But just after first light, some of the men happened across a large, odd-looking cavity in the ground. It was eight to ten feet deep and about fifteen feet wide across the top, with steep sides that looked more like a natural depression or sinkhole than a shell crater. At its bottom was a good-sized pool of the foulest-looking water any of them had ever seen.

"Come on!" one of its discoverers yelled. "We've found a damned well!"

The Marines converged on the hole like starving wolves on a wounded sheep. A corpsman tried to warn them off, saying the water could be poisoned, but most of them paid no heed.

"It ain't beer," said one of the first men to sample it, "but it *is* wet."

"The water was murky and milky-looking, and there were insects floating in it," recalled PFC Bill Leyden, "but none of us cared. We practically dove into it head-first. Some guys climbed down to the bottom, and when they'd drunk what they could hold, they started filling helmets and canteens and handing them up to the rest of us."

Few, if any, Marines took time to treat the opaque liquid with the water-purification tablets they carried. Several became ill after just a few swallows. After watching the man next to him clutch his belly and retch violently, Gene Sledge reluctantly poured out his helmetful of water and helped a corpsman treat the sick Marine.

Leyden, Burgin, and many others tolerated the tainted water with no major problems, however. "God knows what was in the stuff, but I didn't even think about it," Leyden said. "I just gulped it down as fast as I could."

The situation was tailor-made for one of PFC Seymour Levy's favorite passages from Kipling:

It was crawlin', and it stunk,
But of all the drinks I've drunk,
I'm gratefulest for one from Gunga Din.

Ironically, within an hour or so after the episode at the "well," the Marines' first shipments of water began to arrive at the front lines in fifty-five-gallon drums.

To the men's disgust, though, the water in the barrels was even more toxic—and worse-tasting—than the cloudy liquid from the hole. The barrels had originally been used to store gasoline and hadn't been properly cleaned before being pumped full of water. Their contents were heavily contaminated with petroleum residue and rust, but most men drank it, anyway, and scores of them were sickened.

PFC Vincent Santos had a special reason to feel chagrined about the "high-octane" water—a reason he had no wish at the time to share with his fellow Marines. Back on Pavuvu, Santos had been among a small group of men assigned to the chore of filling the barrels, and he clearly remembered how lax the detail had been in rinsing them out.

"Nobody told us what the water was going to be used for," Santos admitted, somewhat sheepishly, many years later. "If we'd known we'd end up having to drink the stuff ourselves, we'd have been a whole lot more careful."

As PFC Sterling Mace observed: "When I tasted the water from the barrels, I was glad I still had some from the hole. If you have to make a choice, coral grit goes down better than gasoline any day."

Soon after full daylight on D-plus-1, the Japanese mortars and artillery opened up again. The Navy's big guns and the Marines' artillery immediately replied, and the men stayed low as they listened to the incoming and outgoing rounds whistling overhead and scrambled to collect their gear. They knew what was coming next. There'd be no further delay in the attack to wrest control of the airfield from the enemy. It was now or never.

"Get ready and stand by," the men were told.

Crouching NCOs raced along the line, yelling for everybody to hug the deck until they got the order to move out, then run like blazes and not look back. It was approximately 1,500 yards across the airfield—over eight-tenths of a mile—and every inch of it was flat, wide-open, and swept by constant enemy fire. Except for the craters that pocked its surface and scattered debris from wrecked Japanese planes and other equipment, there wasn't a speck of protective cover along the way.

Every available man in all three battalions of the Fifth Marines, plus the Second Battalion of the First Marines, would make the charge simultaneously, with 3/5 anchoring the right end of the line and crossing the southernmost end of the field.

"Once you get out there, keep going and don't slow down," Platoon Sergeant John Marmet instructed his K/3/5 mortar section. "The faster you move, the better chance you've got of getting where you're going. Don't stop for anything, and don't bunch up."

At about 8:30 A.M., officers up and down the line shouted, "Let's go!" They waved their arms toward the airfield, and thousands of Marines stood up, then surged forward in staggered waves. As they broke into the clear, the men scattered out, distancing themselves from each other and trotting alone or in pairs.

The scene reminded Gene Sledge of desperate infantry charges he'd seen in World War I movies like *All Quiet on the Western Front*. Shells screeched overhead and exploded on all sides, sending up clouds of smoke and dust. Rifle bullets whined, and waist-to-head-high tracers from enemy machine guns streaked past. Coral splinters stung men's faces, and shrapnel clattered like steel hailstones against their helmets. Here and there, men stumbled and fell, but the rest kept running straight ahead without looking to either side.

It seemed impossible to Sledge that any of them would live to reach their destination. He clenched his teeth, gripped the stock of his carbine, and whispered under his breath as he ran:

"The Lord is my shepherd; I shall not want . . . Yea, though I walk through the valley of the shadow of death, I will fear no evil . . ."

About halfway across the field, a large shell hit just to Sledge's left. He stumbled and fell among the ricocheting fragments, and it took him a second to realize he hadn't been hit. A few feet to his right, Sledge heard a groan of pain and turned to see Snafu Shelton doubled up on the ground clutching at his waist.

Sledge scrambled over to Shelton's side. He looked for blood, but he didn't see any. "Snafu? Are you hit?"

"I dunno. Feels like sumthin' busted me in th' side."

Sledge quickly located the culprit: a hunk of metal about an inch square and a half-inch thick. The shell fragment was still hot enough to burn his fingers when he picked it up, and big enough to kill a man if it hit him in the right spot. Fortunately, it had been partially spent, and Shelton's thick, webbed pistol belt had absorbed most of its force. It left a silver-dollar-sized bruise but nothing worse.

Shelton motioned for Sledge to stick the fragment in his pack as a souvenir. A moment later, he was back on his feet. He picked up his mortar, pushing away Sledge's attempted helping hand.

"Let's go," he grunted, and ran on.

Sledge, who poured several ounces of sweat out of each of his boondockers afterward, called the attack across the airport his "worst combat experience" of the war. He described being shelled in the open by massed artillery and mortars as "terror compounded beyond the belief of anyone who hasn't experienced it."

Many of his comrades concurred.

"The way those tracers were coming across there—just at the right height to rip through a man's head or chest—I don't see how any of us lived through it," said Corporal Burgin. "But by the time we got to the other side of the airport, we could tell that our biggest problem was the Jap guns up in that high ground to the north."

Japanese gun crews positioned on the slopes of Hills 200 and 210, two forward points extending south from the main mass of Bloody Nose Ridge, commanded a field of fire that encompassed the whole airfield. But enemy observers on these slopes could also direct fire onto the advancing Marines from heavier artillery in the ridges further north.

Meanwhile, the structure that had served as the Japanese airfield headquarters presented another formidable obstacle at closer range. With four-foot-thick walls of steel-reinforced concrete, the building was large enough to house a full company of troops. It had been converted into an enormous blockhouse bristling with weaponry and surrounded by a network of a dozen pillboxes.

Like most of the major defensive fortifications on Peleliu, the blockhouse had survived the pre-invasion naval bombardment virtually untouched. Now its guns directed a murderous concentration of fire on Marines crossing the northeastern portion of the airfield, particularly Major Raymond C. Davis's First Battalion, First Marines.

"The blockhouse didn't appear to have been hit at all, and it was cutting us up pretty bad," said Captain Everett Pope, whose C/1/1 was among its main targets. "We lost quite a few Marines before we were able to call in Navy fire to knock it out."

A distress call from Davis brought a quick response from the battleship *Mississippi,* whose fourteen-inch guns hurled a combination of armor-piercing and high-explosive shells that pulverized the concrete walls of the structure and killed most of the Japanese inside. The Marines then used field pieces, tanks, and infantry to silence the protective pillbox network, and the advance continued.

"The way that blockhouse was built was incredible," K/3/5's Corporal Burgin recalled. "I passed within a few yards of it, and even after most of the concrete was blown away, a lot of the reinforcing steel was still standing as straight as you please."

Miraculously, K/3/5 lost only seven men in the crossing. PFCs Robert Oswalt and Walter Reynolds were killed, and five others were wounded. Afterward, the rest lay panting, spent, and dripping with perspiration among the scrub brush at the northeast edge of the airport. Within a few minutes, several had to be evacuated with severe heat prostration.

Burgin took Oswalt's death especially hard. The young aspiring brain surgeon was the first fatality in Burgin's mortar squad, but it was the irony of Oswalt's death that troubled Burgin most that evening. All he could think of when he heard the news was how he'd almost shot Oswalt the night before when the frightened, thirsty teenager had crawled up to Burgin's foxhole in search of water.

"After what I'd seen in combat, I'd come to the conclusion that when a man's number came up, there was nothing anybody could do about it," Burgin said later. "But if Oswalt had to die, I was damned glad it hadn't been me that killed him."

Bloody Nose Ridge had already lived up to its name—in spades—but the struggle to dislodge the Japanese embedded there hadn't even begun. Except for the Point, not one square yard of Peleliu's high ground was yet under American control.

And on the Point itself, a handful of bleeding, surrounded, exhausted Marines were barely hanging on.

CHAPTER SEVEN

POINT OF NO RETURN

To Captain George Hunt's small band of surviving K/3/1 Marines on the Point, the night of December 15–16 was an ordeal that tried men's souls as severely as it tested them physically. On D-Day morning, in one of the most savage fights in Marine Corps history, they'd captured the gnarled, thirty-foot-high knob of rock hugging the water's edge at the extreme northern tip of the beachhead, only to find themselves trapped on it by sundown that evening. During the living nightmare that followed, memories of their victory soon evaporated. Not a man among them expected to see the light of a new day.

At dawn on D-plus-1, against all odds and logic, they still held the Point, but their situation could hardly have been more desperate. Thirty men had remained in fighting condition after wresting the rocky knob from the enemy around 10:00 A.M. the day before, and about ten others had slipped through enemy-infested territory to join them that afternoon.

Now just eighteen of Hunt's Marines were still alive, including the captain and Lieutenant Willis, and several of them were nursing wounds ranging from painful to life-threatening. They were cut off from their comrades by a strong force of Japanese who had seized control of a semicircular area of rocks and jungle growth bracketing the landward side of the Point. From there, enemy machine guns, mortars, and small arms dominated a 100-yard strip between the Point and the rest of the beachhead. Enemy infiltrators could easily slip into the shallow water after dark to attack the trapped Marines from the sea, and a few men had been stationed on ledges at the water's edge and in hollows just above to counter this threat.

Any attempt to resupply Hunt's men or evacuate wounded had to be done by water and was fraught with risk. It meant sending an amtrack through a gauntlet of hostile fire to reach the sheltered seaward side of the Point, then back to the beachhead over the same perilous route. Meanwhile, the batteries in the Point's only radio had long since gone dead, leaving Hunt and the others with no outside contact and almost no hope.

But in the early light, they felt a measure of bitter pride as they looked down from their vantage point and counted the strewn bodies of nearly 400 Japanese soldiers killed during a series of nocturnal attacks.

Corporal Swede Hanson lay motionless on a slight slope facing the beach beneath the seaward side of the Point. He was weak from loss of blood, wounded in three places, covered with bruises and abrasions from head to foot, and utterly amazed to be alive. A round from a Japanese knee mortar had mangled his right arm, severing an artery, and shrapnel fragments from the same shell had buried themselves in his back and buttocks.

Hanson had finally gotten the external bleeding stopped, but the arm had bled internally until it was blue-black and swollen to twice its normal size. Still, he'd managed to keep throwing grenades with it for the rest of the night. Meanwhile, close beside Hanson, Corporal Bob Anderson had given the enemy attackers continuous hell with the Nambu light machine gun captured by PFC Fred Fox.

"I wish you could get up here and see what you guys've done, Swede," Captain Hunt shouted down from the top of the Point. "There's dead Japs piled everywhere."

Probably only the enemy's failure to realize how fragile and thinly stretched the Marines' defenses were—plus unimaginable courage and determination—had spared Hanson, Anderson, and the rest of Hunt's little crew thus far. In the darkness, they'd endured hours of intermittent mortar attacks and relentless stalking by ghostly infiltrators who came at them from all sides.

Now, with the return of daylight, they could hope once more of being reinforced or relieved soon. Otherwise, their time was rapidly running out, and they all knew it.

Still they hung on while the enemy continued to rake their positions with sniper and mortar fire. As they surveyed the tableau of death and carnage on the beaches below, their minds swept back over the events of the past twenty hours or so.

After securing the Point, the remnants of Hunt's First and Third Platoons had devoted the rest of the morning and early afternoon to strengthening their meager defenses. Each man staked out about a ten-foot circle for himself and began piling up loose rocks and debris around it. They also dragged up a few fallen logs for additional cover. At intervals, they rested, lit up sweat-sodden cigarettes, and talked about what had happened that morning.

Word had it that they'd killed well over 100 Japanese during their assault on the Point, but there was no minimizing the fact that their own losses had also been grievous. By Hunt's estimate, the company's casualties totaled about two-thirds of its strength, and every survivor had lost close friends.

In the confusion of the assault, Fred Fox and his assistant flame-thrower operator, PFC Whitey Hudson, had gotten separated, and Fox didn't know whether Hudson was dead or alive. But Fox was even more concerned about his best buddy, PFC Bill "Arky" Elderton, a bazooka team leader from Springdale, Arkansas. Fox hadn't seen Elderton since they'd left *LST 227* on separate amtracks, and he started buttonholing the guys around him for any information they might have.

"Yeah, I saw him when we hit the beach," one Marine finally said. "He was right behind me two or three minutes later when a Jap machine gun opened up on us."

Fox felt a sinking feeling in his gut. "What happened? Did he get it?"

The other Marine nodded. "He was hit right across the middle. I think he was dead before he hit the ground. Sorry, man."

While the radio was still working, Hunt and Lieutenant Willis were able to report their seizure of the Point to battalion headquarters and ask for help. "We need water, grenades, ammunition, and barbed wire—and as many reinforcements as you can scrape together," Hunt told Major William McNulty, the battalion exec.

"Okay, bub," McNulty replied. "I'll get the stuff up to you as soon as I can by tractor along the reef. Be on the lookout for L Company. They're moving into the gap on the right, and they'll make contact with you."

The news from other quarters was less encouraging. Lieutenant Stramel radioed that most of the company's machine gun platoon had been lost on the beach. Only about eight men were left, and all the guns had been ruined.

Corporal Swede Hanson, who'd managed to make his way back to the beach, reported that the mortar section was okay but had no phone communication with the Point. Any mortar fire supporting Hunt's position or Lieutenant Sellers's position down the beach would have to be directed by radio, and the batteries were fading fast. Sellers, meanwhile, was bracketed by enemy mortars and unable to move, and the fate of the Second Platoon was still unknown.

Here and there, Hunt encountered a few bits of good news as well. Sergeant Dick Webber and Corporal Henry Hahn paused from getting the remnants of their Third Platoon dug in to have a smoke with Hunt and tell him how they'd captured an enemy heavy machine gun and wiped out its crew.

"We came around some big boulders, and we were on top of the Japs before we knew it," Hahn said. "Luckily, I had a grenade in my hand. I threw it just in time, and it went off in the middle of them."

With the smaller Japanese machine gun dragged up to the Point by Fred Fox, the Marines now had two valuable additions to their limited arsenal, and plenty of ammunition for the captured weapons was stowed in vacated enemy pillboxes.

Hunt, Hahn, and Webber shared a laugh about PFC Lindsey Jones, a lanky BAR man with a Deep South accent. Crouched in a little patch of brush below the Point at the height of the assault, where he was calmly picking off enemy soldiers on all sides, Jones had been heard to drawl matter-of-factly: "My, my, they sho' is lots of Japs around heah."

As Hunt made his way along the line, other men talked of their personal experiences. Platoon Sergeant Paul Slovik told about a Japanese who approached his lines just after the Point had been seized, claiming he wanted to surrender.

"He had his pack on, and he was carrying his weapon," Slovik said, "so we shot him, just to be on the safe side, and damned if he didn't blow up. He must've been loaded with dynamite and grenades."

"Yeah, they're tricky little bastards," said another Marine, "and you've got to watch 'em. There's lots of 'em running around out there with our helmets on."

In the coming night, these revelations would come back to haunt Hunt and his men.

While bolstering their defensive line, the Point's captors had plenty of other pressing matters to demand their attention on D-Day afternoon. An enemy anti-boat gun was still firing on some of their positions from near the water's edge. The gun was so close that before Navy planes or long-range artillery could silence it safely, the Marines had to put out red cloth panels to mark their own line.

When the panels were in place, a call on the faltering radio for naval air support brought speedy results in the form of four F4U Corsairs. Within minutes, the planes appeared as specks far over the ocean, then swooped down and leveled off about 1,000 yards off the beach, streaking in at breathtakingly low altitudes with their wing guns blazing. For several seconds—red markers or no—they seemed to be aiming directly at the Point itself, giving the Marines who watched from the top of the promontory a sensation of helpless fright that none would ever forget.

"They weren't over ten feet off the water, and I swear it looked like they were coming straight at us," said Fred Fox. "And there was nothing we could do—nowhere to dig, no way to get any lower than we were, no place to hide. They came in over the edge of the cliff one at a time and pulled up sharply, clearing us by maybe twenty or thirty feet while their spent .50-caliber shell casings rained down all over us. I don't think they were really shooting at us, probably aiming thirty or forty yards to our front, but, my God, they scared the hell out of us."

Fox was near enough to Hunt to hear the captain screaming at the Navy over the radio until the planes were called off, then asking for naval gunfire. A few minutes later, a destroyer appeared just beyond the reef. It was as close as it could get to the shoreline and moving very fast parallel to the beach.

Seconds after Hunt reported the location and approximate range of the anti-boat gun, the destroyer's forward battery opened fire. One of three five-inch rounds from the ship struck the target dead-center, and the enemy gun emplacement disappeared in a fire-tinged cloud of smoke and dust.

"We had no more trouble with that particular Jap gun," Fox reported, "and things actually got quiet for a while."

While the break in the frenzied action of the morning was welcome, it also gave the men time to think about how hot and thirsty they were. Almost no one had any desire for food, despite the fact that many of them had eaten practically nothing since the night before. But, to a man, they were starving for water, and without constant danger to distract them, their thoughts locked on their thirst and made it even more unbearable.

As a native of southeastern Texas, Fox was more accustomed than most of his mates to extreme heat and humidity, but now he was suffering as much as any of the others. His lips were cracked, and his mouth felt like it was full of talcum powder, even while the rest of him was soaked with sweat. Both his canteens were bone-dry.

In a dehydrated daze, Fox looked out beyond the red panels that had spared the Marines from their own Navy planes, and his eyes drifted to the bodies of two Japanese officers a few yards further away. Both bodies had clearly been lying there for some time, probably ever since the first day of the pre-invasion bombardment. They were swollen and crawling with maggots, but Fox noticed that both were still wearing their samurai swords, pistols, field glasses—and canteens.

He couldn't take his eyes off those canteens, and he couldn't stop wondering how much water they might contain.

Fox knew there was a better than even chance that the bodies were booby-trapped, but he quickly made up his mind that getting water was worth the risk. Taking advantage of the lull in enemy firing, he crawled out along the edge of the cliff below the Point until he reached the two decomposing bodies. Then, holding his breath against the stench, he carefully cut the two canteens loose from their straps with his Ka-Bar knife.

He felt a burst of elation when he discovered that both canteens were more than half-full. But he resisted the urge to stop for a drink until he made his way to his left for a few yards, eased himself into the ankle-deep seawater below the cliff, and worked his way back to safety.

Fox took a hard-earned swallow of water—the first he'd had in hours—then passed the canteens down the line to his eagerly reaching comrades.

"I felt like I'd struck gold," Fox said. "But if I had, I'd have traded it for just one of those canteens."

The quiet interlude didn't last long. Captain Hunt was sitting behind a large boulder, having a smoke, looking for any sign that

L Company might be approaching and brooding about the dead Marines on the slope below the Point when the Japanese launched a new concentrated mortar barrage. This time, their aim was dead-on.

The very first explosion was much too close for comfort. It put a jarring end to Hunt's cigarette break and sent him ducking. The second round hit even closer. Then the blasts came in rapid succession squarely in the midst of the Marines' line, sending shards of shrapnel ricocheting among the rocks. A chunk of steel smacked the boulder to Hunt's left, spraying him with coral chips.

"Looks like I'm hit," Hunt heard a calm, analytical voice saying nearby. "Yeah, I'm hit, all right. Got me in the leg. Feels like the bone's broken."

Out of habit, Hunt waited for someone to call for a corpsman. When nobody did, Hunt moved toward the voice and tended to the wounded man himself. He still seemed calm and composed—"cool as ice," as Hunt described him—but his face was gray, and he was bleeding profusely. Two Marines carried him to the water's edge to wait for the promised tractor to take him to an aid station.

In all, five men were wounded by mortar and sniper fire over the next half-hour or so. A few more concentrated mortar barrages, Hunt thought grimly, and there might be no Marines left to defend the Point. Then again, maybe the Japanese didn't know how few of them there were.

A few minutes later, Hunt brightened when he saw Sergeant Blandy of the Second Platoon scurrying over the rocks toward him. Blandy was the first member of the Second that Hunt had seen since the landing, and he felt a brief surge of excitement at the sergeant's sudden appearance.

"What happened?" Hunt asked. "Where's the Second Platoon?"

Blandy had to catch his breath for a moment before he could speak. He swiped his sleeve at the sweat running down his forehead into his eyes.

"Most of us got caught in a big tank trap about 150 yards in from the beach," Blandy gasped. "We tried to fight our way out, but we got shot up really bad by machine guns on both sides of us and a pillbox up ahead. Lieutenant Woodyard was killed, and the rest of the platoon's in bad shape. I got cut off from everybody out in that gap, and I just now spotted you guys."

"Good God!" Hunt said. He grabbed the radio and called Lieutenant Sellers to alert him to the Second's predicament.

"We just got the same word down here," Sellers said. "We're gonna try to evacuate what's left of the Second Platoon as soon as we can. Battalion's bringing up some tanks."

Hunt sighed and shook his head. There was no help coming from the Second Platoon for the men on the Point. That much was clear, even if the Second hadn't been totally wiped out by now. The sole remaining hope was that L Company could close the gap to the right of the Point and link up with Hunt's dwindling force.

But where the hell *was* L Company? For that matter, where was the tractor with the promised ammo, water, and other supplies?

The questions fairly screamed in Hunt's mind, but so far there were no answers.

At the moment Hunt was receiving Blandy's distressing report, PFC Joe Dariano was still lying in a daze in the sweltering heat at the bottom of the tank trap, along with the rest of the decimated Second Platoon. Dariano felt as if he'd been there forever. The trench was hotter than hell itself, and despite the drugs he'd been given, his wounds were giving him considerable pain.

Still, he knew he was better off than a lot of other guys. Twice within the past few hours, the bodies of fatally wounded Marines had rolled down the sides of the trench and landed practically on top of him. Anyone exposing any part of his body above the edge of the ditch risked instant death.

On the other hand, the spot where he lay in the tank trap wasn't the safest place in the world either. Streams of bullets from two or three Japanese machine guns raked the lip of the trench every few seconds, and snipers in nearby trees also kept up a steady rate of rifle fire.

Around the middle of the afternoon, a Marine scrambled past Dariano shouting, "Nips! Nips! You better get outta here. They're in the trench and heading this way!"

Slowly and painfully, Dariano dragged himself in the direction the Marine had gone until he reached the south end of the tank trap. He found several Second Platoon guys already huddled there, but he was so exhausted and woozy from the drugs that he passed out almost immediately. One of the other men tried to keep Dariano awake by slapping his face.

Soon a few more Second Platoon survivors joined the little group at the end of the trench. There was no place left to go except over the top into the murderous enemy fire. Dariano looked around at the other wounded men slumped nearby.

Corporal John Schleyer, the platoon demolition man, had been shot through the pelvis and couldn't move. PFC Jack Henery had been machine-gunned so severely through his wrists and forearms that his hands were hanging by a couple of tendons. Another Marine lay motionless and glassy-eyed at the bottom of the trench. To determine if he were dead or alive, somebody removed his helmet, and the top of the man's skull came off with it.

Dariano closed his eyes. He'd decided they'd all be dead in a matter of minutes when he heard a familiar sound. He looked up and saw a Sherman tank clanking to a halt at the edge of the ditch. It was as though an angel had materialized in front of him.

Seconds later, the tank's machine gun and cannon opened fire on the Japanese pillboxes that had kept the Second Platoon pinned down all day. Then the men around him helped Dariano and the other wounded up the side of the trench, and they took cover behind the protective shield of the tank.

Dead Japanese were sprawled everywhere. He watched the tank run over their bodies as it rumbled slowly toward the beach.

Dariano spent the night with three other Marines in a shell hole near the water's edge because there weren't enough operable amtracks to evacuate all the wounded. He didn't give a damn. The shell hole was the safest place he'd been all day.

• • •

Late in the afternoon, two squads from L Company's machine gun platoon managed to work their way through continuous sniper fire and reach the Point. So did a five-man observation group from K/3/1's heavy mortar section. But to Hunt's chagrin, no friendly troops had yet moved into the gap on his right, and any hope of help in that area before nightfall was rapidly fading.

Hunt and Lieutenant Willis were taking stock of their increasingly desperate situation when Lieutenant Monk Meyer and another Marine appeared unexpectedly over the edge of the cliff. The pair had been sent out from Colonel Puller's regimental headquarters to find out what was happening with the beleaguered Third Battalion. They'd just come through a coconut grove east of the Point, and they'd been lucky to make it alive.

"You're isolated up here and surrounded by Japanese," Meyer said, looking Hunt straight in the eye.

"I know that," Hunt said. "Nobody's made contact with us."

"A Company and L Company have been trying all afternoon. They had the hell shot out of 'em when they tried to move into the gap. Do you think you can hold out?"

"Sure we can. Looks like we'll have to." Hunt's tone was a lot more positive than he felt.

"Take it easy and good luck," Meyer said.

A moment later, he and the other Marine were gone. They decided to swim back outside the reef, rather than risk another trip through the coconut grove. Meyer had described the grove as "lousy with Japs."

After the visitors left, Willis offered the only positive note he could think of under the circumstances. "Well, anyway, we'll be able to kill some more of the bastards," he said.

It was approaching dusk when the amtrack finally arrived, dodging sporadic mortar fire as it came. It was manned by a crew of black Marines—the first any of the men on the Point had ever seen.

Fred Fox felt relief beyond description as the tractor dropped its ramp and began unloading cases of ammunition, boxes of hand grenades, crates of C rations, and rolls of barbed wire. Fox was down to two clips of ammo for his tommy gun, although he'd found a good Japanese rifle with several belts of cartridges and had them lying nearby as a backup.

Hunt talked the tractor crew into leaving two of their .30-caliber machine guns with the Point's defenders, which, in Hunt's words, "strengthened our scanty line considerably." In addition to the sorely needed supplies, the amtrack also carried a few reinforcements in the persons of a half-dozen K/3/1 Marines who'd gotten separated from the rest of the company during the day's frantic action. When the unloading was done, the Point's seriously wounded were put aboard the amtrack to be taken back to an aid station for evacuation. Within minutes after it arrived, the tractor departed again, still drawing fire from enemy mortars but escaping without casualties or damage.

Along with the other supplies, the amtrack had brought a barrel of the same tainted water that would be delivered all over the beachhead within the next twelve hours. It was eagerly received at first, but one taste was enough to convince most of the men that they wanted no part of it.

"To us, water was the most precious thing of all right now, but this stuff was awful, sickening," said Fox. "For the time being, we decided we'd just keep doing what we'd been doing over the past few hours to get water—slipping out and cutting the canteens off dead Japs."

Initially, Fox was elated when he saw that the amtrack had also delivered a flamethrower to replace the defective one he'd left behind that morning. But this, too, turned out to be a disappointment. The tank of nitrogen that came with the weapon had been out in the broiling sun for hours and had built up so much pressure that the valve burst when Fox opened it. The broken valve released a fine, cold spray of diesel fuel into the air, and Fox actually found it refreshing.

"It sounds crazy, but I was so hot and dirty, and that diesel felt so cool and good that I just sat there and let it spray on me until the tank went dry," Fox recalled. "There was nothing I could do about it anyway—the thing was useless without the nitrogen valve—so I just told the other guys not to light up any cigarettes around me for a while."

The accident with the valve led to an eye-opening—and unnerving—revelation for Fox a few minutes later. After the diesel fuel evaporated enough to keep a spark from turning him into a walking torch, he decided to go down to the beach and try to locate his original flamethrower. Its igniter wasn't working, but it still had half a tank of fuel and a functioning valve, which might allow him to use the new weapon.

He knew there were enemy snipers around. They'd fired on the Marines laying the barbed wire around the base of the Point a short time earlier. But Fox had little doubt that he could make it to the beach and back without serious problems.

When he started in that direction, he heard an urgent yell from a Marine above and behind him: "What the hell you think you're doin', Fox?"

"I'm just going down to get my old flamethrower out of the hole where I left it," Fox called back.

"Man, you can't go back down there. There's Japs all over the place between here and the beach. You'll never make it."

"What're you talking about?" Fox demanded. "Hell, we just cleared that area not long ago."

"Yeah, but they've come in behind us now. We're cut off up here. Didn't you get the word?"

"Hell, I don't believe it," said Fox.

"Okay, it's your funeral," the other Marine said.

Still determined, Fox walked a few feet further, then hesitated. "You really think it's that bad?" he asked the other Marine.

"If you want to commit suicide, just keep walking," the guy said. "Otherwise, get back up here on the double."

Reluctantly, Fox turned and retraced his steps. He'd barely flopped down behind his little pile of rocks when he heard a shot off to his right. His eyes followed the sound and caught a brief movement in a tree about 100 yards away. Fox knew someone was hit when a Marine nearby shouted for a corpsman.

"I think I see this one," Fox said softly. He picked up the captured Japanese rifle, eased into a sitting position, and took careful aim at the top of the tree. He fired, and a second later, a body plunged to the ground.

"Hey, you got him!" several Marines chorused. "You got the son of a bitch!"

Fox nodded, but his satisfaction was diluted by the queasiness in his belly. As darkness slowly settled over the beach, he was shaken by the thought of how close he'd come to being a sniper's next victim. He closed his eyes and saw the faces of friends he'd already lost that day—PFCs Bill Elderton and Whitey Hudson, Sergeant George Sutkaitis, Corporal Calvin Smith, Platoon Sergeant John Koval, and several others. Then his thoughts jumped to the approaching night and the danger lurking just yards away on all sides. The radio was dead, and there was no way to call for support from the artillery. The Point's defenders were totally on their own.

Fox made no further attempt to leave his ten-foot circle of space. Instead, he piled up more rocks around himself while PFC Braswell "Stringbean" Deen, a rail-thin BAR man from Georgia, did likewise nearby. Fox carefully arranged a row of grenades so that he could find them in the dark, placed his tommy gun and the Japanese rifle by his side, and fashioned a pillow out of his cartridge belt. Then he lay on his back with his feet toward the beach, watching the stars appear in the darkening sky.

For the first time he could remember, he knew exactly how a trapped fox felt.

Except for a few rifle shots and occasional mortar fire, the first two or three hours after nightfall passed uneventfully, but none of the three dozen men remaining on the Point doubted that the Japanese were coming. Swede Hanson was pretty sure he could smell them already.

Ever since the 'Canal, he'd heard guys claim they could smell the bastards, and with every passing moment, he became more convinced it was true.

Hanson had prayed for hand grenades that afternoon, and not long afterward, the amtrack showed up with box after box of them. Now, with the contents of one of those boxes positioned within easy reach, he faced the open beach from a slight slope that curved back under the seaward side of the Point, praying that his nose would warn him in time.

The first attack came just after 11:00 P.M. It announced itself in jabbering voices and the muted scraping of boots on the rocks below.

"Japs! Japs!" a voice hissed nearby.

Hanson couldn't see anything in the pitch blackness in front of him, but he grabbed a grenade and pulled the pin. He held it as long as he dared—about three seconds—then threw it in an arc so that it would explode high and scatter its fragments over a wide area.

The echo of the blast was still ringing in Hanson's ears when he hurled a second grenade, followed by a third and a fourth. He paused to listen and heard the low-pitched *brrrrr!* of the captured Nambu light machine gun as Corporal Anderson blazed away with it just below. It was impossible to tell what kind of damage Anderson was doing, but he kept pouring a steady stream of fire into the darkness.

Hanson hurled two more grenades. Then, frustrated with his inability to see through the curtain of blackness, he stood up for a better look. Just as he got to his feet, a star shell from a Marine mortar somewhere to the south lit the sky.

The shell bathed the Point and the surrounding area in brilliant white light, revealing enemy troops on the move all across Hanson's field of vision. More importantly, it silhouetted the outline of a Japanese soldier charging at him from no more than ten feet away.

"I had my M-1 by my side, holding it by the pistol grip," Hanson recalled. "I came up with it and fired from the hip, and the Jap wasn't there anymore."

With hardly a pause, Swede started throwing grenades again. He threw them until his right arm was so tired he could barely lift it. Each time another star shell went off, he could see more Japanese bodies in front of him, but others still kept coming.

All along the company's tenuous line, Marines were taking similar action. Just as the tension intensified Hanson's sense of smell, it made their hearing so acute that every falling pebble brushed by a Marine's sleeve sounded like a landslide. It may have been a simple case of raw nerves, but some believed they were alerted to the enemy's approach by an indefinable sixth sense.

"You just got the feeling that something was going to happen," said Fred Fox. "My foxhole mate felt it, too. I dozed a little, but he didn't sleep at all, so we were ready for them when they came."

Fox and others around him threw dozens of grenades at targets they couldn't see. But they heard "a helluva lot of screaming" amid the explosions, which told them their grenades were hitting home. Then flares fired intermittently by Marines on the beach made it less of a guessing game.

The ground attack was broken within fifteen or twenty minutes with staggering Japanese losses, and the attackers who were able withdrew to positions roughly fifty yards away. In the silence that followed, powder smoke and the reek of cordite hung heavy in the air.

"You guys okay?" asked Corporal Henry Hahn, pausing to check on two other Marines crouching near the entrance to one of the Point's interior pillboxes.

"Yeah, just trying to catch our breath," one of them said. "The bastards want this place back pretty bad, don't they?"

Hahn nodded, but he scarcely heard the other Marine's words. His own sixth sense was working overtime, and he felt an overwhelming premonition of danger.

Quietly, he moved to the entrance of the pillbox and peered inside. In the fading light of a flare, he saw five Japanese soldiers applying dressings to wounds on their legs.

Hahn raised his tommy gun and fired a long burst. There was no further movement in the pillbox.

The end of the frontal assault on the Point didn't mean the Japanese had given up. After a brief interlude, the enemy mortars started up again, firing concentrations from a range of just fifty yards or so.

"If anything, the mortars were worse than the Japs charging straight at you," recalled Swede Hanson, "because you were so helpless. You couldn't do anything but pray and wait to see if the next one was going to blow you to hell."

The mortar shell that hit Swede came a couple of hours before daylight during a relative lull in the barrage. Fortunately, it was a small-caliber knee mortar round that exploded just a few feet behind him. If it had been one of the enemy's heavy mortars, he'd have been blasted to pieces. (Despite their name, the knee mortars carried by many Japanese infantrymen couldn't be fired from the human knee because of their strong recoil. Their fifteen-inch barrel made them easy to carry and set up and extremely hard to spot from a distance. "Sometimes it seemed as if every Jap in the Pacific had one of those damned things," Hanson recalled many years later.)

It was bad enough as it was, however. One large fragment knifed into his right arm, and several smaller ones struck him in the lower back. The arm wound was bubbling blood, and he knew instantly that it was a bad one.

Since he'd lost two of his best buddies at Guadalcanal and Cape Gloucester, Hanson purposely avoided cultivating close friendships with the guys around him. He was known in the company as a loner, but he didn't care. As an S-2 intelligence scout, his willingness and ability to operate on his own were valuable assets. And even now, he had no intention of forcing another Marine to expose himself to enemy fire by crying out for help.

"I'm hit," Hanson said matter-of-factly, clamping his arm at the elbow and squeezing hard to try to slow the bleeding.

"Hang on," said PFC Snowy Hibbard, the nearest Marine to him. "I'll get a corpsman."

"Never mind," Hanson replied. "The corpsmen don't have any medical supplies left anyway. I'll take care of it." He tore off the sleeve of his shirt and managed to tie it around the arm as a tourniquet.

As severely injured as he was, Hanson had two concerns that outweighed the importance of his own wounds. First, if someone came to help him, it would give the enemy a better fix on his position and make it even more dangerous to stay where he was. Second, if the Japanese knew he was hit, they might try to slip past him and overrun Hunt's makeshift command post.

For the rest of the night, Hanson kept hurling grenades at regular intervals. His right hand was too swollen for him to pull the trigger on his rifle, and firing it could have betrayed his location anyway. His arm looked like hell. It hurt like hell, too, every time he drew back to throw, but he was too erratic when he tried it left-handed, so he kept using the bad arm anyway.

"It's the bottom of the ninth," he told himself between clenched teeth. "Two out and the bases loaded. Just a few more good pitches and we'll win this game."

With daylight, the Point's defenders could see the damage they'd done, but there was little time to congratulate one another. A renewed mortar barrage soon started, and volleys of sniper fire came from bushes, trees, and a natural dip in the ground only about thirty yards away. The Japanese were serving notice that they were still determined to reclaim the prize they'd lost the day before.

Hoping against hope that the radio's batteries had regained enough strength overnight to transmit for a few moments, Hunt's operator tried desperately to get a message out. If he succeeded, Hunt was ready to holler as loud as he could for reinforcements.

"Hello Five, this is control. Hello Five, this is control. Can you hear me, over?" The only reply was static.

Sergeant Red Haggerty crawled over to Hunt, his carrot-colored hair powdered gray with coral dust. "I can get through, skipper," he said. "I can make it to Battalion and get us some help. I'll get 'em to send a tractor around by the reef."

Hunt had no other options. Their backs were to the wall, and he had only about a dozen men left who were fit for combat.

"Go ahead," he said. "Bring some more people up here—anybody. I don't give a damn. Hurry and take care of yourself."

By now, wounded Marines outnumbered the able-bodied, and more casualties were mounting fast. Rounds from an enemy heavy mortar in the nearby ravine rained down on all sides, and snipers firing from elevated positions peppered Marines in the outlying rocks with fire.

Corpsman Bill Jenkins, the only medic still alive on the Point, had set up a crude little hospital in one corner of a pillbox, where he tended to a half-dozen badly wounded men with almost no bandages or medicines. Private Wilburn Beasley lay dying of a gaping grenade wound in his side. One wounded Marine had been hit again as Jenkins carried him on his back toward safety. PFC Wayne Hook, Hunt's only other S-2 scout besides Swede Hanson, had been hit in the shoulder by mortar fragments while hurling grenades from the outer defensive perimeter.

Meanwhile, two wounded men with their legs full of shrapnel dragged themselves up onto the shelf above the beach where Hanson was watching mortar shells bursting out in front of him. With most of the action now on the landward side of the Point, Hanson was able to leave his vantage point long enough to help them to cover, but he kept his remaining grenades handy.

"Our line's getting awful thin," Lieutenant Willis told Hunt. "Looks like we'll have to draw in and tighten up."

"But that'll mean pulling back about twenty yards," Hunt said. "The Japs'll move in on us covered by those boulders. We'd be worse off than we are now."

A Japanese grenade sailed over Willis's shoulder, smacked a boulder, and rolled to within ten feet of where he and Hunt sat. Everyone around them dove away from it, but the grenade was a dud.

"We've gotta get these wounded boys out of here," Willis said when he regained his breath. "Where the hell is that tractor?"

Hunt leaned out and took a long look down the beach. He saw nothing but mortar shells crashing on the sand and the reef. They were exploding just below the cliff, and their fragments were pelting down only yards from the ledge where Hanson and the two other wounded men lay.

"Hey, Swede," Hunt shouted, "can you hear me?"

"Yeah, I'm here." Hanson ventured out far enough for Hunt to see his face and his grossly discolored arm.

"I'm going to put you in for the Silver Star for what you did last night," Hunt said. "Now you need to go to an aid station. That arm looks bad. I don't want you to lose it to gangrene."

"But, hell, Captain," Hanson protested. "How am I supposed to get there through all those Japs?"

"Go through the shallow water along the reef," Hunt told him. "It's only 150 yards or so to our lines on the beach. You can make it."

"Whatever you say, Captain."

"There's just one other thing, Swede."

"What's that?"

"I'll see you get another medal if you'll take those two other wounded guys with you," Hunt said. "They can't walk, but maybe with your help, they can float over there."

For a moment, Hanson stared at Hunt as if he were crazy. Then he raised his left arm and waved. "Okay," he said, "I'll see what I can do."

Hanson handed his rifle and canteen up to Hunt, then dragged the wounded men to the water one at a time. Once they were afloat, they were able to use their arms to paddle a little while Swede supported one with his left arm and had the other hang on to his shirt.

The trip through the chest-deep water seemed to take hours. By the time Hanson spotted a group of Marines just forty or fifty feet ahead, he could feel the last of his energy ebbing away. For the germ of an instant, he felt immeasurable relief. Then he heard a warning cry that sent a chill up his spine.

"Hey, here come the Japs! They're coming through the water!"

Bolstered by a burst of adrenaline, Hanson bellowed out his fear, pain, and frustration in the worst string of profanity he'd ever uttered: "Hold your goddamn fire, shithead! We're Marines, you asshole! We're Marines!"

Then he started singing the Marine Hymn as loudly as his cracking voice would allow.

Hunt got back to his command post just as hawk-nosed Sergeant Dick Webber rushed up. Webber was breathing hard, and his face was smeared with sweat and dirt, but he was also grinning. Hunt couldn't understand why until Webber spoke.

"McComas just knocked out the big mortar that's been hitting us so hard," Webber said in his unmistakable Boston accent, "and I think we've nearly cleaned 'em out on the right."

Hunt hurried to get a look. He reached a vantage point in time to see Marines surge over the rocks down below, hurling grenades and firing BARs. Within seconds, the enemy line in the ravine disintegrated before their onslaught. The Japanese were falling back.

At almost that same instant, Red Haggerty reappeared. "I've got some men, extras from other outfits I found on the beach," he yelled, "and we laid a phone line along the reef from battalion."

Hunt saw about fifteen fresh troops clamber out of the amtrack to make way for the rest of the wounded. He let out a heavy sigh as he watched the tractor crew unload more grenades, cans of water, boxes of medical supplies, and stretchers. It wasn't all he'd hoped for, but it was a damned sight more than they'd had.

Another round in the fight for the Point was over. There would be others before the final bell.

CHAPTER EIGHT

DEATH AND DENIAL

At no juncture in its history has the U.S. Marine Corps faced a darker, more desperate period than the first two and a half days on Peleliu. Between the initial D-Day landing and the morning of D-plus-2, Colonel Chesty Puller's First Marines lost close to 1,000 men. By 8:30 A.M. on September 17—forty-eight hours after the regiment came ashore—about one man out of every three in its ranks had either been killed or put out of action with serious wounds.

Today, many historians, military observers, and Marines who witnessed this bloodbath firsthand insist that many of these losses should never have happened, and they direct a major share of the blame at two men: Puller and General Rupertus, the division commander.

Initially, they say, Puller himself appeared strangely unmoved by the debacle. As a battlefield rule of thumb, when a regiment suffered 15 percent casualties, it was considered unfit for further front-line combat. Since the First Marines' two-day losses were more than double that percentage, the whole regiment would have been withdrawn and placed in reserve under normal conditions.

Yet Puller kept throwing his decimated units at the enemy, downplaying the severity of his losses during that crucial early period, and roundly berating his field commanders when they fell short of the objectives he laid out for them. Meanwhile, Rupertus's obsessive determination to win the quick victory he'd predicted undoubtedly put pressure on Puller and may have been at least as large a factor in the high casualty toll as Puller's own obstinacy.

When Rupertus came ashore at mid-morning on D-plus-1 to oc-cupy the divisional command post set up for him in a deep tank trap, he gave every indication that he still sensed—despite massive evi-dence to the contrary—a speedy victory in the offing. His projec-tions of a "rough but fast" fight of just two or three days had already been drowned in Marine blood. But as the body count mounted over the next few days, Rupertus steadfastly refused to call for read-ily available Army troops to bail out his division.

"The overall feeling seemed to be that a breakthrough was immi-nent," one of Rupertus's staff officers later wrote. "Enemy resistance would collapse, or at worst, disintegrate as had happened on Saipan, Tinian, and Guam."

The division commander had been grumpy and irritable, leaning on a cane and favoring his injured ankle, as he was helped off the am-track. His first act after a briefing by his executive officer, General Oliver Smith, was to banish Smith from any further role in the cam-paign. Smith had personally directed the operation for the past twenty-four hours.

After that, Rupertus called for reports from his regimental com-manders. Colonel Bucky Harris's Fifth Marines had absorbed sig-nificant losses, but they now controlled the airfield and adjacent installations and were ahead of schedule on a drive to the eastern coast of Peleliu. At the southern tip of the island, Colonel Herman Hanneken of the Seventh Marines reported heavy resistance but predicted that his area would be secure by nightfall.

Rupertus was visibly disturbed, however, by the bad news about Puller's Second and Third Battalions—not so much by their losses, it seems, as by their failure to keep up with the planned pace of ad-vance.

"Can't they move any faster?" Rupertus demanded, referring to Colonel Russell Honsowetz and Major Ray Davis, Puller's battalion commanders. "Goddamn it, Lewie, you've got to kick ass to get re-sults. You know that, goddamn it!"

The attack was losing its momentum, Rupertus complained, but all it needed to get back on track and achieve the early triumph he'd predicted was to "put more fire in the bellies" of his field commanders and their troops.

By late afternoon on September 16, D-plus-1, the stalemate on the Point and White Beach 1 had shown little improvement. The Third Battalion was still under intermittent fire from Japanese-held high ground beyond the airfield, and casualties continued to mount.

Every effort at permanently plugging the gap separating Captain Hunt's small force on the Point from the rest of the shallow beachhead had thus far failed. Despite reinforcements and supplies slipped in over the reef to Hunt's men, they remained in desperate straits. They were still cut off, still outnumbered, and still subjected to mortar fire and one probing attack after another throughout the day.

The Japanese now realized the opportunity they'd missed to overrun the Point on D-Day afternoon and night. Consequently, as historian George McMillan observed in *The Old Breed,* that first day would, in effect, drag on for Hunt's battered survivors until the morning of the third day, September 17.

In other words, a second terrible night lay just ahead.

Even so, as the afternoon wore on, Hunt felt far more confident than he had the night before. Late that morning, the remaining ten men from his Second Platoon had reached the Point by tractor, and other amtracks arrived at intervals with additional men and supplies. One brought the company's mortar section, which set up its guns among the rocks. Another carried a radio-equipped artillery observation team to communicate with the Eleventh Marines' batteries on Orange Beach. Hunt and the lieutenant in charge of the observation team worked out the range to cover a 600-yard-deep area in front of their lines.

"We'll put as much explosive in there as you ask for," the lieutenant assured Hunt.

"You're liable to have a busy night," Hunt replied. "The Japs want this Point."

That night Hunt would have more to fight back with than just rifles, tommy guns, and grenades. He'd also have more men to help repel the attacks that were sure to come. There were close to fifty Marines on the line now instead of a mere eighteen, seven machine guns instead of two, radios that worked, and two functioning phone lines to battalion headquarters.

With his position significantly strengthened, Hunt was able to relax a little. He lay down on one of the stretchers that had been brought up and closed his eyes for a few minutes. He thought of his wife, Anita, back in New York, and wondered if she could somehow sense where he was and the danger he faced. As the tension of the past thirty-plus hours eased slightly, he realized more clearly how close he and his men had come to annihilation in the predawn darkness that morning.

In his mind, Hunt pictured happier times and places—the gray skyline of Manhattan stretching out as far as the eye could see, Anita's laughing face, the two of them riding together on the Long Island Rail Road. He almost smiled at the striking contrast between the sophisticated, urbane existence he'd once known and the death-smelling hunk of coral that he now called home.

"Y'know, skipper," he heard Red Haggerty saying, "when I went to get help this morning, those people back there looked at me like they'd seen a ghost. They'd just about crossed us off the list."

Hunt nodded. "We had a close call, all right," he said, "but it'll be different tonight. We're well prepared for 'em."

Harassing Japanese mortar, machine gun, and sniper fire continued through the afternoon. The mortar barrages grew heavy at times, and Hunt had to call once for air support to shut them down. Later, he sent out two rifle squads on patrol to check out the enemy's strength in front of his line. They'd advanced less than 100 yards when they were jumped by swarms of Japanese hiding in holes among low ridges with rifles and grenades. The cost was one Marine killed and three wounded, including both squad leaders, Corporal Henry Hahn and Sergeant Joe Dailey.

After alerting battalion headquarters that the Japanese were mass-ing for a possible night attack, Hunt ordered his own mortars and artillery into action.

About an hour later, another patrol reported friendly troops moving toward Hunt's lines. B Company had finally fought its way through the massed enemy to fill the gap on Hunt's right. Within minutes, the two units were firmly spliced together. Some thirty hours after being cut off and surrounded, what was left of K/3/1 was no longer isolated, but its ordeal wasn't over.

In the darkness now descending, the Japanese were preparing one final, desperate attempt to reclaim the Point.

Late that afternoon, the mood of the troops along Hunt's bolstered line had brightened noticeably as word spread of B Company's breakthrough into the gap and tractors ferried in machine guns, mortars, and more men.

PFC Fred Fox saw Sergeant Blandy, guide of the Second Platoon, step almost jauntily off one of the amtracks with his gangster-style tommy gun slung over his shoulder.

"As bad as things had been the night before, we were ready to fight," Fox recalled, "and seeing those guys we'd been separated from for so long really got us juiced up. They were handing out cases of hand grenades, and just about everybody got his own case. There was also plenty of M-1, BAR, and tommy gun ammo being distributed."

At about 5:30 P.M., with the sun still shining brightly, the Japanese launched a ferocious mortar barrage. Fox and his buddy, PFC John C. Duke, hugged the bottom of their shallow foxhole, but most of the rounds narrowly missed the Point. They either hit twenty to thirty yards beyond it in the shallow water of the reef or fell slightly short of the Marines' defensive perimeter.

"At the time, we thought their range was just off," Fox said many years later. "But now I think they were purposely targeting any defenses below the cliff on the seaward side, where they couldn't see, in preparation for a night attack on our left flank through the shallow water."

The far edge of that left flank just happened to be where Fox and Duke were located.

When the barrage let up, Hunt moved up and down the line, checking to see that everybody was alert and ready for whatever came next. The captain stopped for a minute to talk to Duke and Fox.

"Are you guys set for trouble?" he asked. "I figure we're gonna get it for sure after dark, and I'm a little worried about this area over here." Hunt nodded toward the reef. "There's a depression out there, and I'm not sure how big it is. If the Japs could get thirty or forty troops in it and hit us directly on the left flank, it could be big trouble. They'd be too close for our mortars or artillery to help, and we've got no barbed wire out there."

"We're as ready as we can get, skipper," Fox said. "I was out there earlier to get some canteens off dead Japs, and I found a place where I could crawl down to the water's edge along the cliff. I can go out again when it gets dark and listen. It'll be hard for 'em to move around on that coral without making some noise. If I hear anything, I'll let you know on the double."

"Good idea," Hunt said. "But you be damned careful, Fox."

"I'll do my best to cover him, Captain," Duke said, patting his BAR.

"Duke can keep my tommy gun, too," Fox said. "I'll just take my .45 and a couple of grenades. That way, I can get back here in a hurry if I have to."

For several hours after full dark, Hunt received scattered reports of chattering voices and the sound of scrambling movements beyond the center of his perimeter. At one point, Hunt ventured out himself to have a look.

"Hear anything?" he whispered to a man who was unrecognizable in the gloom.

"Think I did," the Marine said. "Sort of excited jabbering."

Just then, someone threw a grenade toward the woods. When the sound of the explosion faded, Hunt could hear low squeals of pain.

"They're there, all right, and pretty damn near," another Marine said.

"Keep throwing grenades, and don't open up with your guns till you can see 'em," Hunt told them.

He moved quickly along the line to where Lieutenant Willis was sound asleep and shook him by the shoulder until he woke up with a start.

"Yeah, yeah, whatsa matter?"

"Japs milling around in front of our center position," Hunt said. "Shift a couple of men over there to strengthen it."

He also woke up Lieutenant Stramel and told him to check his machine guns. Then he had Haggerty get on the phone to alert the artillery to stand by. After that, there was nothing to do but wait.

It was close to midnight when the Japanese unleashed their final, all-out assault. First their mortars opened fire with a vengeance, but this time they got an instant response, both from K/3/1's 60-millimeter guns on the Point and the battalion's 81-millimeter heavies. Moments later, the Eleventh Marines' 105 howitzers joined the uproar.

Bursting flares flooded the inky sky with brilliance. Every rock, ravaged tree, and blistered clump of brush around the Point stood out starkly in the false daylight. So did scores of Japanese troops, scrambling over and past the bloated, decomposing bodies of their fallen comrades.

"There they are!" came a chorus of hoarse cries. "They're coming in on us!"

Every rifle, BAR, and machine gun in the center of the Marine line erupted at once. The noise rose to a deafening crescendo, but Hunt's angry voice could still be heard above the din.

"Give 'em hell!" he bellowed. "Kill every one of the bastards!"

•   •   •

When the bedlam of fire and noise broke out, Fred Fox had been lying alone by the foot of the cliff for nearly four hours within a few feet of the shallows on the reef. With nobody near enough for conversation, except for a couple of dozen dead Japanese, Fox had nothing to do but listen, think, and try to ignore the smell. For a long time, the only detectable sound had been the soft splashing of water against the rocky bank as the tide moved out, but a jumble of memories kept flashing through Fox's mind like old, faded snapshots.

Although Peleliu was his first combat, Fox had no fear of being on his own—never had, as far as he could remember. In fact, he rather relished it. He'd been more or less fending for himself ever since his father's death when he was just thirteen. Soon afterward, he was sent to military school at Allen Academy in Bryan, Texas, where he'd gotten the drilling-marching-saluting routine down pat long before joining the Marines at age seventeen. He proved as much by being named the top recruit in his boot camp graduating class in San Diego. As a reward, his instructors made him "sergeant for a day" and let him command the detail during its final drill. He thought it would've made his father proud.

Around 11:30 P.M., Fox heard a single rifle shot, followed by some yelling and a brief volley of other shots. Then it grew quiet again—but not for long.

When the storm of shooting broke out, Fox stayed still, flattening himself against the rocky ledge and holding his breath. The firefight raging on the landward side of the Point, where most of his mates were, was the loudest and hottest Fox had ever heard—a constant, thunderous roar. But as nearly as he could tell, there was no activity at all down by the reef. He strained his eyes and ears to detect any movement on his left, but there seemed to be nothing going on there either.

He tried to lie as quiet and motionless as one of the dead Japanese, and he did a pretty good job of it. The only thing that might have betrayed him was the furious pounding of his heart.

After about fifteen minutes, the volume of firing tapered off. A short time later, the night grew relatively quiet again. There were still a few stray shots here and there between periods of total silence. The minutes dragged by, but Fox maintained his position and kept listening intently for any sound from the reef.

Several times, drowsiness crept over him, and he almost dozed. But each time, he was able to rouse himself and reclaim his grip on consciousness. By his best guess, it was around 2:00 A.M. when he heard a soft voice speaking Japanese out in the water directly in front of him.

The voice sounded as though it came from thirty or forty feet away. Fox tensed, gripped his .45 hard in his fist, and made a split-second judgment that turned out to be a big mistake.

There's a whole column of Japs coming along the bottom of the cliff, he told himself, *and that voice I heard in the water was the lead man in the column. I've got to get off this ledge and crawl down the cliff toward Hunt's command post to sound the alarm.*

Fox turned and stepped down into the shallow water—barely two inches deep with the tide out—but he'd taken only a step or two when he heard something behind him. He whirled to face the sound, but a Japanese bayonet was already slashing through the air toward him. He ran into it with his chest and knocked it out of the way, but not before its blade carved a four-inch gash across the left side of his rib cage.

Fox swung his .45 as hard as he could, hitting his assailant squarely in the face with the barrel. The impact knocked the pistol out of Fox's hand, but the Japanese soldier also dropped his rifle. Fox caught it as it fell and drove the bayonet through the soldier's belly.

"Nips!" he screamed. "Nips!"

Seconds later, three more Japanese lunged at him out of the dark. Fox saw their bayonets glinting in the light from a distant flare, but he didn't see the grenade until it exploded a few feet behind him. He wasn't sure whether it was thrown by Duke or one of the Japanese, but it sent a half-dozen steel fragments knifing into his left side and knocked him down.

"Nips!" he yelled again as he tried to crawl away.

Out of the corner of his eye, Fox saw another bayonet-wielding Japanese charging at him. He rolled out into the water, trying to avoid the thrusting blade and get into the flare light, where his friend, John Duke, might be able to give him some help with the BAR or the tommy gun.

Fox didn't roll fast enough. He felt the bayonet stab into his neck, then rip another gash across his back. As he lay bleeding in the water and unable to move, he heard Duke open fire from the top of the cliff. For a few seconds, Fox was dimly aware of the Japanese firing upward at Duke's position. Then he felt himself lapsing into unconsciousness.

It was still dark when Fox reawakened, and he had no sense of how long he'd been lying there. Time seemed to have lost all meaning. Several fresh Japanese corpses were in the water with him, some of them almost close enough to touch if he was able to reach out toward them. Somewhere nearby, a machine gun chattered. Fox was surprised that he was still alive.

After that, he drifted in and out of consciousness. Once, in the light of the flares, he thought he saw his dead father standing beside him. They were talking very earnestly to each other about Fox's wounds and the fact that no one seemed to realize where he was or what a predicament he was in. Fox heard his own childlike voice pleading with his father to help him:

If you'll only get me out of this place, Daddy, I'll be the best little boy you ever had.

When he woke up again, seawater was splashing in his face and getting in his mouth. It was almost daybreak, and the tide was coming in. He realized, with no particular sense of panic, that if he didn't move soon, he'd surely drown.

"Corpsman!" he called out as loudly as he could.

Immediately, a voice shouted back: "What the hell're you doin' out there?"

"I dunno," Fox said, "but I can't get up."

"Hang on," the voice said. "I'll come get you."

After a moment, a Marine came tromping out into the water. It was PFC Andy Byrnes, who'd been manning a machine gun on the ledge nearby. Byrnes gathered Fox in his arms and lifted him, stumbling back toward the safety of the ledge as rifle shots rang out, and enemy bullets whined past them, smacking the rocks.

"Damned brave thing you're doing," Fox muttered.

"Just don't die on me, man," Byrnes panted. "I'd hate like hell to think I'd wasted the effort."

Marine mortar and artillery fire continued to hit Japanese positions in the woods, gullies, and basins north and east of the Point until shortly before daylight. An attempt by about fifty enemy troops to attack through the shallow water of the reef where Fox had raised the alarm ended with most of the attackers killed. The few who survived retreated into niches in the coral cliff near the waterline, so that bullets and ordinary grenades couldn't reach them. But Hunt's men burned them out of their hiding places with thermite grenades that filled the indentures with white-hot flames.

Screaming in agony, the Japanese ran into the water with their uniforms blazing and the ammunition in their belts exploding "like strings of firecrackers," in Hunt's words. They rolled in the surf trying to douse the flames, but it did no good. They burned in the water, their cries so loud and piercing that Hunt realized for the first time that the din of battle had abruptly stopped.

As dawn broke, an unfamiliar calm enveloped the area around the Point. Fox and Duke lay close together on the beach in a line of wounded men on stretchers. Moments after Fox fell, Duke had taken a bullet in his arm and suffered a leg wound from a samurai sword. But as an amtrack approached to ferry them to an aid station, neither was aware of the other's presence.

Nearby, several Marines stumbled down to the water, scooped up handfuls of the incoming tide and splashed it over their heads and shoulders. Others smoked quietly or opened cans of C rations and scraped out the contents with their Ka-Bar knives. Some slumped exhausted, staring out at the carnage surrounding them. They all seemed numbed and dazed by the silence.

Hunt moved among them to conduct a preliminary headcount of the K Company men still fit for duty. Of the 235 men who had landed on D-Day, he could locate only seventy-eight. The other 157 were either wounded or dead.

On all sides, enemy dead covered the ground, floated in the surf, or hung in pieces from shattered trees. In some places, their bodies were piled four-deep. Hunt and Lieutenants Willis and Stramel counted enough enemy corpses—many freshly killed but others dating to the first day of fighting—to determine that more than 500 Japanese had lost their lives in the struggle for the Point.

Now the struggle was finally over.

Someone handed Hunt a field telephone, and he heard Colonel Puller's voice crackling over the line: "I Company will take over your positions at 0800 and continue the advance. You'll go into reserve and get a rest."

A medic pressed a small bottle of brandy into Hunt's hand, and Stramel gave him a ham sandwich that one of the amtracks had brought in. The sandwich tasted fresh and good, and the brandy had a bracing effect, but only for a few minutes.

A deep weariness soon closed over Hunt, and all he wanted to do was sleep.

Taking and holding the Point was the first significant victory for Chesty Puller's First Marines. Elsewhere, however, the news from the front was all bad. Elements of the First assaulting the high ground due north of the White Beaches had run into a veritable meat grinder.

On the morning of D-plus-2, with the regiment's depleted Third Battalion tied down in support of Captain Hunt's men on the Point, Puller ordered Colonel Russell Honsowetz's Second Battalion to attack enemy positions on a coral rise designated as Hill 200. A high point along Bloody Nose Ridge on the southern edge of the Umurbrogol, the hill was a major source of Japanese artillery, mortar, and machine gun fire still plaguing the beachhead and the airfield. Puller didn't mince words as he handed Honsowetz the job of taking it.

"I want that ridge before sundown, and I mean, goddamn it, I *want* it," Puller said.

At age thirty, Honsowetz was among the youngest battalion commanders in the Corps. He was known as a hard-nosed officer who was solidly respected by his troops, and he'd handled tough assignments before. Unfortunately, Honsowetz and his men were about to have the Marines' first major encounter with a new, calculated enemy strategy designed to extract the maximum price for every inch of Peleliu's rugged interior.

Over the next few hours, the Second Battalion's Marines would become the first Americans to come face-to-face with the painstakingly constructed enemy strategy in the ridges. They'd learn to their dismay how deeply and deceptively the Japanese were dug in and how each of their positions was part of an intricate defensive chain, usually supported by others, higher up. It would be an eye-opening —and brutally costly—introduction to a whole new style of defensive warfare.

With a Sherman tank and two amtracks in the lead, the battalion moved north quickly along a narrow, twisting road. The first 300 yards or so were a piece of cake. The Marines covered the distance in five minutes or less, encountering only occasional small-arms sniper fire. But as they reached the lower slopes of Hill 200 and wheeled west to mount their assault, all hell broke loose. From every fold and crevice in the ridge, an avalanche of fire swept down on Honsowetz's men. Wheeled 37-millimeter field pieces appeared suddenly in the mouths of caves, spewed shells at point-blank range, then vanished. Volleys of heavy machine gun rounds and mortar bursts raked the slope from concealed emplacements. Rifles cracked from hidden sniper pits.

Within seconds, the Sherman and both amtracks were knocked out, leaving the rifle squads at the mercy of enemy gunners who moved with lightning speed through tunnels cut through the hill to connect a complex of caves. As the Marines advanced foot by foot up the slope, Japanese infantrymen jumped from their hiding places to meet them head-on with rifles, bayonets, and grenades.

"We got partway up the ridge, and then the hills opened, and fire poured down on our heads," recalled Private Russell Davis, a young 2/1 rifleman. "We could do nothing but huddle together in terror. We couldn't go ahead. . . . We couldn't go back. We were witless and helpless with nothing to do but lie and take it."

Honsowetz called in artillery strikes from Navy ships and the Eleventh Marines' 105-millimeter howitzers on the beach. Then demolition teams hurled satchel charges of TNT into the warren of caves and tunnels to finish off the job. By twilight on D-plus-2, 200 men of the Second Battalion held the crest of Hill 200. But the cost in casualties had been fearsome, and the battalion was still under fire from still higher enemy positions on nearby Hill 210.

The first call received after phone lines were strung to Honsowetz's hilltop command post was from Puller.

"How are things going?"

"Not too good," Honsowetz said. "I lost a lot of men."

"How many did you lose?"

"I don't have a firm count yet, but I think I lost a couple of hundred."

"How many Japs did you kill?"

"Well, we overran one position that had twenty-five in it, and we got 'em all," Honsowetz said. "There were a lot of Jap bodies around, but I don't know how many. Maybe fifty."

"Jesus Christ, Honsowetz!" Puller exploded. "What the hell are the American people going to think? You lost 200 fine young Marines and only killed fifty Japs? I'm putting you down for 500!"

. . .

It was never possible to make an accurate count of Japanese casualties in the First Marines' sector of the battlefield during this gory opening phase of the Peleliu campaign. But based on all available information, Puller's losses probably far exceeded those of the enemy.

Later casualty figures showed that the Second Platoon alone suffered 429 casualties between D-Day morning and the afternoon of D-plus-2, including the dead and wounded left on the slopes of Hill 200 that day. But whether out of shock, disbelief, or sheer vanity, Puller couldn't admit—either to himself or higher-ranking commanders—that he was pushing his regiment to the brink of destruction. His denial was compounded by that of Rupertus, who also seemed incapable of facing up to the gravity of the situation.

During the evening of September 17, D-plus-2, Puller finally contacted division headquarters and asked for reinforcements. Although he could only estimate his losses, he knew the regiment had taken a terrific beating during the first sixty hours of combat. A detailed accounting of casualties would later show that 1,236 men of the First Marines had been killed or wounded by the time Puller placed his call. But from Puller's perspective, his troops' failure to gain control of Hills 200 and 210 was even worse than the losses.

"I've got to have replacements if I'm going to continue the attack as ordered," Puller told Colonel John Selden, General Rupertus's chief of staff.

"I'm sorry, but there's none available," Selden responded.

"Well, give me some of those 17,000 men on the beach," Puller said, referring to the rear-echelon engineering, supply, communications, and other specialized troops who had landed since D-Day.

"You can't have them," Selden said. "Those men aren't trained infantry."

"You give 'em to me, and, by God, they'll *be* trained infantry by nightfall tomorrow," Puller flared.

"You'll have to do the best you can with what you've got for now," Selden said and hung up.

The bad news was just beginning—not only for Puller but for the entire division. What had happened so far was a minor foretaste of what lay ahead for the Marines in the maze of ridges and caves where most of Peleliu's defenders had taken refuge.

Any remaining illusions about a speedy American victory would soon be gone. The struggle—and the killing—had barely started.

CHAPTER NINE

HILLS, HORRORS, AND HEROES

Even with staggering casualties, hellish battlefield conditions, and agonizingly slow progress, the Marines' first three days on Peleliu followed a reasonably predictable scenario. It was essentially the same one that U.S. forces had dealt with time and again in their island-hopping campaign across the South Pacific.

First, they established a foothold ashore and set up a defensive perimeter against enemy counterattack. Then they achieved their primary early objectives, in this case by seizing the airfield and the Point. Meanwhile, they brought in massive amounts of men, equipment, and supplies, expanded their beachhead, and prepared for an offensive to gain control of the whole island.

For the most part, the initial phase of the battle had been fought on the beaches and nearby flat ground against a foe who was, with a few notable exceptions, lightly entrenched. Since it took place amid surroundings closely resembling those on Guadalcanal, Tarawa, New Britain, and other previously taken Japanese strongholds, veterans could rely on their earlier experiences for guidance.

But as the Marines began their first major moves against the nearest of Peleliu's twisting interior ridges late on September 17, the pattern was permanently broken. Nothing in the past thirty-plus months of fighting had prepared them for the almost unassailable defenses now staring down at them from the hills of the Umurbrogol.

As Colonel Honsowetz and his men had discovered in the disaster on Hill 200, they now faced an entirely different kind of warfare—one in which nothing was familiar, where every inch of ground was gained at high cost, and where each passing minute brought a new experience of terror.

There would be no more mass banzai charges or armored assaults, no more large-scale enemy attacks of any kind. Instead, there would be a methodical, guerrilla-style war waged around the clock by phantom adversaries who seemed to be always watching but never seen. Thousands of Japanese lurked in hundreds of mutually supporting caves in every spot of high ground—some spacious enough to house up to a battalion of troops plus large artillery pieces.

Men of Honsowetz's Second Battalion, First Marines, were the first Americans to run headlong into this new kind of warfare, but the Fifth and Seventh Marines would feel its sting soon enough.

"The First Marines got the worst of it in the early part of the fighting, no question about it," said Sergeant Jim McEnery of K/3/5. "But as time went on, and we replaced them in the ridges, our casualties caught up with theirs pretty fast."

By the morning of September 18, D-plus-3, Honsowetz's troops had been driven from the crest of Hill 200 by counterattacking Japanese. The Marines were taking heavy fire on their front and flank on the slopes where they were bogged down, and their plight was compounded by enemy mortar and artillery fire from nearby Hill 210, which the Japanese still held.

This, however, was only a preview of what lay ahead. Just to the north stretched a formidable ridgeline that would soon become known to the Marines as the Five Sisters. Each of its five separate hills was more than 200 feet high, and each was separated from the others by steep cliffs. Together, they posed a baffling combination of natural and man-made obstacles that defied imagination.

Enemy pressure on Honsowetz's battalion was so great that, despite reluctance at division headquarters, the Second Battalion of the Seventh Marines was sent in to help hold the line. Chesty Puller also scared up a few reinforcements from his own headquarters company, where every officer and enlisted man not assigned to a vital job was told to grab his weapon and head north. In all, about 115 replacements were recruited from the rear-area ranks and placed on frontline duty.

Early that fourth morning, Puller moved his command post to a more forward position near the edge of the bluffs and within 150 yards of the nearest Japanese positions. It was already miserably hot, with the temperature on its way to an afternoon high of 112 degrees, and Puller was stripped to the waist, his trademark corncob pipe clenched between his teeth. Enemy mortar and small-arms fire was heavy in the area, and the move had barely been completed when Japanese snipers started firing directly into the CP from higher ground just to the north.

"Send out a patrol and get rid of those bastards," Puller told one of his staff officers.

For three or four minutes, occupants of the CP continued to dodge bullets. Then they heard several sharp bursts of automatic weapons fire from the Marine patrol, and the shooting stopped.

At 8:00 A.M., Puller ordered the assault on Hills 200 and 210 to resume, but as the day wore on, the impasse continued. Early that afternoon, it triggered another fiery exchange between Honsowetz and Puller. As Honsowetz later recounted their conversation:

HONSOWETZ: Our situation's desperate. We've had to fall back.
PULLER: You've got to come into the flank and take the ridge.
HONSOWETZ: Christ, we can't do it. The casualties are too much, and we've been fighting day and night.
PULLER: You sound all right. You're there. Goddamn it, you get those troops in there, and you take that hill!

Infuriated by his commander's refusal to face reality, Honsowetz did his best to obey the order, but the assignment was more than his battalion's depleted ranks could handle alone. Puller did send in elements of Major Ray Davis's First Battalion to help, but the best the

Marines were able to do before the end of the day was capture Hill 205. This was a point of high ground separated from the main ridge-line, but it at least provided a good observation point.

The report issued that evening by regimental headquarters was bluntly worded but still attempted to put a hopeful face on an increasingly grim situation. "Little ground had been gained," it said, "but the center of Japanese resistance had been detected and the weakest spots probed."

Despite his mounting frustration, Puller could now see that his own bluster and iron will weren't enough to dislodge the Japanese from their hilltop strongholds. To his credit, the colonel went out on foot after dark, accompanied only by a sergeant, to meet face-to-face with Honsowetz and Davis in their CPs.

"We press the attack again at 0800 in the morning," Puller told them. "There's no change in our orders. Full speed. Use every man."

As he made his way back to his own CP, Puller was distressed by the condition of his troops and the growing futility of the situation. Without a massive infusion of reinforcements, the impasse—and the losses—could only be expected to continue.

A short time later, he received a call from Colonel Selden at division headquarters, who asked pointedly if Puller understood his orders.

"Yes, Colonel," Puller said. "I just came back from my battalions, and we're going to take ground tomorrow without replacements. But we're also going to add 10 to 15 percent to our casualties. Don't forget that."

Puller was again assured that no replacements could be had—but the statement had no basis in fact. With the troops of the Seventh Marines originally held in reserve now committed, it was true that no additional *Marine* replacements were readily available. Yet the Army's Eighty-first Division, which had just captured the island of Angaur, south of Peleliu, had plenty of fresh, uncommitted troops that could have been sent into action on short notice. The reason they weren't was General Rupertus's continued insistence that this was the Marines' fight, and the Marines, by God, would finish it.

In truth, however, it was Puller's regiment that stood perilously close to being finished. By nightfall on September 18, the First Marines was barely a skeleton of what it had been on D-Day morning. In the space of just four days, it had lost 1,500 men killed and wounded. Half its total strength had been bled away, and the bloodletting would start again as soon as the sun rose.

After crossing the airfield on D-plus-1, Captain Andy Haldane's K/3/5 and the rest of the Fifth Marines had encountered mostly light resistance as they pushed toward the eastern side of the island. Their advance toward the small section of Peleliu's eastern coastline designated as Purple Beach was hardly a stroll in the park, however. As the company moved east, the jungle grew thicker, and the terrain turned increasingly swampy and treacherous.

On the morning of September 17, D-plus-2, as PFC Sterling Mace's rifle platoon picked its way through thickets of brush and past the bodies of dead Japanese, a sudden blast flung mud high in the air and sent everybody scrambling for cover.

"What was it?" Mace yelled to nobody in particular. "A booby trap or a grenade?"

"I don't know," a voice beside him said, "but we've got a man hit."

Mace turned and saw his Kipling-quoting buddy, PFC Seymour Levy, a few yards away. Levy was holding the lower half of his face with both hands while blood dribbled between his fingers and ran down his neck.

"What the hell happened?" Mace asked.

Levy seemed to be in a semiconscious stupor, and if he said anything, Mace couldn't hear him.

A corpsman showed up almost immediately and tried to stanch the bleeding with a field dressing. Levy's chin was a mangled mess, and the shrapnel hadn't missed the jugular vein by much. With all the blood, it was hard to tell how many fragments there were. Mace thought Levy must be hurting like hell, but his injuries were also enough to get him off Peleliu for good.

"Hey, cheer up, man," one of Levy's squad mates said. "I think you just got yourself a ticket home."

"Yeah, it's a million-dollar wound for sure," said another. "The rest of us should be so lucky."

A short time later, Levy was evacuated, and the platoon moved on. The corpsman said Levy would be on a hospital ship within an hour or so, and Mace almost envied his friend. He also felt a deep sense of loneliness and loss.

"I thought I'd never see that crazy kid again," Mace recalled.

He was wrong.

Ahead and a bit to their left, the men of K/3/5 slogging through the muck and mangroves could see the eastern end of Bloody Nose Ridge. On the afternoon of D-plus-2, as they moved up to relieve the First Battalion, Fifth Marines, they also began to take heavy flanking fire from its heights. Japanese observers on the ridge had a clear, unobstructed view of the advancing Marines, and intense enemy mortar and artillery fire briefly pinned down PFC Gene Sledge's mortar section.

"The Japanese ceased firing when our movement stopped," Sledge later said. "Yet as surely as three men grouped together or anyone started moving, enemy mortars opened up on us. If a general movement occurred, their artillery joined in."

Complicating matters, K/3/5's mortars were unable to return the fire on their left flank for fear of hitting other Marine units in that area, where some of the opposing lines were only a few yards apart.

"They need ta git some more damn troops up here," said Snafu Shelton, voicing his standard complaint as he flattened himself on the soggy ground.

The experience gave the men of K Company increased appreciation—and sympathy—for what some of the First Marines were enduring. They were charging squarely into the withering fire from the ridge, rather than merely skirting the edge of it.

Over the next several hours, K/3/5 tied in with units of the First

Marines on their left and troops from 2/5 on their right. As members of the two regiments swapped stories, Sledge and his squad mates learned firsthand of the First's brutal losses and realized what an easy time they had had by comparison.

"I pity them First Marines," said Snafu. "They flat catchin' hell."

"Somebody told me they got those poor guys chargin' that ridge with fixed bayonets, and they can't even see the Nips that're shootin' at 'em," said Corporal R. V. Burgin.

"I just hope they take the damned thing soon, so we don't have to go up there," said somebody else.

"Don't worry," Burgin assured him. "Our turn'll come."

Meanwhile, down on the extreme southern tip of Peleliu, well removed from the gory crags of Bloody Nose Ridge, two battalions of the Seventh Marines had been caught up in their own separate version of hell.

When the original battle plan was drawn for the Peleliu campaign, its framers correctly anticipated that the First Marines would meet the stiffest enemy opposition. But they fully expected the Seventh to secure the southern sector of the beachhead with minimal difficulty during the first twenty-four hours after landing, then swing north to bolster the First Marines' assault on the ridges. By the morning of September 18, D-plus-3, the Seventh was supposed to be mopping up the last pockets of Japanese resistance in the south. In fact, Lieutenant Colonel John Gormley's 1/7 and Major Hunter Hurst's 3/7 were still in the fight of their lives against seemingly impregnable enemy fortifications on two large promontories jutting out into the Pacific.

These rocky headlands were many times larger than the Point where Captain Hunt's company had been isolated for two days, and they were similarly studded with networks of pillboxes, block-houses, gun pits, and embrasures. The narrow approaches to both promontories had also been heavily mined by the Japanese.

The largest of the outcroppings was identified on maps as

Ngarmoked Island, although it was actually more like a peninsula, connected to Peleliu proper by a 100-yard-long sand spit that could be crossed on foot at low tide. It extended slightly southwest from the island's main landmass and was separated by a 200-yard-wide inlet from another, smaller promontory that formed a southeastward extension of Peleliu.

By late morning of September 17, following naval shelling and air attacks, a perilous two-hour foray by a Marine demolition team under Captain Frank Knoff had cleared a newly discovered minefield in the path of the planned attacks. Then a rifle company from 1/7, supported by several tanks, had stormed the smaller promontory. In about three hours of hard fighting, the objective was secured, and the bodies of 441 Japanese were found scattered among the rocks and crevices. Marine losses were seven dead and twenty wounded.

But when a second tank-supported infantry company from 3/7 simultaneously attacked Ngarmoked, it ran into a juggernaut of enemy resistance. One platoon and one tank managed to get across the sand spit before Japanese machine gun, mortar, and small-bore artillery fire stopped them cold and forced them to retreat.

The Seventh's weapons company and every available tank were called in to pound Ngarmoked with mortars and 37-millimeter artillery, followed by more air strikes. Then the infantry tried again with a trio of Sherman tanks leading the way. This time, the Marines breached the enemy's first defensive line and chased the Japanese from some of the high ground. But once more the attack stalled.

"Every few yards, the Japs had coral bunkers, concrete blockhouses, reinforced foxholes, earthen trenches, caves, and sandbagged positions," noted Sergeant Jeremiah O'Leary, a combat correspondent. "Every position was located to cover its own approaches and the approaches to surrounding defense works."

That afternoon, Major Hurst was forced to commit his entire battalion to the fight for Ngarmoked, but even that wasn't enough to break the enemy hold on the promontory. After running into a large swamp that threatened to divide two of his rifle companies, Hurst decided to set up a defensive perimeter and wait for additional armor to be brought up to spearhead a new attack the next morning.

Early on September 18, D-plus-3, the assault resumed with an all-out push by the Seventh to smash through the Japanese lines and reach the seaward end of Ngarmoked. Orders from regimental head-quarters were relayed to all rifle platoons to bypass any small groups of live Japanese remaining in areas that had already been overrun. Whatever mopping up needed to be done would be handled by special teams of reserves, the units leading the assault were told.

It was an ill-advised strategy that left dozens of concealed enemy troops in position to strike the Marines' flank. Most of one platoon was almost immediately pinned down by Japanese firing from strong positions. The situation had all the earmarks of a catastrophe in the making—until husky, nineteen-year-old PFC Arthur J. Jackson grabbed his BAR and sprang into action.

A native of Cleveland, Art Jackson had spent his early boyhood in Canton, Ohio, but after moving with his family to Washington state, then to Oregon, he'd come to consider the Pacific Northwest his home. During high school in Portland, he'd lettered in football and track. By his senior year, he weighed close to 200 pounds, and his friends and fellow athletes called him "Bull."

Following graduation in the spring of 1942, Jackson signed on with a construction crew and went to Sitka, Alaska, to help build a naval air station. A few months later, with his eighteenth birthday approaching, he returned to Portland and joined the Marines.

Fresh out of boot camp, Jackson was picked to attend a two-month combat conditioning course, where he was trained to utilize his size and strength as assets in hand-to-hand combat. He learned to fight with knives, clubs, sticks, and just about anything else he could lay his hands on.

"We did a lot of swimming, long marches, night maneuvers, and landing exercises," Jackson recalled. "The guy in charge was an ex–football coach at Northwestern, and he worked our fannies off."

By the time he reached the Pacific, Jackson was in the best condition of his life, both physically and mentally. From all accounts, he excelled in every job he was given, first as a member of a .30-caliber machine gun section, then as the designated BAR man in a rifle squad.

In January 1944, on infamous Hill 660 at Cape Gloucester, he was credited with carrying a wounded buddy, PFC Frederick Rigby, through enemy fire to safety. Although Rigby later died of his wounds, Jackson received a letter of commendation from General Rupertus for his "outstanding service."

"I was a good AR man, and I guess I was made to be in the infantry," Jackson said. "I was just totally gung ho and always ready to go for broke."

Those qualities were never more evident than on Ngarmoked on D-plus-3, when the men of Jackson's platoon found themselves trapped, outnumbered, and largely helpless to return the enemy fire. Both the platoon's senior sergeant and its CO had been killed, and the pinned-down survivors had no sense of leadership or direction.

With small-arms rounds whining off the rocks around him, Jackson heard the breathless voice of Sergeant Warren Scheidt, his squad leader, a few feet away: "My God, they're all over our left flank. Sounds like a hundred of them, but they're so well dug-in I can't see a damned thing to shoot at. What about you?"

Jackson hugged his twenty-pound BAR against his chest. He trusted the weapon implicitly. If you treated Mr. Browning's gun right and kept it in good repair, it would fire just about forever. He also knew how much havoc it could wreak. He'd seen it with his own eyes on numerous occasions.

Jackson craned his neck to look into a shallow depression nearby. It sloped out toward the cluster of Japanese positions that had the Marines hemmed in, and Jackson thought he might be able to follow it all the way to the base of a large concrete pillbox that seemed to be the linchpin of the enemy fortifications.

"If I can get in that ditch with my AR and enough ammo, I might be able to get close enough to stick it to 'em," Jackson said.

"How much ammo you got?" Scheidt asked.

Jackson felt in his pouch and counted thirteen one-pound magazines for the BAR, each containing twenty rounds.

"Plenty to last for a while. But it'll take grenades and maybe a TNT charge to knock out that big bunker."

"As soon as I hear you quit firing, I'll come up fast and toss you what you need," Scheidt said.

Jackson inched his way toward the edge of the depression and took another look. The more he thought about it, the more certain he felt that he was in exactly the right spot. What he had in mind meant moving out beyond his own line into an area where none of his comrades could provide him with covering fire, and where nobody but Scheidt would be close enough to help. But cowering where they were and waiting for the Japanese to pick them off one at a time seemed an even worse option.

"Okay," he said, "I'm going out there."

Dodging bullets, Jackson slid into the ditch and scrambled forward at a low crouch. A dozen feet from the target, he flattened himself against the rocks at the bottom of the depression, holding his breath and listening. There was no letup in the enemy fire, but since none of the rounds hit anywhere near him, he figured he hadn't been spotted.

He crawled the rest of the way, then jumped to his feet, rammed the muzzle of the BAR into the narrow slit in the side of the bunker, and opened fire. When the first magazine was empty, he paused to listen. All he heard was the frenetic clatter of Scheidt's boondockers on the rocks behind him.

Two bulky satchels tumbled into the ditch as Scheidt raced back to take cover. One was packed with phosphorus grenades, the other with fused charges of TNT. Jackson tore open the first satchel and stuffed three or four of the grenades through the pillbox aperture and hurled himself away from the searing heat of the blasts. He followed up with three charges of high-explosive, then ran for all he was worth.

Seconds later, the pillbox erupted like a small volcano, spewing the remains of its concrete crown twenty feet into the air and pelting Jackson with debris. None of the thirty-five Japanese inside survived.

The determined young Marine was far from finished. Now with covering fire from his comrades, Jackson methodically attacked and destroyed no fewer than eleven other fortified Japanese positions over the next hour. He was credited with killing a total of fifty enemy soldiers.

"As I came to each position, I just unloaded a magazine into it," he recalled many years later. "Then I reloaded and moved on to the next one."

In single-handedly obliterating the last remaining bastion of enemy resistance on Ngarmoked, Jackson displayed levels of self-lessness and courage rarely seen on any battlefield. When it was over, his grateful buddies grabbed him and pounded him on the back "like I'd won the biggest football game of the year."

But Jackson himself shrugged the whole thing off. "Afterward, I was so exhausted I just fell down, and the only thing I wanted to do was go to sleep," he recalled. "The action I was involved in was just one small part of what happened on Peleliu that day, and the only reason I was able to do some things was because I got a lot of help from my buddies. I never considered myself a damn hero. I was just a good Marine, trying to do what any other good Marine would've done under the same circumstances."

His country and his commander in chief disagreed. Slightly more than a year later, then-Lieutenant Arthur Jackson would become one of only three living Peleliu veterans to be awarded the Congressional Medal of Honor. The accompanying citation, signed by President Franklin Roosevelt, read in part:

"Stouthearted and indomitable despite the terrific odds, PFC Jackson resolutely maintained control of the platoon's left flank movement throughout his valiant one-man assault, and by his cool decision and relentless fighting spirit during a critical situation, contributed essentially to the complete annihilation of the enemy in the southern sector of the island. His gallant initiative and heroic conduct in the face of extreme peril reflect the highest credit upon PFC Jackson and the U.S. Naval Service."

Slightly more than two miles due north of Ngarmoked, in the wilderness of gaunt cliffs, coral boulders, and scorched brush marking the forward approaches to the Five Sisters, first light on the morning of September 19, D-plus-4, revealed a scene of sheer desperation and utter horror.

The dead of Colonel Honsowetz's 2/1, Major Davis's 1/1, and Lieutenant Colonel Spencer Berger's 2/7 littered the slopes. Wounded men, left behind when the Marines were forced to fall back, screamed for help over field telephones and walkie-talkies, but none of their pinned-down comrades could reach them. In battalion and company command posts, officers buried their heads in their hands, cursed, and prepared for more of the same.

Every attempt to dislodge the enemy from his heavily fortified hilltops had failed. Each brief, costly advance up the rugged heights below the Five Sisters had been beaten to a halt. Most had been driven back with calamitous losses.

Part of the problem was that no one in a command position in the First Marine Division fully grasped the true nature of the terrain or the diabolical tricks it could play. The Five Sisters and the high ground just to the south—the string of hills originally nicknamed Bloody Nose Ridge—formed a sheer wall blocking any northern movement through the Umurbrogol. It was no accident that the Japanese had made this aggregation of sawtooth ridges and sheer cliffs the cornerstone of their interior defenses on Peleliu.

As for the Marine riflemen charged with taking them, they didn't know the difference between the Five Sisters, Bloody Nose Ridge, and the numbered hills on their officers' sector maps—much less how they all related to one another. Many of them would never fully comprehend the giant topographical puzzle they'd been ordered to solve. All they knew was that they were being cut to ribbons and still gaining little or no ground.

Nevertheless, the haggard remnants of the three battalions climbed out of their foxholes at 0700 on D-plus-4 and stumbled forward for another frontal assault.

"Crawling and clawing up the cliff went platoons that were no more than squads and companies that were no more than large platoons," recalled 2/1 rifleman Private Russell Davis. "I counted one platoon. It mustered eighteen men on that push. But they went up."

Marine artillery and mortars had started bombarding the highlands some forty minutes before the assault troops moved out, and Navy guns joined the barrage soon after. But as was so often the case on Peleliu, the shelling had little apparent effect on the enemy.

Colonel Puller threw all the manpower and firepower his regiment could scrape together into the fight that morning, holding nothing in reserve. Every man who could walk and carry a weapon, including those of the Fourth War Dog Platoon, was recruited for the attack. They were joined by all available tanks and amtrack-mounted flamethrowers to give the infantry as much mechanized muscle as possible.

Among the decimated rifle companies joining the D-plus-4 assault was Company C, First Battalion, First Marines, commanded by Captain Everett Pope, the scholarly Phi Beta Kappa from Bowdoin College. By now, Pope's friend and ex–Bowdoin classmate, Captain Andy Haldane, and his K/3/5, had finished clearing the island's eastern shore of Japanese and were getting a welcome rest on Purple Beach. Pope and his company, on the other hand, were about to experience the most terrible twenty-four hours of their lives.

Under anything akin to normal circumstances, C/1/1 would've already been relieved. After the firestorm on White Beach 1, the company had run squarely into the strongest enemy fortifications at the airfield, including the reinforced-concrete blockhouse that had served as the Japanese headquarters. Pope's unit had absorbed one of the division's highest casualty rates thus far.

The young Marines who fought at Peleliu came from across America and were part of a unique brotherhood. At age seven, future Sergeant Fred Miller (top left photo, second from left) posed with his siblings at home in St. Joseph, Missouri. Future Lieutenant Ed Jones (top right) was known in Whiteford, Maryland, for his musical talent, and Seymour Levy (above left) was a poetry-loving mama's boy in Brooklyn before becoming a Marine at seventeen. Charles "Red" Womack (above right) of McComb, Mississippi, had only a few weeks with his bride, Hilda, before shipping out for the Pacific.

The Marines were told that the battle would be over in two or three days, but their fiery reception en route to the beach (above) and after reaching shore told them otherwise. PFC Joe Lambert (below left, foreground) and other men of K/3/5 huddle under an amtrack, pinned down by enemy fire. Sergeant Fred Miller (below right) was severely wounded within the first hour and a half. A corpsman (bottom) tries to aid a dying Marine on the beach.

Before the Marines could secure their first major objective—Peleliu airfield—they had to repel a fierce Japanese tank-infantry attack (top). All thirteen enemy tanks were destroyed, but crossing the airfield the next day was still a nightmare. Marine riflemen (middle) took advantage of what scant cover they found, but for most of the way they were in the open. The metal framework of a huge Japanese blockhouse guarding the field (bottom) remained standing after its concrete skin was blown away.

12

13a, b

14

Plaguing the beachhead on the north was the Point, a hollowed-out knob of rock bristling with enemy fortifications. K/3/1, commanded by Captain George Hunt (top left), had the job of capturing the Point, then holding it against repeated Japanese counterattacks while cut off from the rest of the division. PFC Fred Fox (top right and above right) almost lost his life on the Point but lived to return twenty years later and retrieve the rusty Ka-Bar knife and Japanese canteen he left there during the fight. Gravely wounded was Corporal Wilfred "Swede" Hanson (above left), shown with the Silver Star he was awarded fifty years later. Below are the Point and White Beach 1 as they appear today.

15

16

17

18

Captain Everett Pope (above left) lost most of his company on a ridge north of the beachhead, but held off an all-night Japanese attack with a few grenades and a large supply of rocks, earning a Medal of Honor. PFC Arthur Jackson, decorated by President Truman (above right), won the same honor for wiping out a dozen enemy pillboxes. As casualties soared, Division commander General William Rupertus (left, third from left), Fifth Marines commander Colonel Bucky Harris (second from left), and III Amphibious Corps CO General Roy Geiger disagreed on assault tactics. Rupertus urged speed, but gains against enemy-held cliffs often came in inches (below).

19

22

With close air support by Corsair fighters (above left), K/3/5 seized the islet of Ngesebus in one day, killing 470 Japanese, but the Marines also paid a high price. Among dozens wounded that day was PFC Bill Leyden (top right), hit in the face by grenade fragments. Corporal R. V. Burgin (above right) and his mortar squad got help from a tank and flamethrower to "cure" an enemy pillbox. The attacking Marines included PFC Gene Sledge (below left) and PFCs John Redifer, Vincent Santos, and Gene Farrar (below right).

23

24

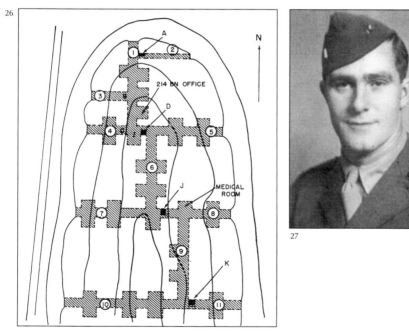

The tortured terrain of the Umurbrogol Pocket (top) was honeycombed with interconnected, multilevel Japanese caves (diagram, above left), which kept Marines under constant fire from unseen mortars, artillery, machine guns, and small arms. Enemy marksmen inflicted a fearsome toll on American forces, including more than 300 officers. Among their victims was Captain Andy "Ack-Ack" Haldane (above right), popular commander of K/3/5, killed by a sniper as he peered over a ridge two days before his company was withdrawn from action.

Among the last Marine units pulled off the line, K/3/5's weary survivors—numbering just 85 men out of 235 who had landed on Peleliu on D-Day—posed for a Corps photographer (above) before shipping out for a rest camp. They included only five senior noncommissioned officers: (below left, from left to right) Sergeant Dick Higgins, First Sergeant David Bailey, Sergeant Donald Shifla, Sergeant Jim McEnery, and Platoon Sergeant John Marmet. Just two commissioned officers remained with the company (below right): First Lieutenant Thomas "Stumpy" Stanley (standing), who replaced Captain Haldane as CO, and Second Lieutenant Charles "Duke" Ellington.

Of the 235 men under his command at the time of the landing, Pope had only ninety survivors still fit for duty. The rest had been killed or evacuated with serious wounds. For the action on September 19, his company was detached from Davis's 1/1, its regular battalion, and temporarily assigned to Honsowetz's 2/1. Its mission was to slip out ahead of the main assault force on a flanking movement to seize what appeared on sector maps as Hill 100. This rocky knob lay to the rear of the Five Sisters and to the left of the East Road, a trail running north and south between the Umurbrogol ridges and the eastern coast of the top pincer of Peleliu's lobster claw.

Map designations for various hills were derived from their altitude, meaning that Hill 100 was only 100 feet high—less than half the elevation of the enemy-held heights of the Five Sisters. But Honsowetz believed that if C/1/1 could capture Hill 100, it might provide an opening to strike at the core of the thus far impervious Japanese defenses.

Typical of the extremes in Peleliu's landscape, the most direct approach to the base of the hill was through a small swamp. When Pope's men tried it, they ran into heavy machine gun fire from two enemy pillboxes and were forced to withdraw and regroup.

A brainy young officer who had graduated magna cum laude, Pope quickly spotted another route via a causeway across the swamp, where his riflemen could be supported by Sherman tanks. Honsowetz gave his okay to try it, but it took two hours, with Pope and his men under constant harassing fire from enemy machine guns, to scare up four Shermans—and then the tanks proved ineffective. One slipped off the side of the narrow causeway, and when a second tried to pull out the first one, it also slid off, on the other side, effectively blocking the causeway to other armored vehicles.

"We can either sit here and keep taking casualties while we wait to see if those tanks can be cleared out of the way," Pope told Lieutenant Frank Burke of Scranton, Pennsylvania, one of the company's handful of surviving officers, "or we can take our chances and run across on foot a few men at a time."

Although it was a considerable gamble, Pope decided the latter course of action made more sense, and he passed the word to get ready.

"We'll go one squad at a time," he said. "Just run as fast as you can, and don't slow down till you get to the foot of the hill."

The high-risk footrace apparently took the Japanese by such surprise that every Marine made it safely across the causeway. Then they caught their collective breath, regrouped, and charged on up the hill.

With some support from their own machine guns and mortars on the other side of the swamp, Pope and his riflemen reached the top of Hill 100 with amazing speed, although not without substantial casualties. Within ten minutes, about twenty-five of them were at the crest—but a bitter surprise awaited them there.

Hill 100 wasn't actually a separate hill at all. It was only the leading edge of a long, angular ridge dominated by higher ridges to the north and west. Looking down on them from no more than fifty yards away were more Japanese armed with machine guns, mortars, and light artillery. Instead of seizing a vital vantage point, Pope's men had climbed directly into an enemy crossfire.

"The maps are wrong," the captain fumed as his Marines scurried for what scant cover they could find among the rocks. "And we're in one helluva bad spot."

With twilight falling, Pope and his men had no reliable contact with battalion headquarters or their own mortar and machine gun squads, and the small amount of ammo they'd been able to carry with them on their charge up the slope wasn't nearly enough for a prolonged fight. Their cramped defensive perimeter was defined by the steep edge of the cliff, and by Pope's reckoning, it wasn't much larger than one of the courts on which he'd once played intercollegiate tennis.

Here, virtually surrounded and totally on their own, they'd try to hold out until morning. If there was any consolation in their situation, it was that, as long as they held the hilltop, their presence would provide a protective shield for American positions to their rear.

"The line is flimsy as hell, and it's getting dark," Pope noted in his journal. "We have no wires and need grenades badly." An infantry unit could fight a few days without food and a few hours without water, Pope told himself, but it couldn't last long without ammunition. Besides their rifles and several dozen hand grenades, the Marines on Hill 100 had a lone .30-caliber machine gun, two tommy guns, and a few BARs. Rounds for all the weapons were in short supply.

"Let's gather up plenty of rocks," Pope told his noncoms. "We're going to need them." The idea, he explained, wasn't so much to hit attacking Japanese soldiers with the rocks as to confuse them and slow them down. "You throw three or four rocks over the side of the cliff before each grenade. In the dark, they won't know which is which, and they'll stop to take cover just as fast for a rock as they will for a grenade."

That night was an endless series of enemy onslaughts, some of them stealthy probes by a few knife-wielding infiltrators, others screaming charges by groups of twenty or more Japanese. Each of the assaults was repelled, but the cost in casualties was brutal.

Because so little distance separated Pope's small force from the enemy, no fire from the Eleventh Marines' artillery could be directed into the area. The only help from beyond C/1/1's own perimeter came from a mortar platoon near the foot of the ridge, which kept up a steady rate of fire on the approaches to Pope's position from about 500 yards away. PFC Barney Bell, a twenty-two-year-old mortar man from Georgia, estimated that he and his comrades fired more than 3,000 rounds in support of the trapped men.

"We knew Captain Pope needed all the help he could get," Bell said later, "and we did our best to provide it."

Hand-to-hand combat raged on the hilltop until dawn. By then, the Marines *were* using rocks as weapons, along with rifle butts, Ka-Bar knives, empty ammo boxes, and bare fists. They also hurled several attackers bodily over the cliff.

Pope watched a fellow Bay State native, PFC Philip Collins of

Gardiner, Massachusetts, scoop up grenades thrown by the Japanese and hurl them back before they could explode.

"He kept doing it until one of them went off in his hand," Pope said. "Then he picked up a rifle and fired it until he was too weak to reload."

Counting Pope, only nine of the twenty-five men who had reached the crest of the hill—and of the ninety who had attacked it the day before—survived to see dawn, and most of these had at least minor wounds. Seven of the company's eight junior officers were dead, and Lieutenant Burke, the sole survivor, suffered a serious bayonet gash in his leg before knocking his assailant unconscious.

"I had one round left in my .45," Pope said. "I wasn't about to let the Nips take me."

With first light on September 20, D-plus-5, the Japanese finally broke off the attacks, but heavy artillery fire immediately began to pound the hilltop. Within minutes, it was clear that the situation was untenable for Pope's men and that no reinforcements could reach them. At that point, Honsowetz was able to make contact with Pope and order what was left of C/1/1 to withdraw.

Getting back down the hill was a white-knuckle process in itself. With the help of smoke shells that partially obscured their movement, the Marines slid and skidded, rolled and tumbled their way to the bottom. Not all of them made it alive. Pope's radio man was shot dead during the descent as he talked on his field telephone. Pope himself was targeted by one Japanese machine gun and escaped only by throwing himself behind a stone wall beside the causeway.

Within minutes, Hill 100 was reoccupied by the Japanese, and enemy guns were again firing down from its heights on the Marines below.

Only after reaching safety did Pope take note of several grenade fragments that had buried themselves in the backs of his legs. After resting for a while, he limped to an aid station, where he unceremoniously pulled them out with a pair of pliers.

Then Pope returned to duty in the ridges, unaware that his gutsy leadership in the lost cause of the night of September 19–20 would shortly earn him the Medal of Honor.

When the First Marines were finally pulled off the line for good on September 22, after eight days on Peleliu's killing ground, well over half the men in Chesty Puller's regiment—a disastrous 56 percent— would be dead or wounded. Despite his ordeal and the loss of nearly nine-tenths of his company, Captain Everett Pope held the distinction of being the First's only company commander to escape death or serious wounds.

The total number of casualties in the First Marines, plus the losses sustained by 2/7 in the assaults on the hills, now stood at 1,838.

The Japanese, too, had paid a stiff price in human casualties, but although the Marine commanders didn't realize it at first, the enemy's strategic losses were of even greater long-range importance. Because of faulty intelligence and grossly inaccurate maps, no one knows the precise moment or hour when enemy positions on Hills 200 and 210 were finally neutralized. As the battle seesawed, heights were often seized by Marines, then reoccupied by Japanese, then taken again by Americans. Neither of these so-called hills was actually an isolated peak at all, but rather a small part of a complex system of connected ridges, and during September 21, D-plus-6, the Marines had pushed far enough along the northern extensions of these ridges to gain permanent control of them.

Only later did the full significance of this action become clear. The Five Sisters would remain a major thorn in the side of U.S. forces for weeks to come, but once Hills 200 and 210 were firmly in American hands, the last Japanese positions from which artillery and mortar fire could be visually directed at the airfield and the beachhead had been eliminated.

By seizing these key pieces of high ground, the Marines had made it virtually impossible for the Japanese to drive them off the island. Yet Colonel Nakagawa, the Japanese commander, had never expected that to happen. In fact, the battle was proceeding exactly as Nakagawa had planned it. His forces had already inflicted heavy losses on the Americans, and with the fighting now moving deeper into the ridges, the rest of the battle would be fought strictly on Japanese terms.

The bloody chunk of rock known to Pope and his men as Hill 100 would remain in enemy hands for many days to come, during which it would take on a whole new identity. It would be renamed Walt's Ridge for Colonel Lewis Walt, whose Fifth Marines would also struggle and die to control its heights.

For the invaders, each ridge of the Umurbrogol would become a grinding, pulverizing, seemingly endless battle of attrition. According to Nakagawa's reasoning, if the Japanese defenders could exact a high enough price in Marine blood, the struggle might end in an American withdrawal from Peleliu's killing ground *by choice*— simply to be spared further slaughter. That was the ultimate goal for the enemy commander, whose men were prepared to fight until the last one was dead.

If such a fate was to be avoided, it would be up to the Fifth and Seventh Marines to stay the course and complete the job. As a combat unit, the First Marines was done, but that didn't keep Puller from ordering a new assault on Hill 100 within a few hours after Pope's withdrawal.

This time, the Navy's big guns and those of the Eleventh Marines were fully utilized in advance of the ground attack, and all available mortars, machine guns, flamethrowers, tanks, and LVTs were thrown into the fray to bolster the infantry.

The result was yet another huge disaster. Once more, the weary Marines charged the slopes. Some of them gained a foothold on the high ground, only to be killed by the Japanese. Their bodies fell among those of Pope's men. They would lie there for days before they could be recovered.

Private Russell Davis was caught up in the midst of the carnage as a witness to his regiment's swan song. By some miracle, he was among the few who survived to recall it.

"I picked up the rifle of a dead Marine, and I went up the hill. . . . I didn't worry about death anymore. I had resigned from the human race. I only wanted to be as far forward as any man when my turn came. . . . As a fighting outfit, the First Marine Regiment was finished. We were no longer even human beings. I fired at anything that moved in front of me. Friend or foe. I had no friends. I just wanted to kill."

CHAPTER TEN

NORTH THROUGH SNIPER ALLEY

While the First Marines and 2/7 were being chewed to pieces south of the Five Sisters, the Fifth Marines was enjoying what turned out to be its longest respite from combat of the whole Peleliu campaign. Between September 19 and September 24, K/3/5 had almost no contact with the enemy, and after Orange Beach and the airfield, its losses during the five days seemed almost negligible by comparison. Only three members of the company were wounded during those five days. One also died, but not from hostile action.

The Fifth's basic assignment during this interval was to keep an eye out for enemy movements on the southern claw of Peleliu and establish defensive positions to prevent any possible counter-landing by the Japanese on small, isolated Purple Beach. In the words of PFC Bill Leyden: "It wasn't exactly R&R, but it was pretty tame compared to what those poor devils in the First and Seventh Marines were going through."

Even during the lull, however, conducting small overnight patrols through the swamps and jungles north and west of Purple Beach was exhausting, nerve-jarring duty that took a heavy physical and mental toll on the men assigned to them.

On September 21, D-plus-6, with Lieutenant Hillbilly Jones in command and pillbox-busting Sergeant Hank Boyes as the senior NCO, a forty-man patrol from K/3/5 set out on a prolonged foray through the heavy undergrowth. In addition to several rifle squads, the patrol also included two machine gun squads, a mortar squad, and a Doberman pinscher war dog to help sniff out the enemy.

Sergeant Jim McEnery was glad to have the Doberman along.

"They say these mutts can smell a damn Jap fifty yards away," McEnery told PFC Sterling Mace.

Division intelligence suspected that up to 2,000 enemy troops were trying to slip past the American line and cross the large swamp in the center of Peleliu's southern claw to rejoin the main Japanese force in the Umurbrogol ridges. If the patrol should confirm this suspicion, the whole regiment was to hold the enemy at bay until artillery, air strikes, and reinforcements could be called in.

PFCs Gene Sledge and George Sarrett were among the mortar men chosen for the patrol. Sledge could hear the distant rumble of battle from Bloody Nose Ridge as they marched warily in single file past marshes choked with mangroves and tangled vines. Conflicting feelings ran through him—a sense of closeness with the men around him, on one hand, and a hollow, lonely sensation on the other.

Deep in the jungle, the patrol halted for the night, and Jones set up a CP in a bunker built of logs and coral rocks that had recently housed a Japanese machine gun emplacement. About thirty feet away, almost at the edge of the swamp, Sledge and the rest of his squad dug a mortar pit and set up their 60-millimeter gun. At least the dirt here was soft and conducive to digging, unlike the solid rock they'd encountered elsewhere. Everybody was tense and jumpy as they ate their rations, checked their weapons, and got ready for a long night.

With sundown came a drizzling rain and the densest, blackest darkness Sledge could ever remember. He huddled close to Sarrett in their foxhole and listened to the Cape Gloucester veteran talk in low tones about friends, family, and his boyhood in Denison, Texas.

"There's a girl back there named Anna Lee," Sarrett mused. "She's not but sixteen or so. She was just a freshman when I was a senior in high school, but I've been thinkin' about writin' her a letter sometime. Maybe I will when we get through with this mess here."

In the next foxhole, just a few feet away, Sledge could hear his other squad mates also whispering back and forth. The quiet chatter continued until Gunnery Sergeant Elmo "Pop" Haney, the oldest man in K/3/5, made his way along the line, demanding the password and warning men to knock off the noise and stay ready for trouble.

Haney was a legend in the outfit. At fifty-something, he was older than most of the men's fathers, and although he never talked about it, he'd supposedly fought with the doughboys in France in 1918. But Haney's greatest notoriety among the youngsters of K/3/5 stemmed from the weird ritual he'd gone through each morning on Pavuvu. It included a fierce scrubbing of his whole body—genitals included— with a stiff-bristled shower brush that would've taken the hide off anyone else, followed by a rigorous bayonet drill with Pop as the only participant.

More than a few guys thought Haney was either getting senile or a certifiable nutcase, but nobody ever dared say so to his face. Even with his eccentricities, they respected him. He'd won a Silver Star for gallantry at Guadalcanal and served with distinction at Cape Gloucester. He'd also volunteered for this patrol, which was more than any of the rest of them could say.

"You guys be on the alert now, you hear?" Haney said. "Check your weapons, and make sure you got a round in the chamber."

All was quiet for a while after Haney disappeared back in the direction of the CP. But in a half-hour or so, he was back.

"Okay, stand by with that mortar," he told Sarrett and Sledge after they gave him the password. "If the Nips come through this swamp at high port with fixed bayonets, you'll need to fire as fast as you can."

"Wish to hell that ole boy'd settle down," Sarrett grumbled after Haney left again. "He's startin' to make me nervous. Hillbilly needs to grab him and keep him anchored in the CP."

The feeling was shared by Marines up and down the line. Maybe Haney could sense something that the others couldn't, but each time he made his rounds, the tension mounted. To Sledge, every jungle sound became sinister. A soft splash in the water of the swamp made his heart pound and his muscles draw up in knots.

It was after midnight when the men in the foxholes heard a different kind of noise. It started as a low moan, trailed off for a second, then grew louder.

"Ooooh! Ahhhh! Ooooh . . ."

"What's that?" Sledge whispered.

"Sounds like some guy havin' a nightmare," Sarrett said.

Now there were scuffling, thrashing sounds accompanying the moaning—all of it coming from the direction of the CP. The moaning rapidly escalated into a series of bloodcurdling shrieks that rose in volume until their source was obvious to every Marine within earshot.

Rubbed raw by the real or imagined dangers of the night, some guy's nerves had snapped. A comrade was cracking up. Worse yet, his anguished cries could bring every enemy soldier within a half-mile down on the patrol's necks unless someone managed to shut him up.

"Oh God, help me!" he screeched. "They're gonna kill me. Ohhhh, God, please don't let 'em kill me!"

"Quiet that man down!" Lieutenant Jones snapped. "Get a corpsman over here." A moment later, the others could hear Hillbilly talking to the guy in a low voice, doing his best to calm him. "It's okay, son. Everything's going to be all right. Just take it easy, and we'll get you taken care of."

It did no good. The screams became more piercing, and the tormented Marine lashed out wildly at his comrades. Someone tried to grab the man's flailing arms as he pleaded to the Doberman pinscher: "Help me, dog! The Japs've got me! They're gonna throw me in the ocean! You gotta save me, dog!"

A corpsman gave the man a shot of morphine, then another. But they had no effect. If anything, the man screamed louder, punching and kicking at everyone around him.

"For God's sake, hit him with something," someone said. In desperation, another Marine grabbed a trenching tool and swung it hard at the man's head. Sledge heard a sickening thud—like one of Pavuvu's rotten coconuts hurled against a concrete wall.

Finally, abruptly, the screaming stopped.

The men sat in stunned silence. For a long time, nobody moved or spoke, and the only sound anyone could hear was his own breathing. Then Pop Haney began making his rounds again, repeating his monotonous inquiry at each foxhole along the line:

"What's the password?"

"What's the password?"

"What's the . . ."

Nobody slept for the rest of the night. At dawn, the men gathered around the CP and stared down at the body of the berserk Marine, now covered by a poncho. Jones and Sergeant Boyes didn't look at anyone or say anything, but their expressions told the story. The man was dead, killed in self-preservation by one of his own.

Hillbilly turned to his radio man. "Get Battalion for me," he said. "I'm taking this patrol in."

A moment later, Jones was talking to Major John F. Gustafson, recently assigned to command the Third Battalion, replacing the wounded Colonel Shifty Shofner.

"I really need you to stay put for a day or two, Lieutenant," Gustafson said. "Just until G-2 can figure out what the Japs are doing."

"We haven't seen a Jap or fired a shot, Major," Hillbilly said, "but we've got a tragic situation here, and the men's nerves are shot to hell. I feel strongly that I need to bring them in now."

After a long pause, Gustafson replied: "Okay, I'll send a relief column with a tank so you won't have any trouble getting back."

Hillbilly bowed his head, his eyes avoiding the lump under the poncho. "Thank you, sir," he said.

After struggling out of the swamp with the rest of his patrol, PFC Sterling Mace was exhausted, soaked to the skin, and demoralized. But when he got back to the battalion bivouac area and saw PFC Seymour Levy waiting for him, Mace's demeanor changed in a split second.

The kid looked pale and tired, but under the bandages that

swathed the lower half of his face, Mace could tell that Levy was grinning as widely as his mangled chin allowed.

"What in the hell are you doing back here?" Mace demanded. "I thought you'd be halfway to the States by now."

"I sneaked off the hospital ship and bummed a ride back to the beach on a ferry," Levy mumbled around the gauze. "I just wanted to be back with you guys. It's where I belong."

"Jesus, Sy, you must be nuts," Mace said, but he couldn't keep from grinning, too.

By the next day, September 22, everyone in the company, from Captain Haldane on down, knew that the quiet interlude was almost over. Late that afternoon, when the first hollow-eyed survivors of Chesty Puller's battered regiment came stumbling down from the ridges, it was clear that the Fifth Marines would soon be back in the thick of things. With total casualties of thirty-seven dead and wounded, K/3/5 was one of the least beat-up rifle companies in the entire division. But its turn in the crucible was coming.

In a way, the sight of the First Marines' battered ranks was more appalling to their comrades in K/3/5 than their own losses since D-Day. It showed just how close a company could come to total annihilation in a matter of a few days.

"I'd been envying the First Marines because they were gettin' relieved and we weren't," said Jim McEnery. "Then I saw the poor bastards, and I didn't envy 'em anymore."

As the Fifth Marines marched along one side of a narrow road, and Puller's withdrawing troops filed past on the other side en route to the rear area that the Fifth Marines were vacating, Gene Sledge was shocked at how few they were. During training camp and later on Pavuvu, he'd gotten to know a lot of the men from the First. Now an incredible number of familiar faces were missing.

"How many men left in your company?" Sledge asked a former buddy from his Camp Elliott days.

The man stared at him with empty, bloodshot eyes. "Twenty's all that's left, Sledgehammer," he said. "They nearly wiped us out. I'm the only one out of the old bunch in my company that was with us in mortar school."

Sledge shook his head and bit his lip. "See you on Pavuvu," he said lamely.

"Good luck," said the other Marine as he shambled off.

On the morning of September 25, D-plus-10, the men of K/3/5 loaded up their gear and moved out on Peleliu's East Road. Their march led briefly south, but only to a rendezvous point where they were to board trucks that would take them to the opposite side of the island. From there, the entire Third Battalion had orders to move north on a main road along the western coast of Peleliu to the island's extreme northern tip, where they'd replace troops from 2/5 and await further orders.

The road hugged the craggy shore, but it also lay in the shadow—and within easy mortar, machine gun, and rifle range—of the Umurbrogol ridges. Among those who had attempted to travel it over the past few days, it was already known as Sniper Alley.

As the men marched toward the trucks, they again passed some of the battered survivors of the First Marines, who were heading in the opposite direction toward Purple Beach to await the arrival of ships that would take them back to Pavuvu. For the First, the ordeal was over. For the Fifth, the worst of it was just beginning.

Andy Haldane didn't immediately recognize Captain Everett Pope when he saw him making his way down the road that morning. But when the figure drew nearer, Haldane squinted and finally recognized his old college chum. Pope was a year or two younger than Haldane, but his face had aged markedly since the last time they'd been face-to-face, and his gait was slow and painful.

"Hey Ev, you old Polar Bear," Haldane yelled. "Is that really you?"

Pope stared blankly for a moment. Then his drawn features formed a smile, and he grabbed Haldane's hand. "Good to see you, Andy. Where's your outfit headed?"

"Someplace up toward the northern tip of the island, I hear. That's about all I know."

"Well, thank God you're not bound for those damned ridges," Pope said. "I lost almost my whole company up there. It was a miracle any of us got off that hill alive."

"Jeez, Ev, I'm sorry. Looks like you're a little dinged-up yourself."

Pope shrugged. "Picked up a few pieces of shrapnel—enough for a junior-grade Purple Heart, I guess. Anyway, the best part is we're done here, Andy. At first, Puller told us we'd get three days' rest and then go back on the line, but even he could tell the regiment's not fit to fight anymore. We'll be on our way back to Pavuvu pretty soon. Maybe you and your guys won't be far behind."

"Well, we're certain to get a trip home when this one's done," Haldane said. "Man, would I love to be there to see the Notre Dame-Dartmouth game this year. Sometimes it seems like we've been out here forever."

Pope nodded. In February 1942, he'd married his high school sweetheart, Eleanor Hawkins, and they'd had just three months together before he shipped out. It had been nearly two and a half years since he'd seen her.

"Hope you make it," said Pope. "With luck, maybe we'll both be home for Thanksgiving—or Christmas, anyway."

For a long moment, Pope gazed into his friend's handsome, square-jawed face. Even covered with dirt and sweat, and with a bristly beard, Andy Haldane still looked every inch the Saturday afternoon hero he'd been a few years before. It seemed uncanny how fate had woven their lives together and how similar—yet different—they were.

They'd both been raised in modest circumstances on opposite sides of Boston, Pope in North Quincy, Massachusetts, and Haldane in Methuen. They'd met at tradition-steeped Bowdoin College in Maine, where they'd graduated in the same Class of '41. Both had excelled in sports, and both had signed up for the Marines with the same campus recruiter. They'd reached the South Pacific within a few weeks of each other. Each had risen to the rank of captain and assumed command of a rifle company.

In some ways, though, they were also a study in contrasts. Haldane was unquestionably the finest athlete Pope had ever known—a "man's man" in every sense. But Haldane readily admitted being a mediocre student who was happy to make Cs, while Pope's forte was scholarship, and his Phi Beta Kappa key proved it. If the war hadn't come along, Haldane most likely would've been coaching football somewhere right now, and Pope probably teaching English lit.

"See you stateside," Andy said as they shook hands again. "If you get there before I do, tell everybody I said hello."

As their trucks bounced along the road past the airfield, the men of K/3/5 could hardly believe how different it looked from the last time they'd seen it. The bomb and shell craters and mangled wreckage were mostly gone, replaced by heavy equipment. A neat tent city had been erected beside the field, and American planes would soon be flying dozens of daily combat missions from its runways.

Meanwhile, battalions of Seabees and Army and Marine service personnel were going about their business in fresh, clean uniforms. They looked as if they were in Hawaii or San Diego instead of less than 1,000 yards from the nearest enemy fortifications, and the haggard, unshaven men on the trucks found the contrast both striking and depressing.

This transformation was the one positive result of the blood sacrifices in the ridges. Puller's regiment, with substantial help from the Seventh Marines, had managed to push the Japanese far enough north to put the airfield beyond the effective reach of enemy mortar and artillery fire.

Most of the Umurbrogol was still firmly in Japanese hands, but rather than continue the suicidal frontal assaults on the Five Sisters and the ridges beyond, division headquarters had decided to try a different tactic. Instead of driving straight ahead, the plan was to skirt the enemy stronghold with a northward thrust up the West Road. The mission was to secure the entire northern sector of Peleliu, and the Fifth Marines' Third Battalion would lead the attack.

The trucks transporting K/3/5 proceeded up the West Road for a short distance, then stopped to let the men off. Along the roadside, they saw the first Army troops they'd encountered on Peleliu—members of the 321st Regiment of the Eighty-first Infantry Division. These soldiers had just captured the island of Angaur seven miles to the south and were now relieving the First Marines. General Rupertus could no longer deny his division's desperate condition and had reluctantly agreed to accept limited help from the Army.

As the Marines passed through the Army lines, the two groups mingled briefly and traded information, and it was soon apparent that the dogfaces wouldn't be accompanying the gyrenes on their march north. The Army troops were moving into the area previously occupied by the First Marines and would remain in the southern sector of Peleliu for the time being.

"Looks like we'll be walkin' the rest of the way up Sniper Alley by ourselves from here," said Corporal John Teskevich as he sat by the roadside with Jim McEnery, waiting for the order to move out. "That don't sound like such a hot idea to me."

"I hear they're sending up some tanks to go with us," McEnery said. "If we get lucky, maybe we can hitch a ride."

Teskevich leaned back against a rock with his hands clasped behind his head. The ex–coal miner had never made any attempt to regrow the flowing mustache that he'd worn with fierce pride for most of the time on Pavuvu. One side of the handlebars had been neatly shaved off by an unknown culprit one afternoon on Banika while Teskevich was sleeping off a drunk. Teskevich had threatened to whip everybody in camp until Sergeant Jim Day had cooled him off. Now the corporal's face was covered with a thick stubble of beard.

"One way or another, I'm ready to get outta here," Teskevich said. "My old man damn near collected my $20,000 worth of life insurance when I got hit on the 'Canal, but my luck's held pretty good since then. Hell, if we make it through this crapshoot, Mack, both of us oughta be home free."

"Damned straight," McEnery said. "Christ, they *gotta* send us stateside as soon as this one's over."

It was well past noon by the time several Sherman tanks rumbled into sight and the Marines received the order to move out. As they collected their weapons and started up the narrow coral road, Japanese machine guns were raking American positions at the southern end of the Umurbrogol. The men of K/3/5 could see streams of blue-white enemy tracer bullets passing high above their heads.

At first, the terrain was flat with only a few scattered trees and bushes, but the roadway soon became littered with debris and choked in spots with tangled undergrowth and vines as it crossed ravines and crevices. A few dozen yards to the left was the ocean, and not much further away to the right rose the nearest of the crags known collectively as Bloody Nose Ridge.

The layout was ideally suited for snipers, and it didn't take them long to announce their presence. "Somebody would get hit before you even heard the shot," said PFC Sterling Mace. "You'd see a plume of pinkish dust, then a thud, and a guy would fall. Most of the time, we never saw a target to shoot back at, but we'd just fire in the general direction and hope we hit something."

Mace felt a rush of relief when a tank drew up beside him, and Lieutenant Bill Bauerschmidt, the flamboyant young leader of the Third Platoon, waved Mace and several others over.

"Go on and climb aboard," said Bauerschmidt, a Pennsylvania Dutchman who packed a "hogleg" pistol that his father had carried in World War I. Bauerschmidt's order was one that any infantry grunt would welcome, and Mace quickly clambered up onto the platform beside the turret, along with Sergeant Jim McEnery, Corporal John Teskevich, and PFCs Jesse Googe and Seymour Levy.

The tank rumbled forward, but it hadn't traveled more than a few feet when Mace heard a shot. He turned and saw Teskevich clutching his belly, blood oozing between his fingers and his face contorted with pain. At the same instant, Mace heard Googe let out a yell from the other side of the tank: "God, I'm hit! I'm hit!"

Mace's eyes jerked toward the sound of Googe's voice. The other Marine's right arm hung limp, and his shirtsleeve was stained bright red. As Googe moaned in pain, Mace raised his BAR and looked for something to shoot at, but he saw nothing.

"Stop the tank!" McEnery shouted at the tank commander. "We got two men hit." As the Sherman ground to a halt, McEnery turned to Mace and Levy. "Help me with Teskevich," he said. "We gotta get him down from here before the sons of bitches kill us all. Corpsman! Corpsman!"

A medic came up just as they managed to lower Teskevich to the ground in the shelter of the tank. By this time, the brawny Pennsylvanian's eyes were glassy and his face was the color of ashes.

"Guess I'm gonna make my old man rich, after all," Teskevich whispered through the bloody froth on his lips.

The corpsman stood up and shook his head. "The slug went all through his intestines," he said softly. "Not much I can do for him."

"See about Googe then," McEnery told the medic. "Looks like his arm's busted."

McEnery, Mace, and Levy waited by the roadside until Teskevich died. Then McEnery picked up his tommy gun and turned away. This was why he never got too chummy with anybody in this outfit anymore, he reminded himself. Teskevich was a good Marine, who'd crawled through a firestorm of bullets to save the life of a squad mate at Cape Gloucester, and he and McEnery had served in the same company since the summer of '42. It was tough enough to see a guy you'd spent that much time with get his guts blown out right in front of you, Mack thought, but if he and Teskevich had been big buddies, it would've been even worse.

"Okay, you guys," McEnery said, averting his eyes from the others. "Let's haul ass. Move it! Move it!"

They stood up, slung their weapons over their shoulders, and started walking north again.

. . .

The company proceeded slowly and with great caution as sporadic sniper fire continued during the rest of its mile-and-a-half march straight up the western coast of Peleliu. But K/3/5 suffered no additional losses along the way, and casualties for the whole battalion were lighter than expected, thanks to the tanks and amtrack-mounted flamethrowers that led the way.

By late afternoon on September 25, the Marines had covered more than half the distance to the furthest point of the island's northern claw and Colonel Bucky Harris, the battalion CO, ordered a halt. Harris extended his lines back to the perimeter held by Marines and Army troops to the south, rested his flanks on the beach, and told his men to dig in for the night along the thirty- to forty-yard-wide strip of ground between the ocean and the road.

Warnings were quickly passed for the men to stay alert for infiltrators. During 3/5's stay in the vicinity of Purple Beach, after-dark enemy incursions had been rare, but the battalion now confronted a far more threatening situation, with strong Japanese positions at close range in two directions. Enemy artillery emplacements looked down on the Marines from deep caves no more than 300 yards to the east. But Captain Haldane sensed that the greater danger would come from small groups of bayonet-wielding enemy foot soldiers attacking from the west, or seaward, side.

"This is no time or place for us to get too comfortable," Haldane told his platoon leaders while members of the company hurriedly stacked up low piles of rocks as makeshift foxholes. "We've got to be on our toes tonight and take every possible precaution. I guarantee we'll have some visitors before morning."

After studying his maps by the light of a flashlight in the gloom of his CP, Haldane got on the phone and asked for the artillery's help in emphasizing his point.

"Give us some high-explosive rounds from your 75s out to our front," he told the Marine at the other end of the line.

"But there's no report of enemy activity in that area, Captain," the Marine said. "It's probably a waste of ammunition."

Ack-Ack's voice remained pleasant but firm. "Maybe so, but my boys' security is more important to me than a few shells. I'm expecting trouble from that direction, and I want the Japs to know we're not asleep."

Within a few seconds after he hung up the phone, Haldane heard the first of the 75-millimeter rounds whistling overhead and blasting the dark undergrowth on the east side of the road.

The northwestern coast of Peleliu had no sandy beaches like those to the south. The shoreline was solid coral but remarkably smooth, and between the barrier reef and the shore, there was plenty of shallow water. Enemy soldiers could wade down the coast from their complexes of defensive fortifications on the northern tip of Peleliu, or even from the adjacent island of Ngesebus, then slip ashore behind the American lines. Japanese in the ridges to the east, meanwhile, could either approach the Marine positions directly or circle the north end of Peleliu through the water.

In essence, 3/5 faced trouble on three sides, and as night fell, Japanese artillery opened fire from caves in the ridges. Once full darkness descended, the night stalkers also got busy. Fortunately for the Marines, the skies were relatively clear, and a pale moon was shining.

Under the usual high-security arrangements, one Marine in each two-man foxhole was to stand watch while his comrade slept, with the men alternating roles every four hours. Corporals R. V. Burgin and Jim Burke, both squad leaders in K/3/5's 60-millimeter mortar section, bunked together only occasionally, usually sharing a foxhole with one of the men in their respective squads. But on the early morning of September 26, D-plus-11, they were in adjoining foxholes, and both were wide awake when the first of the intruders came calling.

"Hey, Burgy," Burke whispered from a couple of feet away, "I hear something out in the water."

Silently, Burgin stared toward the ocean and listened intently. Sure enough, after a few seconds, he could make out a faint chatter of voices just offshore. After all the times the Japanese had tried to sneak up on him in the dark, Burgin still couldn't understand why they always seemed to jabber at each other loudly enough to give themselves away.

"They're there, all right," Burgin hissed. At the same instant, he noticed a flicker of movement in the water. Then a head and a pair of shoulders appeared several yards out.

"Gimme your rifle for a second," Burke muttered to his foxhole mate. "I see the son of a bitch plain as day."

Burke waited until the infiltrator was waist-deep in the surf and about twenty yards away. Then he fired a single shot, and the figure flopped backward into the water without making a sound.

"You got him, Jimmy," Burgin said. "I saw him go down."

"Watch out, you guys," Burke shouted. "You can bet your ass there's more of 'em out there somewhere."

PFC Gene Sledge stood watch while his foxhole mate, Corporal Snafu Shelton, slept fitfully, grinding his teeth and snoring. Directly in front of Sledge, the West Road stood out plainly in the moonlight, a bright band of coral framed against a dark tangle of undergrowth just beyond.

Sledge was about to turn to look in the opposite direction when he saw two figures abruptly materialize out of a shallow ditch on the other side of the road. His heart skipped a beat as the figures waved their arms, yelled hoarsely in Japanese, and ran toward him. One of them cut sharply to Sledge's right, raced down the road for a short distance, and disappeared into an adjoining area occupied by another company. The remaining enemy soldier, waving a bayonet over his head, ran straight at Sledge's foxhole.

Sledge raised his carbine and flipped off the safety, lined up the charging Japanese in his sights and tightened his finger on the trigger. Then he hesitated. Directly between Sledge and the enemy soldier was another Marine foxhole, and if one of its occupants should jump up to meet the attacker just as Sledge fired, he might kill a buddy by mistake. He waited, his heart pounding and frenzied questions echoing in his brain:

What's wrong with you guys? Don't you hear that Jap coming? Why don't you fire?

With one final shout, the Japanese leaped into the hole. A wild, thrashing melee of hand-to-hand fighting followed. Sledge heard yells, curses, grunts, and the sounds of men hitting each other. The intruder jumped back out of the hole and ran a few steps toward the K/3/5 command post before a Marine caught up with him and clubbed him to the ground with a rifle butt.

At the same time, piercing screams and the sound of another fierce struggle came from the adjacent company area where the second intruder had disappeared. After a few seconds, the screaming stopped. Then a rifle shot exploded nearby.

"I got him," Sledge heard a Marine say from the adjacent foxhole.

As Sledge and his buddies caught their breath and tried to assess the situation, they heard someone groaning faintly in the shadows nearby.

"How many Nips were there?" someone asked.

"I saw two," Sledge said.

"Must've been more than that," another Marine said. "If there was only two, what's all that groanin' over there?" Sledge thought the man was pointing toward the Japanese who'd been knocked senseless with the rifle butt.

"I didn't see but two Nips, and I'm sure of it," Sledge insisted.

"I'll check it out," said a Marine in a nearby hole. The others waited silently as he crawled over to the groaning man. Then a .45 pistol shot rang out, and the groaning ceased.

Numerous similar attacks occurred up and down the line during the next few hours, but Sledge's area remained quiet for the rest of the night. In the first light of morning, when Sledge was able to see the body of the groaning man clearly for the first time, he made an unnerving discovery: The dead man was wearing Marine dungarees and leggings. Either one of the Japanese infiltrators had on an American uniform, or . . .

Shaking and queasy, Sledge crawled toward the body. But its identity was obvious to him even before he rolled it over and looked into the dead face of teenage PFC William S. Middlebrook.

"My God," Sledge gasped. "It's Bill."

A sergeant ran over to look. "Did he get shot by one of those Japs?" he asked.

Sledge was too sick inside to reply, but he realized with crushing certainty what had happened. Middlebrook had been shot through the temple by mistake by one of his own comrades.

Later that morning, Captain Haldane conducted an investigation into the death, during which he questioned Sledge and others in the vicinity at the time of the shooting about what they'd seen and heard. Sledge repeated what he'd said before: He'd seen only two Japanese, and one of them had run into another company's area.

"Do you know who killed Bill?" Haldane asked.

"Yes," Sledge said.

Haldane nodded. "Well, what happened was a tragic mistake— one that any of us could've made under the circumstances. There's nothing we can do or say to bring Bill back, and the conscience of the Marine responsible won't ever stop punishing him for what happened. So I'm asking you not to discuss the matter any further or mention the name of the man who did it to anyone—not ever. Okay?"

As their eyes met, Sledge could tell that Ack-Ack was feeling as much grief over Middlebrook's death as any man in the company, yet Haldane was also hurting for Middlebrook's killer. Sledge felt a surge of admiration and compassion for his commanding officer that went beyond mere respect.

"Yes, skipper," he said.

During the course of that day, Sledge walked down to the next company area to find out what had happened there the previous night. He learned that the agonized screams he'd heard had come from the Japanese intruder.

"He jumped in a foxhole with one of our guys," an eyewitness told Sledge. "All the Jap had was a bayonet, and the Marine had an M-1, but in the struggle, they both dropped their weapons, and the Marine killed the Jap with his bare hands. Jammed his finger through the bastard's eye socket right into his brain."

The normally sensitive Sledge scarcely winced. Like many other Marines, he was almost becoming immune to the brutish realities of Peleliu.

CHAPTER ELEVEN

NIGHTMARE ON NGESEBUS

PFC Bill Leyden was awakened from a light sleep by the first of a series of violent abdominal cramps. It was a little after eight o'clock on the night of September 26, D-plus-11, and Leyden realized instantly that something was seriously wrong. In all his eighteen years, he could never remember feeling so sick to his stomach.

Leyden groaned as his bowels churned furiously. He knew he was only seconds away from an explosive diarrhea attack, but he couldn't see any safe place to relieve himself except in the bottom of the foxhole. The nearest Japanese positions were only a few yards away, and moving even a step or two beyond the pile of rocks that Leyden shared with a squad mate, PFC Louis Swonger, meant risking death. If an enemy bullet didn't get him, he could easily fall off the edge of a fifty-foot precipice in the dark. Venturing forth in search of a makeshift emergency latrine was out of the question.

Leyden and Swonger, along with the rest of K/3/5, had finished their march north and replaced troops of the Second Battalion, Fifth Marines, early that afternoon atop a hill a short distance from Peleliu's northern coast. After days of slogging through swamps and dodging crocodiles in the island's southeastern sector, then spending the night along the West Road, the company was experiencing the tortuous ridges of the north for the first time, and it had inherited one of the steepest of the lot.

"What's the matter with you?" Swonger whispered, reacting to Leyden's moans. "Are you sick?"

The identity of the culprit behind his sudden illness dawned on Leyden even as Swonger spoke. Earlier in the day, he'd come across some canned Japanese delicacies in an abandoned cave. He'd hardly been hungry since the landing, and for close to a week, he'd eaten almost nothing except a few bites of cheese. But the canned shrimp and condensed milk from the cave had awakened his appetite, and he'd consumed them with gusto a couple of hours earlier. The stuff had tasted fine at the time, and Leyden had quietly dozed off when he finished eating. But then . . .

"Christ, yes, my belly's killing me," Leyden said. "I think I've got food poisoning, and I gotta go really bad, but I don't want to do it right here. We'll be looking for another foxhole if I do."

"There's some C ration cans in my pack," Swonger said. "You can use them, and then throw 'em over the cliff."

"Jesus, anything," Leyden said. "Toss 'em over here—and hurry!"

There were five or six empty cans, and Leyden filled them all. When he was done, he pulled up his dungaree pants, crawled cautiously to the edge of the precipice, and dropped the cans one by one into the dark void below. He heard them clatter sharply against the sides of the canyon, splattering their contents over the rocks as they fell.

A few seconds of silence followed. Then Leyden and Swonger heard a furious voice from somewhere below them, screaming and cursing in Japanese. As nearly as Leyden could tell, the voice came from no more than thirty feet away. If words could've killed, he thought, he'd be dead where he lay.

Swonger laughed. "Looks like the shit just hit the fan downstairs," he said.

They discovered later that a cave carved into the side of the hill just beneath them housed a large Japanese kitchen and mess hall. Before dawn the next morning, an enemy infiltrator was overpowered by a Marine and thrown to his death from the same cliff. But the doomed man's cries on the way down were no louder or more charged with emotion than those of the unsuspecting Japanese victimized by Leyden's "bombs."

．　．　．

By the morning of September 27, D-plus-12, the main offensive action on Peleliu was concentrated in the island's extreme northern sector.

In the south, the Seventh Marines and units of the Army's Eighty-first Division continued to apply pressure on the central phalanx of Japanese caves in the area of the Five Sisters. But with the First Marines now effectively out of the fight and awaiting evacuation, the costly strategy of frontal assaults had been abandoned in favor of a more methodical squeezing approach. Advances were rare, coming a few feet—or even a few inches—at a time, and the American lines had remained fairly static for the past five days.

The Fifth Marines, meanwhile, was at the center of operations in the north, facing Japanese entrenched among low ridges and in an old phosphate plant converted into a huge blockhouse. The regiment's main objective went beyond wiping out enemy resistance on the north end of Peleliu proper, however. Heavy fire from Ngesebus, the small, separate landmass located north of the main island across several hundred yards of shallow reef, also had to be silenced.

The Japanese had landed a sizable number of reinforcements on Ngesebus within the past few days. The enemy troops had been transported on barges from Babelthuap, the largest island in the Palaus group. The Navy had sunk some of the barges, but several hundred Japanese soldiers had made it ashore.

This news wasn't well received when it reached the men of K/3/5 on the small, isolated hill they occupied overlooking the north coast of Peleliu.

"Sounds just like Guadalcanal," a veteran groused to PFC Gene Sledge. "About the time we think we got the bastards boxed in, the Nips bring in reinforcements, and it'll go on and on."

The threat posed to the Marines' northern flank by Japanese troops already entrenched on Ngesebus and others who might soon arrive—plus the presence there of an auxiliary enemy airstrip for fighter planes—made the small island the next high-priority objective of the Peleliu campaign.

Colonel Bucky Harris, the regimental commander, called in a series of artillery strikes by Navy ships and the Marines' own batteries to pound Japanese positions on Ngesebus well in advance of the landing. No detailed information was available on enemy fortifications on the island, but they would prove to be a smaller, less complex version of the Umurbrogol's interwoven system of caves and bunkers. No amount of shelling would be enough to dislodge the island's deeply dug-in defenders. That would be up to the infantry.

Another amphibious assault was in the offing. On the morning of September 27, Harris handed the assignment to Major John Gustafson's Third Battalion, Fifth Marines.

"Tomorrow morning at 0800, our whole battalion will board amtracks and hit the beach on Ngesebus," Lieutenant Duke Ellington told his mortar section later that day. "Regiment expects us to secure the island in one day, so get ready for a tough fight."

Corporal R. V. Burgin, one of Ellington's squad leaders, took the news with a sour grin. "Just sounds like more of the same old crap to me," he told his friend, Corporal Jimmy Burke. "Nuthin' ever comes easy in this damned place."

Burgin's observation was undeniably true, but the assault on Ngesebus was destined to be tougher than anything he and the rest of K/3/5 had seen thus far.

As dawn broke on September 28, D-plus-13, the men of 3/5 gathered their gear and moved down to a narrow strip of sand along the shore. At a point about 1,000 yards from Akarakoro Point, the easternmost tip of Peleliu's northern claw, the Marines stood by to board the thirty amtracks that would take them to Ngesebus. As they waited, they stared across the strait at their objective—now separated from them only by several hundred yards of shallow water—and wondered what the next few hours held in store.

PFC Gene Sledge listened to some of his buddies argue over whether they'd earn another battle star for the Ngesebus landing, but Sledge, nervous as usual, had little interest in the debate. He was busy praying that the morning wouldn't be a repeat of the holocaust on D-Day.

There was ample reason for Sledge and his mates to be concerned. Casualties had reduced 3/5 from its pre–D-Day strength of about 1,000 men to just over 700, and its three rifle companies could expect no help from other Marine or Army infantry units in this particular fight. Thirteen tanks were assigned to spearhead the attack, but otherwise, the Third Battalion's depleted ranks would have to do the job alone.

About forty minutes before H-hour, heavy guns on the U.S. battleship *Mississippi* and the cruisers *Denver* and *Columbus* opened fire, sending scores of sixteen- and fourteen-inch shells rumbling overhead and raising clouds of smoke and coral dust on the smaller island. Corsairs of Major Robert F. "Cowboy" Stout's Marine Fighter Squadron VMF-114—flying from the Peleliu airfield's newly repaired runways—also joined the attack, blasting Japanese positions along the beach with bombs, rockets, and machine gun fire.

"We're gonna have plenty of support on this one," a passing platoon sergeant assured the men as they boarded the amtracks.

The infantrymen watched the Marine pilots' precision flying with appreciative awe, punching the air with their fists and cheering on the low-flying Corsairs. Sledge had never seen fighter pilots take such risks by waiting until the last possible second to pull out of their dives. Several times, a plane seemed headed for certain disaster, but all completed their missions without mishap.

Despite enthusiasm for the spectacular flying, no man in K/3/5 was naive enough to believe that the destructive force raining down on Ngesebus meant his job would be easy once the three assault companies went ashore. The Corsairs' precision strafing, which would continue until the first wave of amtracks was barely thirty yards from the waterline, made beach defense by the Japanese virtually impossible. But the bloody lessons of D-Day, and each day since, had taught the infantry that enemy troops entrenched further inland would have to be rooted out one by one the hard way.

The loaded amtracks moved down to the water's edge, pausing there until the barrage and bombardment ran its course. Then, just after 0900, with the squadron of amphibian tanks out in front, each mounting a 75-millimeter cannon and two .50-caliber machine guns, the tractor drivers received the signal to get underway. They revved their engines, and the first of four waves of assault troops shoved off in perfect formation.

Gene Sledge felt his heart pounding, and he wondered if the good luck or divine providence that had sustained him thus far would hold out. "The Lord is my shepherd," he whispered, squeezing the stock of his carbine.

It took about six minutes for the ponderous tractors to navigate the shallows on the reef and reach the opposite shore. While they were still a couple of minutes from land, the amtracks' .50-caliber machine guns went into action, peppering the shoreline and the jungle just beyond.

Unlike on D-Day, this time there was no discernible response from the Japanese. To the Marines' relief, no artillery or mortars kicked up the surf. No machine gun tracers or small-arms rounds whined past their ears. The only sounds from Ngesebus came from the continuing naval barrage as it moved inland ahead of the landing parties and from the Corsairs wheeling over the beach at treetop level.

PFC Sterling Mace was encouraged by the absence of enemy fire. A couple of weeks earlier, going into his first combat, he would've been downright elated. Mace had learned a lot since then about Japanese tricks and tenacity, however, and suspicion tugged at his mind. As the amtrack carrying his rifle squad covered the last few yards toward shore, he peered over the gunwale and saw something that worried him.

"We were pointing out targets for the gunner to aim at," Mace recalled, "but there was one that he couldn't seem to get a bead on. It was a pillbox set some thirty yards into the brush, and I had the feeling it was going to give us hell when we hit the beach."

Mace was right, but the pillbox in question was just one small part

of the problem. Ngesebus was defended by 500 well-led Japanese troops, nearly all of them hiding in bunkers and caves bored into a low coral ridge that ran from south to north up much of the length of the island. These heavily fortified emplacements sheltered at least two large naval guns, several 75-millimeter field pieces, and dozens of mortars—and in each of them, patient enemy gunners lay waiting.

Corporal R. V. Burgin motioned his seven-man mortar squad to stay low as he crouched behind a rock and eyed the massive gray shape of an enemy pillbox jutting out of a coral ledge just a half-dozen yards away. The squad had been ordered to set up its 60-millimeter guns on the inland side of the pillbox, which meant the men had to make their way past it, and one crew was already moving toward its firing position. Along with the order had come assurances that the bunker had been neutralized and that no live Japanese remained inside. Burgin wasn't so sure.

Armored vehicles, rifle squads, and weapons units working in close coordination against enemy positions had enabled the Marines to penetrate the first line of Japanese defenses on Ngesebus with relative ease. They'd found at least fifty dead Japanese soldiers on or near the beach—mostly victims of the Corsairs' strafing runs. After silencing several enemy machine guns and overrunning a few pillboxes, they'd crossed the island's small airstrip and pressed steadily north. Now, with the invasion about two hours old, the advance was slowed by a network of larger, more formidable bunkers embedded in the north–south coral ridge. It was the only appreciable high ground on the island, and it ran squarely across K/3/5's sector.

Although most of the ridge rose only about fifteen to twenty feet above the surrounding area—mere anthills compared to cliffs in the heart of the Umurbrogol—it dominated the otherwise flat terrain of Ngesebus, and the enemy had built a formidable network of underground defenses along it.

The operation had gone well enough so far, but much of the mile-and-a-quarter-long island was still in enemy hands, and Burgin was

certain that the area nearby was crawling with Japanese troops. A short time earlier, a burst of sniper fire from the rear had sent the whole squad diving for cover and left one man bleeding from a wound in the left arm.

The sniper had been quickly silenced, but Burgin was still uneasy about the pillbox. It was almost close enough to spit on—only a few feet from where they'd been told to set up one of their mortars. Despite Gunnery Sergeant W. R. Saunders's insistence that the bunker was empty and harmless, its lack of outward damage made Burgin uneasy.

He blotted the sweat on his forehead with his shirtsleeve to keep it from running into his eyes. Burgin had sweated plenty as a kid in Texas, but the sweat here was different. Hell, everything here was different—in the worst imaginable way. It had cooled off a few degrees since D-Day, but the daily high temperatures still averaged well above 100, and the humidity seemed as thick as ribbon-cane syrup.

At least the air on Ngesebus still smelled reasonably fresh, Burgin thought. On Peleliu, the buildup of unburied corpses, spoiled food, and human waste made every breath sheer agony. The full impact of the odor hadn't reached Ngesebus yet, but it wouldn't take long after today's battle. In the dank tropical heat, dead bodies started decomposing as soon as they hit the ground, and the Japanese left most of their corpses where they fell.

Burgin kept his eyes glued to the pillbox as he rang Sergeant John Marmet, platoon leader of the three-squad mortar section, for firing orders. In two weeks on Peleliu, Burgin had learned not to take anything for granted. The pillbox was one of the largest he'd seen since D-Day, and he decided to mention his concern about it to Marmet, a hard-bitten Ohioan who knew the enemy as well as any man in the Corps.

Before Burgin could make the connection with Marmet, however, he heard a startled yell from one of his ammo handlers: "Hey, Burgy, I hear Nips in there!"

Hugging the deck, the corporal scrambled over to where PFCs Vincent Santos, John Redifer, and Gene Sledge were staring and

pointing at a vent in the side of the pillbox. Sledge was the one doing most of the yelling.

"What's the matter, Sledgehammer?" Burgin drawled, keeping his voice calm. "You ain't crackin' up on me, are ya?"

"No, no, I heard 'em," Sledge said. "Listen."

As he leaned closer to the barred vent hole, Burgin heard the sounds himself—a babble of low, excited Japanese voices coming from inside the bunker. After peering through the bars and seeing a pair of eyes looking back at him, he jammed the muzzle of his .30-caliber Browning carbine through the hole and squeezed off two quick rounds. Gritting his teeth, he then emptied the rest of the clip through the opening. "Take it right in the face, you sons of bitches!" he shouted.

There was silence for a moment. Then a grenade came sailing out of the bunker and bounced on the ground a few feet away.

"Grenade!" Sledge shouted, diving behind an L-shaped sand breastwork protecting the front of the pillbox. PFC Jay d'Leau, the squad's bazooka man, dropped his bulky weapon and scurried to get out of the way. Burgin, along with PFC George Sarrett, huddled close to one of the bunker's blank concrete walls to keep the Japanese inside from spotting them. Sarrett's close friends, Redifer and Santos, along with Corporal Snafu Shelton, jumped on top of the pillbox and flattened themselves there. For the next two or three minutes, Japanese grenades kept flying out of the bunker and exploding at irregular intervals. Then everything got quiet.

"Take a look, and see what's in there," Burgin called to Sledge, who was nearest the pillbox entrance.

Sledge obeyed the order—and narrowly missed getting his head blown off as a result. He peeked over the edge of the sand barrier, straight into the face of a Japanese machine gunner. A burst of fire from the enemy weapon missed Sledge by an inch or two.

Shaking and breathless, Sledge struggled to the top of the pillbox, joining Redifer, Santos, and Shelton there. When Burgin yelled up at the unnerved young Marine to see if he was okay, Sledge could manage only a hoarse grunt in reply.

"Those Japs have an automatic weapon in there," Redifer said.

"I ain't so sure about that," Snafu countered in his usual megaphone voice. "Could be just rifles." The wiry little Cajun would've argued with God himself, Burgin figured, if he ever got the chance.

"Oh, yeah?" Redifer snorted. "Just ask Sledge if you don't think it's a damn automatic weapon."

"Shut up, you guys," Burgin said. "We don't have time for that crap."

While Redifer and Shelton argued, Santos busily checked out the top of the pillbox. The pint-sized Latino youngster was so good-natured that his closest buddies called him "Smiley," and he seemed capable of laughing off almost anything. He often acted as if warfare was just another game, like the ones he'd played as a boy along the Medina River near San Antonio with slingshots and rubber-band guns.

But there was a serious side to Santos as well. He was one of the mortar section's most skillful gunners, and if he had a grain of fear in his makeup, none of his squad mates had ever noticed it. Santos was also endlessly curious—as Redifer would attest after following him into an "empty" cave and being scared out of his wits by a dead Japanese, sitting upright in the gloom—and his curiosity now led to a striking discovery.

"Hey, look at this," Santos said, waving Redifer, Sarrett, and Sledge toward him and pointing to another vent pipe protruding a few inches above the top of the pillbox. The end of the pipe was open with no protective grate covering it.

Santos was already dropping grenades down the hole by the time the others crawled over to him. When he'd used all of his own grenades, Redifer and Sledge handed him theirs, and Santos dropped them through the opening, too. They could clearly hear a series of muffled explosions below, and they glanced at each other, wondering if any of the Japanese were still alive.

The answer came soon enough when two of Santos's grenades were tossed back outside through the pipe. The four Marines hurled themselves away from the opening a split second before the grenades went off. Redifer took several fragments in one forearm as he raised it to shield his face, but his wounds weren't serious, and the others were unhurt.

"Let's get the hell outta here," Burgin shouted. "Pull back a few yards, and take cover in those shell craters we passed. We're gonna need help to clean this thing out. I'll see if I can find a tank and maybe a flamethrower."

As Burgin took off toward where he'd seen a tank earlier, he glanced back to see three enemy soldiers dart out of the pillbox, running toward a nearby thicket. Several Marines opened fire from the craters, and all three Japanese fell.

Burgin had gone about 200 yards without spotting any tanks close by when he ran into a two-man flamethrower team from the battalion weapons section. He instantly recognized the gunner, Corporal Red Womack, whose brawny build and flaming red beard had made him a familiar figure on the streets of Melbourne during happier times. Womack was actually a soft-spoken, good-natured guy, but he reminded Burgin of the fierce-looking Vikings in his tenth grade world history book. They'd gotten to know each other fairly well from swapping stories about their big games as high school football players on teams 500 miles apart.

Now, Womack's face was streaked with sweat and dirt, and he was panting from lugging the flamethrower's heavy fuel cylinders on his back. His assistant gunner, PFC William Lewis, trailed close behind him.

"I need your help, Red," Burgin said. "We've got a pillbox full of Japs up the way, and we can't set up our mortars until it's knocked out."

"I got plenty of fuel in this thing," Womack said. "Just show me where."

Burgin pointed. "It's back that way a couple hundred yards. Soon as I find a tank, I'll meet you there."

Seconds after Womack and Lewis departed, a tank rumbled into view, and Burgin hailed the sergeant commanding it. A couple of minutes later, the bulky Sherman was in firing position parallel to where the mortar squad had taken cover. Several more Japanese soldiers, apparently realizing what was about to happen, darted out of the pillbox and tried to run. The Marines opened fire, and the enemy soldiers fell to the ground, their rifles clattering against the coral and their helmets rolling away.

"You think there's any more in there?" the tank commander asked Burgin.

"Hell, yes," Burgin told him. "There's no tellin' how many's left. Just blow the whole damn thing open if you can."

"Fire away," the tank commander said.

The gun turret swung slowly around as the gunner sighted in on the pillbox. Then he fired three armor-piercing 75-millimeter shells at the bunker in rapid succession from point-blank range. The blasts made Burgin's ears ring and filled the air with coral dust. They ripped a four-foot hole through the center of the pillbox and rained debris on the mortars, bazooka, and other equipment the mortar squad had left nearby.

"Hold it," Burgin yelled. "Our guns and stuff are in your line of fire."

"Christ, nobody could still be alive in there anyway, could they?" Santos muttered. "Not after all that." The wisecracking youngster looked slightly spooked for once.

But even as Santos spoke, a Japanese soldier appeared through the swirling dust of the pillbox. He was drawing back his arm to hurl a grenade when Sledge and several others raised their carbines and fired. The soldier fell, and the grenade exploded at his feet.

"Bring the flamethrower up, Red," Burgin shouted to Womack. "Everybody else keep shooting. Shoot anything that moves."

Grunting under his load, Womack moved to within fifteen feet of the smoking fissure in the pillbox. Lewis was a half-step to one side and slightly to the rear, holding his combat shotgun steady with one hand and reaching out with the other to open a valve on Womack's fuel tank. As the nozzle of the weapon erupted in flame, a pinkish orange stream of it spewed directly into the fissure.

The flamethrower made a sharp, sucking *whoosh,* accompanied by a sound like distant thunder as a gust of 1,000-degree heat turned the pillbox into an inferno, searing waves radiating outward. Burgin heard a few screams, then silence.

As the squad began to relax, three Japanese ran out of the pillbox with their clothes on fire. They struggled to pull off their blazing uniform pants, but they couldn't get them below their knees because of the tightly wrapped leggings they wore. Redifer, Santos, Shelton, and Sarrett leveled their carbines and sent all three of them tumbling.

As Sarrett helped kill the burning enemy soldiers, he watched Santos, his best buddy, shoot one of the dying Japanese squarely in the bare butt. Santos's face was expressionless, without the slightest hint of mirth, but Sarrett had to stifle his own momentary urge to laugh.

Meanwhile, a hundred or so yards north of Burgin's position, PFC Bill Leyden and others of his rifle squad were trading grenades and small-arms fire with an undetermined number of enemy troops holed up in a large, fortified cave.

In the two weeks since the slender teenager from Long Island had first come under fire and seen men die on D-Day, his fortitude had been tested to its limits. But he'd learned a lot in that time, both about how to kill the enemy and how to keep from being killed. In the process, his early inner doubts had given way to grim self-confidence.

Leyden couldn't explain it, even to himself, but he felt almost invulnerable. Neither a hundred close calls from Japanese fire nor his recent bout with food poisoning could shake that feeling. If anything, they'd only served to strengthen it.

When he'd seen four enemy soldiers dash into a cave ahead of him seconds earlier, Leyden had raced forward without hesitation and thrown a grenade in after them. Several of his squad mates had done likewise, and five or six grenades had exploded almost simultaneously near the cave's entrance. A dense cloud of dust still swirled there as Leyden approached with his M-1 at the ready. He was only about twenty-five feet away when a dim figure materialized in the opening and lurched forward out of the dust.

"Here I am, Marine!" a Japanese soldier screamed in perfect English. "Kill me! Kill me!"

Leyden obliged as fast as he could pull the trigger. He fired an eight-round burst at the figure and saw the man's body jerk as bullets tore through him. The enemy soldier, now dead on his feet, stumbled another step or two toward Leyden before he fell, detonating a grenade no more than five yards from where Leyden was instinctively jamming a fresh clip into his rifle.

The whole world seemed to blow up in Leyden's face. The explosion knocked him cold momentarily, and when he came to, his cheek and one side of his head were covered with blood. An anvil chorus was ringing in his ears, and he couldn't see out of his left eye.

He shook his head and tried to sit up as another Japanese staggered toward him out of the cave. At the last possible moment, Leyden managed to raise his rifle and fire. The mortally wounded soldier's momentum carried him so close that he almost fell on top of Leyden. Seconds later, the wounded Marine passed out again.

When the firing stopped and the smoke cleared around the pillbox, Corporal Burgin ordered his men to set up their mortars in a large crater nearby, then spent a few minutes taking stock of the situation. Burgin was gratified to find that, despite the intensity of the firefight, Marine casualties were light. Of the dozen mortar men involved, only Redifer and PFC Lewis Porter had been wounded, both by grenade fragments, and neither was hurt seriously enough to require evacuation.

While most of the men worked with the mortars, Burgin ventured inside the still smoldering bunker. Redifer, whose arm wounds prevented him from performing his duties as an ammo handler, tagged along, and they quickly solved the riddle of how so many of the enemy had survived the repeated grenade blasts and shell fire.

The pillbox was divided into a number of compartments, each separated from the rest by thick concrete walls and connected by small passages. Each compartment was designed to hold three or four soldiers, and each was equipped with its own gun ports to the outside. Without the tank's 75 and Womack's flamethrower, Burgin realized, the bunker's occupants might have held out for hours, even days.

Burgin counted at least ten enemy bodies littering the floor of the various compartments. Then, as he stepped through a shattered wall into the last of the small chambers, he caught a flicker of movement and stopped.

"What is it?" Redifer whispered.

In a single unbroken motion, Burgin drew his .45 and fired, killing a wounded Japanese huddled in one corner of the chamber, pretending to be dead.

"Stay away from him," Burgin warned Redifer. "Son of a bitch is probably loaded with grenades."

Seven other Japanese bodies were found outside, making a total of at least seventeen enemy dead from the pillbox. Gunnery Sergeant Saunders, who had vowed a half-hour earlier that the bunker was empty and harmless, seemed stunned when he saw the mortar squad's handiwork.

"Sorry about the mix-up," Saunders said sheepishly.

Burgin nodded, clenched his fists, and turned away.

When Bill Leyden awoke, he had no idea where he was or how long he'd been unconscious. He soon realized that he was lying on the rear of an amtrack along with several other wounded men, and that a corpsman was hovering over him. He was dazed and hurting, and his left eye was covered by a bandage. What vision remained in his other eye was badly blurred, but he could, at least, see something out of it.

The realization that he was seriously wounded, out of the fight—and as vulnerable to pain, disability, and even death, as any other human—brought the anger Leyden had felt earlier surging back. He felt for his rifle, but it was nowhere to be found. A disparaging inner voice whispered to him, making the anger worse:

Some Marine you are! You probably couldn't aim a rifle or fire it if you had it in your hands.

"How is it up there on the line, son?" another voice inquired close beside him. Its tone was sympathetic, but somehow it only added to Leyden's rage. When he turned toward the voice, he could make out the fuzzy outline of a Marine uniform and helmet, but he couldn't tell anything about the face.

Just some damn rear-echelon type trying to be cute, he thought.

"Why don't you get off your ass and go inland about two hundred yards," Leyden growled. "Then you can see for yourself."

An awkward pause followed. "Well, uh, don't worry, son," the man said finally, clearly taken aback. "You'll be okay."

As the amtrack clattered slowly away toward an aid station, one of the other wounded Marines nudged Leyden. "Hey, man," he said, "do you know who that guy was—the one you just told off?"

"What the hell difference does it make?" Leyden snapped.

"None, I guess," the Marine said. "But just for the record, it was Colonel Walt, the regimental exec."

Leyden was soon on his way to a hospital ship, then to Pearl Harbor and two months of delicate treatment to save his left eye.

Years later, Leyden met Walt, then a retired two-star general and former deputy commander of the Marine Corps, at a reunion. Walt told Leyden he was so shocked by the young PFC's outburst that he'd backed off the amtrack and almost broken his ankle.

By five o'clock on the afternoon of September 28, the Marines had gained control of all but the extreme northern tip of Ngesebus. The last diehard Japanese defenders were bottled up in an area measuring about 300 by 500 yards, with no hope of reinforcements or relief. But like their cohorts on Peleliu proper, they clearly intended to hold out as long as possible, so the Marines were ordered to dig in for the night and leave the final mopping up until the next morning.

As Corporal Burgin's mortar squad fired a few rounds to register in its guns for the night and chipped out shallow foxholes in some of the softer coral, a brisk breeze sprang up, and the darkening sky grew heavy with clouds, portending rain. Up and down the line, men pulled their ponchos out of their packs and prepared to get wet. The brewing storm reminded Gene Sledge of hurricanes he'd seen as a boy along the Gulf Coast.

The wind intensified, fanning the embers inside the gutted Japanese pillbox into flame, and gusts of it blew the smell of burning human flesh over the bivouac area. Brief series of explosions broke out occasionally, announcing that the fire had reached stocks of enemy ammo and grenades left behind in the bunker.

Sometime before midnight, the rain descended in torrents, finally putting the fire out. After that, the explosions stopped, and the putrid odor became less noticeable.

Sledge and his squad mates stayed alert for enemy infiltrators, but none appeared in their area. The storm, along with frequent star shells fired by Navy ships to illuminate the island, apparently kept the Japanese deep in their holes, marshaling their flagging strength for a final stand the next morning.

At full daylight on September 29, D-plus-14, Sergeant Jim McEnery's Third Platoon resumed its advance and almost immediately ran into trouble. It happened to be McEnery's birthday, and although there was no time to celebrate, he did get a present of sorts as he and the others went back to work against the enemy caves. Somebody, maybe Gunnery Sergeant Tom Rigny, who'd been killed the day before, had left behind a Thompson submachine gun, and McEnery claimed it as his own.

"I don't want to waste no ammo with this tommy," he yelled to his men as they moved north, "but if you riflemen spot any Nips you think are dead, shoot 'em anyway. If their guts or mouths ain't wide open, put a few rounds in the bastards just to be on the safe side."

PFC Sterling Mace, his squad's designated BAR man, had no qualms about taking McEnery's warning to heart. Earlier that morning, Mace and his mates had heard how two Marines from L Company had been killed in an ambush when they stopped to examine a supposedly dead enemy soldier.

By now, some of the Japanese had seen enough of the Marines' bunker-busting tactics—in which all available weapons, from heavy armor to grenades and rifles, were used in relentless coordination—to opt for taking their chances on the outside. In a way, this was good for the Marines, because it brought more of the enemy into the open, but it also heightened the risk of both friendly fire and unexpected encounters with enemy soldiers.

To guard against these possibilities, scouts were especially wary, and group leaders moved stealthily between units, calling out today's password to identify themselves: "Hey, Zero! Hey, Zero!"

K/3/5's Third Platoon had drawn the left-flank position, so McEnery knew he and his men would be seeing plenty of action. The platoon's authorized strength was forty-five men, but casualties had already cut that number by close to a third, and there'd be more by afternoon.

A few yards ahead of McEnery and Mace, Corporal Thomas "Nippo" Baxter, a group leader and one of the platoon's best scouts, was checking the terrain. Baxter's head had a way of jerking back and forth like a chicken's when he was looking for the enemy, and a lot of guys laughed about it, but Nippo had a rare talent for spotting hiding Japanese. He did it better than anyone McEnery had ever known. That was how Baxter had gotten his nickname.

Screened by underbrush, Baxter was approaching a low ridge overlooking a small clearing when he abruptly froze, raised his M-1, and fired a single round. As the squad behind him crouched, Baxter turned and made eye contact with Mace, then motioned him forward. Baxter fired again at something beyond the brush—a full volley this time—and when Mace reached his side, Baxter pointed downward toward a cave only about fifteen feet away.

Three enemy soldiers were clustered just inside the cave's entrance. Two of them had their rifles aimed in Baxter's direction while the third peered around, trying to locate where the firing was coming from.

"I musta missed the bastards," Baxter breathed. "Take 'em out if you can."

Mace stuck the muzzle of his BAR over the edge of the ridge. One of the Japanese looked up, and their eyes met an instant before Mace squeezed the trigger. Seconds later, all three enemy soldiers lay dead.

Mace and Baxter tossed a half-dozen grenades into the cave, ducking as the blasts shook the ground. For insurance, McEnery brought up a bazooka man to fire a couple of rounds deep into the cave's innards. Then a flamethrower followed up with a stream of fire.

Finally, as the platoon skirted the cave and went down the incline toward the clearing, a demolition team moved in to seal the cave entrance with dynamite charges.

"That was the way we had to do it to 'cure' a cave," McEnery recalled later. "Sometimes it seemed like we had to kill every Nip on Ngesebus three or four times before they'd stay dead."

A communications breakdown between K/3/5's three rifle platoons kept runners busy as the northward advance continued. After the third platoon took up new positions at the far edge of the clearing, Mace's group leader, Corporal Richard Van Trump, ordered Mace and his assistant gunner, Private Charlie Allman, to move out about twenty yards ahead of the main force.

"The Nips to the north of us know they're surrounded by now," Van Trump said. "They may attack and try to punch through our lines. Keep a sharp eye out, and if you see any Nips coming this way, beat it back here on the double and let us know."

Crawling slowly, the two of them struck out alone, Mace carrying the BAR and Allman hauling several heavy tins of ammo. Within a few minutes, they located a shallow trough, well concealed by natural camouflage, and set up their gear there.

At intervals over the next hour or so, they could hear Van Trump moving among the squads, shouting, "Hey, Zero!" to keep his own men from opening fire on him. In the distance behind them, Mace could also detect the rattle of canteens and the sound of Marines talking in low voices.

As the afternoon dragged on, sporadic outbursts of small-arms fire echoed in the distance, but Mace and Allman saw nothing of either the enemy or other Marines. They avoided conversation, communicating mostly by hand signals to avoid giving away their position to any Japanese in the vicinity, and listening intently for the snap of a twig or the swish of movement in the brush that could betray an approaching enemy.

Gradually, Mace realized that he could no longer hear any sounds of activity. He had no idea when the sounds had stopped, only that they weren't there anymore. He crawled over and nudged Allman, who'd also noticed the eerie silence. They looked at each other and frowned.

"Something's wrong," Mace whispered. "We'd better head back."

They crawled back to the clearing to find it deserted. On the ground were a bloody Marine poncho and thirty or forty unfired rounds from a Thompson submachine gun, the same type of weapon that Jim McEnery had been carrying that morning.

"Damn," Mace said, "the platoon must've pulled out and left us."

"Why didn't Van Trump let us know?" Allman demanded. "You think he just forgot about sending us out there?"

"I don't know," Mace said, "but I sure as hell intend to find out."

Unnerved and angry, but trying to remain cautious, the two Marines picked their way along a narrow path toward the beach. With each step, their fury and feelings of abandonment escalated. Soon, they were stumbling and tripping, their boondockers tangling in the knotty vines crisscrossing the trail.

Gasping for breath, they finally burst out of the thick jungle growth and onto the open beach, where they saw the rest of their platoon waiting near the water's edge.

As they approached, Mace saw Van Trump being carried away on a makeshift stretcher. When he ran up to the stretcher and looked down at his group leader, Mace saw only mangled flesh and shattered bone where the bottom half of Van Trump's face had been. His entire lower jaw and most of one cheek had been blown away.

As Mace averted his eyes from the wound, he saw his buddy, Seymour Levy, staring at him, and he felt Jim McEnery's hand on his shoulder.

"Why'd you go off and leave me and Allman?" Mace asked McEnery.

"What're you talkin' about?" McEnery said. "Where were you?"

"Twenty yards out ahead of the line, watching for Japs. Been out there for hours—on Van Trump's orders."

McEnery shook his head. "I guess nobody knew but Van Trump," he said. "The Nips picked up on his code call and started callin' back to him. Lured him right into an ambush and shot him in the face. After that, he wasn't in no shape to tell nobody nuthin'."

A short time later, amtracks arrived to take the surviving members of the Third Battalion, Fifth Marines, back to Peleliu. An Army unit was moving in to relieve them and hunt down the few remaining Japanese holdouts. In its thirty-plus hours on Ngesebus, 3/5 had lost forty-eight men—fifteen killed and thirty-three wounded—a toll officially described as "only light casualties."

This was a reasonably accurate description when compared to the 470 Japanese killed and captured during the operation. But two-thirds of the Third Battalion's losses were sustained by a single company—K/3/5. Captain Andy Haldane's unit recorded eight men killed and twenty-four wounded—almost as many as the company had lost during the first thirteen days of the Peleliu campaign.

As they prepared to board an amtrack for the short ride back to the main island that evening, PFCs Sterling Mace and Seymour

Levy felt a huge sense of relief. Word was already circulating that 3/5 would shortly be joining the First Marines back on Pavuvu. On hearing this news, Mace and Levy were energized enough to perform an impromptu "trucking dance" for the lone newsreel cameraman who showed up to record their moment of victory.

The rumor, of course, was a lie.

CHAPTER TWELVE

PICKING SATAN'S POCKET

In Marine Corps annals, 3/5's decisive victory on Ngesebus still ranks as a textbook example of how a quick-strike amphibious operation should be carried out. Much of the brass on Peleliu came over in person for a close-up look at the well-coordinated assault.

With its comparatively low American casualty rate, speedy completion, effective use of close air support, and refined tactics for "curing" enemy caves and bunkers, Ngesebus was the best news to come out of the Palaus campaign thus far. Although General Rupertus, the First Marine Division commander, spoke disparagingly—and inaccurately—of "meager" Japanese resistance, he and his staff were elated. As the division's battle diary phrased it: "Infantry and armor performed with a ruthless efficiency unequaled in any previous Pacific operation."

Colonel "Silent Lew" Walt, the Fifth Marines' executive officer and overall on-site commander of the operation—the reason he happened to be on an amtrack with the wounded PFC Bill Leyden during the height of the battle—gave Major John Gustafson and his men most of the credit. "Major Gustafson and the officers under his command used excellent tactics and made maximum use of supporting arms," Walt wrote.

In a separate report, Gustafson added these thoughts: "It should be emphasized that, with the terrain most suitable for an infantry-tank attack, with both elements coordinating perfectly, the operation was made to appear easy. The tanks should get a great deal of credit, but, on the other hand, the tank commanders said they never experienced such coordination from the infantry."

On September 30, D-plus-15, Rupertus announced that "organized resistance has ended on Ngesebus, and all of northern Peleliu has been secured." In the view of the Army troops who replaced 3/5 to mop up on Ngesebus, the statement was both premature and deceptive. Army Major General Paul J. Mueller told of "determined" Japanese resistance to men of the Second Battalion of his 321st Regiment along the north–south strip of high ground on Ngesebus.

At any rate, instead of earning Gustafson's troops a one-way ticket back to Pavuvu, their success turned out to be a mixed blessing at best. It convinced Rupertus to send K/3/5—its ranks now reduced by nearly 30 percent from its D-Day strength of 235 officers and men—and the rest of the Fifth Marines into the Umurbrogol Pocket, the bristling core of enemy defenses in the ridges. There Gustafson's men would try to repeat their performance on Ngesebus.

Hard practicality no doubt played a prominent role in Rupertus's decision. The Seventh Marines had continued to attack embedded Japanese in the Pocket without pause during the eight days since the First Marines had been relieved. Now, the Seventh was almost as weakened and worn-out as Chesty Puller's regiment had been when it was pulled off the line to await evacuation.

The Fifth, battle-scarred and shorthanded as it was, offered the least-depleted Marine infantry units available. But it was hard to convince men like PFC Gene Sledge that he and his K/3/5 comrades were capable of fighting on much longer.

On the afternoon of September 29, as the company had waited on the beach on Ngesebus for transport back to Peleliu, Sledge overheard fellow mortar men talking about a squad mate who'd been virtually blown in half by an enemy shell. The man's body had come apart as his buddies tried to load it on a stretcher. Then Sledge had watched a K/3/5 rifleman idly toss pebbles into a gaping hole in the skull of a dead Japanese machine gunner. The normally sensitive Sledgehammer had even found himself preparing to pry gold teeth from the mouths of enemy corpses as souvenirs, until Navy corpsman Ken Caswell dissuaded him. Later, Sledge confessed shock when he thought back on his own brush with barbarism.

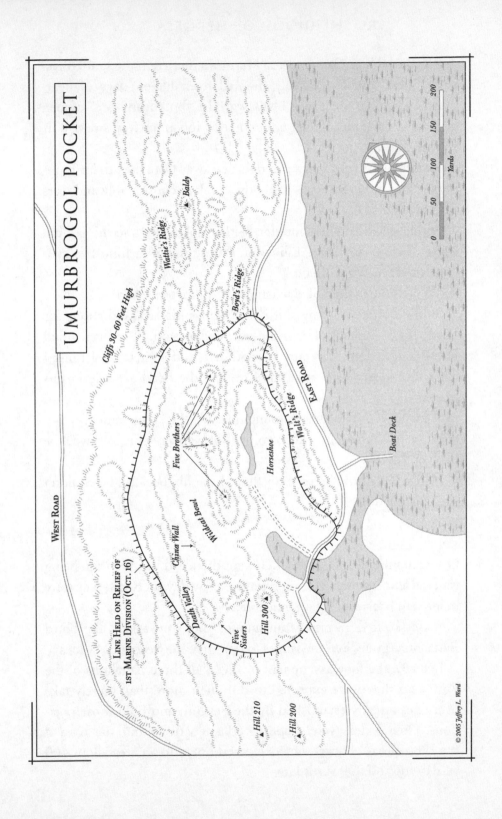

UMURBROGOL POCKET

West Road

Cliffs 30–60 Feet High

Wattie's Ridge

Baldy

Boyd's Ridge

Five Brothers

Horseshoe

Walt's Ridge

East Road

Boat Dock

China Wall

Wildcat Bowl

Line Held on Relief of
1st Marine Division (Oct. 16)

Death Valley

Five Sisters

Hill 300

Hill 210

Hill 200

Yards

0   50   100   150   200

© 2005 Jeffrey L. Ward

All around him, Sledge noted Marines slumped in the sand, physically spent and emotionally drained from fifteen days of near-constant combat, their eyes blank with the "bulkhead stare" of men pushed to the limits of their endurance by too much fear, stress, horror, and death.

He felt himself choking up and turned away from the others, burying his face in his hands as his body shook uncontrollably and tears streamed down his face.

Feeling a hand on his shoulder, Sledge looked up to see his section leader, Lieutenant Duke Ellington, staring down at him. His eyes were tired but sympathetic.

"What's the matter, Sledgehammer?" Ellington asked.

Sledge swiped a grimy shirtsleeve across his face and shook his head. "I just feel sick and wrung-out, sir," he said. "I've been afraid for so long I don't have any strength left, and sometimes I think I can't take it anymore. It seems like only the dead are safe in this place."

"I know what you mean," Ellington said. "I feel the same way, but take it easy. We've got to keep going. It'll be over soon, and we'll be back on Pavuvu."

Sledge felt a little better after that—but only because he couldn't see into the future.

On September 30, D-plus-15, 3/5 got the word. Rather than being relieved and evacuated, or even getting a few days of R&R, they were being sent back into action immediately.

"Stand by to draw rations and ammo," they were told. "The Third Battalion is going into the ridges to reinforce the Seventh Marines."

Actually, the new assignment involved all three battalions of the Fifth, and they were expected to do much more than merely take over lines already established by the Seventh and hold those positions. Their orders were to spearhead a new thrust into the maze of the Umurbrogol Pocket, now squeezed down to an area about 400 yards wide and 900 yards long.

First, though, there was one last enemy stronghold that had to be cracked near the northern coast of Peleliu. It was called Radar Hill, a dome-shaped cliff jutting 200 feet above densely wooded flatlands and swamps. It bristled with enemy mortars, rockets, and artillery capable of reaching a large area, including Ngesebus. The assignment to take the hill was handed to Lieutenant Colonel Robert Boyd's First Battalion, already reduced by casualties to 500 men—half its original strength.

"If northern Peleliu was secured [by this point], no one bothered to tell the Japs on Radar Hill," Boyd later noted.

On the morning of September 30, Boyd divided his force and attacked the hill from two sides with all the firepower hc could muster. Resistance was stiff in some spots, where well-entrenched Japanese fought to the death, as expected. But it was surprisingly weak—almost nonexistent—in other places, where many enemy soldiers "simply hid, abjectly awaiting death with little effort to defend themselves or kill the attacking Marines," as a battalion diarist put it.

By afternoon, 1/5 rifle squads held the summit of Radar Hill and a communications team was stringing telephone wire to the top. Soon after, battalion troops arrived in force, enabling Boyd to set up a forward command post and Colonel Walt to notify regimental headquarters that Peleliu North *was* finally secure.

That night, the Marines could hear Japanese soldiers in caves that had been bypassed along the slopes, as well as occasional grenade blasts and bursts of machine gun fire, but the remaining enemy force in the area was too weak to attempt any counterattack during the night.

Meanwhile, some 500 yards to the north of Radar Hill, Major Gordon Gayle's 2/5 had moved against about 200 Japanese holed up in the wreckage of the phosphate plant and along a nearby ridge. By nightfall, they, too, were in control of the situation, but a few enemy soldiers still held out in several caves.

To spare his riflemen the task of storming these last enemy positions, Colonel Bucky Harris, the regimental CO, had a giant 155-

millimeter artillery piece brought up and directed its crew to use it in a way it had seldom been used before. Normally, the long Tom was employed only against far-distant targets, but Harris ordered it zeroed in on caves only a few dozen yards away. The gun crew had to stay under cover to keep from being hit by fragments from their own shells, but within half an hour, all remaining Japanese fortifications had been blasted into oblivion.

Once these positions were secured, the encirclement of Japanese Colonel Nakagawa's last bastion in the Umurbrogol Pocket was complete, and any possibility of Nakagawa's remaining troops fighting their way out of the Pocket was eliminated.

Yet the longest and most confounding phase of the battle was still to come as the Marines tried to sew up the Pocket for good.

PFC Seymour Levy had never been quite the same since getting his chin ripped open by a Japanese grenade. On occasion, he showed flashes of his old high-spirited self, but even his poetic wit and prankish humor were tinged with a grimness that hadn't been there before.

It had been days, for example, since PFC Sterling Mace had heard his friend quote a single line from Kipling. Consequently, Mace was a bit surprised on the night of September 30, as the two of them shared a foxhole, when Levy quietly began reciting a poem. Mace didn't know the name of it, but it definitely wasn't "Gunga Din."

"God of our fathers, known of old," Levy murmured, his voice slightly muffled by a bandage on his lower jaw that looked like a dirty white beard. "Lord of our far-flung battle line . . . beneath whose awful hand we hold—"

"What the hell is that, Sy?" Mace interrupted.

"It's Kipling's 'Recessional,'" Levy said. "Haven't you ever heard it before?"

"No, and it sure doesn't sound like Kipling—more like something out of the Old Testament. Where's the Cockney accent?"

"I guess he was in a more serious mood when he wrote it," Levy said.

Mace turned away and soon lost interest, but Levy continued his recitation: ". . . drunk with sight of power, we loose . . . wild tongues that have not Thee in awe . . . such boasting as the Gentiles use . . . or lesser breeds without the law . . ."

"Hey, just lay off the Gentiles, okay?" Mace said. "I don't think I like this poem much."

Levy ignored him. "Lord God of hosts, be with us yet . . . lest we forget—lest we forget!"

As Mace drifted off to sleep, Levy was still at it. Even when Mace awoke briefly an hour or so later, he could hear Levy continuing to recite verses in a low monotone, but it wasn't the same poem as before. This time, it *was* something from the Old Testament. Mace recognized it as the Twenty-third Psalm.

While 1/5 and 2/5 were completing the final mopping up in the north, the Fifth's Third Battalion turned south to take up positions facing the cave-riddled ridges of the Five Sisters—the same mass of fortified crags and crevices that had broken the back of the First Marines more than a week earlier.

By October 1, D-plus-16, elements of Colonel Herman Hanneken's First Battalion, Seventh Marines, continued to contain Japanese forces in the southern portion of the Umurbrogol and along the West Road. But Hanneken's depleted ranks were stretched thin, and the best they could do was prevent the enemy from breaking out of the Pocket. Recent advances were marked in feet and inches, and the opposing lines remained perilously close together.

While the Fifth Marines conducted operations on Ngesebus and the northern coast, the Seventh Marines' other two battalions had been pressing the attack on the Pocket from the north, but they, too, lacked the strength to gain much ground. With units from the Army's Eighty-first Division assuming a growing role in the battle, any remaining chance for troops of the First Marine Division to collapse the Pocket now rested squarely on Bucky Harris's regiment.

Early on October 1, a convoy of trucks and amtracks reunited the dog-tired rifle companies of 1/5, 2/5, and 3/5 at a bivouac area a short distance south of the Five Sisters. Then the three battalions began moving into position to launch a major assault on the five-headed coral juggernaut, beginning on the morning of October 3.

The men of 3/5 knew the reputation of the Five Sisters as they approached them, but otherwise they had no real sense of place. Like the numbered hills dotting officers' maps, the names attached to various formations of jagged rock had little meaning for the Marines who gazed up at them. Within a few hundred yards of the Five Sisters were the Five Brothers, the China Wall, Baldy Ridge, Death Valley, and the Horseshoe. Other heights were named for Marine officers who had led attacks against them, including Walt's Ridge, named for Lieutenant Colonel Lew Walt, executive officer of the Fifth Marines, and Boyd's Ridge, named for Colonel Robert Boyd, commander of 1/5.

Regardless of what they might be called, most of the ridges looked exactly the same to the Americans who fought and died on them. Each harbored its own anthill of Japanese soldiers, its own arsenal of enemy weaponry, and they seemed to have no beginning or end. When a ridge was finally taken, another one, identical to it, inevitably loomed beyond.

"We were usually told the name of this or that coral height or ridge when we attacked," said PFC Gene Sledge. "To me, it meant only that we were attacking the same objective where other Marine battalions had been shot up previously."

Countless efforts have been made over the past six decades to describe the Umurbrogol ridges in adequate terms. Words inevitably fail to capture their grotesque symmetry, but an observation by PFC Sterling Mace comes closer than most.

"The terrain was like the surface of a waffle iron," Mace recalled, "only magnified about a million times."

. . .

The deeper the men of K/3/5 moved into the ridges, the more it seemed as if every inch held unseen dangers. Well before Captain Andy Haldane's unit reached the jumping-off place for the planned attack, concealed Japanese marksmen watched from above, searching in their gun sights for the slightest hint of movement. Now and then, an isolated shot rang out, and a Marine fell. The briefest momentary exposure—a peek over a ledge or around a boulder—invited sudden death.

When opposing fire was identified as coming from a fortified enemy position, mortar and artillery could be directed against it long enough for a rifle squad to scramble from one protective outcropping to the next. But isolated snipers were extremely hard to locate, even after they fired on the Marines.

Time correspondent Robert Martin described the Japanese system of mountainside caves as "the incarnate evil of this war" and like nothing U.S. forces had encountered previously. "They were built at staggered levels," Martin wrote, "so that it was impossible to reach one without being fired at from another."

On the afternoon of October 1, Sergeant Jim McEnery's Third Platoon was inching its way along a jagged ridge overlooked by higher ground where Japanese riflemen were known to be entrenched. There'd been no enemy fire for a couple of hours, but McEnery knew this was no time for complacency or carelessness.

"Watch it now, you guys," McEnery told the men around him. "Just take it easy, keep your heads down, and don't take any unnecessary chances. Play it safe, and we'll be all right."

Crouching a few feet away, Sterling Mace stuffed his pack and pockets with extra ammo for his BAR, then searched in vain for somewhere to put the fresh package of cigarettes he'd just opened. The ammo was important, but so were the smokes, and he hadn't left any room for them.

Mace glanced over at his buddy, PFC Seymour Levy, who squatted a couple of arm's lengths to his left. "Hey, Sy, you got room in your pack for my cigs?" Mace said. "I got no place to put 'em where they won't get mashed."

Levy shrugged. "Sure, toss 'em over."

"You better be careful," said PFC Frankie Ocepek. "Levy's liable to smoke the damn things while you're not lookin'."

"He better not," Mace warned. "It's the only pack I got." They both knew Levy didn't smoke.

Levy shook his head as he slipped the plastic-wrapped cigarettes into his pack. Because of the bandage on Levy's chin, Mace couldn't tell if his friend was smiling or not.

As the men scattered out and took up positions about ten feet apart, Mace moved down the line and found a fairly comfortable spot some twenty or thirty yards from where he'd left Levy. Several other Marines scrambled past him in single file, their boondockers kicking loose pebbles. But once everybody got settled, it grew very quiet.

Mace leaned against the coral, cradling the BAR in his arms, his senses drifting back and forth across the invisible line between fear and boredom. He pictured his family's house in Queens and wondered if he'd ever see it again. He remembered a great play he'd made as third baseman on the company baseball team. It had been a little over a month since the team's last game on Pavuvu, but it seemed like half a lifetime.

Somewhere down the line to Mace's right, the silence was broken by the sharp crack of a single gunshot, not unlike the sound of a bat making solid contact with a baseball. He jerked at the sound. He'd heard thousands of shots in the past sixteen days—almost enough not to notice them anymore—but the fact that this one was solitary made it different. He tensed for a moment to listen, but when he heard no other shots or cries of "Corpsman!," he relaxed a little.

After ten or fifteen minutes, the order came down the line to move ahead for another short advance. As the men closed ranks around him, the first thing Mace wanted was a cigarette. "Hey, where's Levy?" he asked. "He's got my smokes, and I need one bad."

Frankie Ocepek stared at Mace for a second, then looked away.

"What's the matter with you?" Mace demanded. "Where's Levy?"

"Nobody wanted to tell you," Ocepek said softly. "He got it in the head a while ago. Never had a chance."

As Ocepek's words sank in, Mace thought back to the lone shot a few minutes earlier. He felt a sinking sensation in the pit of his stomach as he heard Jim McEnery's voice behind him.

"Sorry, kid," McEnery said. "I kept warnin' Levy to stay down, but he was antsy as hell, and he wouldn't listen. The longer we were stuck here huggin' the dirt, the worse he got. Finally, he said, 'I'm sick and tired of this shit,' and he raised up to take a look. They nailed him before you could bat an eye."

"I was only eight or ten feet from him," said Corporal Tom Matheny, a quiet mortar man from east Tennessee. "Just a minute before, we'd been sitting there talking, and then, wham! If it's any consolation, he never knew what hit him."

Mace felt tears on his cheeks and a choking sensation in his throat. "Where is he?" he asked. "What happened to his body?"

"Stretcher-bearers took him down the hill," McEnery said. "It was tough going. Lucky they didn't get hit themselves."

Mace gestured with his BAR toward the enemy-held ridge. "I'm gonna go up there and wipe out the whole damned bunch of those assholes," he said.

McEnery laid his hand on Mace's shoulder and gave it a little shake. "You're one of the best BAR guys in the platoon, but I ain't lettin' you get yourself killed for nothin'," he said. "You'll have plenty of shots at the Nips later, so just cool off. You can handle this, kid. Hell, you *gotta* handle it."

Mace locked eyes with McEnery for a few seconds, then turned away and sank down onto the coral, holding his head in his hands.

Why'd you have to come back here, you dummy? Why couldn't you just take your million-dollar wound and go home, like any sane person would've done? Why in God's name did you have to come back?

Seymour Levy was killed exactly two weeks after the injuries to his chin. He was only seventeen years old.

. . .

On the morning of October 3, the men of 3/5 launched an attack from the south on the Five Sisters. In a simultaneous strike, 2/7 attacked from the east against Walt's Ridge—the same strip of high ground held briefly two weeks earlier by the thin ranks of Captain Everett Pope's C/1/1 before they were driven off. Meanwhile, 3/7 advanced from the north on Boyd's Ridge.

The primary objective of the latter two coordinated attacks was to push the enemy off the cliffs that dominated the East Road, making it impossible for American forces to move supplies or evacuate wounded over the route. The Five Sisters action by 3/5 was intended to draw enough attention from the now encircled enemy defenders to ensure that the East Road was cleared. In other words, it was primarily a diversionary attack, but no one had bothered to tell the Marines who made it.

For an hour or more preceding H-hour for the 3/5 rifle companies, massed 75-millimeter batteries of the Eleventh Marines lashed enemy emplacements on the five peaks with intense artillery fire. Unlike many previous softening-up operations, this barrage was basically a continuation of about two weeks of systematic pounding of the Five Sisters by the Eleventh's guns. It remained impossible, however, to tell how effective all this shelling had been in reducing the estimated 1,500 Japanese embedded in the area.

Corsairs from the Peleliu airstrip also flew dozens of missions against the ridges. Most of their sorties lasted only about a minute from takeoff to landing—so brief that Marine pilots never bothered to retract their landing gear. Tons of napalm were dumped on enemy positions, but, again, the depth and complexity of the Japanese positions made it difficult to assess the impact of these searing blasts.

PFC Gene Sledge and the rest of his K/3/5 mortar section joined in with a heavy barrage from their 60-millimeter guns, then briefly ceased firing as the company's rifle platoons surged up the lower slopes below the Five Sisters. When the riflemen's advance was stalled by enemy machine guns, mortars, and artillery, Sledge and his mates resumed firing, this time more rapidly than before, to provide cover for the retreating riflemen.

It was the same brutal process that had repeated itself time and again, first with the First Marines, then with the Seventh Marines. Now it was the Fifth's turn, and some of its rifle companies seemed to enjoy amazing success in the early going on October 3. By around noon, 3/5 had taken four of the jagged heights comprising the Five Sisters, and only Sister 2 remained in Japanese hands. But within three or four hours, enemy fire intensified from all directions, and the situation deteriorated. As in the past, the Marines were forced to give up their gains and pull back to approximately the same line where they'd jumped off that morning.

"Each time we got orders to secure the guns after the riflemen stopped advancing, the mortar section stood by to go up as stretcher-bearers," Sledge recalled. "We usually threw phosphorus and smoke grenades as a screen, and the riflemen covered us, but enemy snipers fired as rapidly as possible at the stretcher-bearers."

To Sledge, it seemed a miracle that any of the wounded men or those who struggled to carry them out of danger ever reached a rear area alive. He marveled at the confidence shown by wounded Marines toward their stretcher-bearers, even under the most desperate circumstances.

"Most of the time, it took four stretcher-bearers to get one wounded man down off those ridges," recalled Corporal R. V. Burgin. "That's how steep and treacherous the terrain was, and they were almost always under fire."

There was plenty of need for stretchers throughout the day on October 3, when K/3/5 recorded twenty casualties—five killed and fifteen wounded. It was one of the costliest days of the war for the company, equaled only by the first day on Ngesebus, and a disproportionate number of those who fell were comrades of Sterling Mace and Jim McEnery in the Third Platoon.

"We started out that morning with the ridges on our left and an open space on our right where you could see all the way to the airstrip and the ocean past the old beachhead area," Mace recalled. "We took out some Jap caves on our way up the slopes, but we must've bypassed several more because we started taking hostile fire from the rear as well as the front."

Lieutenant Bill Bauerschmidt, the tall, young Pennsylvanian who led the Third Platoon, was crouching on a hillside, directing his troops through an open area, when he was hit in the stomach by rifle fire.

"I don't get it," Bauerschmidt gasped to a Marine who braved blistering fire to come to his aid. "The shot came from behind. Are our own men shooting at us?"

Bleeding profusely, Bauerschmidt groped at his side for the long-barreled .45 revolver on his belt, his most treasured possession. But before he could draw the pistol from its holster, he lapsed into unconsciousness. By the time stretcher-bearers got him to an aid station, Bauerschmidt was dead, and his platoon had been forced to fall back.

About twenty yards from the spot where his platoon leader fell, PFC Lyman Rice was killed instantly by another enemy bullet, and PFC Raymond Grawet, another Third Platoon rifleman, was fatally wounded as he ran toward the entrance to one of the bypassed Japanese caves.

Mace was still reeling from Sy Levy's death when he learned that three more members of his platoon had been killed. He was numbed by the news, but when he heard about Bauerschmidt, the first thing that crossed his mind was a comical exchange he'd had with the lieutenant on Pavuvu. It had happened one evening when Bauerschmidt dropped by, as he frequently did, to socialize with the enlisted men.

BAUERSCHMIDT: Any of you guys want to take in a movie?
MACE: Yeah, we want to see *The King's Hand*. Ever heard of it?
BAUERSCHMIDT: I don't think so. What's it about?
Mace (with a straight face): Oh, about halfway up the queen's ass.

All the guys had laughed, and Bauerschmidt had chased Mace around the tents for ten minutes, threatening to kick his butt for being a smart-aleck.

The affable officer with the mane of blond hair had been that kind of guy—one who was never afraid to joke around with the grunts who served under him. For a second or two, Mace smiled at the memory. Then the smile withered on his face, and he felt a hard ball of emptiness in his gut, like before.

As dusk approached on October 3, the high price paid by K/3/5's third platoon and other units had seemingly accomplished nothing. As far as Mace and his comrades could tell, they were right back where they'd started that morning, only with lower spirits, wearier bodies, and considerably fewer men.

Undoubtedly, they'd try again tomorrow. Somewhere, somehow, there'd be another attack. There was always another attack. Now their challenge was to survive the night.

It was barely full dark when the first of the enemy infiltrators descended on K/3/5's thinly manned front. Some obviously came for the express purpose of killing or crippling as many Marines as possible. Others may have crept out of bypassed caves to the battalion's rear, trying to slip past American positions to reach their own lines. In either case, the intruders brought mayhem with them.

Most of them wore tabi, the notorious "black pajamas" that made them next to invisible at night. They knew every inch of the terrain, and their ability to move noiselessly through the darkness over rough, rock-strewn ground was uncanny.

Like most of the men in K/3/5, R. V. Burgin was by himself that night in a shallow breastwork of piled-up rocks and sticks. The swelling tide of casualties no longer allowed the company to fill its required space in the line with two Marines per foxhole. Instead, one-man foxholes were spaced about six feet apart—close enough to allow their occupants to reach out and touch each other in case of trouble—and every second man was supposed to stay awake.

"By now, we were standing watch in one-hour shifts," Burgin recalled. "We were so exhausted that we couldn't count on anybody to keep his eyes open much longer than that."

A few yards from Burgin's foxhole, one side of the ridgeline on which they were dug in fell away into a sheer seventy-foot ravine. Between Burgin and the edge of this chasm were two other one-man outposts.

Shortly after 1:00 A.M., while the Marine adjacent to Burgin was on watch and both Burgin and the next man over were sleeping, a black-clad Japanese soldier scurried past and jumped into the hole with the other sleeping man. Seconds later, Burgin awoke to the sounds of painful grunts and thrashings.

He reached for his carbine and turned toward the other foxholes in time to see the intruder sitting astride his groggy victim, choking him with both hands. Burgin didn't dare fire at the attacker for fear of hitting the man he was attacking, but he and the Marine on watch both scrambled in that direction.

In a fist-swinging, hair-pulling, eye-gouging frenzy, the embattled Marine managed to free himself before his comrades could join the fray. He threw the smaller Japanese soldier to the ground, then picked him up and hurled him off the edge of the cliff. His piercing scream echoed off the walls of the canyon all the way to the bottom, then abruptly stopped.

"You okay?" Burgin asked.

The Marine was coughing and rubbing his severely bruised neck, but he finally nodded. "Everything anybody ever taught me about self-defense flashed through my mind just now," he croaked, "and I think I used every damn bit of it, too."

Although there were no reports of other infiltrators jumping into K/3/5 positions that night, a number of suspicious movements were observed among the rocks and debris in front of the company's lines. With the first light of a new day, it soon became apparent that a dozen or more enemy soldiers had crept into the area and taken cover.

PFC Jay d'Leau, the bazooka man in Burgin's mortar squad, was carrying an armload of rations from the command post back toward his foxhole when he jumped over a fallen log—and landed squarely on top of two hiding Japanese soldiers.

"Nips! Nips!" d'Leau yelped, dropping the rations and grabbing at the carbine on his shoulder as he sprang back. He swung the carbine around and tried to squeeze off a shot, but nothing happened. A spent cartridge was jammed in the chamber, and the weapon wouldn't fire.

One of the enemy soldiers darted away and disappeared behind some rocks, but the second chased after d'Leau, brandishing a grenade. By now, d'Leau's comrades had heard the ruckus and turned to look. One was a BAR man with his automatic weapon in his hands.

"Shoot him!" d'Leau shouted. He threw down the useless carbine, veered toward the BAR man, and pointed at the Japanese. "For God's sake, shoot him!"

The BAR man took aim, then hesitated. For what seemed an eternity to d'Leau, the Marine stood there waiting as the pursuing Japanese closed the gap between them. To make matters worse, d'Leau had been troubled for a day or two with diarrhea, and his bowels were rumbling ominously.

"Shoot him, damn it!" he screamed.

The Japanese was only two or three steps behind d'Leau when the BAR man finally opened fire. In one furious volley, he poured most of a twenty-round magazine into the enemy soldier's midsection. For a second, the force of the blast held the soldier suspended in midair. Then his body fell in a heap, and the grenade rolled harmlessly away.

D'Leau glared at the BAR man and shuddered as cold sweat streaked his face and something worse dribbled down his pantlegs. "What were you waiting for?" he demanded. "An engraved invitation?"

The BAR man shrugged. "It was just kind of an experiment," he said. "I wanted to see if I could cut the son of a bitch clean in half with one burst." He seemed disappointed that he hadn't quite succeeded.

Moments later, as d'Leau made his way in a stiff-legged waddle back toward the battalion CP for a fresh pair of dungaree pants, he passed a puzzled Gene Sledge, who'd obviously missed the whole episode.

"What happened to you, Jay?" Sledgehammer inquired.

"Aw hell," d'Leau replied sheepishly, "I'll tell you later."

On October 4, D-plus-19, the attacks on the Pocket resumed. While 3/5 applied pressure on the Five Sisters and the Horseshoe, a U-shaped ridge system just southeast of the Sisters, from the south, the tattered remnants of 3/7 and 2/7 tried to secure a draw between Walt's Ridge and Boyd's Ridge and another between Boyd's Ridge and an unnamed hill to the north. Securing these two draws was essential to end the enemy threat to the East Road.

For 3/5, the day was a depressing repeat of the day before. About 10:00 A.M., the guns of the Eleventh Marines began pounding the ridges again. An hour later, the rifle companies stormed up the slopes and made quick progress, just as they had on October 3. Then, once more, everything began to go sour.

PFC Ray Rottinghaus and his comrades in K/3/5's First Platoon got to the top of their assigned ridge within five minutes after the advance began, with Rottinghaus and several other BAR men leading the way. He took cover behind some rocks, quickly laid out several magazines of ammo for his BAR, and got set to go to work.

The ex–Iowa farmboy had seen about a dozen Japanese heads bobbing up and down on the other side of the ridge, and he whispered to the guy beside him to get ready.

"We waited as long as our nerves would stand it," Rottinghaus recalled. "Then we all fired at once, and all the Japs crumpled. But then a Jap pillbox opened up on us from an adjoining ridge about 100 feet away, and all hell broke loose."

A fusillade of automatic weapons fire tore off the index finger on Rottinghaus's left hand, splintered the stock of his BAR, and slammed another bullet into his shoulder. Two of the Marines nearby also fell with wounds.

"I'm hit, John," Rottinghaus muttered to PFC John Huber, who crouched next to him. "I think I'm hit pretty bad."

"For God's sake, hang on," Huber said. "I'll try to find a corps-man."

But Rottinghaus didn't wait for the medic. Holding his dungaree shirt around his mangled hand, he stumbled down the hillside on his own, leaving his ruined BAR behind. The barrel of his weapon was too hot to touch, anyway, after firing close to 500 rounds within two or three minutes.

When two stretcher-bearers finally appeared, Rottinghaus assured them he could make it the rest of the way to the nearest evacuation point without help.

"You're in no shape to walk, man," one of them told him. "Now lie down, damn it."

So he did.

Although 3/5's losses were lighter than the day before, K Company had a total of eight additional casualties on October 4. PFC Alden F. Moore was killed, and Rottinghaus was among the seven wounded.

The men of 2/7 and 3/7—already battalions in name only when the day's action began—fared far worse. Remnants of F/2/7 and I/3/7 made short work of the enemy in the draw between Walt's and Boyd's Ridges, and L/3/7 had similar initial success in the second draw, seizing three key outcroppings.

Major Hunter Hurst, commanding 3/7, tried to maintain this momentum by ordering tank support for a drive by L Company against Hill 120, between Baldy and Boyd's. Late that afternoon, however, the Japanese sprang a clever ambush. One platoon of L/3/7 came under concentrated automatic weapons fire from atop Baldy while it was exposed on the crest of Hill 120. As the platoon tried to retreat down the slopes, it found its escape blocked by other Japanese troops firing from below them on Boyd's Ridge.

With the company caught in a murderous crossfire, Hurst called on the tanks for help, but the Japanese gunners were so well concealed that the tanks couldn't get at them. Finally, a smoke screen allowed the surviving handful of Marines to make their way out of the draw. They left their company commander, Captain James V. "Jamo" Shanley, and executive officer, Second Lieutenant Harold Collins, mortally wounded on the battlefield.

Shanley, a Navy Cross winner at Cape Gloucester, was blown to pieces when a mortar shell hit within a few feet of him as he tried to rescue a wounded Marine. Collins was killed by an anti-tank gun seconds later, attempting to reach his fallen captain. Lieutenant James Dunn, leader of the trapped platoon, was hit by rifle fire and fell off a cliff to his death. Of the forty-eight Marines who attacked Hill 120, only eleven survived, and six of these were wounded.

The carnage of that afternoon marked the swan song of the Seventh Marines at Peleliu. Like the First Marines before them, Colonel Hanneken's regiment simply didn't have enough able-bodied men left to continue the fight. Its casualties now stood at 1,486 killed and wounded—more than 46 percent of its authorized strength.

In its final two days as an operational unit, Major Hurst's Third Battalion was especially hard-hit. Its L Company was reduced to the strength of a single platoon, and its Company I came off the line with just thirty-one men and one officer.

A hodgepodge of supporting troops manned gaps in the Seventh's lines to guard against any attempted Japanese outbreak to the west until the withdrawal was completed. These included artillerymen from the Eleventh Marines, members of the First Pioneer Battalion, men of several amphibian tractor battalions, and volunteers from various other units.

General Geiger, commander of the III Amphibious Corps, told

General Rupertus that the Seventh was too shot-up and beaten-up to continue, but Rupertus at first refused to admit it. "Give 'em a little more time," the division commander insisted. "They'll take the Pocket, and the battle will be over."

On the morning of October 6, even as the Fifth Marines was replacing the Seventh's remaining front-line troops in the ridges, Rupertus finally yielded to common sense and the inevitable. Shortly before noon, he ordered Hanneken to withdraw his troops and prepare for evacuation.

As they departed, the Japanese grip on the Pocket appeared as tenacious as ever. The division's last hope of breaking it now rested with the Fifth Marines.

CHAPTER THIRTEEN

A STINKING, TIMELESS VOID

Members of the Fifth Marines who lived through what would be the regiment's last ten days on Peleliu have trouble recalling the dates of specific events. The constant danger, the ever-present stench of death, and the exhaustion from nearly three weeks of combat melded days and nights into an indistinguishable blur.

The attacks against the Pocket continued. Men bled, screamed, and died. Enemy caves were blown out. Now and then, a few feet of ground were wrested from the enemy, but there was no sense of victory. Beyond the gains were only more hills, more caves, more ridges, more Japanese. For the men of the Fifth, only two things about this final phase of the battle stand out clearly in their collective memory. One was a level of mental and physical fatigue that defied description. The other was an odor too revolting to imagine.

The fatigue undoubtedly posed more danger, but the smell—the inescapable stench of death, rot, and human waste—remains foremost in the minds of those who survived. It, and the swarms of flies it attracted, hung over Peleliu like a shroud. As the combat dragged on, both grew progressively worse.

"Everywhere we went on the ridges, the hot, humid air reeked with the stench of death," said PFC Gene Sledge. "A strong wind was no relief; it simply brought the horrid odor from an adjacent area."

Pilots who flew in and out of the Peleliu airstrip later told their infantry comrades that the smell was readily detectable at 1,500 feet.

· · ·

On October 5, the day the Seventh Marines ceased to function as an active infantry regiment, the three-day "quickie" operation predicted by General Rupertus was three weeks old. During those twenty-one days, it has been conservatively estimated, more than 8,000 Japanese either died in action or committed hara-kiri. The enemy made little effort to retrieve or bury its dead, so thousands of bodies were left to rot where they fell.

American troops did their best to collect the bodies of their fallen comrades as soon as battlefield conditions allowed and turn them over to graves registration personnel for proper burial. Sometimes, though, this proved impossible—especially in the seesaw fighting in the ridges. The bodies of men from Captain Everett Pope's company killed during their attack and retreat on Walt's Ridge on September 19–20 couldn't be recovered until October 3, when Marine and Army troops regained the ridge for good. There were numerous other instances of American dead being left behind during a retreat.

Late one afternoon, Sergeant Jim McEnery discovered the bodies of four dead Marines strewn in an isolated ravine below the Five Sisters. "They'd all been dead at least two weeks," McEnery said. "I cut off their dog tags and told the graves registration guys where to find them, but I never knew how much longer they lay out there."

A short time later, Corporal R. V. Burgin came across the several-days-old remains of four other Marines piled together in a shallow depression. Burgin guessed that the bloated bodies were those of intelligence scouts from regimental headquarters who'd been ambushed by the Japanese.

He recoiled in horror when he saw that all four bodies had been severely mutilated. Two had been decapitated and their hands severed at the wrists. One had been hacked into numerous pieces, and the other's penis and testicles had been cut off and stuffed into his mouth.

Overcome with sickness and rage, Burgin turned away. "I already hated the Japs," he recalled many years later, "but I'd never hated them as bad as I did that day. I knew then why we didn't take prisoners, and I wanted to kill every one of the bastards."

• • •

Even when American bodies were removed promptly from the scene of combat, conditions could delay their burial in the new division cemetery near the airfield. At times, the bodies remained for days in rear areas near the front, laid out on stretchers and covered with ponchos only yards from where living Marines were fighting, until they were in advanced stages of decomposition.

Enemy dead were denied even these crude niceties, but the Japanese did go to the trouble of booby-trapping dozens of their corpses, allowing them to keep killing and maiming Americans after death. "I think they purposely left behind the ones that weren't booby-trapped, too," said Burgin, "just to make it as unbearable as they could for Marines who had to take up positions right next to the bodies."

As platoons moved back and forth through the ridges, enemy corpses often became gruesome landmarks amid a maze of deceptively similar rock formations. As the days passed, Marines witnessed some enemy dead passing through the whole cycle of decay—from freshly killed bodies, to bloated and discolored corpses, to maggot-infested carrion, and finally to partially exposed skeletons.

For several days in a row, PFC Sterling Mace watched Jim McEnery aim a burst from his tommy gun at the same dead Japanese soldier as their platoon rounded a bend in a trail along one of the ridges. Mace could tell it was purely a reflex action on McEnery's part. The soldier was in a sitting position on an adjacent ridge about 100 feet away, and at first glance, he looked alive. Eventually, he turned black and his flesh started falling away.

Now adding to the odor problem—and the flies—was three weeks' worth of feces deposited on the coral by thousands of men. Once the Marines moved inland, most of the ground they fought on was solid rock, where latrines were nonexistent and established field sanitation practices became meaningless. Men had no choice but to relieve themselves wherever they could and leave the results exposed.

"Field sanitation during maneuvers and combat was the responsibility of each man," said Sledge. "In short, under normal conditions, he covered his own waste with a scoop of soil. . . . But on Peleliu, except along the beach areas and in the swamps, digging into the coral rock was nearly impossible."

The problem might have been worse except for the fact that many Marines in assault units lost their appetite, eating so little that it wasn't uncommon for them to go a week or more without a bowel movement. On the opposite extreme, however, hundreds of others suffered recurrent bouts of diarrhea.

"I don't ever remember being really hungry on Peleliu, and when I did try to eat something, the flies fought me for every bite," McEnery said. "They came in swarms the second you'd open a can of rations, and you couldn't shoo 'em away. You damn near had to scrape 'em off the food to keep from swallowing 'em."

To reduce the fly population, the newly developed pesticide DDT was employed in a combat zone for the first time on Peleliu, but the Marines noticed no appreciable improvement. The insects rose into the air just after dawn each morning in buzzing, black clouds that sometimes blotted out the sun for a second or two. Many were so large, lazy, and glutted that they could barely fly, and nothing intimidated them. Sledge recalled a standard chow time ritual of balancing a can of stew on one knee and simultaneously spooning it up with his right hand while picking the flies off it with his left hand.

For obvious reasons, tons of uneaten rations were tossed aside and abandoned by American troops during the course of the battle. To a lesser extent, the Japanese also discarded substantial amounts of food scraps. Within hours, all of it soured and spoiled, contributing more fodder for the flies and another component to the cauldron of nauseating odors.

"I felt as though my lungs would never be cleansed of all those foul vapors," Sledge recalled. "It may not have been that way down on the airfield and in other areas where the service troops were encamped, but around the infantry in the Umurbrogol Pocket, the stench varied only from foul to unbearable."

Few news reports mentioned these terrible conditions, but a notable exception was a dispatch from *Time* correspondent Robert Martin, who wrote: "Peleliu is a horrible place. The heat is stifling, and rain falls intermittently—the muggy rain that brings no relief, only greater misery. The coral rocks soak up heat during the day, and it is only slightly cooler at night. . . . Peleliu is incomparably worse than Guam in its bloodiness, terror, climate, and the incomprehensible tenacity of the Japs. For sheer brutality and fatigue, I think it surpasses anything yet seen in the Pacific."

The fatigue that Martin mentioned was like a debilitating disease. Physical and psychological exhaustion stretched the limits of human endurance. Men went through the motions of battle like glassy-eyed zombies, drained of energy, almost devoid of emotion, and dead on their feet. Yet sleep or genuine rest was impossible because the enemy was always there—around the clock, often no more than a few feet away—and the tension never eased.

When men did manage to catch a catnap, it was usually for only a few minutes, and many Marines went for days with no sleep at all. While remaining at forward positions to direct his squad's mortar fire, R. V. Burgin endured one stint of more than seventy-two hours when he never closed his eyes.

During that period, Burgin saw a drowsy Marine at his side killed instantly by a sniper's bullet squarely through the center of his forehead. Keeping the incident fresh in his mind helped snap Burgin back to alertness whenever he felt himself drifting off or losing concentration.

"After three days, I finally told Johnny Marmet, my platoon sergeant, that I had to come off the line," Burgin said. "I was so punchdrunk I couldn't focus my eyes anymore. I made it back to my squad's position, crawled up behind some rocks, and passed out like a light. I didn't stir for about twelve hours straight, most of that time with two 60-millimeter mortars firing right over me."

The few remaining officers of K/3/5 were as sleep-starved as the enlisted men, if not more so. Captain Andy Haldane stayed constantly in the company's most forward positions and as close as possible to the action, helping to position his mortar and machine gun units and spotting targets for the artillery. When somebody had to go to the relative safety of the battalion CP, Haldane preferred to send his executive officer, Lieutenant Thomas "Stumpy" Stanley, and stay with his troops.

Haldane had long ago earned the respect and admiration of his Guadalcanal and Cape Gloucester veterans, but since D-Day at Peleliu, every man in K/3/5 had come to recognize their company commander's courage as well as his compassion for the men he led.

"He was more than just a CO; he was a real friend," said Sergeant Dick Higgins, a personal aide to Haldane whose brother had played football with Ack-Ack back in Maine. "Anytime he told men they had to go up front, he was right there with them."

In addition, there was a rock-solidness about Haldane, almost an aura of indestructibility, that inevitably boosted the spirits of those who served under him. As Gene Sledge put it: "We were thankful that Ack-Ack was our skipper, felt more secure in it, and felt sorry for other companies not so fortunate."

But now, even Haldane was showing the effects of weeks of unremitting stress and bloodshed—weeks that had left more than half his company dead or wounded.

"You could tell how tired the captain was, just by looking at him," said Corporal Jim Anderson, a Wisconsin native whose severe wounds at Cape Gloucester had cut short his service as a scout and landed him in headquarters platoon as a runner for Haldane. "But he still seemed calm and steady, never flustered, never yelling at anybody."

By the first week of October, even as the slaughter continued unabated in the heart of the Umurbrogol, nine-tenths of Peleliu was firmly under American control. Although the men of the Fifth Marines were too busy fighting to take much notice, most of the island was now as secure as any noncombat zone. As a result, it had split into two strikingly opposite worlds. Physically, they were separated only by a few hundred yards of land, but when it came to living conditions, they were oceans apart.

In rear areas around the airfield and the old beachhead, service and supply personnel slept in comfortable tents, took their meals in tidy mess halls, patronized a well-stocked PX, attended nightly movies, and safely went about their jobs with neither helmets nor weapons.

Instead of fear, exhaustion, and constant danger, their main complaint was often boredom. In search of diversion, adventure, and potentially valuable souvenirs, hundreds of men who had never been near actual combat were drawn out of their safe havens into areas where bullets were still flying. There, they frequently got a rough reception from front-line troops, some of whom resented these "rear-echelon Charlies" enough to let them wander into serious trouble.

Sledge recalled one incident during a lull between attacks on the Five Sisters when a pair of fresh-faced youngsters, wearing green fatigue caps instead of helmets and carrying no weapons, sauntered through K/3/5's lines, heading straight for concealed enemy positions.

After a few paces, one of them turned around and called back: "Hey, you guys, where's the front line?"

"You just passed through it," Sledge said.

The souvenir hunters froze in their tracks, staring at Sledge in astonishment. Then they glanced at each other, grabbed their caps, and ran like rabbits toward the rear.

"Hell, Sledgehammer," complained a nearby rifleman, "you shoulda let 'em go, so they'd get a good scare."

"But the way they were headed, they might've walked right up on a sniper," Sledge said.

"Serve them rear-echelon bastards right," the other Marine grumbled.

Major Joseph E. Buckley, who commanded the Seventh Marines' Weapons Company, had his own way of dealing with unwelcome visitors from the rear. Those without legitimate business at the front were detained, issued rifles, and put in the line with the combat troops. If they behaved, Buckley notified their unit commanders of their whereabouts and "present employment." If not, Buckley didn't bother, and the visitors were listed as AWOL as long as he chose to keep them there.

Hordes of souvenir hunters and curious noncombatants became almost as much a nuisance as Japanese infiltrators. Most were aviation ground personnel, sailors from Navy transports, or service troops with excess time on their hands and delusions of finding jewel-studded samurai swords.

On the other hand, many Marines from rear areas came to the front with a sincere desire to help their embattled comrades. They volunteered to bring up supplies, serve as stretcher-bearers or gravediggers, and even fill gaps in the lines for shorthanded rifle squads. Ground crewmen from the Second Marine Air Wing were especially active as volunteers, and they paid a high price for their courage— ten men killed and sixty-seven wounded.

At one of the darkest hours in the history of the Seventh Marines, the casualty-riddled regiment received significant help from an unexpected source. As the exhausted survivors of an I/3/7 rifle platoon rested near a northern beach in 110-degree heat, Top Sergeant Bill Mulford was approached by a young, muscular black man.

"I heard you all were looking for replacements," the black man said. "We've had some infantry training, and we want to volunteer."

Corporal Edward "Eddy Lee" Andrusko, a squad leader who was standing nearby, saw a look of stunned surprise cross Mulford's face. "Well, I don't know," the top sergeant said. "Who are you guys? Are you Army, Navy, Seabees, or what?"

"I'm a sergeant in the U.S. Marine Corps," the black man said, "and all my men on this beach are Marines, too. We're in an ammunition depot company, but we've finished our work here, and we're cleared with division to volunteer anywhere we're needed. We know how to handle weapons, and we want to help."

Mulford stood there for a minute, chewing his lip, and Andrusko could tell what was going through his mind. I/3/7 had a large contingent of unreconstructed Southern "rebels"—some of whom had given Andrusko a hard time just for being from New Jersey and who might balk at the idea of serving next to blacks—but the company was also dangerously shorthanded.

As the men of the supply unit picked up their weapons and fell into line behind their sergeant, Mulford tried to discourage them. "Nothing you people have seen on this beach is gonna prepare you for the hell you're gonna face if you go with us," he said. "So don't say I didn't warn you."

"We can take it," the black sergeant assured him.

For the rest of the day, the African-American Marines made dozens of trips between the front lines and rear areas. They carried dead and wounded in one direction and hauled back ammo, food, and other supplies on their return trips. That night, they moved into vacant foxholes along the line and helped fight off a Japanese counterattack. The next morning, in several hours of bloody fighting, they charged and took an enemy-held hill shoulder to shoulder with what was left of I Company.

Andrusko marveled at their courage, strength, and endurance. "I saw more than one of them gently carrying a wounded man on a stretcher with one hand and firing an automatic weapon simultaneously with the other," he said. "I heard one badly wounded Southerner say he felt like he'd been saved by 'black angels sent by God.'"

Today, the Black Angels of Peleliu are still remembered by grateful survivors of the battle for their unflinching tirelessness, fighting ability, and heroism under fire. When an Army infantry unit finally moved in to relieve I/3/7, one of the soldiers inquired derisively as to who "those black boys" were. Mulford's reply echoed the sentiments of the whole company—and demonstrated how much his own feelings had changed in a short time.

"Why, hell," he bellowed, "they're some of the best damn Marines you'll ever see—that's who!"

. . .

Perhaps the most tragic volunteer story to come out of the fighting around the Pocket was that of Colonel Joseph L. Hankins, a former First Marines battalion commander at Cape Gloucester and a renowned sharpshooter on several Marine Corps rifle teams.

Before the Peleliu landing, Hankins had been promoted to full colonel, appointed division provost marshal, and given command of General Rupertus's large, unwieldy Headquarters Battalion, which included the division's Military Police Company. Hankins chafed under the inaction and heavy loads of paperwork entailed by his new assignment, and when Japanese snipers began targeting his MPs on security details along the West Road, the colonel decided to take a personal hand in the matter.

"I'm going to do a little counter-sniping on my own," he told his executive officer, loading an M-1 and a pair of binoculars into his jeep. Then, without informing Rupertus or any of the general's staff of his plan, Hankins sped away.

A short time later, Hankins came across an amtrack and several trucks, deserted by their drivers and blocking the road. Despite heavy small-arms fire from a nearby cliff, he climbed out of his jeep, ran into the road, and persuaded the drivers to return to their vehicles. The crucial supply and evacuation route was almost cleared for traffic when an enemy bullet struck Hankins in the chest.

He died instantly, the highest-ranking Marine officer to be killed in action on Peleliu.

The advanced state of exhaustion now affecting the entire Fifth Marines wasn't lost on the Japanese. Enemy documents captured on October 6, D-plus-21, reported that the Marines appeared worn out and dispirited and that their assaults on the Pocket were less aggressive than before. This doubtlessly lent encouragement to an adversary resigned to his eventual fate but committed in the meantime to two simple objectives: Keep fighting to the last breath and kill as many Americans as possible.

By now, Colonel Nakagawa, commanding enemy forces on Peleliu, had lost telephone communication with most of his troops, and his only way of checking on the condition of individual units was by furtive nighttime visits. But Nakagawa still had radio contact with Lieutenant General Sadae Inoue on the island of Koror, twenty-five miles north of Peleliu, and Inoue had approved a last-ditch campaign of attrition. Foreseeing the communication breakdown, Nakagawa had given his individual unit commanders advance authority to act on their own initiative. As the battle neared its end stage, their instructions were to use every guerrilla warfare tactic available to inflict maximum harm on their foe.

"They couldn't hope to drive us off by then or to be reinforced themselves," Sledgehammer observed. "From that point onward, they killed solely for the sake of killing, without hope and without higher purpose."

For the Fifth Marines, this meant a stepped-up threat from snipers, infiltrators, and suicide squads. The Japanese machine guns and mortars in concealed embrasures were often silent now, their ammunition being saved for short volleys at the most opportune moments. Sudden, small-scale attacks still could come at any moment, twenty-four hours a day—and the deeper the Marines sank into feelings of fatigue, futility, and fatalism, the easier prey they became.

Amid the stress of constant combat, Corporal Matt Rousseau had all but forgotten the premonition of disaster that he'd first felt the night before D-Day. On the beach that first day, he'd thought for sure his time had come when he and several other Marines made the mistake of taking cover in a gun emplacement still inhabited by live Japanese. Two of his buddies had been killed, but Matt had gotten away clean.

Now, more than three weeks later, he was filthy, emaciated, and almost too weary to move, but he was still leading his battered B/1/5 rifle squad against enemy positions south of the Five Brothers, and so far he hadn't suffered so much as a scratch at the hands of the enemy. In fact, he'd gone for days without even thinking about his earlier fears.

On the morning of October 6, Rousseau was observing for the company mortar section atop a ridge to the right of the Brothers when the unit came under sudden, heavy fire from short-range enemy mortars.

"We can't tell where the Nips are," one of the mortar men yelled. "The CO says for us to get the hell down from here as fast as we can."

On their way down the slope, Rousseau and two other Marines were running past a large, ravaged tree trunk when a mortar shell hit a few feet behind them, knocking all three of them down. Matt lost consciousness for a minute, and when he came to, he could hear one of the other men moaning nearby. He tried to lift himself, but he couldn't.

There wasn't much feeling where the shell fragments had torn into Rousseau's lower back, but when he reached to feel the wound, he found a gaping hole, and his hand came away covered with blood.

As he started to pass out again, he heard someone shouting for a corpsman and stretcher-bearers.

Damn it, I knew I was gonna get my ass shot off, he thought. *And now I have!*

Rousseau remembered nothing else until he awoke several hours later aboard a hospital ship. He never saw the two other wounded Marines again.

Corporal Red Womack slumped in his foxhole, weighted down by weariness and almost oblivious to his surroundings. It was just after nightfall, but Womack no longer cared whether it was morning or evening. He thought he'd heard somebody say that today was October 5, but he wasn't sure. He had no interest in the date, anyway.

Likewise, it made no difference to Womack which of the ridges 3/5 would attack the next day or which cave would become his flamethrower's next target. The ridges all looked alike now, and the days all felt the same. He'd long ago quit counting the caves and bunkers he'd hit since D-Day. The number, like the date, was meaningless. Nothing meant anything anymore except getting off this stinking island alive, but Womack was too dazed and drained even to worry about that very much.

Besides having his sense of time go haywire, he found it next to impossible even to sort out the names and faces of all the friends he'd lost. One buddy, PFC John Louder, had been shot dead during the first few minutes on the beach. Another, PFC Chick Meyer, had been wounded a few days later, then returned to duty only to be hit again. Corporal Frank Wiley, a squad leader in the flamethrower section, had been cut down by a machine gun and died on a hospital ship. PFC William Lewis, Womack's original assistant gunner, had been ripped across the face and chest by grenade blasts on Ngesebus.

Yet, by some miracle, Womack had made it through without a nick so far. The closest he'd come to being wounded was getting a few fragments in the soles of his boondockers from the same grenades that had bloodied Lewis. There'd been two or three other assistants since Womack had picked up Lewis in his arms and carried him to an aid station, but for the life of him, he couldn't remember any of their names.

After all, what's the point? he asked himself. *Before long, they'll most likely be dead or wounded, too. It's just a few less names to keep track of.*

There hadn't been as much demand for handheld flamethrowers since the battalion had moved into the Pocket. Japanese caves here were so deep and hard to reach that even tank-mounted flamethrowers weren't very effective. Caves in the ridges invariably called for a "rope" of fire, rather than a "roll." Womack preferred rolls—fat bursts of flame like the one he'd used against the big pillbox on Ngesebus—but rolls were only good at close range. Ropes, on the other hand, were thin streams of the jellied fuel shot deep into a cave from a considerable distance, before igniting. Under the right circumstances, Womack could use either, but the uncooperative terrain offered few opportunities.

For the past few days, Womack had mostly just tagged along with one of the rifle squads, carrying a carbine and trying to be helpful without getting in the way. As long as he was in combat, he could keep his mind focused on the job at hand. But during lulls in the action, gloomy thoughts could overwhelm a man. They could be as dangerous in their own way as enemy fire.

In self-defense, Womack had tried out a couple of ways to ward off negative thoughts and loneliness for his young wife. One was to make his mind a total blank, but he was never able to do that for more than a few minutes at a stretch. Another was to cram his brain with so many memories of happier times that no room was left for anything else. That was why Womack had spent so much time lately thinking back to his final football game for the McComb High School Tigers in December 1941.

He recalled every detail of the trip to New Orleans that Friday—just two days before the raid on Pearl Harbor—where the Tigers played a team from St. Stanislaus High in Bay St. Louis in a special benefit game called the Toy Bowl, for what amounted to the Mississippi state championship. Womack could still picture the 27,000 howling fans who'd made City Park Stadium shake as he lined up at starting right tackle. He could close his eyes and see the bruising, 198-pound running back named Felix "Doc" Blanchard, who led the St. Stanislaus offense. He could still hear the public address announcer describing one of the first plays from scrimmage:

Blanchard takes the ball on a fullback draw, but Womack hits him behind the line and drops him for a loss . . .

McComb had won the game convincingly, 25–6, touching off the biggest victory celebration in the town's history, and Womack had helped hold Blanchard in check all night. It was the only time the two ever met face-to-face, and fate had soon carried them in sharply divergent directions. Within a few months, Womack was in the Marine Corps, headed for the South Pacific, while Blanchard had gone on to West Point, where he was now one of the top college football stars in America.

Funny how things worked out sometimes, he thought. *No, not really funny—not ha-ha funny, anyway. Maybe "odd" was a better word.*

A startled shout from a few yards to Womack's left abruptly halted his musings. "Who goes there?" a Marine yelled. "Give the pass-word, damn it!"

"Chevrolet," a voice responded. "It's Chevrolet."

"That's yesterday's. Give me the password for today, or I'll shoot you, so help me God."

"No, man, don't shoot. I swear I thought it was Chevrolet. I can't remember nothin' anymore, but it's *me,* for Chrissake!"

"You got one last chance," the first Marine said grimly. "What's the damn password?"

"Chevrolet. That's all I know."

A rifle cracked in the darkness, followed by a brief silence. Then Womack heard a pained but surprisingly calm voice: "Well, you son of a bitch, I hope you're satisfied now. You *did* shoot me."

It was soon established that the injured man was, indeed, a Marine who'd simply forgotten the password, or maybe never heard it in the first place. Luckily, he was only grazed by the shot, and the shooter—now even more jittery and unstrung than before—quickly summoned a corpsman to patch him up.

After a few minutes, the men along the line settled down, and it grew quiet again. Womack leaned against the low pile of rocks at his back and adjusted his helmet to a more comfortable angle under his head, hoping to get a little sleep.

His mind drifted back to the Toy Bowl. He wondered what Doc Blanchard was doing at that very moment.

On October 6, Colonel Robert Boyd's 1/5 finally secured the crests of Walt's Ridge and Boyd's Ridge, parts of which had been seized two days earlier by men of the Seventh Marines in one of their final actions. Boyd's battalion repelled all Japanese attempts to regain these heights, putting the east wall of the Pocket in American hands for good.

This victory further compressed the boundaries of Colonel Naka-gawa's last bastion and increased the pressure on his dwindling garrison. But these achievements were small consolation for the battered survivors of the Seventh Marines as they limped down from the ridges to await evacuation.

The condition of Colonel Herman Hanneken's Seventh Regiment when it had been relieved on October 5 rivaled that of Chesty Puller's First Marines at the time of its withdrawal two weeks earlier. It also illustrated the merit of the methodical battle plan favored by Colonel Bucky Harris, commander of the Fifth Marines. Harris considered a deliberate, unhurried approach as the surest and least costly way to obliterate Japanese resistance. He believed in taking the time necessary to send engineering troops with bulldozers to clear paths through the coral rubble for howitzers and tanks. He also sent amtrack-mounted flamethrowers to burn off any remaining brush around the caves.

With these steps taken, armor and howitzers were moved into close range and ordered to fire into caves until their entrances were sealed with tons of rock and their occupants either dead or trapped inside. Only then were the rifle squads sent in to finish the job. It was a slow, carefully calculated process—the direct opposite of the frontal-assault strategy that had shattered the First Marines—but it paid dividends. In three days of heavy fighting, Harris's battalions secured high ground that other units had been denied for nearly three weeks.

During the same period, Major Gordon Gayle's Second Battalion, Fifth Marines, breached another enemy stronghold to capture a portion of Baldy Ridge and the complex of spurs and knobs surrounding it in a firefight spanning almost seventy-two hours. About 100 Japanese were killed, while 2/5 sustained about two dozen casualties, mostly wounded.

Still, the results weren't fast enough to suit General Rupertus, who was determined to see his division credited for the final knockout punch in the Pocket. Fresh regimental combat teams of the Army's Eighty-first Wildcat Division were massed on the sidelines, ready to replace the Marines, and General Roy Geiger, commander of the III Marine Amphibious Corps, repeatedly urged Rupertus to let them take over the fight.

Rupertus refused to yield. He stayed on the phone lines to Fifth Marines headquarters, prodding Harris to quicken the pace of the attacks. "Hurry it up," he demanded. "Don't let the advance stall. Don't lose your momentum."

On October 7, D-plus-22, K/3/5 and the rest of Major John Gustafson's Third Battalion launched an attack across a long, rugged valley just north of Walt's Ridge, aimed at enemy caves and bunkers on the ridges beyond. The valley was commonly known as the Horseshoe because of its concave shape. To the north, east, and west loomed the cave-riddled heights of the Five Sisters, Five Brothers, and Hill 300. Together, they formed a multifaceted center wall that had to be penetrated to reach the heart of the Japanese cave system.

As always, the infantry attack was preceded by an artillery barrage, but this one was longer and more intense than most of the previous ones. The heavy shelling by the Eleventh Marines' 75-millimeter guns lasted for two and a half hours. Dozens of the Eleventh's pack howitzers had been hauled by hand up sheer cliffs from which they could fire across yawning canyons directly into enemy positions. They were joined by all of 3/5's available mortars, now operating in close conjunction with the artillery.

The length and ferocity of the barrage reflected Harris's theory that not sparing firepower before an assault would save the lives of infantrymen later. It may have helped compensate for the withdrawal, several days earlier, of the Marine First Tank Battalion, which was described as "badly depleted and debilitated."

Prior to early October, the Marine tankers had supported every major infantry assault on Peleliu. But with many of the armored unit's vehicles disabled or in disrepair from weeks of fighting in rough terrain, its effectiveness in the extremes of the Pocket was too doubtful to justify keeping it in action.

The terrain of the Horseshoe was well suited to armor, however, and six Army tanks were sent to support K/3/5's portion of the attack. Armored vehicles outfitted with bulldozers had been sent out in advance to cut paths through the narrow ravines at the foot of the slopes on the far side of the valley, allowing the tanks to bring their cannon and machine guns to bear on enemy caves from devastatingly close range.

To avoid disaster in the tight quarters of the Pocket, tanks and rifle squads had to support and protect each other. The tanks, of course, served as armored shields for the riflemen, and their heavy weapons were a decisive factor in silencing enemy guns inside the caves. But without the riflemen who rode atop the tanks or followed in their tracks, the Shermans were highly vulnerable to Japanese suicide teams armed with explosive charges.

Jumping off at 9:00 A.M., K/3/5 drove to the right through the mouth of the Horseshoe, toward the Five Brothers, and achieved surprising early success. Within about an hour, the company penetrated to within 100 yards of the Brothers, where the advance was halted by a shallow pond. Several of the tanks were hit, but none was seriously damaged.

At mid-morning, a withdrawal was ordered to replenish fuel and ammunition, and a second attack was launched shortly after noon, joined by two flamethrowing amtracks and a platoon of engineers to handle demolitions and mine removal. Again, the company advanced briskly but was later stymied by heavy enemy fire from the dominating high ground.

Meanwhile, L/3/5 attacked to the left through a narrow pass between the Brothers and the Five Sisters. It advanced beyond where any American unit had gone before, to the foot of the so-called China Wall, a line of almost-vertical cliffs encompassing the inner sanctum of the Japanese cave system. At this point, the attack bogged down under a firestorm from multiple layers of enemy positions carved into the buttressed heights. Unable to gain a foothold, the company was driven back.

Simultaneously attacking up the main valley, I/3/5 drove forward for about 200 yards—as far as its supporting tanks could travel—then hit the entrenched Japanese with all the power the rifle squads and armor could muster. Although no detailed estimate of enemy casualties was made, scores of Japanese were believed killed before the tanks ran out of ammo and the infantry's position became untenable.

Major Frank O. Hough, author of *The Assault on Peleliu,* an official Marine Corps monograph on the battle, described the combined attacks by the three companies of the Third Battalion as the
"largest single dose of destruction" delivered thus far to the Japanese
defending the Horseshoe.

Among the positives: More than a dozen large Japanese caves,
including several housing heavy mortars and field pieces, were
"sanitized." At least seventy-five Japanese were killed by Marine
small-arms fire, and an unknown number of others were buried inside seared, shell-blasted caverns.

Overall, considering the ferocity of the fighting, American casualties were lower than expected. Incredibly, not a single member of
K/3/5 was reported killed or wounded in the day's action. But,
again, the gains proved only temporary, as all three units had to fall
back to their previous lines.

Colonel Harris had already held serious doubts about the wisdom
of sending his battalions into more major attacks on the Pocket from
the south. The actions of October 7, plus careful air and ground reconnaissance of the Pocket's peculiar terrain, convinced Harris to
change his strategy drastically. The Fifth Marines' best hope of securing the Pocket without massive, crippling losses of its own, he
concluded, was to reverse "the direction of all prior attacks" and
strike from the north instead.

As Harris later explained: "The methodical reduction of enemy
positions was possible in driving southward due to the compartmen-
tation of the terrain. It was this slow but steady eating away of the Jap
defenses that gave the real payoff."

Despite relentless pressure from division headquarters for more
speed, Harris was determined to bide his time, conserve his forces,
and give his tactical concept a chance to work. He placed 3/5 in reserve to give the men a brief rest before sending them north, and he
ordered Colonel Boyd's 1/5 to hold its position and content itself for
the moment with anti-sniper fire.

He directed Gordon Gayle's 2/5 to conduct small-scale patrol
missions aimed at locating enemy strong points and prepare for an

impending attack, a couple of days hence, against a westward extension of Baldy Ridge, designated as Hill 140.

On October 8, D-plus-23, Harris called in new artillery strikes to maintain pressure on the Pocket from both north and south, while Marine Corsairs dumped more napalm and 1,000-pound bombs on the Brothers and Sisters.

At the same time, several 105-millimeter howitzers, the heaviest field guns in the Eleventh Marines' arsenal, were assigned to fire point-blank at the cliffs west of Baldy in an effort to alter the acute angle of their sides. Giant shells relentlessly pounded the coral on the sheer face of the ridge, pulverizing large sections of it and turning them into rock slides. Slowly, the shelling transformed the precipice into a more gradual slope—one that would give 2/1 a much easier route to the top when the time came.

On October 9, the men of 3/5 left their bivouac area in the south and headed for an area north of Baldy. The next day, they would move against the Pocket again—this time from a different direction.

CHAPTER FOURTEEN

LOST LEADERS AND
FALLEN FRIENDS

Many Marines who endured the constant, prolonged grind of combat on Peleliu developed a potentially lethal psychological condition known to division veterans as the "don't-give-a-damns." It filled tired, dispirited men with feelings of futility and inevitable doom. At the same time, it made them less concerned about danger and more prone to take risks. Their senses eroded by stress and exhaustion, some forgot the basic precepts of their training and such simple precautions as staying alert and under cover.

One veteran officer, quoted in George McMillan's *The Old Breed*, told of seeing a group of riflemen following tanks "sit down in their lees and light cigarettes" when the tanks ran into a ravine and had to stop briefly. "It is a common observance," the officer said, "that in a long campaign, men tend to get more careless about taking cover as the campaign progresses, partly due to fatigue and partly, I suppose, to fatalism."

Nowhere was this phenomenon more prevalent than in the Umurbrogol Pocket, and no unit experienced more of it than 3/5, the last Marine battalion to be withdrawn from the ridges. The longer its men fought there without rest and relief, the more acute—and costly—this particular malady became.

The progression of the condition was totally predictable. As front-line troops gradually adjusted to the ever-present threat of sudden death, their initial terror gave way to more tolerable levels of fear, then to controlled tension, and finally to numb resignation. Denied rest and relief, they came to accept flying bullets, exploding shells, and dead or mangled comrades as battlefield norms, inescapable parts of their daily routine.

Eventually, if these troops lived long enough, some developed an amazing indifference to personal danger. Sometimes, their lack of self-concern could become the very essence of bravery, at least as most people define the term. But it also could kill—and frequently did.

"Many men I knew became intensely fatalistic," recalled PFC Gene Sledge. "Somehow, though, one never could quite visualize his own death. It was always the next man. But getting wounded did seem inevitable. In a rifle company, it just seemed to be a matter of time. One couldn't hope to escape the law of averages forever."

In a battle that ground on with no end in sight, some men openly hoped for a million-dollar wound that would allow them an honorable escape from Peleliu's meat grinder to the safety and comfort of a hospital ship.

"Tempting fate got to be kind of a game after a while," recalled Sledge's mortar squad buddy, PFC Vincent Santos. "When we were up in the ridges where one false move could get your head blown off, I remember one guy sticking his foot out in the open and saying, 'I'm gonna get hit, so I can get outta this place.' We used to dare each other to do it."

Corporal Jim Burke, another mortar man, showed so little emotion in the face of danger that he earned the nickname "the Fatalist" among his mates. Burke had demonstrated his nerveless detachment earlier in the fighting when he calmly borrowed Sledge's carbine to kill a Japanese infiltrator creeping up behind company lines along the West Road.

According to Burke's best buddy, Corporal R. V. Burgin, the Fatalist's legend may have started on New Britain, when a sniper's bullet smashed through a canteen cup just as Burke picked it up for a drink. Without flinching or changing his expression, Burke had turned to Burgin and remarked: "On second thought, I don't think I'm very thirsty, after all."

During their final few days in the Pocket, however, this same lack of concern about their personal safety reached levels that neither Burke nor Burgin had ever experienced before.

"Jimmy and I had never been excitable types," Burgin recalled, "but on Peleliu, it was different from just being able to stay calm under pressure. There toward the end, we got to the point where we didn't feel much of anything. We still wanted to kill Japs, but there were times when it didn't seem to matter if you lived or died. You were so damned tired and worn-out, you just didn't care. I can honestly say I never felt that way anywhere else. Sometimes I think not caring was the only thing that kept us from going completely nuts."

By October 9, D-plus-24, the Fifth Marines had been fighting almost continuously for nearly four weeks under some of the worst combat conditions in the history of modern warfare. Four days earlier, they had replaced the last elements of the Seventh Marines, and now the full responsibility for preserving the First Marine Division's fading hopes of achieving final victory in the Pocket rested squarely on Colonel Bucky Harris's thin ranks. It was an onerous load on sagging shoulders. Like Burgin, the rest of the men in the regiment were "damned tired and worn-out."

In the words of one officer on Harris's staff: "I don't think there can be any true picture of that final drive without some description of the great weariness of the Marines who participated in it. The division had optimistically said that the Fifth would be one of the first outfits to leave Peleliu, yet after securing the northern end of the island, everyone knew that we would be committed again. The men and officers were superb . . . but very, very tired."

Weary, bedraggled, and desensitized as they were, the men of the Fifth who were still able to stand upright and function had become methodical killing machines. It was impossible to surprise or rattle them anymore. They'd seen every trick the Japanese could pull.

"Every Marine fighting in these hills is an expert," said Major Gordon Gayle, commanding 2/5. "If he wasn't, he wouldn't be alive."

As one outgrowth of this hard-won expertise, their hatred of the enemy had become a more passive, impersonal thing, frequently tempered with bitter, but genuine, respect. Even in the midst of their own agony, many Marines were perceptive enough to realize that the Japanese had to be suffering, too. Most of Colonel Nakagawa's remaining troops had lived underground for weeks, subsisting on small daily rations of rice and dried fish, with only rainwater to drink and barely enough oxygen to breathe. Now, undoubtedly short of ammunition and medical supplies, and with no chance of resupply, they had little besides bushido, their ancient warrior's code of honor, to keep them going.

"I still hated the little bastards, but they were damned good fighters," admitted PFC Herbert Mizner, an eighteen-year-old 2/5 flamethrower operator from Chicago. "I don't know how they took it, but they did, and they still fought like sons of bitches all the way."

On the morning of October 9, Gayle's battalion was still trying to solve the riddle of Baldy Ridge and the maze of outcroppings around it. A rifle platoon from G/2/5, commanded by Second Lieutenant Robert T. Wattie, set out to try a new approach to the puzzle by making its way up the previously mentioned precipice that had been reshaped by artillery fire into a more gradual slope.

Climbing the blasted coral with relative ease and meeting little resistance, the platoon quickly reached the top of a narrow ridge forming a western spur of Baldy. This formation was tactically important for both defensive and offensive reasons. For one thing, it commanded a clear field of fire to the West Road, posing a danger to traffic as long as the enemy had use of it. For another, it connected directly with Baldy, providing a hitherto-untested route of attack to portions of the ridgeline still held by the Japanese.

Wattie and his men moved south along the crest for about 100 yards and knocked out several Japanese positions before coming under heavy fire from an adjacent ridge and a large enemy cave in an intervening gulch. In keeping with Harris's overall battle plan, Wattie ordered his men to fall back to a more secure position a short distance to the north and wait for artillery, aircraft, armor, and flamethrowers to come to their support.

By now, the engineers' bulldozers had enabled amphibious tractors to bring flamethrowers close enough to reach all remaining vegetation on Baldy and the jumble of ridges just east of it. When the flamethrowers finished their work, Baldy lived up to its name.

Meanwhile, the cave in the gulch was targeted from the air, but because of its location, Marine Corsairs couldn't bomb it without endangering their own troops. Later in the day, howitzers were positioned to fire on the cave, and their salvos touched off a massive landslide. When demolition teams moved in to finish the job, they found the cave's entrance already sealed tight.

The next morning, Wattie led his men back over the same ground they'd given up the day before, along with the rest of G/2/5 and E/2/5. This time, they kept going, using rifles and grenades to blast their way through a skirmish line of Japanese. After overrunning the enemy position, they swept along the crest of the ridge against weak opposition, destroying several other Japanese fortifications along the way.

By noon on October 10, the whole ridgeline was secure, and within another hour or two, E/2/5 was also in control of the neighboring piece of high ground known as Hill 120. The formidable crest of Baldy itself, which, as it turned out, had been used primarily as a Japanese observation post, would never again be available for directing enemy mortar and artillery fire against American forces.

Beginning that day, Baldy also received a new identity. From then on, it would be identified on U.S. military maps as Wattie's Ridge.

After its attack on the Horseshoe on October 7, most of Major Gustafson's 3/5 had gone into reserve for a day or two, then taken up new positions north of Baldy. During this interval, K/3/5's mortar section was temporarily detached from the rest of the company and ordered to set up its 60-millimeter guns along the West Road in positions screened by large rocks and a strip of thick foliage.

Mortar men were now being called on to help shorthanded rifle platoons cope with large numbers of Japanese snipers. As the enemy's major underground emplacements were systematically destroyed and its heavy weapons silenced, more of Colonel Nakagawa's remaining troops took their rifles and moved out into the rocks to wreak havoc. Some had managed to infiltrate back into previously secured areas, including the ridges overlooking the West Road. Their random fire seemed to come from everywhere—and nowhere.

"The enemy were firing from positions that were almost impossible to locate, and they shot any and everybody they could—even casualties being evacuated by amtracks," said Gene Sledge. "More than one desperate amtrack driver, as he raced down the West Road toward the regimental aid station, arrived only to find his helpless cargo slaughtered where they lay."

With Baldy finally in friendly hands, the bulk of 3/5 moved into an area between it and the Five Brothers and prepared to drive south. But by now, none of the Marines laboring in the ranks had any clear idea of where they were or where they were headed. "North and south didn't mean a thing to us anymore," said Burgin. "Every hill looked the same, and as near as we could tell, they were all full of Japs."

When K/3/5 pulled back to a rear area on the evening of October 8, Lieutenant Ed "Hillbilly" Jones had his first chance in twenty-five days of near-constant combat to remove his ravaged shoes and peel off his rotted socks. He also unbandaged the week-old bullet wound in his left hand, decided the gash was healed enough to be left open, and threw the soiled dressing away. Then he stretched out and went through a small stack of mail from home that had finally reached

him. There was a letter from one of his sisters, Clara, with a dozen or
so recent family photos tucked inside; a package from his mother,
containing a comb, some razor blades, and a calendar; and a note in
his mom's neat handwriting, filled with small talk about the fall canning and his brother Kenny's sore throat.

In spite of everything Ed had been through in the nearly four
weeks since D-Day, he felt okay. He'd lost some weight, but his
health was fine, and he still had an appetite like a horse. He still usually managed to feel upbeat, too, because he knew the fighting
couldn't last much longer. And once it was over, he'd be headed
home for the first time in . . . He paused to count.

Thirty-nine months? Could it possibly have been that long?

America had still been at peace that summer of '41, and everybody
said if war came, it would be in Europe, not the Pacific, where Ed
was going. He and his two oldest sisters, Clara and Anna, had paid
for a trip for the whole Jones clan from the family home at Whiteford, Maryland, to Atlantic City. It had taken several cars to carry
them all, and they'd had a great time on the big steel pier. Frank Sinatra had been there, singing with Tommy Dorsey's band. Ed still remembered how skinny Sinatra had been and how all the girls had
swooned over him.

Ed smiled at the memory as he downed his C rations. Then he
slept like a log. He awoke the next morning, October 9, thinking
about Christmas. God willing, he'd be back in Whiteford by then.
That afternoon, he dug out some paper he'd found in an abandoned
Japanese cave and wrote a letter. It was mainly to his mother, but he
made the salutation all-inclusive:

Dear Mamma, Daddy & Kids,
  Well, I hope this finds you all well and keeping warm around
the big stove. Hope Kenny is feeling much better. I am also glad
that canning is all over. I know that is much too hard for you to do
now—especially with all the house work you have to do.
  I can hardly wait to get home and for you and Daddy and I to

go to Baltimore shopping. We should take all the children along to
help carry the packages. I would rather wait until I get home to
buy clothes for the kids, as I know nothing about sizes, etc., yet I get
a lot of enjoyment from buying for them. I'll draw a check and
send you so you can buy all the Christmas presents. I wish I could
send it to you now, but that is impossible as we have no paymaster
here.

Hillbilly pictured the little ones' faces as they opened their gifts. He signed the letter "Lots of love to all, Edward."

On the morning of October 10, while most of the Third Battalion remained in regimental reserve, K/3/5 went back into action to eliminate an especially active concentration of enemy snipers, firing from one- or two-man positions along an adjacent ridge well behind the front lines. The snipers had a clear shot down a long draw, threatening any passing traffic along the West Road.

The series of recent attacks by 3/5 had pushed K Company's casualty rate above 40 percent, and Lieutenant Jones's First Platoon was among the more seriously depleted units, operating with slightly more than one-third of its authorized strength. Only about fifteen riflemen and one officer, Jones himself, remained fit for combat as the platoon occupied a position opposite the sniper-infested ridge and facing the Five Brothers from the north.

Several tanks had been brought up to add firepower to the counter-sniper operation and provide cover for the riflemen. Within the next day or so, the company was scheduled to relieve elements of 2/5 on the front lines, but for now, its main responsibilities were holding its present position and thinning out the sniper population.

As the sun rose higher, the snipers grew increasingly aggressive, firing from about 100 yards south of Jones's platoon. Now and then, from his vantage point behind a stationary Sherman tank, the lieutenant could spot a puff of smoke as a Japanese knee mortar fired from the ridge, then watch its shell explode seconds later down the line. At irregular intervals, rifle bullets twanged like broken guitar strings off the tank's armored hide or struck nearby. Numerous small caves were visible on the ridge, but the unyielding sameness of the terrain made it impossible to pinpoint the shooters' locations.

During the next couple of hours, two K/3/5 riflemen were hit within minutes of each other, and another, PFC Charles R. McClary, was fatally wounded by a sniper's bullet through the abdomen. The casualties made Jones uncharacteristically edgy as he stared toward the ridge over the treads of the sheltering tank. He saw no sign of the enemy, but he thought if he could climb up beside the turret of the tank, the added height would give him a better view, and he might be able to tell the tank's gunners where to aim their .50-caliber machine gun and 75-millimeter cannon. It would be like a blindfolded man swatting at flies with a pile driver, but it was worth a try.

As Jones dropped to the ground behind the tank, Major Clyde Brooks, a staff officer from battalion headquarters, trotted up and squatted beside him.

"The Japs on that ridge are giving us fits," Brooks said. "Major Gustafson sent me over to see what we could do to get rid of 'em. You got any ideas?"

Hillbilly gave the officer a wry grin. He knew Brooks fairly well and respected his judgment. "I've been thinking about climbing up on the tank to see if I can spot something for the gunners to shoot at," he said. "What do you think?"

"I think it's awful damn risky," Brooks said.

Jones wiped at the sweat on his face and shrugged. "Sure, but I figure it's either that or sit here all day in this Nip shooting gallery."

"Okay then, give it a try," the major said. "Just watch yourself."

Leaving his tommy gun behind, since the snipers were well beyond its range, Jones clambered onto the rear deck of the tank, crawled up behind the turret, and pounded on its side to alert the tank commander. "I'm gonna try to find you a target," he yelled down the opening. "Get ready."

Crouching low, Brooks eased up to the protected side of the tank. "Are you sure you want to do this?" he asked.

"So far, so good," Hillbilly said.

"I'm going for some satchel charges," Brooks told him. "We may need TNT to cure those sniper holes up there." He turned and quickly moved away.

As Jones's men watched, he inched cautiously forward, leaned around the turret, and peered intently toward the ridge. Seconds later, the silence was broken by a single shot.

The bullet struck Jones in the left side below his rib cage, and its impact propelled him backward and sideways. He tried for an instant to steady himself, but then he fell off the side of the tank and tumbled to the rocky ground.

"Corpsman! Corpsman!" somebody yelled. "Hillbilly's hit!"

To the amazement of the Marines around him, Jones struggled to his feet and reeled toward the tank again. Dazed, in obvious pain, and with blood saturating his shirt, he somehow managed to pull himself back aboard the Sherman. But just as he stood up, a second bullet tore through Jones's chest. He slumped to the deck of the tank, one arm dangling over its side, and this time, he didn't move.

Brooks heard the shots and came running back in time to see a corpsman and another Marine risking their own lives to lift Jones's body down from atop the tank and get it on a stretcher.

"He's dead, sir," the corpsman said. "That last round went right through his heart."

Word spread quickly up and down the line that Hillbilly had been killed. Corporal Burgin was about fifty yards away, directing mortar fire against other snipers on the same adjacent ridge, when the news reached him. PFC Sterling Mace saw Corporal Ted Barrow sitting near a poncho-covered corpse, and Mace was stunned when he lifted the poncho and recognized Hillbilly. Burgin reached the scene a few minutes later, but by then stretcher-bearers had already removed the body.

The young lieutenant with the engaging smile and easygoing manner left something of himself with almost everyone in K/3/5. As Gene Sledge observed years later: "Between this man and all the Marines

I knew, there existed a deep mutual respect and warm friendliness. He possessed a unique combination . . . of bravery, leadership, ability, integrity, dignity, straightforwardness, and compassion."

Even in Burgin's numbed state, he found it hard to believe that Jones was really gone. A random stream of memories flowed through his mind: The night on Banika when he'd helped Hillbilly to bed after the whole crew had gotten soused on grain alcohol and grapefruit juice. Sunday mornings on Pavuvu, when Jones never failed to get spruced up and attend church services. An infinite number of storytellings and sing-alongs.

Burgin remembered one particular evening, some thirty-six hours before D-Day, when the singers on *LST 661* had concentrated on old, religious tunes like "Swing Low, Sweet Chariot" and "When the Roll Is Called Up Yonder." He closed his eyes for a few seconds, imagining he could still hear Hillbilly singing his favorite hymn:

> *There's a land that is fairer than day, and by faith we can*
> *   see it afar;*
> *For the Father waits over the way to prepare us a dwelling*
> *   place there.*
> *In the sweet by and by, we shall meet on that beautiful*
> *   shore . . .*

Wherever Lieutenant Edward Allison Jones might be now, Burgin hoped it would, indeed, be a sweet, fair, and beautiful place. If it was, he knew it had to be a long way from the hell on earth called Peleliu.

As it turned out, nobody from K/3/5 had any luck locating the snipers Jones was searching for at the time of his death. Sporadic rifle fire from the crafty Japanese hiding on the ridge continued for the rest of the day, occasionally augmented by a few mortar rounds. The Marines responded by blasting shut every cave opening they could find with relentless fire from tanks, artillery, and mortars. The methodical pounding of the ridge continued until the sniping eventually stopped. Yet at no time during the two-day action did any Marine catch a glimpse of a live Japanese.

On October 11, D-plus-26, two companies of Major Gayle's 2/5 attacked craggy, enemy-held Hill 140, a westward extension of Baldy Ridge. To the uninitiated eye, the hill had little to distinguish it from dozens of others in the Umurbrogol. After studying the latest maps, however, Gayle was convinced that Hill 140 was of immense strategic importance—and could, in fact, hold the key to penetrating the heart of the Pocket.

Major George Bowdoin, executive officer of the Fourth Battalion, Eleventh Marines, and a veteran artilleryman, shared Gayle's opinion. If a 75-millimeter howitzer could be hauled to the top of Hill 140, Bowdoin concluded, it could fire directly into the nearest of the Brothers, much of the Horseshoe, and down the draw between Walt's and Boyd's Ridges. Moreover, its shells could reach almost any point in the Pocket still held by the Japanese.

Despite its value to American forces, Hill 140 was less heavily defended than expected. Troops of 2/5 secured it by mid-afternoon, and a Japanese attempt to regain the hill that night was beaten off with relative ease. The next morning, Bowdoin moved immediately to place an artillery piece on its crest.

The Eleventh Marines' two pack howitzer battalions had been evacuated a few days earlier, but luckily, heavy seas had forced them to leave some of their guns behind. Bowdoin had one of the 75s brought up as close as possible to Hill 140, then broken down, manhandled in pieces up the west side of the hill, and reassembled on top.

The summit was so small and its surface so impenetrable that the gun couldn't be dug in or braced enough at first to fire effectively. On the howitzer's initial shot, the violent recoil injured a member of the gun crew. The problem was overcome when sandbags—the first to be used by U.S. forces in the Umurbrogol—were brought all the way from the beach and hauled by hand to the top of the hill to protect the gun and hold it in place. It took sixty-eight Marines eight hours to get the gun and sandbags up the steep slope, but by daylight on October 12, the job was done. For the next eighteen hours or so, the 75 kept up a steady rate of fire on previously unreachable Japanese positions. All the while, the gun crew fought off repeated grenade attacks by enemy infiltrators.

A second gun, manned by a makeshift crew who called themselves "infantillery," was also positioned in the high ground near Hill 140 under the command of Lieutenant Colonel Edson Lyman. This weapon concentrated on an enemy position on an opposite ridge, where high-ranking Japanese officers had been spotted, indicating the presence of a major command post.

In Lyman's words, the crew's accurate fire "routed out a covey of Nips." Those who were able fled down the far side of the ridge to escape, but the gun soon came under heavy small-arms fire, and, after getting off about forty rounds and suffering several casualties, the crew withdrew to safer positions.

The capture of Hill 140 would be the last organized action of the Peleliu campaign by Major Gayle's Second Battalion. It would be withdrawn from further combat and placed in reserve, along with Colonel Boyd's 1/5, which had already turned over its sector in a rear area to partially rested troops of the Seventh Marines.

On the morning of October 12, D-plus-27, the skeleton-strength companies of 2/5 were replaced on the front line by the equally depleted units of Major Gustafson's Third Battalion. When the transfer was completed, 3/5 would become the last battalion of the First Marine Division actively engaged in the battle.

For the men of K/3/5, it would always be remembered as the most tragic day of the war.

First light that morning brought orders for Gene Sledge's mortar section to pick up its guns and prepare to rejoin the rest of K Company as it took over one of the sectors where 2/5 was being relieved. A few minutes later, Sledge climbed into a jeep along with two squad mates, PFC George Sarrett and Corporal Snafu Shelton, for a wild ride along the sniper-plagued West Road. The driver jerked the jeep to a halt at a supply area, where the mortar men received directions to the company's newly assigned positions, then continued on foot.

Instead of moving into a comparatively calm, reasonably familiar area, the Third Battalion was taking over an active front on ground that had been seized only the previous afternoon. The whole line held by 2/5 was still hotly contested by the Japanese, and the relieving troops of 3/5 had no opportunity to get acquainted with their new surroundings before trouble erupted.

The line held by the Second Battalion formed a deep, narrow salient that was subject to enemy fire from three sides. Further complicating the situation, the line was broken where one side of Hill 140 dropped away into a deep chasm, leaving one company of Marines with no friendly troops to its immediate left. The day's main objective was to straighten out the front by pushing south and west, thus tightening the troops' alignment on more favorable terrain.

As riflemen and machine gunners from K/3/5 climbed toward the top of Hill 140 to take over the shallow holes and crevices being vacated by 2/5, they received strict orders not to look over the crest of the ridge.

"There's Jap sharpshooters everywhere out there," the men were warned. "Even one glance can get you killed instantly."

Early that morning, a small group of Marines from K/3/5 crawled on their bellies to the highest available point on the ridge to undertake a nerve-wracking task. Their challenge was to steal a look over the crest and try to orient themselves to the unfamiliar terrain spread out before them without getting shot by an enemy sniper. Only then could they determine the most effective locations for their mortars and machine guns, and decide how to deploy their rifle platoons. They also had phone contact with the artillery to direct fire on Japanese positions in the valley below and the ridges beyond.

Captain Andy Haldane was the only commissioned officer among the group. Lieutenant Stumpy Stanley, Haldane's exec, was at battalion headquarters, and Lieutenant Duke Ellington was with other members of his mortar section en route to the front. All the others were out of action.

Hugging the ground within a few feet of Haldane were several of his senior NCOs, including Platoon Sergeant Johnny Marmet of the mortar section; Sergeant Dick Higgins, the captain's personal aide and runner; Sergeant Jim McEnery, platoon guide of the First Rifle Platoon; and Corporal Jim Anderson, another trusted runner.

The captain was lying flat on his stomach just below the crest of the ridgeline. McEnery, who'd been with Haldane since Guadalcanal, knew the captain was an "old machine gun man" and that one of Ack-Ack's main concerns was where to set up the company's .50-caliber weapons. The machine gunners of 2/5 were so badly pinned down that they could only aim their weapons by sighting along the undersides of their barrels.

Haldane crawled forward a few feet and raised his head slightly, no more than four or five inches, to glance over the edge of the ridgeline. He said something that sounded like:

"We need to get them as close as—"

The sniper's bullet came instantaneously—not as a loud *bang!* but more of a sharp *smack!* Every man within earshot knew what the sound meant, even before they saw Haldane's head explode.

"I was right beside him," Anderson recalled, "and I can't even describe the shock of it. The sniper must've had his sights zeroed in on that exact spot. I knew immediately the captain was dead, but I still couldn't make myself believe it."

Higgins was also only a few feet away. He saw the bullet strike Haldane squarely in the face. Haldane's head jerked backward, then flopped forward against the coral. Instinctively, Higgins scrambled toward the body, his mind steadfastly denying what he was seeing:

He can't be dead! He's had a hundred near-misses—bullet holes through his hat, bullet holes in his clothes. This has got to be just another one!

Only it wasn't. Higgins started to yell for a corpsman, but the cry died in his throat.

Gene Sledge and his fellow mortar men were still making their way around Hill 140 to find their new positions when Johnny Marmet stumbled down off the ridge toward them. Even before Sledgehammer got a clear look at the platoon leader's face, he could tell that something was terribly wrong. Marmet was more nervous than the squad had ever seen him. He clutched the web strap of his tommy gun with shaking fingers, his face pale and twisted with emotion, his eyes wet and red.

"Hey, Johnny," R. V. Burgin said cautiously as the squad shuffled to a halt. "What's goin' on?"

Marmet stared into space, unable to meet Burgin's questioning gaze. "Okay, you guys, let's get squared away here," he mumbled, fidgeting with the gun strap. He opened his mouth and tried to say something else, but he seemed to choke on the words, and nothing came out.

"What the hell's wrong?" Burgin asked. The rest of the guys paused in their tracks, glancing quizzically back and forth at each other.

Marmet bit his lip and lowered his head. "The skipper's dead," he said. "The Japs got him a few minutes ago up on the ridge."

Burgin felt as if somebody had kneed him in the gut. "Those slant-eyed sons of bitches," he said.

Sledge dropped his ammo bag and turned away with tears running down his face. He pulled off his helmet and sat down on it, feeling as if he might vomit. Behind him, he heard other Marines cursing. Several slammed their gear violently against the coral. Almost everybody in the section was crying.

After a minute or two, Marmet stood up and shouldered his

tommy gun. "All right, let's move out," he said, rubbing his knuckles against his bloodshot eyes. "We still got a job to do."

Stunned and silent, they picked up their weapons and gear, then slowly followed Marmet through the broken shards of limestone on the side of the hill.

Sledge's grief was still fresh and raw when the squad reached its assigned positions. As he helped set up a 60-millimeter mortar among a pile of rocks near the foot of the ridge, he moved like a robot, scarcely aware of the 2/5 mortar men he was relieving.

Then he noticed the agonized expression on one young Marine's face and the anguish in his voice as he spoke: "You guys watch out for Japs at night. Two of the bastards got in this gun pit last night and cut up our gunner and assistant gunner. One guy's dead, and the other one's in bad shape."

Armed with knives, the infiltrators had jumped into the pit while the mortar crew was busy firing at enemy positions, the Marine said. Two ammo handlers had finally killed the Japanese and thrown their bodies into some bushes, but by then the damage was done.

Smears of dark red blood streaked the white coral rocks, and several drying puddles of it coated the bottom of the pit. Once the mortar was emplaced, Sledge found a few scraps of pasteboard and laid them over the worst of the bloodstains to keep from having to look at them.

His heart was like a lead weight in his chest. Death and violence had been his constant companions for almost a month, but nothing had ever affected him like Haldane's death. He understood the young Marine's grief over his two comrades, but mortar men were only human, and Sledge had always thought of Ack-Ack as immortal. Larger than life. An unshakable rock of stability in a world destroying itself.

If Ack-Ack was dead, what was left to believe in?

As a lazy swarm of blowflies circled the bloody rocks, Sledge pondered the stupidity of such expressions as "shedding your blood for your country."

After the captain's body was taken off the ridge, Dick Higgins slowly made his way back down the hill toward the company command post. Higgins was dazed with shock, and his surroundings seemed foggy and unreal. But his mind was crowded with vivid images of Andy Haldane—not the dead officer with the blown-open skull but the friend and leader around whom Higgins's life had centered for many months.

He saw himself carrying a base plate for a 60-millimeter gun on a twenty-five-mile hike outside Melbourne. The plate had been getting heavier with every step Higgins took when he'd heard a voice behind him and turned to see then-Lieutenant Haldane grinning at him.

"You look tired, son. Could you use some help?"

"Of course, sir, but I can manage."

"Give me that thing, and I'll spell you for a while."

It had been one of their first personal encounters, and Higgins had expected Haldane to hand the plate back after five or ten minutes. Instead, he carried it effortlessly—at least it looked that way—for a good three-quarters of an hour.

The scene in Higgins's mind fast-forwarded to Cape Gloucester. He and Haldane were squatting behind a tractor during an enemy artillery attack. A dud shell crashed against the tractor, ricocheted off, and bounced along the ground between them.

Higgins jumped about ten feet and threw himself to the ground. When he looked up, Haldane was standing there, smiling and shaking his head.

"You may as well get up, son," he said calmly. "If that thing was going to go off, both of us would've been blown to bits already."

The reverie continued until Higgins got back to the command post and saw Haldane's gear piled where he'd hurriedly dumped it before going up on the ridge. Then, without warning, Higgins went to pieces. He fell to the ground, screaming, swearing, and sobbing uncontrollably.

"All at once, it hit me, and I totally lost it," Higgins recalled much later. "They sent me to sick bay for four days, and the doctors advised me not to go back on duty even then, but I insisted. It was better to be doing something than just sitting there."

Not even the passage of sixty years could erase the pain. "It was the kind of thing that never gets out of your mind completely," Higgins said, "and it still hurts to think about it. I've wondered a thousand times why I lived and he died, but I guess it's true that only the good die young. Andy Haldane was as good a man—and as good a Marine—as you'll ever find."

In an oddity of war, Haldane's death temporarily put a buck sergeant in command of K/3/5. Jim McEnery, one of the NCOs on the ridge with the captain when he was killed, was thrust into the most peculiar situation of his Marine career.

McEnery had landed on Peleliu as a platoon guide, or third in his platoon's chain of command, but within the past few days, casualties had already elevated him to senior NCO in the platoon. In the period after Haldane's death, Lieutenant Stanley and First Sergeant David Bailey were at battalion headquarters on company business. Lieutenant Ellington and Platoon Sergeant Marmet were with their mortar section some distance to the north, and Platoon Sergeant Harry Spiece was somewhere else on the line and couldn't be reached.

"I was it," McEnery said. "There was nobody else available. So there I was, a mere three-striper, trying to take the place of one of the best COs in the Corps in one of the toughest spots we'd been in."

McEnery remained in charge for several hours, until Stanley and Bailey could be notified and make their way back from battalion headquarters to rejoin the company.

"I did my best to direct heavy weapons fire for the whole company and get fire teams together for patrols," he said. "I also conducted a class in grenade throwing for some aviation Marines who came up to try and help us. It definitely wasn't a job I would've wanted permanently."

McEnery established radio contact with an Army 105-millimeter howitzer in the valley below Hill 140 and directed its fire on Japanese positions visible from the high ground.

When Major Gustafson, the battalion commander, received word that K/3/5 was operating without a CO, he rang McEnery on the phone and asked who was responsible for the continued firing.

"I am, sir," McEnery said. "I'm the senior guy up here, and I didn't think we could afford to quit shooting until one of our officers gets back to take over."

"Carry on, Sergeant," the major said. "Just be careful."

Fierce fighting raged throughout the morning and afternoon of October 12. At dusk, the impasse continued, with the Marines still in control of Hill 140 but unable to gain any appreciable ground against the strongly entrenched enemy. Meanwhile, however, American artillery in the high ground was taking a heavy toll on the Japanese, who were also unable to move offensively.

At about this same time, word reached the front lines that General Roy Geiger, commander of the III Marine Amphibious Corps, had moved his command post ashore for the first time earlier that day and officially declared the "assault phase" of the Peleliu operation at an end. This news brought profanity, bitter laughter, and snorts of derision from Marines huddled in gun pits and behind coral breastworks.

"Oh, yeah?" they growled. "Well somebody from division oughta come up here and tell that to the damn Nips."

By the morning of October 13, D-plus-28, the Third Battalion's gaunt, punch-drunk veterans were the only Marines still actively engaging the enemy. The rest of the Fifth Marines, like the First and Seventh before them, had been pulled off the line and out of the fight.

"Your orders are to renew the offensive," the troops of 3/5 were told early that morning. "Your objective remains the same—to straighten out the salient around Hill 140 and further constrict the enemy-held portion of the Pocket."

It was like a grim replay of the day before—and of all the days before that. It was as if nothing had changed, when, in fact, *everything* had changed.

The battle would inevitably go on, but for the Marines of K/3/5 who were left, the world would never be the same again.

CHAPTER FIFTEEN

LEGION OF THE
ALMOST-DAMNED

By the morning of October 13, the Battle of Peleliu was history, at least as far as top U.S. military leaders and the American public were concerned. The stateside media was fully focused on General MacArthur's triumphant return to the Philippines and the Allied drive across Western Europe. The obscure fortress-island, where U.S. assault troops and Japanese defenders had lost a combined total of more than 18,000 killed and wounded, already was largely forgotten.

Almost a week earlier, Admiral Chester Nimitz, commander of the Pacific Fleet, had concluded that the struggle for Peleliu was basically over. Even before that, high-ranking Navy sources were describing the enemy garrison as "virtually, if not totally, wiped out."

As of that morning, this news had failed to reach the emaciated scarecrows of 3/5—and it was probably just as well. For them, nothing had changed, and they were still too busy dodging rifle and mortar fire in the Umurbrogol ridges to feel any sense of triumph or jubilation. Many had just spent another mostly sleepless night fighting for their lives.

The trouble had started sometime after midnight. BAR man Sterling Mace and PFC Charlie Allman were sharing a hurriedly assembled breastwork of scrap lumber and cast-off strips of corrugated metal, only about sixty yards from the nearest of the Five Sisters. Before dark, they'd come across one piece of metal that was flat enough and large enough to lie on, and to avoid another night on the sharp coral, Mace had been tempted to make it his mattress. He'd given up the idea when he discovered that the metal popped and clattered whenever he moved—a dead giveaway of his location to infiltrators.

To air out his sore, sweaty feet and legs, Mace had peeled off the socks and leggings he'd worn constantly for seventeen days. He was standing watch while Allman tried to sleep when a Marine machine gun opened up a short distance down the line. A moment later, a grenade exploded, silencing the chattering gun. Then the familiar cry echoed down the line:

"Corpsman! Corpsman!"

Mace grabbed his BAR as two indistinct figures darted past in the gloom, no more than five feet away. He raised the weapon but held his fire, not knowing whether the shadows belonged to Japanese night stalkers or corpsmen responding to the call for help. Within a few seconds, he heard a short volley of shots from the direction the shadows had gone. Silence followed, broken only by Allman's rapid breathing.

Must've been Japs after all, Mace thought. *Guess I should've fired, but, damn, I didn't want to hit a medic. Those poor bastards have it tough enough as it is.*

He pulled his socks and boondockers back on, pausing frequently to hold his breath and listen. He could tell that Allman was wide awake now, too, although neither of them said anything.

A half-hour passed, then an hour. Mace was getting drowsy in spite of himself when the sound of running feet jerked him back to high alert. This time, the infiltrators came in a pack—at least three or four of them—sprinting out of the darkness and tossing grenades in all directions.

An opportune star shell exploded somewhere overhead, lighting the sky enough to reveal the infiltrators' running figures. As their grenade blasts pelted Mace's metal barricade with fragments and slivers of coral, he raised his BAR and emptied a full magazine at them. He was reaching for another magazine to reload, unsure whether he'd hit anything, when he caught a glimpse of a Japanese on the ground crawling toward him. Then the star shell faded, plunging his surroundings into pitch-blackness again.

Mace rose to his knees, staring down the barrel of a weapon he couldn't see into an impenetrable curtain of darkness—and waited.

And waited . . .

Then, directly in front of him, Mace heard metal scraping and crunching against coral, and the realization hit him like a lightning flash: The enemy soldier was crawling toward him over the same sheet of corrugated steel that Mace had thought better of using for his bed that night.

I was right, he thought. *The noise was a dead giveaway.* He pressed the trigger, and the BAR spouted twenty rounds toward the sound. He paused to listen, but he heard nothing.

"I think you got him," Allman whispered.

"We'll find out at daylight," Mace said. "Just stay put, and don't move."

When dawn broke an hour later, the dead Japanese soldier lay about ten feet from the two Marines' makeshift fort. Mace's volley had torn his body almost in half, and his hand still gripped a live grenade. He was one of fifteen enemy infiltrators killed in 3/5's area that night.

These continuing nighttime attacks, plus the fact that a new thrust into the Pocket was in the offing, were more than enough to keep any K/3/5 victory celebrations on hold.

By late afternoon on October 13, however, the Third Battalion had essentially achieved the objective it was handed that morning. The salient that had exposed the Marines' lines to relentless enemy fire since the capture of Hill 140 had been straightened considerably. K and I Companies had pushed their front forward up to 150 yards, squeezing the enemy still deeper into his shrinking lair.

Most of the Marines who made the advance were too worn out at day's end even to care how they'd managed the feat, but they knew that Marine air support had played an important role.

Starting around eight o'clock that morning, precision air strikes by napalm-packing Marine Corsairs had turned the enemy-held ridges facing Hill 140 and the intervening draw into one giant fireball. Following up on the aerial attacks, riflemen from K and I Companies had pushed forward into the smoldering gulch at 9:15 A.M., making steady gains, and holding them, against stubborn enemy resistance.

Now they faced yet another night, one indistinguishable from dozens that had gone before—a night haunted by infiltrators with knives and grenades, snipers with rifles, knee mortar blasts from invisible enemy positions, and the ever-present threat of sudden death.

No one can say for certain how much longer their commanders might have kept the Fifth Marines—and particularly 3/5—flailing at the Japanese in the Pocket if intervention hadn't finally come from higher up.

Since the withdrawal of the Seventh Marines from active combat, General Rupertus, the division commander, had been under increasing pressure from his superiors to relieve the Fifth Marines. The Army, with thousands of fresh troops standing by on Ngesebus, Angaur, and Peleliu proper, was ready and waiting to take over the final phase of the battle, and there was no valid reason for further delay.

Any honest assessment of the Fifth's strength showed that it no longer had sufficient manpower to finish off the foe and was being bled white in the effort. The regiment was also woefully short of field leadership. K/3/5's Captain Haldane and Lieutenants Barrett, Bauerschmidt, and Jones were among 358 commissioned Marine officers killed or evacuated with wounds in the Peleliu campaign, and hundreds more senior noncoms were also lost.

For several days, General Geiger, Rupertus's immediate superior, had urged the division commander to relieve the Fifth, but Rupertus still refused to make the call. Even when Geiger stepped up the pressure by leaving the command ship USS *Mount McKinley* and moving his CP ashore, Rupertus remained adamant.

Geiger's patience was severely tested, but if he chose to force the issue, only two options were open to him: He could either summarily relieve Rupertus of his command or give him a direct order to withdraw the Fifth Marines and turn over the Peleliu operation to Army General Paul Mueller's Eighty-first Wildcat Division.

Either course would lead to major problems, but the first was unprecedented and pretty much out of the question. No Marine general had ever been stripped of his command during combat, and such a step would stir up a storm at Corps headquarters and almost surely end Rupertus's military career. The second option would also endanger Rupertus's future, trigger political upheaval in Washington, and possibly give Geiger himself a black eye.

Besides, Geiger was convinced that Japanese resistance was at the point of final collapse. Within a day or two—perhaps even a few hours—he foresaw the last enemy strongholds being obliterated, sealing the Marines' victory, and bringing every square foot of the island under American control. So Geiger kept waiting and hoping for a resolution.

Rupertus's obstinacy may have stemmed, in part, from the fact that, besides having a painful broken ankle, the division commander was dangerously ill with heart disease. Although neither Geiger nor anyone else knew it at the time, Rupertus's failing health may well have affected his judgment, even as his physical condition was aggravated by the stress of seeing his division cut to pieces.

Perhaps Rupertus sensed that Peleliu was his last campaign. Perhaps the realization added to his obsessive determination to see his command credited with the victory, whatever the human cost. No one knows because the division commander apparently kept his feelings strictly to himself. What *is* known is that, within six months, Rupertus would be dead of a heart attack. And it seems reasonable to assume that Peleliu might have cost the Fifth Marines considerably more casualties if its fate hadn't been taken abruptly out of the hands of Rupertus and Geiger.

On October 12, Vice Admiral Theodore S. Wilkinson, overall on-site commander of Operation Stalemate, had been summoned to Hawaii for reassignment by Admiral Nimitz. Wilkinson was succeeded by Rear Admiral George H. Fort, who was already with the Navy armada at Peleliu and who had, in fact, directed the D-Day landing there on September 15.

Fort's first act in his new capacity was to make the decision that both Rupertus and Geiger were avoiding. In a personal visit to First Marine Division headquarters, Fort informed the two generals that the assault phase of the campaign was over, and that the Marines' combat role on Peleliu was about to end as well.

On October 14, according to a timetable set out by Fort, Army troops of the 321st Infantry Regiment would begin replacing units of the Fifth Marines still on the line in the area of Hill 140, Baldy Ridge, Five Brothers, Five Sisters, and the China Wall. Within a few days, all Marine personnel would be in rest areas awaiting evacuation.

When Geiger got the word, he breathed a deep sigh of relief. "I'm glad it's finally over," he said.

Regardless of what bitterness, disappointment, and misgivings may have seethed inside him, Rupertus also took the announcement with outward calm. "I am, too," he said simply.

Actually, though, it *wasn't* over—not quite. For 3/5 and a few rag-tag survivors of 1/7 and 3/7, there was still more fighting to be done.

On the morning of October 13, Corporal Eddy Lee Andrusko and the handful of other members of I/3/7 who were still capable of walking and firing a weapon were rousted out of a Seventh Marines rest area and sent back onto the line. Captain Carl Ferguson, the company commander, and First Lieutenant John Gravitt, the executive officer, had both been killed. The new CO, a stranger who'd assumed command of I/3/7 a few days earlier, was apologetic but adamant. The Army infantry unit that had replaced the company several days earlier had been severely mauled and overrun by counterattacking Japanese, and there was no one else available to hold the line in that area.

"I know you guys have been through hell," the CO said, "but Item Company's been ordered to retake that hill at all costs—no ifs, ands, or buts. We'll rest when it's over. Now let's get with it."

Marine artillery and mortars rained fire on enemy positions above them as Andrusko and his squad started their advance. The barren, treeless slopes over which they climbed were pockmarked with shell holes, natural caves, and bunkers. They reminded Andrusko of a lunar landscape inhabited by enemy soldiers who hid until the Marines moved past, then attacked from the rear.

"Look out, Eddy Lee!" a man in Andrusko's fire team yelled. "There's Japs behind you!"

There were three of them, and they lunged forward, their bayonets gleaming in the sun. Several Marine rifles cracked, and two of the attackers fell quickly. The third charged straight into a withering volley of fire from Andrusko and refused to go down, even when the warning clip popped out of Eddy Lee's rifle, indicating he was out of ammunition.

When the Japanese soldier finally fell, he landed within inches of Andrusko's feet. A Marine rolled the body over. "Jesus, Lee, you hit him seven times, and he still kept coming," the Marine said. "This son of a bitch must be Super-Jap."

Andrusko's hands trembled, and sweat poured down his face as he reloaded his rifle and listened to the pounding of his heart. Then he and the others struggled on to the top of the hill. They dug in among boulders, shell-blasted tree trunks, and enemy dead. They waited for a counterattack, but none came. Instead, the Marines received rations, water, and—of all things—a batch of mail. Andrusko unslung his rifle, dumped his pack, took off his helmet and his sweat-soaked shirt, and leaned back against a large rock to read his three letters.

The first was a notice from his draft board that he was going to be in big trouble if he didn't report immediately for induction. He laughed at that one. The next was from his girlfriend, who told him she was marrying someone else. He cursed at that one.

Andrusko was opening the third letter when a sniper's bullet hit him—not once but three times. It seared its way across his right forearm, dented the cross on a rosary around his neck, creased his left forearm, then ricocheted off the rock behind him, and struck him again in the back. Finally, the spent chunk of lead landed in his helmet, where it rattled around for a second and burned a hole in one of the envelopes from his letters.

"You are one lucky Marine," a corpsman said a few minutes later, after Andrusko's squad mates had killed the sniper. "The only unlucky part is that none of these wounds is serious enough to get you out of combat. Here's some pills if you get to hurting."

It was true, Andrusko thought. He *was* lucky. On D-Day, he'd stepped on a land mine on the beach and walked away with nothing worse than a shredded field pack and a nick in his thigh. Altogether, he'd been wounded three times, and now he'd been hit in three places by the same bullet.

Maybe my archangel is looking out for me, he told himself. *Maybe this means I'll get home alive after all.*

At 8:00 A.M. on October 14, I/3/5 launched yet another attack against the western portion of the Pocket near the West Road, where probes by K/3/5 had met little opposition the day before. Again, the attack was preceded by napalm strikes from the air and a heavy mortar barrage. Despite severe sniper fire from Japanese scattered among the rocks, I Company pushed ahead about 250 yards, taking up a new line late that afternoon near the northernmost knob of the Five Brothers.

At the same time, rifle squads from the First Battalion, Seventh Marines, were rousted out of a rest area, attached operationally to 3/5, and pressed back into action. Attacking north from the Pocket's southern perimeter, they pushed forward approximately 125 yards before heavy enemy fire forced them to halt. Later, however, they regrouped and continued the drive until they converged with troops of I/3/5, consolidating a significant reduction of enemy-held territory and substantially advancing the containing line around the Pocket. After these gains, the enclave still held by the Japanese measured only about 300 yards by 450 yards.

Meanwhile, K/3/5 and L/3/5 concentrated on sealing caves, sending out patrols, weeding out scattered snipers, and lugging more sandbags up Hill 140. They also strengthened their positions and strung concertina wire that would prove instrumental in keeping enemy infiltrators beyond grenade range of Marine foxholes that night. During the day, K/3/5 recorded what would prove to be its last two casualties of the Peleliu campaign as Sergeant Harry Spiece and PFC Earl Shepherd were evacuated with wounds.

Late on the afternoon of October 14, scuttlebutt circulated that Army troops would move in to relieve the Marines the next day. By that evening, the word was supposedly official, but the men of K/3/5 remained dubious. Much as they wanted to believe what they were hearing, they were too near collapse to waste their energy getting their hopes up.

"We were barely making it," said Gene Sledge. "Rumors flew . . . but my cynicism kept me from believing them."

"I'd reached the point where I figured we were doomed to stay on this damned island forever," recalled R. V. Burgin. "We were always going to be relieved 'tomorrow'—only tomorrow never came."

This time, though, it did. Shortly after daylight on October 15, D-plus-30, Sledge, Burgin, and their comrades looked up to see somber-faced Army troops marching single-file into their area.

For once, the rumors had been true.

The Marines' esprit de corps was bruised and raw, and their pride was frayed and dragging, but both were far from dead. On one level, they were glad to see the Army troops, elements of the Second Battalion of the Army's 321st Infantry. On another, more than a few Marines viewed their replacements with a jaundiced eye.

"I don't know about them dogfaces," remarked a squad mate of Sledge's as the soldiers filed past. "Look how many of 'em are wearin' glasses, and some of 'em look old enough to be my daddy. And did you see how baggy their pockets are?"

"They look fine to me," Sledge replied.

But a short distance away, Lieutenant Stumpy Stanley, who'd taken over the company after Captain Haldane was killed, also expressed shock and concern at the soldiers' appearance. Not only did many wear eyeglasses—a rarity in the Marine Corps—but they also looked to be much older, on average, than the men they were relieving. They were thin and somewhat frail-looking as well, even in comparison to the gaunt Marines. Stanley guessed that some of them weighed no more than 115 pounds.

"I felt sorry for them, these guys that relieved us," Stanley recalled. "I thought it was a crying shame. They had no more business being on that island than the man in the moon."

Despite the disparaging observations in some quarters, other Marines gave the Army troops a warm welcome. "We sure are glad to see you guys," Sledge told one of the replacements.

"Thanks," the soldier said. His halfhearted smile made it clear that he was less than overjoyed to be there.

By noon, the transfer was complete in 3/5's sector around Hill 140, and the battalion's survivors were aboard trucks bound for the Army troops' former bivouac area on the north coast of Peleliu. The Marines of 1/5 had to wait until the following day, however, to turn over their positions on Walt's and Boyd's Ridges to the 321st Infantry's First Battalion. At 12:45 P.M. on October 16, command of U.S. operations in the Umurbrogol officially passed to the Army.

Corporal Eddy Lee Andrusko of I/3/7 awoke from a deep, feverish sleep to find a Navy chaplain leaning over him and whispering a prayer. Andrusko sat up with a start, trying to figure out where he was and what had happened to him. Then he remembered: Two or three days after his most recent wounds, he'd started feeling sick. The skin around the wounds had turned reddish black, and the wounds themselves had swelled and started to smell bad. The corpsman who'd checked them frowned and shook his head. "You've developed gangrene," he said. "You need treatment fast, or you're likely to lose an arm. If the infection spreads, you could even die."

Andrusko's luck had finally run out. He'd walked unaided to a field hospital, where a doctor had given him a shot and he'd lost consciousness. Those were the last things he remembered, but he wasn't in a hospital now; that much was clear. He was lying outdoors in an open area crowded with other motionless men on stretchers, and the chaplain who'd been praying over him seemed more stunned than Andrusko was. With his eyes wide and his mouth agape, the priest hurriedly crossed himself and darted back toward the main hospital tent a few yards away.

Moments later, he reappeared, accompanied by a Navy doctor and several other medical personnel. The chaplain was smiling and gesturing toward Andrusko, but he also appeared nervous and uneasy, and he remained behind near the entrance to the tent as the others came forward.

The doctor glanced over Andrusko's wounds, silently read his "wounded in action" tag, then listened to his heart with a stethoscope. "How long have you been out here behind the tent, son?" he finally asked.

"I don't know," Eddy Lee said. "Hours, I guess."

"Well, your right arm's pretty bad, and you've got blood poisoning in your system. We're going to get you evacuated to a hospital ship as soon as we can, and they'll get this thing under control. Good luck."

"Thanks, doc," Andrusko said.

"By the way," the doctor said quietly, "you see that chaplain standing over there? He thinks he just witnessed a miracle. That's the reason he's grinning like that."

Eddy Lee frowned. "I don't understand. What kind of miracle, sir?"

"He thinks he prayed you back from the dead. I don't know how the hell you ended up out here, son, but this is our temporary morgue. You're the only live man out here. All the rest are corpses awaiting burial."

The ride up the East Road covered only about a mile, but when the ragged, grimy men of K/3/5 reached their new area, it was like entering a different world. One of the first things they noticed was how quiet it was and how unaccustomed their ears were to the absence of sudden, explosive bursts of sound. The accommodations—tents with plywood decks, functioning showers, a well-equipped cookhouse and mess tent, and even a screen for outdoor movies—seemed like sheer luxury.

As a precaution against the remote chance of a Japanese counterlanding, the mortar section was directed to set up its weapons facing seaward along the East Road, and the rest of the company established a defensive perimeter. But these were only formalities. The beaches of Peleliu were safe and secure, and no enemy force capable of threatening them remained in the Palaus.

At first, some of the men worried about being sent back into the line, but after a day or two, they began to relax. The muted sounds of intermittent artillery and mortar fire could still be heard to the south, where the Army continued to press enemy holdouts in the Pocket.

As soon as they settled in and went through a few perfunctory military motions, the men were allowed to rest. What virtually all of them craved above anything else was sleep—not a mere catnap of an hour or two but the kind of deep, peaceful, uninterrupted slumber they hadn't enjoyed in weeks. Many had slept even less than usual during their final night on the front. As Sledge explained: "With the end in sight, I didn't want to get my throat slit at the last moment."

The presence of plenty of fresh water was a marvel in itself. Once rested, they cleaned themselves up, shaved off their weeks-long growths of beard, washed their greasy, matted hair, and brushed their teeth multiple times a day. They also took notice of the weight they'd lost and began to regain their appetites. R. V. Burgin hadn't realized how skinny he'd gotten until he stripped off his filthy dungaree shirt and found that he could count his ribs. "I'd weighed right at 180 when we left Pavuvu, and I was down to 138 when we finished with Peleliu," he said.

Even more welcome than hot meals were fresh clothes. Within a day or so, each man in 3/5 was issued a new uniform, new boondocker shoes, and—especially prized—new white socks. Like most of his comrades, Burgin still had on the same uniform he'd worn ashore on D-Day. It was full of holes and stiff enough with dried sweat and encrusted grime to stand by itself. "By now, we were the Raggedy-Ass Marines for sure," he said. "The closest I'd come to a change of clothes in weeks was taking my socks off once in a while and wringing the sweat out of them."

For the first time since D-Day, men had an opportunity to sit quietly and think of other things besides their own minute-to-minute survival.

Burgin's thoughts drifted far from Peleliu, to Florence Riseley, the girl he'd left back in Melbourne and not seen in what seemed like half a lifetime, and to his baby brother, J.D., an eighteen-year-old Army PFC, last reported somewhere in France.

Corporal Red Womack was able to write a letter to his wife, Hilda, halfway around the world in Mississippi, and feel reasonably sure that he'd live to mail it.

PFC Vincent Santos received correspondence from home, telling him that his younger brother Abel, another Army guy, had made it okay through D-Day at Normandy. Santos and his buddy, John Redifer, also went fishing along the beach. Not having any poles, lines, tackle, or bait, they used hand grenades instead and brought back an impressive catch.

It was a time to compare and swap souvenirs, some of which were grisly enough to turn the stomach of even a seasoned combat veteran. Sledge had learned to accept the fact that many of his comrades collected gold teeth extracted from enemy corpses. But he recoiled in horror when a buddy called him aside and proudly showed off the blackened, severed hand of a Japanese soldier.

"I think you're nuts," Sledge told the guy. "Bury it."

Several other Marines came over for a look, and they unanimously agreed with Sledge. "You dumb jerk," said one NCO, "throw that thing away before it starts to stink."

"You ain't goin' aboard ship with me carryin' that," warned another squad mate. "It gives me the creeps."

The Marine finally yielded to peer pressure and threw his souvenir away. But to his buddies, the fact that he could seriously contemplate keeping such a gruesome prize, and justify doing it in his own mind, was striking evidence of how dehumanizing prolonged combat could be. "The war had gotten to my friend," Sledge said. "He had lost—briefly, I hoped—all his sensitivity. He was a twentieth-century savage now."

Sledge contented himself with a much less macabre souvenir of his month-long ordeal. He washed his filthy, but miraculously untorn, dungaree jacket in seawater and dried it in the sun. Then he carefully folded it and put it in his pack as a memento of his good fortune.

Because of a lack of suitable shipping, the Fifth Marines would remain in their rest area on Peleliu for two full weeks, but each passing day made it more apparent that their combat role was truly over. The men's lingering fears of being sent back into the Pocket gradually faded, and speculation turned to when Navy transports would arrive to take them back to Pavuvu.

During this interval, few, if any, of the men of the Fifth gave much thought to what they'd accomplished on those endless, merciless ridges. It would be up to military experts and future historians to calculate how much the blood and sweat shed by the Fifth in the Umurbrogol contributed to the final victory, and many would give them generous praise.

The Old Breed, George McMillan's history of the First Marine Division, credited the Fifth Marines with several key breakthroughs in the Pocket. These included piercing the deadly salient above Dead Man's Curve to make the West Road safe; slugging its way up Baldy Ridge and Hill 140, where other units had been driven back; and fighting off constant Japanese counterattacks to hold the ground they'd won.

Furthermore, Colonel Bucky Harris's regiment was able to achieve these successes with fewer casualties than those incurred by the First and Seventh Marines in fighting for the same ridges. This was remarkable, considering that the Fifth was in combat longer than the other two regiments and captured almost twice as much enemy territory as the First and Seventh combined. The primary difference was Harris's patient, methodical pace and his infantry-sparing utilization of coordinated artillery and air strikes.

But the Fifth's contributions to the overall victory went far beyond what its exhausted troops accomplished in the Umurbrogol. It was the only regiment in the First Marine Division to achieve all the objectives assigned to it during the campaign. These included securing its section of the beachhead on schedule, seizing the airfield on D-plus-1, capturing Ngesebus and wiping out its defenders, breaking the enemy's grip on Peleliu's northern coast and highlands, and, finally, effectively compressing the Pocket.

When the final units of the Fifth departed the Umurbrogol, U.S. military observers believe that fewer than 1,000 of its Japanese defenders remained capable of fighting on in a space the size of five or six football fields. Yet it took Army troops an additional six weeks—until November 27, 1944—to eradicate these last enemy holdouts. This illustrates the near-impregnability of the Japanese defensive core, but it also attests to the fortitude and tenacity of the Marines, who destroyed the other 10,000 enemy combatants on Peleliu in a span of just thirty days.

Statisticians at Corps headquarters later determined that the First

Marine Division fired more than 15.7 million rounds of all types of ammunition on Peleliu, including 13.3 million .30-caliber bullets, 1.5 million .45-caliber bullets, 116,000 hand grenades, and 123,000 artillery shells. All told, it took an average of 1,589.5 rounds of light and heavy ammo to kill each of those 10,000 Japanese.

For most Marines who survived it, any attempts to put the battle into perspective would come much later—if at all. What they *did* begin to ponder, however, as they marked time waiting for a ship, was how close each of them had actually come to doomsday.

In companies like K/3/5, each man could look back on his own personal brushes with fate, where a split second or a fraction of an inch often determined who made it through any given day, and who didn't. As survivors came to understand how narrow their escapes had been—and how totally beyond their control—each was drawn closer to comrades, both living and dead, who shared the agony of Peleliu's killing ground.

They had been pushed to the very brink of damnation, and many had been swept over the edge. All who remained were forever changed. Some were left embittered and scarred by their experiences, others strangely bolstered or even uplifted, but none would ever be the same as before.

"Peleliu took its toll," said Lieutenant Stanley, Andy Haldane's successor as K Company CO. "I saw in the eyes of each survivor the price he paid for thirty days of unrelenting close combat on that hunk of blasted coral. [But] Peleliu was something special for the Marines of K/3/5—for all of the First Marine Division. It has remained so down through the years."

No battle in the history of the First Marine Division forged a tighter, more enduring bond among the men who lived through it. Some of the most dramatic evidence of the selfless love many of these Marines felt for one another can be found in Peleliu's list of Medal of Honor winners. Five of the eight men awarded the nation's highest military decoration there—Corporal Lewis K. Bausell and

PFCs Richard E. Kraus, John D. New, Wesley Phelps, and Charles H. Roan—received the medal posthumously. Each of the five was mortally wounded in the act of throwing himself on top of an exploding grenade to save the lives of his comrades. A sixth Medal of Honor recipient, Lieutenant Carlton H. Rouh, also took the full impact of a grenade blast as he sought to protect the men of his mortar section, but miraculously recovered.

"I know there were many others who deserved the medal more than I did," said Captain Everett Pope, one of two surviving Peleliu Medal of Honor winners still living as this was written, "but I wear it for those who died."

"I don't think I did anything that anybody else in my outfit wouldn't have done," added former PFC Arthur Jackson, the other Peleliu Medal of Honor recipient who survived to wear his decoration. "I feel strongly that only a Marine who was on the scene at Peleliu can understand what took place during that period of time. It was a nightmare, to say the least. Every man there deserved a medal."

Never was membership in the Old Breed more highly cherished or bitterly earned. But within the larger framework of that legendary fraternity, the individual rifle companies that formed its heart and soul took on even deeper personal meaning for their survivors. They became close-knit, lifelong brotherhoods.

For the men of K/3/5, their thirty days in hell not only cemented lasting friendships but became the catalyst for an almost spiritual fellowship—one that will endear them to one another for as long as any of them live.

"The Marines in my company were the finest men I've ever known," recalled PFC Bill Leyden, who recovered sufficiently from his eye wound on Ngesebus to rejoin K/3/5 in time to fight on Okinawa. "Instead of counting sheep when I'm having trouble sleeping, I count the brave and wonderful men I was privileged to know and love as my comrades—forever. I see these men as clearly now as I saw them then, and I always will."

Although Sergeant Fred Miller was wounded and evacuated early on D-Day at Peleliu, he still feels this same kind of affection toward his mates. "I've always thought all the Marines I served with in K/3/5 were heroes," he said recently, "and even though I didn't know the two Marines who came to my aid when I was hit, I knew they were brothers in arms who would fight and die for you. Whenever anyone asks me why Marines are so close and what it is to be a Marine, I think of Peleliu and that pillbox."

Six decades after the battle, R. V. Burgin voiced similar sentiments: "The guys I was with in K Company were my family, my life—and time hasn't changed that. We're like brothers, and I stay in close touch with all the ones that are still alive. But not a day goes by that I don't remember the men who lost their lives on Peleliu, too. In a way, I still feel as close to them as I do the guys I talk to on the phone every few weeks."

On an afternoon in late October 1944, Sterling Mace and PFC Gene Holland, a fellow New Yorker, hitched a ride south from the K/3/5 rest area and made the four-mile trip to the new military cemetery near the Peleliu airfield.

It had been close to a month since a sniper's bullet had killed PFC Seymour Levy, and several days of loafing around with no regularly assigned duties had given Mace plenty of opportunity—too much opportunity, in fact—to think about his dead friend. Finally, he'd asked Holland to go with him to see if they could locate Levy's grave.

"It'll have a Star of David on it, I guess," Mace remarked as the two Marines wandered among the neat rows of fresh white crosses. "At least it should, since he was Jewish."

When they located Levy's marker, however, it was a cross like most of the others, and Mace felt a little miffed by the mistake. When he saw an enlisted man from graves registration nearby, he waved him over.

"This guy was a friend of mine, and he's Jewish," Mace said, pointing at Levy's grave. "He ought to have a Star of David, not a cross."

"So what's the big deal?" the guy said. "He don't know the difference, and I got enough problems as it is. Just pretend it's a star, okay?"

Mace stared at the graves registration man for a second. He thought about how unfair it was for a jerk like him to be walking around sneering at people when Levy was six feet under the ground.

"Isn't there somebody who could fix it?" Mace asked.

"I dunno." The guy shrugged. "Maybe you should check with Admiral Nimitz." He turned quickly away.

Mace clenched and unclenched his fists a couple of times as he glanced from the fresh grave to the retreating figure of the graves registration man, but after a minute, he calmed down a little.

What the hell, he thought, *Levy probably wouldn't care, anyway. Sy always said he wasn't an Orthodox Jew—whatever that meant— so he'd probably just laugh about it. And, Levy's not here in this damned hole. I don't know where he is, but he's definitely not here.*

As usually happened when he thought of Levy, a passage from his friend's favorite Rudyard Kipling poem crossed Mace's mind. He'd never been good at memorizing poetry, but he remembered this one because it was the last part of "Gunga Din":

> *So I'll meet 'im later on*
> *In the place where he has gone,*
> *Where it's always double drill and no canteen.*
> *He'll be squattin' on the coals,*
> *Givin' drink to poor damned souls,*
> *And I'll get a swig in hell from Gunga Din.*

"Let's go, Holland," Mace said. "I don't like it here."

October 29 was designated as "picture day" for the men of K/3/5 who were still physically able to pose for a Marine Corps photographer. As they boarded trucks for the short ride to Purple Beach and their date with the cameraman, word had already spread that this would be their last official duty assignment on Peleliu.

The Navy troopship USS *Sea Runner* was anchored offshore. The next day, God willing, K/3/5 would be boarding her for the voyage back to Pavuvu. But Gene Sledge was among many who found it impossible to believe that he and his mates were actually leaving. He could almost feel Bloody Nose Ridge pulling him back toward it "like some giant, inexorable magnet," ready to soak up the rest of the company's blood.

As the men formed up into irregular rows for the photo session—most of them bare-chested and wearing shorts, others sporting fresh T-shirts and dungarees—they were struck by how few of them there were. The company had mustered just eighty-five men that morning, all that remained of the 235 who had come ashore on D-Day. Twenty-six were either in the cemetery by the airfield or had died aboard Navy hospital ships and been buried at sea. One hundred twenty-four others were hospitalized with wounds at various points across the Pacific. While K/3/5's casualty rate of 64 percent was far from the worst recorded on Peleliu—Captain Pope's C/1/1 had ended up with fewer than a dozen men at the time it was relieved—it was among the highest in the division.

With several battle-scarred palms forming a backdrop, the company's only two surviving officers, Lieutenants Stanley and Ellington, stretched out in the sand in front of the rest of the group. Johnny Marmet, a bandana knotted around his neck, squatted with other platoon and squad leaders just behind the lieutenants. Sterling Mace, gripping a corncob pipe between his teeth, grinned from the back row. A couple of rows in front of Mace, Jim McEnery had his fatigue cap pulled low over his eyes and wore a faint smile under his thin mustache. Tall, lanky R. V. Burgin stood near the exact center of the picture, and Gene Sledge frowned over Burgin's shoulder from a couple of rows further back. Mortar section buddies George Sarrett, John Redifer, and Vincent Santos stood side by side at the end of one row on the photographer's far right.

In a couple of minutes, it was over, and members of the group went their separate ways, laughing and talking and trying not to think too much about those who were conspicuously absent from the picture.

Peleliu had inflicted a terrible toll on the First Marine Division. During the thirty vicious days between September 15 and October 15, 1944, the division had lost 6,526 men—1,252 killed in action and 5,274 wounded in action—or more than two casualties for each of the island's 3,200 acres. Casualties in the division's three infantry regiments averaged more than 50 percent of their total reinforced strength of about 3,000 men apiece at the time the fighting started. The First Marines had lost 1,749 men, the Fifth Marines 1,378, and the Seventh Marines 1,497.

The Army's Eighty-first Division would suffer another 3,278 casualties before the last Japanese resistance was finally snuffed out. Estimates of Japanese battle casualties range from just under 11,000 to about 13,000. The exact number of enemy dead has never been determined, but only about three dozen members of Colonel Nakagawa's garrison lived to surrender, although approximately 200 civilians working for the Japanese survived.

The sea was rough on the morning of October 30 as the Higgins boats carrying K/3/5 plowed up to the *Sea Runner* and cut their engines beside the ship's dangling cargo nets. It had been almost exactly forty-five days since the first waves of Marine assault troops had stormed onto Peleliu's beaches to launch a "quickie" operation that was supposed to be over in seventy-two hours or less.

In countless exercises during their Marine careers, the men in the bobbing boats had routinely climbed cargo nets like the ones now confronting them. But the distance up to the ship's rail had never looked longer, and their bodies had never been more spent.

PFC Jay d'Leau was among many whose arms felt like lead weights long before they made it onto the deck. "Some of the guys were too weak to climb at all by themselves," d'Leau remembered, "and I only got halfway before I had to stop and rest. Three feet from the top, I was totally beat, and some sailors had to reach down and help me."

Sledge also had difficulty with the net, partly because of his weakened condition and partly because the boats were pitching around so much in the heavy sea. He felt like a "weary insect climbing a vine," and he considered it fortunate that nobody lost his grip and fell during the ascent.

On the other hand, the mere thought of the rewards that lay ahead aboard the *Sea Runner* were enough to energize many of the men. "McEnery and I started singing the minute we got on deck," said Sterling Mace. "Just being somewhere else besides Peleliu was a great feeling, and the food and accommodations were fantastic. It was the best sail of my life, except for the one that took me back to San Francisco."

After the men stowed their gear and checked out their quarters, many returned topside as the ship got underway, to sniff the fresh salt air and take a final look at the miserable island they were leaving behind. Sledge was thinking about how ugly it looked, even from a distance, when Sergeant Pop Haney, the oldest man in the company, joined him at the rail, scowling and smoking a cigarette.

"Well, Haney," Sledge asked, "what did you think of Peleliu?" The young Marine had no earlier experience to measure against the battle just past, but if anyone could put it into proper perspective, he thought, it should be Haney, whose previous combat dated back to the slaughter in the Argonne in 1918. Sledge was expecting a typical response from a quarter-century veteran of the Corps—something like "If you think this was bad, you should've seen so-and-so." But Haney surprised him.

"It was terrible," the old-timer said. "I ain't never seen nothin' like it. I'm ready to go back to the States. I've had enough after that."

In those few words, Haney summed up the feelings of every survivor in the company.

At noon on October 30, an hour or so after the *Sea Runner* weighed anchor and departed for Pavuvu, General Geiger turned over command of the conquered islands of the Palaus group to Army

General Paul Mueller, commander of the Eighty-first Division. By mid-afternoon that day, Geiger and General Rupertus, along with most of their top aides, were aboard a B-24 Liberator bomber bound for Guadalcanal.

The Marines' role on Peleliu was finally and officially over. The impact of what happened to them there would last as long as any of them lived.

CHAPTER SIXTEEN

NEXT STOP: OKINAWA

By late 1944, there could be little remaining doubt in Tokyo about who would win the war in the Pacific. The Allied noose was steadily tightening around Japan, and her armed forces were being beaten back in every sector of the combat zone.

But as Peleliu had clearly demonstrated, the Japanese intended to leave every inch of yielded ground stained with American blood. They were rapidly losing their Pacific empire, but they still held two important aces in the hole. One was the extreme defensive strategy first employed at Peleliu. The other was the fanatical willingness of Japanese soldiers, sailors, airmen, and even civilians to die for their emperor.

Unaware that the dawn of the atomic age—and the end of the war —was less than ten months away, U.S. military planners envisioned the same type of scorched-earth struggle for Japan's home islands as the Marines had encountered on Peleliu. It was expected to take as much as two years, with the estimated cost in American casualties ranging from 250,000 to 1 million men. Japan now pinned her last hopes for a negotiated peace on her ability to fulfill these projections.

Only two major obstacles still stood between the approaching Allied juggernaut and an invasion of Japan. One was Iwo Jima in the Volcano Islands, where the Third, Fourth, and Fifth Marine Divisions would land on February 19, 1945. The other was a large island only 325 miles southwest of the nearest Japanese home island of Kyushu. Measuring nearly sixty miles long and up to eighteen miles wide, or roughly ten times the size of Peleliu, the island was known to the Japanese as Okinawa Shima. After four months of reinforcement and recuperation at Pavuvu, Okinawa would be the next stop for the First Marine Division and K/3/5.

Today, many division veterans who fought in both places view the battle for Okinawa almost as a continuation of Peleliu. Okinawa was a much larger operation, and the total number of Americans killed or wounded ran much higher. Yet a sizable percentage of Marines who lived through the two battles still rate Peleliu as the most savage, downright nastiest ordeal they ever faced. Many also believe that Okinawa would have exacted an even greater toll from the Marine and Army troops that invaded the island on April 1, 1945, if not for the bitter lessons learned in the earlier battle about enemy defensive tactics.

"There were caves on Okinawa, too—lots of them," said R. V. Burgin. "But by then, we knew a helluva lot more about cave busting than we had when we first hit Peleliu. Otherwise, we might've spent twice the time we did taking Okinawa and lost God knows how many more men."

Thus, the story of the Marines at Peleliu doesn't really end with the departure of the last battered units of the First Marine Division from that obscure corner of hell. At least, it shouldn't. If it did, the true significance of what happened there between September 15 and October 30, 1944—and its impact on the division's future—would remain unclear.

To a great extent, the rank-and-file Peleliu veterans who went on to Okinawa provided the leadership, toughness, and battlefield savvy that enabled the Old Breed to claw its way back from the edge of extinction. They were, without doubt, the major factor in the division's regeneration as a premier fighting force. This is reason enough to follow them a few steps further.

After an eight-day voyage, the *Sea Runner* and its destroyer escorts steamed into the quiet waters of Macquitti Bay, and the men of K/3/5 lined up along the rail to stare at the familiar, palm-fringed shoreline of Pavuvu.

From a distance, the island appeared little changed from the desolation of mud, moldy canvas, rotten coconuts, and miserable living conditions they remembered. But as they drew closer, they noticed signs of an amazing transformation.

By the time they disembarked from their small boats onto a new steel pier, their still hollow eyes were wide with disbelief. Decorated tables were set up along the beach, and waiting to greet them was a reception line of a half-dozen female Red Cross workers, handing out paper cups of chilled grapefruit juice.

After months without seeing a member of the opposite sex, the sight of young American women brought sharply varying reactions from the Peleliu veterans. Some, including Vincent Santos and John Redifer, rushed to get in line, craning their necks for a better view of this incredible sight. Others, like R. V. Burgin and Gene Sledge, were considerably less receptive.

"My reaction was kind of negative, and I really don't know why," Burgin recalled years later. "I guess those girls were just trying to do their jobs, but at the time, it didn't seem appropriate for them to be there."

A number of the Peleliu veterans felt uncomfortable enough at this unexpected welcome to ignore the women, or at least pretend to. They sat sullenly on the beach and waited for orders to move out to their assigned camp areas, but few were able to keep from stealing occasional glances in the women's direction.

Sledge accepted a cup of juice from a smiling Red Cross girl, but like Burgin, he felt a resentment that he couldn't explain in logical terms. Even as he thanked her and moved away, an angry voice inside his head complained:

What the hell's she doing here? She's got no more business here than some damned politician.

But when Sterling Mace spotted the women and an attractive new Red Cross canteen/club building under construction near the beach, his initial reaction was more pleasant surprise than anything else. "I thought, 'Hey, this is nice,'" he recalled, "but that was about all there was to it."

Neither the Red Cross girls nor the new canteen was ever very widely accepted by the Marines. "Not many of the guys went over there," Mace said. "We just felt more comfortable relaxing in our own bivouac area." Men who did become regular visitors to the canteen were saddled with the derisive nickname "Red Cross Commandos."

Part of the reason for the Marines' standoffishness was simple mathematics: There were, after all, only six women and more than 15,000 men.

As they arrived, the men also noticed plenty of other indications that substantial changes had taken place on Pavuvu since the previous August. Clusters of sunbathing Marines relaxed on the beach while others splashed in the surf, but unlike the old days, they all wore swimming trunks. Further evidence that coeducational civilization had reached the island could be found in the fact that all its heads were now discreetly screened with burlap. Bare butts and men relieving themselves in the open were clearly out of fashion on the new Pavuvu.

Other changes, however, earned the returnees' full approval. During the weeks they'd been gone, Seabees and Marine engineers had built a neat network of streets and roads paved with hard-packed coral, plus a fifteen-acre parade ground. Replacing the ragged, leaky Army tents the men remembered were new ones with wooden decks and electric lights. There were showers, screened mess halls, laundries, and a fully stocked PX. Each man had access to a three-can-per-week beer ration as well as such all-but-forgotten luxuries as Coca-Cola, ice cream, current movies, up-to-date magazines, and plenty of sports and recreation equipment.

Pavuvu was still no fancy seaside resort—and the land crabs still abounded—but when these Marines compared the island to where they'd been, it was hard to find much to complain about. Corporal Red Womack found the accommodations "real nice" the second time around. He appreciated the large new refrigeration unit that allowed fresh meat to be served regularly, and he especially liked his area's well-lighted, concrete-floored mess hall, where men could spend their free time playing cards, reading, or writing letters protected from mosquitoes and other insects. He found the atmosphere a little like sitting on a screened-in porch back in Mississippi.

Womack was also gratified to see PFC William Lewis, his friend and former assistant gunner, recovered from his wounds on Ngesebus and waiting on Pavuvu when the rest of the division got there.

A few days after its arrival, a new commander was named to replace General Rupertus: Major General Pedro A. del Valle, a Puerto Rico–born Naval Academy graduate whose command experience had started in World War I and who held the Legion of Merit for bravery on Guadalcanal. The new CO and his spit-and-polish style —which placed proper dress and divisional pride above collecting rotten coconuts—were generally welcomed by both officers and enlisted men.

In the words of Lieutenant Colonel Harold Deakin, a member of Rupertus's staff who stayed on to serve under del Valle: "The spirit of the division changed overnight." Deakin described del Valle as the "best leader" he'd encountered in the Corps, and even Admiral Halsey observed that high morale was "characteristic" of del Valle's units.

Few Marines who remembered their former commander's ill-fated promise of a "quickie" two- or three-day battle at Peleliu were sorry to see Rupertus go.

Now a new fight lay ahead. No one in the ranks knew yet where or when it would take place, only that it was coming. Meanwhile, del Valle and his staff faced the mammoth task of rejuvenating their ravaged division and honing it into as strong a combat machine as it had been on D-Day at Peleliu.

This meant that throngs of green recruits and untested "ninety-day wonder" officers—4,500 of whom were already waiting on Pavuvu when the veterans returned—had to be initiated, fully and quickly, into the ways of the Old Breed. And, with such well-seasoned NCOs as Sergeants Johnny Marmet and Jim McEnery finally due to be rotated stateside within the next few weeks, the initiation would be left largely to men who'd been raw replacements themselves only a few months earlier.

As Sledge, Mace, and other Peleliu veterans reached the K/3/5 camp area, they found self-conscious newcomers eyeing them nervously. When some of the recruits hurried out to help the returnees with their gear, they realized for the first time that they were now among the "old men" of the company. It was a sobering thought. Sledge had turned twenty-one aboard the *Sea Runner*, and Mace was still just nineteen.

Among the new replacements were a number of men who'd been drafted into the Corps—the first nonvolunteer Marines the veterans had ever met. To Sledge, the replacements seemed so innocent and unaware of what lay ahead that he felt a surge of sympathy for them.

Soon, the division would resume a regular training schedule with long, rigorous days of combat maneuvers and practice landings. The newly paved parade ground would be trampled from daylight to dark by marching feet of companies, battalions, and even full regiments in close-order drill. For large-scale amphibious exercises, however, it would still be necessary to travel to Guadalcanal.

During the veterans' first week or two back on Pavuvu, their main duties were resting and recuperating. Although the replacements were already being sent out on daily work details, the men from Peleliu had plenty of time to catch up on their mail, play baseball and basketball, toss horseshoes, swim, fish, read, or simply loaf.

Evenings, however, took on a more serious tone during this period of recuperation. They became a time for renewing old friendships, sharing smokes, trading stories, and seeking out news from other outfits. Inevitably, that news included reports of comrades who hadn't come back.

"You didn't really know until you got back to Pavuvu how many of your buddies were gone," explained one old-before-his-time corporal, quoted in *The Old Breed*. "Up to then, you kept telling yourself that they'd turn up back at Pavuvu, that they were only slightly wounded or not even wounded at all, just lost from their units. But at Pavuvu you couldn't fool yourself any longer."

Guys from other companies who remembered the young, guitar-playing officer named Hillbilly Jones often came around looking for him. Whenever they asked where he was, the question triggered a momentary sense of sorrow and loss among Jones's comrades. But such moments were brushed aside, sometimes roughly. Every man in the outfit had lost close friends on Peleliu, and dwelling on their losses only made them feel worse.

One evening, Sledge noticed Lieutenant Stumpy Stanley toss an armload of maps and papers into a trash can, then angrily throw a large, hardbound book into the can on top of the other stuff. Curious, Sledge wandered over to examine the discards after Stanley left and discovered that the book was *Men at War* edited by Ernest Hemingway. When he opened it and found the name "A. A. Haldane" written on the flyleaf in Ack-Ack's bold hand, Sledge realized that Stanley's gesture had been one of grief, rather than anger. With a lump in his throat, he pitched the book back into the trash and walked away.

As Thanksgiving 1944 came and went, men who had put in their twenty-four months in the Pacific combat zone—and, in many cases, a great deal more—packed their gear and prepared for their long-awaited trip back to mainland U.S.A. They held high hopes of being home by Christmas, and their excitement grew with each passing day.

Those being left behind were in no mood to celebrate, however. For them, the impending departures drove home a gloomy realization: Because of the heavy losses at Peleliu, virtually every company in the division was already pitifully short of battle-seasoned NCOs. Many of the platoon, squad, and fire team leaders who were key parts of the unit's organizational framework, as well as the glue that held it together, were dead or recovering from wounds. Now, the shortage of experience and leadership was about to become even more acute.

"We envied them, but we hated to see them go," said Mace, who knew he'd especially miss Jim McEnery, the fellow New Yorker who'd passed along many of the combat lessons learned at Guadalcanal and Cape Gloucester to younger men in his platoon. "We knew that guys with just one battle under their belts—even grabasses like me—were going to have to take up the slack now. It was kind of scary."

By virtue of his service at Peleliu, Mace had earned a corporal's stripes, but his promotion hadn't dampened his taste for horseplay. When his pranks interrupted a lecture to company personnel, Lieutenant Stanley showed his irritation as forcefully as Mace's old platoon leader, Lieutenant Bill Bauerschmidt, had—only in a different, more long-term manner.

"Instead of chasing me around the camp and threatening to kick my butt like Bauerschmidt did, Stumpy put me on corporal of the guard duty for two weeks straight," Mace recalled with a grin many years later. "My buddies said it was some kind of modern record."

Although Mace still mourned the death of Seymour Levy, he struck up a friendship with PFC Bob Whitby, one of the new replacements assigned to Mace's platoon. In age, personality, and general demeanor, Whitby was almost Levy's direct opposite. He was small, serious, and almost thirty years old—ancient by K/3/5 standards—with a wife and twin daughters back home in Ohio. Whitby missed his family desperately, and Mace did his best to keep the new man's spirits up, but sometimes he questioned the wisdom and justice of sending a guy like this into combat.

On an evening in late November, Johnny Marmet dropped by R. V. Burgin's tent for a visit. For the most part, the eighteen-month relationship between the taciturn platoon sergeant from Ohio and the wiry young squad leader from Texas had been strictly business. Marmet had never been overly chummy with anyone who served under him in the mortar section, and sentimentality wasn't his style. But he and Burgin had learned to respect and trust each other implicitly in countless life-and-death situations. Now, with only a day or two left until Marmet shipped out for the States, he'd come to say goodbye.

"Your promotion to sergeant's in the works," Marmet said. "But I guess you know that already."

"Yeah, I heard," Burgin replied. "I know you put in a good word for me, and I appreciate it."

"You're a good troop, and you damn well earned the extra stripe." Marmet paused, frowned, and lowered his eyes. "There's something else I thought I ought to tell you, but you may not like to hear it."

Now it was Burgin's turn to frown. "What is it?"

Marmet's dark eyebrows were knit as he stared directly at Burgin's face. "A few days before the skipper was killed, he told me he was gonna recommend you for a Silver Star for the job you did knocking out that pillbox on Ngesebus. The way things happened, Ack-Ack never had a chance to put the recommendation through, but I know he would've if he'd lived. I figured he'd want you to know."

Burgin felt himself relax a little. From Marmet's tone, he'd thought he was going to hear something really bad. He smiled tightly and shrugged.

"Thanks for telling me," he said. "But, hell, if I had a choice, I'd give a hundred Silver Stars to have the captain back."

Marmet nodded and stuck out his hand. "Take it easy, Burgy," he said. "See ya stateside."

In early December, some of the less seriously wounded Marines evacuated from Peleliu began to find their way back to Pavuvu to rejoin their comrades. Among them was PFC Dan Lawler, a machine gunner whose hand had been mangled by mortar fragments while crossing the airfield on D-plus-1.

Lawler was glad to get back to K/3/5, although he knew it meant he'd be in another battle soon. More awful than his own wounds, in

Lawler's estimation, had been a job he'd undertaken on the Navy hospital ship that took him from Peleliu back to Guadalcanal. As an ambulatory patient, he'd assisted in burials at sea for many men who died of their wounds during the voyage.

"Throwing those dead Marines into the ocean was my worst experience of the war," he recalled. "Nobody forced me into it—I volunteered—but it was the most painful thing I ever did, and it weighed on my mind for a long time afterward."

His injured eye miraculously saved by Navy doctors, PFC Bill Leyden also arrived back on Pavuvu shortly before Christmas, along with his Third Platoon buddy, PFC Marion Vermeer, who'd been wounded on Ngesebus at about the same time as Leyden.

On their return, both Leyden and Vermeer were promoted to fire team leaders, but by this time, the quota of promotions to corporal had already been reached, so there was no extra stripe or pay raise for either of them. "We were kind of ticked off about that," Leyden said, "and our Purple Hearts weren't much compensation."

Among the first scuttlebutt to reach the ears of Lawler, Leyden, Vermeer, and other returnees were rumors that a magnificent Christmas feast was being planned for the First Marine Division. As a general rule, the quality of Marine chow rated well below that of Navy fare, and enlisted men considered any shipboard dining opportunity a genuine treat. But on three or four occasions each year, the Corps went to special pains to provide fresh, enjoyable food, and Christmas was at the top of the list.

"They say we're gonna have turkey and all the trimmings for Christmas dinner," men confided to one another.

"Oh, sure," the skeptics responded, "but the turkey'll be dehydrated, and the trimmings'll be C rations."

Even the naysayers were pleasantly surprised, however, when a massive shipment of frozen turkeys arrived a few days before the holiday, and the preparations for a lavish banquet proceeded as promised.

On Christmas Eve, many of the men of 3/5 gathered for church services in a palm-thatched regimental chapel. Afterward, they sat on coconut logs to watch a Christmas program and sing carols. Sledge echoed the sentiments of many when he said: "I enjoyed it a great deal, but I felt pretty homesick."

The next day's main event was eating. "Man, I've never seen such huge turkeys before or since," said Lawler. "They had to have weighed between forty and fifty pounds apiece, and they were delicious. That was the best meal I ever had in the Marine Corps."

Along with generous servings of turkey, a souvenir menu listed tomato juice cocktail, green pea soup, giblet gravy, dressing, cranberry sauce, whipped potatoes, buttered peas and corn, apple pie, coffee, and fruitade. In addition, each man received a mimeographed letter of greeting signed by General del Valle.

"We are all conscious at this time of our loved ones at home, and all of us wish we could be with them," the general wrote. "We can be with them in spirit by the exercise of our Christian faith on the anniversary of the birth of our Lord, and by resolving . . . to work and fight harder than ever, to the end that our country's enemies may be quickly beaten, that peace may come on earth to men of good will, and that we may return to our loved ones serene in the assurance that we have done our duty."

For some, the celebratory mood lasted through New Year's Eve. After chow that evening, several Marines from K/3/5 diverted the attention of cleanup crews in the battalion mess hall while others "requisitioned" a couple of leftover Christmas turkeys. For the rest of the night, warm beer and a potent fermented concoction called "jungle juice" flowed freely, washing down freshly carved slabs of turkey. The sound of guitars, fiddles, singing, and laughter rolled through the coconut groves until sometime before dawn.

"It was the kind of party Hillbilly Jones would've loved," said R. V. Burgin.

In mid-January, the full division boarded a convoy of LCIs (Landing Craft, Infantry)—a newer, smaller version of the LSTs that had taken it to Peleliu—for its first trip to Guadalcanal and ten days of field problems and practice landings. The intensifying pace of the training was a clear indication to the veterans that time was growing short.

The exercises also demonstrated how much the dozens of officers newly arrived from the States still had to learn. This was especially apparent in K/3/5, where Lieutenant Stanley was the only remaining commissioned officer with combat experience.

Second Lieutenant Robert "Scotty" MacKenzie, the young New Englander who succeeded Lieutenant Ellington as commander of the company mortar section, was a prime example. "Scotty had gone straight out of college into OCS [officer candidate school], and he was green as a gourd," Burgin recalled. "He was as gung ho as a junior high kid playing his first football game, but he was also a good guy who grew up in a hurry and became a good Marine."

Not all of the mortar section's numerous veterans were quite so charitable toward their new boss. When MacKenzie talked excitedly about "taking my Ka-Bar between my teeth and my .45 in my hand" and charging the enemy, men like George Sarrett, John Redifer, and Snafu Shelton tended to smirk and roll their eyes. They also speculated among themselves about what the "big-mouthed Yankee boot" would do when he came under fire for the first time.

"I felt embarrassed for Mac," said Gene Sledge. "He wouldn't listen to the few words of caution from some of us who suggested he had a shock coming."

During the last week of February, a steady stream of news reports about the battle raging on Iwo Jima began to reach the men on Pavuvu, making it plain that the Japanese were employing the same defensive tactics used on Peleliu. "It sounded like Bloody Nose Ridge all over again," said Burgin, "only bigger."

Casualty figures for the three Marine divisions in the Iwo Jima campaign would mount to roughly three times those suffered by the First Marine Division at Peleliu, although the battle on Iwo would last several fewer days.

Meanwhile, rumors were rampant about the men's next destination. One widely circulated story claimed the division was being integrated into an Army force to invade China, Formosa, or even Japan itself. Since the current round of training emphasized both street fighting and coordinated tank-infantry strikes in open country, each of these possibilities seemed plausible. Adding to the confusion and speculation, the men also repeatedly practiced scaling a sheer cliff on ropes. They were told to be ready to do the same when they reached their objective.

When Red Womack's turn came to go up the wall, he had yet another reason to appreciate his newfound seniority and his recent promotion to squad leader. As the man in charge of three two-man flamethrower teams, Womack was no longer required to carry one of the bulky weapons himself. Now he had only a pistol and a carbine to weigh him down, and climbing walls with seventy pounds of molten death strapped to your back was someone else's problem.

Only when the men were shown a map of a long, narrow island—without any identifying names—did they realize that the recent rumors about their destination were off-target as usual. Soon afterward, a friend from another company showed up at Sledge's tent, pointing excitedly to a *National Geographic* map of the Pacific and an island whose outline and description matched the one with no names. It was, of course, Okinawa, and word spread quickly.

During the last two weeks of February, the division went back to Guadalcanal for more rigorous landing exercises and field problems. It seemed strangely prophetic that the men's bivouac area on the 'Canal was the same one recently vacated by the Third Marine Division, now locked in the fight of its life on Iwo Jima. Following long days of repetitious maneuvers in the big island's hills, grass fields, and jungles, they returned to Pavuvu, where, a few days later, two events of note took place.

On the warm afternoon of Sunday, March 4, a group of about thirty K/3/5 veterans of Peleliu and Cape Gloucester participated in the dedication of a new multipurpose athletic field in one corner of Pavuvu's parade ground. With the veterans forming an honor guard, a chaplain spoke briefly, taps sounded, and a three-volley rifle salute was fired. Then a sign was unveiled, designating the area as "Haldane Field" in honor of Captain Andrew A. Haldane.

Afterward, according to an unnamed officer quoted in a Marine Corps press release, there was a baseball game "because that's the way Captain Haldane would've wanted it." A team of enlisted men beat a team of regimental officers by a score of 2–0.

On March 15, the division boarded a convoy of troopships and sailed for Ulithi Atoll, a major Navy anchorage in the central Pacific some 250 miles northeast of Peleliu, where the Okinawa assault force was gathering. When the convoy arrived six days later, the Marines looked out over a huge invasion fleet—scores of ships of every description, including more aircraft carriers than any of them had ever seen.

"This is expected to be the costliest amphibious campaign of the war," an officer told the men of K/3/5 at a briefing. "We can expect 80 to 85 percent casualties."

"How's that for boosting the troops' morale?" someone in the audience whispered.

"Well, hell," countered another voice, "at least they're not tellin' us it'll be over in two or three days."

The first month on Okinawa was relatively easy duty for the men of 3/5. By virtue of its lead position in the first wave of the assault on Peleliu, the battalion was initially placed in regimental reserve for the Okinawa campaign. The landing was unopposed—a piece of cake, even for the first units ashore—and U.S. forces advanced at a steady pace through the rolling countryside and small villages in the southern portion of the island.

But the Japanese had planned it that way. True to form, in a series of east–west ridges to the north, characterized by terrain and a network of mutually supporting fortifications reminiscent of Peleliu, the bulk of a 110,000-man Japanese army lay waiting with massed heavy artillery, including eight-inch siege guns.

Lieutenant General S. B. Buckner Jr., commander of the U.S. Tenth Army, which included the First, Second, and Sixth Marine Divisions, had a total of nearly 542,000 men at his disposal. Before the slaughter was over, more than one man out of every dozen in this vast force would become a casualty, and Buckner himself would be mortally wounded by enemy artillery fire.

Unlike the close-order combat on Peleliu, where Marines could often smell the enemy and hear him breathing, Sergeant R. V. Burgin found that most of the danger on Okinawa was of the long-range variety. Heavy Japanese siege guns rained death on American lines from miles away, and even machine guns could threaten from distances that would've been unheard of on Peleliu.

On a day in early May, Burgin was in a forward position near a Marine rifle squad whose advance up a nearby ridge had been abruptly halted by a Japanese machine gun. The enemy gunner was firing from at least a third of a mile away, as nearly as Burgin could figure. Nobody had been able to spot his location, but the gunner's pinpoint aim had the whole squad pinned down.

For several minutes, Burgin studied the situation and watched the same scene repeat itself: Each time a Marine moved around the east side of a nearby mound of dirt, the machine gun instantly opened fire, and the Marine either got hit or barely managed to duck in time.

"You guys lay low for a spell," Burgin yelled at the squad leader. "I want to try somethin'."

He moved stealthily toward the mound of dirt and started around the east side of it. But instead of moving normally, he turned around and walked backward, staring toward the distant ridge and purposely trying to draw the machine gunner's fire so that he could spot the gun's location.

The instant Burgin showed himself, a spray of machine gun rounds slammed into the mound beside him and pelted the ground under his feet. As he hurled himself backward and hit the deck, he saw three smoldering bullet holes in the legs of his dungaree pants.

But in that split second, he'd also seen exactly where the fire was coming from.

"You okay?" one of the riflemen shouted.

"Yeah," Burgin drawled. "Just hold on till I can get my mortars in action. It won't take long." He picked up his walkie-talkie. "I got a target for you," he told a mortar man some distance behind him. "Range 600 yards . . ."

Almost immediately, one of the mortar squad's 60-millimeter weapons opened fire. On the second round, as Burgin later put it: "The Jap machine gun went one way, and the gunner went the other."

Two weeks later, on May 20, 1945, the streak of luck that had carried Burgin safely through two major battles and most of a third finally came to an end. He was struck in the neck by fragments from a Japanese shell and taken to a field hospital.

That same day, a short distance from where Burgin was hit, a blast from a Japanese eight-inch gun miles away blew Corporal Sterling Mace out of his foxhole. As the dust settled, his comrades rushed forward, certain that Mace was dead, but the explosion had only knocked him cold and punctured his eardrum.

Mace was evacuated two days later and was soon on his way to San Francisco. But after having his wound patched up and getting a couple of days' rest, Burgin rejoined his mortar squad and remained on the line until the island was declared secure.

For risking his life to locate and knock out the Japanese machine gun, Burgin was awarded the Bronze Star.

On the morning of May 25, PFC Bill Leyden was sitting on the edge of his foxhole on a ridge called Half Moon Hill, talking to PFC Marion Vermeer. At least, he was *trying* to talk to Vermeer, but his friend wasn't responding. Vermeer was lying on his back in the bottom of the hole, his right leg resting on Leyden's boondockers, but he might as well have been on another planet.

"What the hell's wrong with you?" Leyden demanded after a long pause. "Do you even hear what I'm saying?"

Vermeer didn't move or make a sound. His glazed, vacant eyes were fixed on the sky in what the men of the First Marine Division had come to know all too well as the 1,000-yard stare—the telltale symptom of the combat fatigue now reaching epidemic stage on Okinawa. Only minutes earlier, the young rifleman from Washington state had seemed okay, but now he was totally out of it.

"Hey, man," Leyden said, extricating his feet from beneath Vermeer's leg and pulling himself to his knees. "I think you need to go to an aid station and talk to a doc."

Leyden heard the incoming 75-millimeter shell a second or two before it hit. He knew from the sound it was going to be close, but not as close as it actually was. Then the whole world seemed to vanish in a ball of fire, a cloud of dust, and an ear-splitting burst of sound.

Leyden was dimly aware of his own body flying through the air, but he felt nothing when he hit the ground, and he heard nothing, either. One of his eardrums was blown out, and the little finger on his right hand was torn off. Worse, his body was sprayed with shrapnel from his chest to his knees, and blood oozed from a dozen puncture wounds in his abdomen. There was nothing much left of Vermeer or PFC Roy Baumann, the other occupant of the foxhole. In the next foxhole over, PFCs Archie Steele and Luigi Verga had also been killed by shell fragments.

As shock settled over Leyden, dulling the pain, the events of the next few minutes came in disjointed flashes between periods of unconsciousness: Marines loading him on a stretcher. . . . The stretcher-bearers struggling and stumbling through ankle-deep mud to carry him out. . . . The mangled corpses of other dead Marines littering the ground, at least 100 of them. . . . The medics at the aid station, their faces and bare arms spattered with blood, looking at rows of bodies on stretchers, then methodically covering the faces of the dead. . . .

Oh God! Leyden thought. *Please don't let them cover me up!*

Only when he awoke in a field hospital following surgery did he know for sure that they hadn't.

Okinawa was the largest, costliest battle of the Pacific war. By the time it officially ended on June 21, 1945, it had claimed more than 49,000 American casualties, some seven and a half times the number of killed and wounded at Peleliu. However, records indicate that more than 26,000 of those Okinawa casualties were attributed to neuro-psychiatric causes, similar to the condition that affected Marion Vermeer just before his death, rather than to actual battle wounds.

The First Marine Division lost 7,665 men killed, wounded, and missing—about 1,100 more than on Peleliu. Most of these were in the division's three infantry regiments, which suffered combined losses of more than 150 percent in the two battles—a total of 14,191 men. More than 107,500 enemy bodies were counted on Okinawa, and an estimated 20,000 more Japanese dead were either sealed in caves or buried by their comrades. Only about 10,000 were taken alive.

A high percentage of the American casualties at Okinawa, both physical and psychological, was caused by long-range artillery fire. "An incredible number of guys cracked up under the constant strain of not knowing when or where the next shell was going to hit," said Bill Leyden. "Peleliu was hell, but we always knew we could fight back because the enemy was so close. On Okinawa, there was this feeling of helplessness because most of the Japs who were firing at us were completely beyond our reach."

There were also some striking similarities between the two battles, however. Like Peleliu, Okinawa also had its Pocket, an interlocking network of fortifications in rugged terrain that could neither be bypassed nor effectively attacked by tanks. In a single week between June 11 and 18, the First Marine Division sustained 1,150 casualties in the battle to dislodge the enemy from a ridge system called the Kunishi-Yuza-Yaeju escarpment. Once the Marines won the fight, organized Japanese resistance ended on Okinawa.

When the battle was officially declared over, on June 21, only twenty-six of the approximately sixty-five K/3/5 Peleliu veterans who landed on the island on April Fool's Day remained with the company. Several of these, like R. V. Burgin, had been wounded but returned to duty after treatment. Lieutenant Stanley had been evacuated a few days earlier with a severe case of malaria.

"Of the fifty-three men who joined K Company with me in Melbourne in March 1943," Burgin noted, "only three were still there after Okinawa. But of the three major battles I was in, Peleliu was the ugliest, dirtiest, most exhausting one of all. The heat, the dead bodies, the flies, the god-awful terrain, those damned caves, the continuous day and night combat with no relief—those were what made Peleliu the worst in my book."

Although Bill Leyden's wounds on Okinawa were more serious than those he suffered on Peleliu, he agrees wholeheartedly. "For a lot of reasons, Peleliu was probably the worst campaign of the war, at least in the Pacific," he said. "It was the Marines' biggest surprise in World War II, and it made a terrible battle like Guadalcanal seem like a picnic by comparison."

Many men who fought at Guadalcanal, Tarawa, Iwo Jima, and Okinawa would doubtlessly disagree. But Burgin's and Leyden's eyewitness assessments are solidly supported by various historians and military analysts.

"One can argue fruitlessly over which was the most hard-fought and fearful campaign of the Pacific war," wrote historian Harry A. Gailey in his book *Peleliu 1944*. "However, the testimony of many Marines seems to prove conclusively that Peleliu ranks with Iwo Jima in any listing of the most difficult major Marine campaigns."

"They talk of Tarawa and Iwo Jima and all of that," added Lieutenant Colonel Lewis J. Fields, a Marine officer who was present when plans for Operation Stalemate were drafted. "But Peleliu was just as difficult—and more so to some degree—but its publicity was practically nothing."

Major Frank Hough offered a similar appraisal in his Marine Corps monograph *The Assault on Peleliu*, describing the battle as "one of the most stubbornly contested campaigns in the history of this or any other war." And Colonel Harold Deakin, a member of General Rupertus's staff, put it even more strongly. Peleliu, he said flatly, was "the worst campaign in the history of warfare—far worse than Iwo Jima or the others."

The ever-philosophical Gene Sledge stopped just short of calling Peleliu worse than Okinawa. "On Okinawa, I would be shelled and shot at more, see more enemy soldiers, and fire at more of them . . . than on Peleliu. But there was a ferocious, vicious nature to the fighting on Peleliu that made it unique for me. Many of my veteran comrades agreed."

Sledge, Vincent Santos, George Sarrett, Jim Burke, and Snafu Shelton, all members of Burgin's mortar section, and Red Womack of the 3/5 weapons company were among a handful of Third Battalion Marines who came through both Peleliu and Okinawa without a scratch. In Sledgehammer's words: "The few men like me who never got hit can claim with justification that we survived the abyss of war as fugitives from the law of averages."

The First Marine Division had already received one Presidential Unit Citation for "extraordinary heroism" at Peleliu. It was awarded a second for its performance on Okinawa.

EPILOGUE

More than six decades have passed since the last shots were fired on Peleliu. Yet history buffs, students of military tactics, and aging veterans who were there still snipe back and forth over two lingering questions:

- Were Operation Stalemate and the assault on Peleliu actually necessary, or was this merely a costly campaign of no genuine strategic importance?
- How much did faulty intelligence and reckless or ego-driven command decisions—particularly by General Rupertus and Colonel Chesty Puller—contribute to the high toll of Marine dead and wounded?

Few, if any, of the Marine infantrymen most directly affected by these questions gave them any thought during the battle. They were on Peleliu to carry out an assignment, and they did it. They were trained to obey orders without hesitating or asking why, and they didn't. Their philosophy was: If we weren't doing this dirty job here, we'd be doing another dirty job somewhere else.

But once the firing stopped and they went home, the questions refused to go away. When some people implied that the Marines' suffering and misery had been for nothing, that their buddies had been maimed and slaughtered for no legitimate purpose, it stung. Some veterans shrugged it off. Others felt anger and bitterness, and some still do.

"In my opinion, we never should've hit the damned island in the

339

first place," said R. V. Burgin. "We never used it for anything after we took it, and we could've bypassed it just as well. It still makes me mad to think about all the lives that were wasted there."

Marines who shared Burgin's views coined a nickname for Peleliu that summed up their feelings about its ultimate value: "Nothing Atoll."

Even Admiral Jesse Oldendorf, whose ineffective pre-invasion shelling of the island must share blame for the carnage when the Marines went ashore, came to believe that the Palaus campaign was a massive mistake. Writing after the war, Oldendorf admitted a lack of foresight by himself and other military leaders and concluded that the assault on Peleliu should never have been attempted.

Historian Harry Gailey has argued that criticism of the decision to invade Peleliu shouldn't be based on what became known after the war but rather on what military planners knew—or thought they knew—as of mid-1944. But even at that time, he added, both the collapse of Japanese naval and air-power and the increasing dominance of U.S. forces were obvious. Likewise, the tactic of bypassing non-essential enemy strong points, thereby isolating their garrisons, was already well established.

"Thus, if the planners had chosen to ignore Peleliu, they would not have been introducing a new concept," Gailey noted. "The Palau area was at first considered important because, in the spring of 1944, intelligence estimates gave the Japanese forces in the Central Pacific retaliatory powers which they, in fact, did not possess."

"The intelligence we had was no intelligence at all," said Burgin. "We had no reliable maps, no accurate information on terrain or enemy defenses, and not a hint that all those caves were there. We didn't have any idea what we were getting into."

The bitterness of many surviving Peleliu veterans toward the high command's decision not to bypass Peleliu also extends to Rupertus and Puller at the battlefield level. "I don't think Chesty Puller was the greatest thing since sliced bread," said Captain Everett Pope, whose company was slaughtered on Hill 100 (Walt's Ridge) under Puller's orders and who won the Medal of Honor for leading the heroic stand there. "I had no use for Puller. He didn't know what was going on, and why he wanted me and my men dead on top of that hill, I don't know."

George McMillan, author of *The Old Breed,* labeled Puller "a tragic caricature of Marine aggressiveness" who, in the minds of many fellow officers, "crossed the line that separates courage and wasteful expenditure of lives."

Largely because of the carnage inflicted on Pope's company and other First Marines units, Puller has been frequently characterized as a butcher who callously disregarded the lives of his men. But in a 2002 report entitled "The Truth About Peleliu," Marine Colonel Jon T. Hoffman, deputy director of the Marine Corps History and Museums Division, argues otherwise. While not totally blameless, Puller "has gotten a bum rap," Hoffman contends.

According to Hoffman and others, a much larger share of the blame rests with Rupertus, whose obsessive rush to take Peleliu consistently sacrificed lives in the name of speed. "The cold fact," said Lieutenant Colonel Arthur M. Parker Jr., executive officer of the Third Armored Amphibian Battalion, "is that Rupertus ordered Puller to assault impossible enemy positions at 0800 daily till the First was decimated."

Colonel Bucky Harris also felt that he and his Fifth Marines were "roughly used" later in the battle when Rupertus pushed them too hard. Harris believed that only General Geiger's intervention kept Rupertus from stripping him of his command.

Admiral Nimitz and General MacArthur, the top military leaders in the Pacific, who bore the ultimate responsibility for Operation Stalemate, also come in for their share of scorn and criticism. Neither ever commented publicly on their differences concerning the operation, and Nimitz stipulated in his will that all his personal papers be destroyed.

In the view of historian Gailey, American possession of Peleliu and its neighboring island to the south, Angaur, had little influence on either MacArthur's Philippines campaign or any other subsequent Pacific action. "Colonel Nakagawa could have been left to his caves," Gailey wrote, "and the only change in the outcome of the war in the Central Pacific would have been the surrender of . . . more Japanese to the Americans in the fall of 1945."

By many accounts, Nimitz was less in favor of the Peleliu invasion than MacArthur, but noted historian Samuel Eliot Morison faults Nimitz, in particular, for not heeding Admiral Halsey's advice to cancel Operation Stalemate. "Considering that the capture of Peleliu and . . . Angaur cost almost as many American lives as the assault on Omaha Beach," Morison observed, "it would seem that CinCPac [Nimitz] here made one of his rare mistakes."

"I'd still like to get my hands on MacArthur and Nimitz for sending us into that terrible place for no good reason," said Corporal Swede Hanson, one of the heroes of the Point. "I still dream of that stuff all the time, and I still feel the Japs coming at me out of the night."

"Peleliu was a political thing that got a lot of people killed for nothing," added Navy corpsman Bill Jenkins, who treated Hanson's wounds, was himself wounded at the Point, and later returned to serve on Okinawa. "It makes you sick to think about it, but it's the truth."

Thus, the debate simmers on. It seems likely to continue even after the last Peleliu veterans are gone.

Okinawa turned out to be the First Marine Division's final combat assignment of a war that ended sooner than almost anyone on either side anticipated. As many Cape Gloucester veterans completed their twenty-four months in the combat zone and rotated stateside, and another new batch of replacements appeared, rumors predicted that the division would be heading for Japan itself by early fall. Based on past experience, no one had much reason to think otherwise during July and early August 1945. Then came word that the most powerful explosions ever seen had devastated the cities of Hiroshima and Nagasaki. Suddenly, the war was over.

At first, the Marines were stunned and filled with disbelief, but when the full meaning of what had happened hit home, they felt jubilation and indescribable relief. There would be no house-to-house, street-by-street battle for the Japanese homeland. Instead, the division was sent to north China, where it remained on occupation duty until January 1946.

When the announcement came that the division was shipping out for home, it touched off a sharp clash of emotions in many of the men. Mixed with their elation were feelings of gloom and pain. Buddies who had shared at least two—and in many cases three—major campaigns were about to be separated for good.

"I've never felt as close to anyone as I did to my comrades in K/3/5," said Bill Leyden. "There are no words in the language to describe the feeling, and it didn't end when we went our separate ways. Years later, we could look at each other and feel the tears start rolling down our cheeks."

"We'd forged a bond that time would never erase," added Gene Sledge. "We were brothers. I left with a sense of loss and sadness, but K/3/5 will always be a part of me."

After the extraordinary life-and-death experiences shared by the veterans of the First Marine Division, the majority would return home to unremarkable lives of quiet obscurity. In an emerging peacetime world, they would become largely indistinguishable from other "typical Americans" around them—as unrecognized among their fellow countrymen as the Battle of Peleliu itself. There would, of course, be exceptions. A few notable examples:

PAUL DOUGLAS, who left the faculty of the University of Chicago to join the Marines as a fifty-year-old private, quickly advanced to captain, was slightly wounded at Peleliu, and suffered permanent disability in one arm on Okinawa, became a U.S. senator from Illinois. WILLIAM LUNDIGAN interrupted a budding acting career to become a Marine Corps combat cameraman with the rank of corporal, then returned to Hollywood for a long string of starring and leading-man roles in feature films and TV. ROBERT LECKIE, a young noncom whose experience on D-Day beaches from Guadalcanal to Peleliu formed the basis for his 1957 best-seller, *Helmet for My Pillow,* went on to write some twenty books, mostly on military history. GEORGE HUNT, whose K/3/1 captured the Point on D-Day at Peleliu, then held it against everything the enemy could throw at it while cut off from the rest of the First Marines, also scored with a hit postwar book called *Coral Comes High.* Hunt later served as editor of *Life* magazine.

Despite a 90 percent disability from wounds suffered with Hunt's company at the Point, FRED FOX earned a degree in petroleum engineering from the University of Texas after the war, then made a fortune by inventing a specialized mechanism now used on every oil drilling rig around the world. Fox has undoubtedly made more trips back to Peleliu than any other veteran of the battle—about twenty-five in all. On his first visit in 1964, he found his rusted Ka-Bar knife, identifiable because of its badly bent blade, lying precisely where he'd dropped it twenty years to the day earlier. Through influential friends in Washington, Fox has helped Peleliu and the rest of the Palaus obtain Peace Corps volunteers, economic development funds, and even assistance in setting up their present form of home rule government. He lives in a posh penthouse apartment overlooking downtown Austin.

For every Peleliu Marine who achieved some measure of fame or distinction in the postwar world, many others returned home to lives of virtual anonymity or remained in the Corps long enough to see action in more recent U.S. wars. And there were, of course, those—like Jones and Haldane—who didn't survive the battle but whose memory has been preserved by former comrades, family members, or others close to them.

WILFRED "SWEDE" HANSON, another decorated survivor of the Point, recovered sufficiently from the severe wounds he suffered there to fight—and be wounded again—on Okinawa. He was discharged from the Marines in 1946 but soon reenlisted for another eight-year hitch, during which he also saw action as a platoon sergeant in Korea. When he finally became a civilian for good, Hanson settled in Florida and turned his attention to higher education, earning a bachelor's degree from the University of Tampa and a master's in education from the University of South Florida, and later serving as a police officer in Tampa. In April 1993, nearly fifty years after the fact, Hanson was finally presented a Bronze Star for his bravery on Peleliu. Still later, the decoration was upgraded to a Silver Star. Hanson and his wife, June, make their home in Lutz, Florida.

EUGENE B. SLEDGE, who returned to his native Alabama after the war and became a biology professor at the University of Montevallo, also achieved recognition as an author. Sledgehammer's introspective memoir, *With the Old Breed at Peleliu and Okinawa,* originally published in 1981, has gone through eighteen printings to date and become one of the more widely acclaimed works of its type to come out of World War II. Before his death in 2002, Sledge was also featured in several televised documentaries on Peleliu and often served as a spokesman for veterans of this "forgotten" battle.

On the other extreme, EDWARD A. JONES came to symbolize those unknown heroes who fell at Peleliu and are now almost totally forgotten, except by a dwindling handful of relatives, friends, and former comrades. Jones was posthumously awarded the Silver Star for his actions against the enemy snipers who threatened his platoon. In October 1947, Hillbilly's body was returned from Peleliu and buried with full military honors in the Slate Ridge Cemetery at Delta, Pennsylvania, near his family home at Whiteford, Maryland. He was survived by his mother, Mrs. Reba Allison Jones, and seven brothers and sisters, all of whom lived at the time in the Whiteford area. As this is written, only three siblings are still alive, and only Jones's sister, Anna Mosher of Westport Point, Massachusetts, retains clear personal memories of him. His two surviving brothers, John (Jack) Jones of Red Lion, Pennsylvania, and Gary Jones of San Jose, California, were only six and eight years old respectively when

Ed came home on his last leave in 1941. "I remember how impressed I was by his Marine uniform," Jack recalled recently, "but that's about all."

The memory of ANDREW A. HALDANE has been kept alive through the efforts of eight of his fellow Bowdoin College alumni who served with him in the First Marine Division. Shortly after returning from the war, the group established a fund for a permanent annual award, to be presented in Haldane's name to a member of Bowdoin's senior class "whose qualities of leadership, sportsmanship, and courage approach those displayed by Andy." Known as the Haldane Cup, the award has been given each year since 1945. In October 1948, Haldane's body was shipped home from its original resting place on Peleliu and permanently reburied, at his father's request, in Arlington National Cemetery.

Among those contributing to the memorial for Haldane was his good friend and onetime fellow athlete, EVERETT P. POPE. After returning in mid-1945 to the bride he hadn't seen in more than three years, Pope was awarded the Medal of Honor for "conspicuous gallantry and intrepidity at the risk of his life" and soon began a highly successful banking career. Five years later, however, he was recalled to active duty with the Marines during the Korean War. In 1953, at age thirty-four, he became the youngest bank president in Massachusetts. Over the years, he has also been a major financial supporter of Bowdoin College and a longtime member and chairman of its Board of Trustees. Now retired, Pope and his wife, Eleanor, divide their time between homes in Florida and Maine.

ARTHUR J. JACKSON, Peleliu's other living Medal of Honor winner, received his decoration from President Harry Truman during ceremonies on the White House lawn on October 5, 1945. Jackson had recovered from a neck wound received in the process of killing four Japanese infiltrators a few days after the action for which he earned the medal (he still keeps the bullet from his neck in a watch fob). By this time, the former PFC had also completed officer candidate school and been commissioned a second lieutenant. He remained a

Marine until 1962, when he resigned from the Corps as a captain, moved back to the Pacific Northwest where he'd spent his boyhood, and went to work for the U.S. Postal Service. Now retired, he lives in Boise, Idaho.

One of the first chores undertaken by the irrepressible STERLING MACE when he got home to New York in June 1945 was to visit the grieving mother of his buddy, SEYMOUR LEVY, and hand her some of Levy's personal effects. "It was the toughest thing I ever had to do," he said. "She never got over Sy's death." After peace broke out, Mace went to art school and later found a job in the art department of the theater at famed Jones Beach State Park, where he became friends with singer Guy Lombardo and many other celebrities, and eventually became theater manager. Since 1983, he and his wife, Joyce, have made their home in St. Pete Beach, Florida, where he stays in close touch with former platoon mate JIM MCENERY, who lives an hour away in Ocala.

Minus a finger, carrying hunks of shrapnel embedded in both knees, and with two Purple Hearts tucked away among his souvenirs, WILLIAM J. LEYDEN returned to Long Island in 1946 after months in various hospitals. Not quite twenty years old—although far more mature than the headstrong youngster who'd joined the Marines on his seventeenth birthday—Leyden's thirst for adventure was still unquenched. Consequently, he shunned routine civilian jobs and parlayed an engaging personality and natural athleticism into a lengthy career as a professional golfer, competing in tournaments around the country. Among his greatest thrills were occasional opportunities to play golf with his former commanders in the First Marine Division. On Veterans Day 2003, Leyden was honored as local "Veteran of the Year" in his hometown of Hempstead, New York. "I owe my life to the Marine Corps," he said recently. "Without it, I probably wouldn't have lived to be eighteen—much less seventy-eight."

After being discharged from the Marine Corps in April 1946, GEORGE SARRETT returned to his hometown of Denison, Texas, and went into railroad work like his father before him. But after marrying Anna Lee, the girl he'd corresponded with from Peleliu, and starting a family, he decided to return to military life. In November 1947, he joined the Air Force—mainly because there were no openings at his grade level in the Marines—and served continuously for twenty-five years, the last twenty as a first sergeant. He saw duty at Da Nang in Vietnam, and after his retirement in 1972, he and his wife settled in the Fort Worth suburb of Benbrook. Sarrett died in early 2004, a few months after the death of his wife.

It wasn't until after the fighting ended on Okinawa that R. V. BURGIN received word that his younger brother, Joseph Delton, an eighteen-year-old Army private, had been killed by German artillery fire in France in February 1945. Burgin made it home to Jewett, Texas, in early 1946, and a year later he was reunited with Florence Riseley, the fiancée he'd last seen in Australia in September 1943. The couple was married in Dallas on January 29, 1947, a few days after Florence's arrival from Melbourne.

To celebrate their tenth wedding anniversary in 1957, the Burgins spent an entire year in Australia and have been back a number of times since, but R.V. has declined several opportunities to revisit Peleliu. "I saw all I ever want to see of that damned place in 1944," he explained recently. However, as secretary of the K/3/5 Veterans Association and publisher of the group's quarterly newsletter, he maintains contact with all the company's surviving World War II members, especially such old mortar section buddies as JIM BURKE, JOHNNY MARMET, and VINCENT SANTOS. Since the mid-1960s, the Burgins have lived in a quiet corner of suburban Lancaster, Texas, where their secluded home, wooded creek bank, large vegetable garden, and the pastoral atmosphere belie the fact that downtown Dallas is only about ten miles away.

After the war, CHARLES "RED" WOMACK returned to his native McComb, Mississippi, and his prewar job as a locomotive engineer. He lives alone today in a secluded house behind a brick wall facing Delaware Avenue, the town's busiest thoroughfare. The rest of the street is dominated for several blocks in both directions by stores, service stations, motels, and restaurants, but the noise and bustle are somehow lost in the small oasis that Womack has built. It's a place of shade trees and shrubs, well-tended flower beds exploding with color, exotic plants in scores of clay pots, and a lazy orange tomcat named Big O. It's probably the last place you'd expect to find a former Marine Corps flamethrower guy.

Only a few graying strands remain of the mane of copper-colored hair that earned "Red" Womack his lifelong nickname, and bypass surgery has left him a frail shadow of the kid who played tackle for the McComb High Tigers in 1941. To a visitor, he displays a strange device that might be mistaken for a farm implement by the uninitiated until Womack identifies it as a Japanese knee mortar. "But you wouldn't want to fire it off your knee," he adds quickly. "The recoil would break your leg for sure." His eyes mist as he gazes at a photograph of his wife, Hilda, now gone these six-plus years. "My wife was a beautiful woman," he says, and the picture bears out his words. In it, she wears the necklace made of black seashells that he collected on Pavuvu.

Womack takes pride in his family's long association with America's military. Both his grandfathers fought for the Confederacy in the Civil War, and a photo on the mantel shows his father, Purser Womack, with his .50-caliber machine gun squad in France in 1918. Red's oldest son, Michael, recently retired as a lieutenant colonel in the National Guard and spent five years on active duty with the Army during the Vietnam era. More recently, grandson Brian Graveley carried on the family tradition, first by serving a hitch in the Marines, then with the Army's Third Infantry Division in Iraq. In a recent letter, Brian assured his granddad that he'd be "going back into the USMC" as soon as his current Army hitch is up. The news makes Womack smile as he reads it to a visitor.

"Mr. Red," as he's affectionately known around McComb, is eighty years old now, and memories of the hell he once endured—and helped to create—on an obscure Pacific island have grown as faded as the pictures on his walls. But in his heart, Red Womack will always be a member of the First Marine Division and its legendary Old Breed. "I just like to go down to the recruiting office sometimes," he says. "They always treat me real well, and it makes me feel good when they shake my hand and call me 'Marine.'"

As a final testimonial to the intricate efficiency of their underground hideouts, a small number of Japanese troops in the Umurbrogol continued to elude capture until late April 1947—nearly two and a half years after combat operations officially ended on Peleliu and twenty months after V-J Day. They subsisted on rations pilfered from a caretaker American detachment of about 100 men and occasionally exchanged fire with U.S. patrols.

One of the holdouts, identified as Superior Seaman Tsuchida, told Marines to whom he surrendered that his cohorts, refusing to believe the war was over, were planning a last-ditch banzai assault on the main American camp near the airstrip.

The camp went on high alert, and more Marines were dispatched from Guam to bolster the small garrison. But on April 21 and 22, after Seaman Tsuchida returned to the ridges with letters from Japan assuring the others that hostilities had ended, the thirty-three other hiding Japanese, led by Lieutenant Ei Yamaguchi, turned themselves in.

Today, the interiors of many of the caves they left behind remain little changed from when their Japanese occupants last saw them—littered with rusting weaponry, countless beer and sake bottles, and, in all likelihood, more than a few skeletal remains. The heavy jungle growth obliterated in 1944 by tons of American napalm and high-explosive shells has returned with a vengeance. A nearly impenetrable mantle of vines and foliage again shrouds the ridges and leaves many of the caves, especially those at higher elevations, beyond the reach of all but the heartiest, most determined adventurers.

But a few score visitors—a high percentage of them Peleliu veterans or their family members—do find their way each year to more accessible caverns at lower levels. Among those who came in 1994, a half-century after the battle, was author Peter Richmond, whose father, Captain Tom Richmond, commanded Company G, Second Battalion, Fifth Marines.

Along with getting himself hopelessly tangled in vines and undergrowth and experiencing momentary panic, the younger Richmond slithered into one of the caves on his belly and explored it with a flashlight. He calculated that the cave was big enough for a dozen or more men—maybe a lot more because it was hard to tell where it stopped—yet its only entrance was a narrow slit about two feet wide, hidden beneath a huge boulder.

"I crawled back into the cave and rummaged around," Richmond wrote. "My hands found untold empty beer bottles. The Japanese had crawled into this cave, got drunk, and died."

In August 1947, Peleliu and the rest of the Palaus were recognized by the United Nations as a U.S. trust territory. In October 1994, fifty years after the First Marine Division was evacuated, the islands were officially designated as the Republic of Palau. Peleliu itself remains an isolated backwater of the Pacific, receiving only a trickle of the 40,000-plus Asian tourists who visit the Palaus annually. Almost all the island's 600 native inhabitants live in three small villages and earn their livelihood from one or more of three sources—tuna fishing, tourism, and growing what is reputed to be some of the world's finest marijuana.

Within a few years after the end of the war, the remains of all the Americans who lost their lives on Peleliu were brought home for reburial, so there is no longer a military cemetery on the island. Peleliu's caves, along with other former combat areas, remain a government-protected historical site, and the removal of artifacts is forbidden. A small airstrip of crushed coral occupies part of the same area as the large military airfield crossed by the Fifth Marines in 1944, but the original field has long since been taken over by jungle.

The only official monument to the Marines who fought, suffered, and died there sixty years ago stands in a cleared area on a low cliff at the southern end of Bloody Nose Ridge and a few hundred yards inland from White Beach 2. A four-foot-tall monument of red granite bears the Marine Corps emblem and a simple inscription:

IN MEMORY OF THE MARINES WHO GAVE

THEIR LIVES IN THE SEIZURE OF PELELIU

AND NGESEBUS ISLAND FROM THE JAPANESE

DURING THE PERIOD 15TH SEPTEMBER

THROUGH 15TH OCTOBER 1944

SOURCES AND NOTES

PROLOGUE

Sources

The reconstruction of the moments just preceding the Marines' landing on Peleliu and the landing itself is based entirely on the author's interviews with R. V. Burgin, Bill Leyden, and Charles "Red" Womack.

1. OLD BREED, NEW BLOOD

Sources

Information on the early history of the U.S. Marine Corps prior to World War I and on the evolution of the First Marine Division was obtained from Heinl's *Soldiers of the Sea,* McMillan's *The Old Breed,* and the official Marine Corps Web site. Author interviews with Burgin, Leyden, Jim McEnery, and Fred Miller provided personal insights, as did Sledge's *With the Old Breed at Peleliu and Okinawa.*

The Bowdoin College Archives contributed important background on Captain Andrew A. Haldane in the form of letters written by Haldane from the South Pacific and various news clippings.

2. A REST CAMP FROM HELL

Sources

Recollections of the sing-along on the deck of the troopship are from author interviews with Burgin and George Sarrett; background information on Lieutenant Ed "Hillbilly" Jones is from author interviews with members of Jones's family, particularly his sister, Anna (Jones) Mosher.

Additional author interviews with Joe Dariano, Wilfred Hanson, Leyden, Sterling Mace, Vincent Santos, and Womack provided personal reflections and general information on Pavuvu. The controversial selection of that inhospitable island as a rest camp and training area for the First Marine Division is discussed at length in McMillan's *The Old Breed,* Ross's *Peleliu: Tragic Triumph,* and

Sledge's *With the Old Breed at Peleliu and Okinawa*. Haldane's letters from the Bowdoin College Archives offered other key information.

Notes

Page 37   *PFC Bill Leyden was even more outspoken:* A sharp division of opinion exists among those interviewed by the author as to the frequency and number of suicides on Pavuvu. Leyden's K/3/5 comrade Burgin, for one, claims that such incidents have been grossly exaggerated over the years.

3. THE ROAD TO PELELIU

Sources

The Marines' final evening aboard the invasion-bound LSTs is based on author interviews with several Peleliu survivors who were there, including Burgin, Sarrett, Mace, McEnery, and Matthew Rousseau. Additional information on Hillbilly Jones was gained from interviews with Anna Mosher and Jones's boyhood friends and former neighbors, Ernest and Dorothy Neeper, as well as a letter from Jones to Mildred Glasgow, dated 4/1/44. Haldane letters and news clips from the Bowdoin College Archives were also utilized.

Books providing useful background on the buildup to the amphibious assault include Davis's *Marine!: The Life of Chesty Puller*, Gailey's *Peleliu 1944*, Hallas's *The Devil's Anvil*, McMillan's *The Old Breed*, Morison's *History of United States Naval Operations in World War II*, Ross's *Peleliu: Tragic Triumph*, Sherrod's *The History of Marine Aviation in World War II*, and Sledge's *With the Old Breed at Peleliu and Okinawa*.

Notes

Page 57   *Four months later, at a meeting at Pearl Harbor:* A detailed account of the Pearl Harbor meeting of Roosevelt, MacArthur, and Nimitz appears in Ross's *Peleliu: Tragic Triumph*. It was the only face-to-face meeting held by FDR with his two top Pacific commanders during the entire war, and the Joint Chiefs of Staff were not invited. Ross described the "jousting" between Nimitz and MacArthur, observing that the soft-spoken admiral was no match for "MacArthur's eloquence." Neither ever commented publicly on the matter.

Page 62   *After the war, in a rare comment:* Hindsight is, of course, always better than foresight. The remark by Oldendorf in the following quotation is cited by several authors, including Ross and Gailey, but the admiral never offered any further explanation for his decision to call off the bombardment early.

4. SEA OF CHAOS; ISLE OF FIRE

Sources

Author interviews with Burgin, Leyden, Mace, McEnery, and Santos revealed the nervousness and tension among the Marines as the countdown to H-hour progressed and the amtracks carrying the invasion force headed for the beaches. Additional interviews with Edgar Brown, Miller, and Womack conveyed the confusion and carnage encountered by the Marines during their first chaotic minutes ashore.

Numerous books helped provide a broad overview of the landing of the first waves of assault troops on Peleliu that morning. Among them are Gailey's *Peleliu, 1944*, Gayle's *Bloody Beaches: The Marines at Peleliu*, Hallas's *The Devil's Anvil*, Hough's *The Assault on Peleliu*, Leckie's *Helmet for My Pillow*, McMillan's *The Old Breed*, and Ross's *Peleliu: Tragic Triumph*. Sledge's *With the Old Breed at Peleliu and Okinawa* provided a unique personal perspective.

Notes

Page 71   *To avoid a repeat of the heavy casualties:* Even with their design liabilities, Higgins boats were vastly superior to amtracks in two key areas—speed and maneuverability. The boats were named for Andrew Jackson Higgins, president of Higgins Industries of New Orleans, which produced most of the World War II landing boats of this type, as well as the Navy's patrol torpedo (PT) boats. Because of the disaster that befell many of the slow, unwieldy amtracks used in the Peleliu landing, the Higgins boats regained favor with Navy brass and were widely used in later landings at Iwo Jima, Okinawa, and Leyte. The book *Andrew Jackson Higgins and the Boats That Won World War II* by Jerry E. Strahan tells the complete story of the Higgins boats.

5. THE WHITE BEACHES TURN RED

Sources

Interviews with Dariano, Braswell Deen, Fred Fox, Hanson, Wayne Hook, and Ray Stramel—all of whom survived the fight to wrest the Point from its Japanese defenders—enabled the author to re-create this bloody struggle in all its agony and valor. Captain George Hunt's dramatic postwar memoir, *Coral Comes*

High, augmented the author interviews and provided many key insights into this portion of the battle and the men who fought it.

Fox's oral history, courtesy of the National Museum of the Pacific War, and Deen's self-published book, *Trial by Combat,* were also valuable resources. Davis's *Marine!: The Life of Chesty Puller,* Gailey's *Peleliu 1944,* and Ross's *Peleliu: Tragic Triumph* provided general background information.

The author's interview with Everett Pope provided perspective on action occurring on White Beach 1 at the same time that the fight for the Point was taking place.

Notes

Page 88   *First Sergeant Schmittou was:* The author was unable to establish Schmittou's first name. None of the half-dozen surviving interviewees who served with Captain Hunt's company on the Point could recall it, although they remembered Schmittou vividly, and Hunt identifies the first sergeant only by his last name in his book. The same is true of Sergeant Blandy, mentioned in Chapter 7.

Page 106   *But Puller provided little information:* This conversation between Puller and General Oliver Smith is recalled by Smith in Ross's *Peleliu: Tragic Triumph.*

6. A BLOODY NOSE AT THE AIRFIELD

Sources

Author interviews with Frank Batchelor, Burgin, Leyden, Mace, James Mason, Pope, and Santos provided a panorama of the action up and down Peleliu's beaches as the Marines clawed out a foothold on the island under relentless enemy fire. A videotaped interview with the late Jay d'Leau and Sledge's *With the Old Breed at Peleliu and Okinawa* also helped paint a portrait of a beachhead still very much in doubt.

Information drawn from Gailey's *Peleliu 1944,* Gayle's *Bloody Beaches,* Hallas's *The Devil's Anvil,* and Lea's *Peleliu Landing* created a broad backdrop for stories of individual heroism.

Notes

Page 120   *From all indications, the enemy onslaught:* Well planned or not, the tank attack was an unmitigated disaster for the Japanese, whose light tanks were helpless against concentrated American fire. As Gayle, who observed the fight at close range, notes in *Bloody Beaches*: "In a very few minutes, it was all over. The attacking tanks were all destroyed, and the Japanese infantry literally blown away."

7. POINT OF NO RETURN

Sources

Author interviews with Dariano, Fox, Henry Hahn, Hanson, Hook, and Bill Jenkins provided the framework for describing the struggle by survivors of K/3/1 to hold the Point against relentless enemy counterattacks. Augmenting the interviews were Fox's oral history, Deen's *Trial by Combat,* and Hunt's *Coral Comes High.*

8. DEATH AND DENIAL

Sources

The final showdown in the fight for the Point was re-created primarily through author interviews with Fox, Hahn, Hanson, Hook, and Stramel, supplemented by Hunt's account in *Coral Comes High* and Fox's oral history.

For the action of other units, the narrative draws on information from Davis's *Marine at War,* Gailey's *Peleliu 1944,* Hallas's *The Devil's Anvil,* McMillan's *The Old Breed,* and Ross's *Peleliu: Tragic Triumph.*

Notes

Page 154   *"The overall feeling seemed to be that a breakthrough was imminent":* This quotation appears in Ross's *Peleliu: Tragic Triumph.*

Page 154   *"Can't they move any faster?" Rupertus demanded:* These quotations from the First Marine Division commander are recorded in Ross's *Peleliu: Tragic Triumph.* Ross also quotes Rupertus's chief of staff, Colonel John Selden, on the general's seemingly obsessive desire to come ashore early on D-Day, ostensibly to put more pressure on his regimental commanders. "It was all I could do to keep him from going in immediately," Selden said. Rupertus's absence from the beachhead and the fact that Puller's command post was cut off from contact with division headquarters for a considerable time was a "made-to-order situation for Chesty," according to one of Puller's staff officers. "He liked nothing better than to do things his own way, without the brass breathing down his neck," Ross quotes the officer as saying.

Page 165   *Puller didn't mince words:* Puller's terse order to Colonel Honsowetz is cited in Ross's *Peleliu: Tragic Triumph.*

Page 166   *"How are things going?":* This exchange between Puller and Honsowetz is detailed in Hallas's *The Devil's Anvil.*

Page 167   *"I've got to have replacements"*: These quotations from Puller and Selden are also included in both Hallas's *The Devil's Anvil* and Gailey's *Peleliu 1944.*

9. HILLS, HORRORS, AND HEROES

Sources

This chapter's close-up account of major actions by all three Marine infantry regiments on Peleliu draws from the author's interviews with Edward Andrusko, Burgin, Arthur Jackson, Mace, McEnery, and Pope. Andrusko's self-published memoir, *Love and War Beneath the Southern Cross,* and Sledge's *With the Old Breed at Peleliu and Okinawa* contributed other valuable perspectives.

Books providing general overview and background include Davis's *Marine!: The Life of Chesty Puller,* Davis's *Marine at War,* Hallas's *The Devil's Anvil,* and Ross's *Peleliu: Tragic Triumph.* Information on the actions resulting in Medals of Honor being awarded to Pope and Jackson was drawn from the citations accompanying those medals.

Notes

Page 171   *Honsowetz: Our situation's desperate:* Honsowetz recounts his conversation with Puller in Ross's *Peleliu: Tragic Triumph.*

Page 172   *"We press the attack again at 0800"*: Quoted from Ross's *Peleliu: Tragic Triumph.*

Page 172   *"Yes, Colonel," Puller said. "I just came back from my battalions"*: Quoted from Ross's *Peleliu: Tragic Triumph.*

Page 180   *But Jackson himself shrugged the whole thing off:* During an interview with the author in September 2003, Jackson continued to protest the fact that Sergeant Scheidt was never recognized or honored for his role in wiping out the enemy positions.

Page 185   *"We knew Captain Pope needed all the help he could get"*: Quoted from Ross's *Peleliu: Tragic Triumph.*

10. NORTH THROUGH SNIPER ALLEY

Sources

A lengthy account of the ill-fated patrol led by Hillbilly Jones and the killing of the berserk Marine by one of his own comrades is included in Sledge's *With the Old Breed at Peleliu and Okinawa.* Author interviews with Burgin, Leyden, Mace, McEnery, and Sarrett produced many additional details.

To re-create the last meeting between Andy Haldane and Everett Pope, the author relied heavily on his interview with Pope, who remembered the event vividly. Again, various documents from the Bowdoin College Archives also proved invaluable.

Personal recollections of the death of Corporal John Teskevich and the wounding of PFC Jesse Googe came from Googe as well as Burgin, Mace, and McEnery, all of whom were nearby when the sniper fire erupted.

The accidental death of PFC William Middlebrook is recounted in detail in Sledge's book, but the victim's name was withheld. Author interviews with Mace and Burgin provided additional information on the tragedy. Background on battle action in general is from Ross's *Peleliu: Tragic Triumph*.

Notes

Page 207   *Later that morning, Captain Haldane conducted an investigation:* For as long as he lived, Sledge kept the vow of silence to which he was sworn that morning by Haldane, and so did others in the company. To this day, the identity of the Marine who killed Middlebrook by mistake remains a well-guarded secret. Several surviving K/3/5 veterans told the author that they knew the man's name but, understandably, declined to reveal it.

11. NIGHTMARE ON NGESEBUS

Sources

To tell the story of the assault on Ngesebus in greater detail than it has been told before—and to weave into it the personal stories of men who took part in it—the author relied heavily on his interviews with Burgin, Leyden, Santos, Sarrett, and Womack. Additional information came from a previously videotaped interview with Leyden and an oral history by Mace.

An account of the attack directed by Burgin against the large Japanese pill-box also appears in Sledge's *With the Old Breed at Peleliu and Okinawa*. Other battle information is from Gailey's *Peleliu 1944,* Hough's *The Assault on Peleliu,* McMillan's *The Old Breed,* and Ross's *Peleliu: Tragic Triumph*.

12. PICKING SATAN'S POCKET

Sources

No surviving member of K/3/5 could have given as well-remembered and richly detailed an account of PFC Seymour Levy's final hours as his best buddy, Sterling Mace. Fortunately, Mace was willing to spend as much time and thought as necessary to provide the author with information about this period. But since Mace was elsewhere at the time Levy was killed, the author's interview with McEnery also provided vital details about the young Marine's death.

Other author interviews with Burgin and Ray Rottinghaus, plus a video-taped interview with the late Jay d'Leau and numerous details gleaned from Sledge's *With the Old Breed at Peleliu and Okinawa,* were essential in piecing together a coherent account of the confusing action in the Umurbrogol Pocket.

Among published sources, Hough's *The Assault on Peleliu* provided the most detailed overview of this phase of the fighting. Gailey's *Peleliu 1944,* Gayle's *Bloody Beaches,* Hallas's *The Devil's Anvil,* McMillan's *The Old Breed,* Ross's *Peleliu: Tragic Triumph,* and Sherrod's *The History of Marine Aviation in World War II* also contain useful information.

Notes

Page 250   *General Geiger, commander of the III Amphibious Corps:* Rupertus's response to Geiger is quoted in *Peleliu: Tragic Triumph* by Ross, who also quotes General Oliver Smith, assistant division commander, on the condition of those members of the Seventh Marines still on their feet. They were, Smith said, "beyond mere exhaustion . . . shot to pieces, beat to a pulp . . . fatigued to where the 'thousand-yard stare' was a common expression on their faces."

13. A STINKING, TIMELESS VOID

Sources

To capture the description-defying conditions on Peleliu in the latter stages of the battle for the Pocket, the author relied on personal interviews with Jim Anderson, Andrusko, Burgin, Dick Higgins, Mace, McEnery, Rousseau, and Womack.

Other key information for this comes from Andrusko's essay entitled "Black Angels on Peleliu" as well as from Sledge's *With the Old Breed at Peleliu and Okinawa,* Gailey's *Peleliu 1944,* Hough's *The Assault on Peleliu,* and Ross's *Peleliu: Tragic Triumph.*

An article in the McComb, Mississippi, *Enterprise-Journal* provided details on the 1941 Toy Bowl football game in which Womack starred and which he enjoyed recalling as a psychological escape from the monotonous agony in the Pocket.

Notes

Page 265   *There hadn't been as much demand for handheld flamethrowers:* In his monograph, *The Assault on Peleliu,* Hough notes that "the most important new weapon" to make its initial appearance on Peleliu was the long-range, amtrack-mounted flamethrower. "This performed yeoman service," he wrote, "yet the vulnerability of the LVT as a carrier for a purely offensive weapon proved a limiting factor throughout the operation. This came as no great surprise; the amtrack was simply the most practical vehicle to which this new device could be adapted in the short time available. With development of a mount suitable to the Sherman tank, the long-range flamethrower went on to play its highly useful part in subsequent operations."

Page 269   *Rupertus refused to yield:* The quotation in this paragraph from the division commander appears in Ross's *Peleliu: Tragic Triumph.*

Page 271   *reverse "the direction of all prior attacks":* The quotations in this and the following paragraph are taken from Hough's monograph, *The Assault on Peleliu.*

14. LOST LEADERS AND FALLEN FRIENDS

Sources

The remembrances of Marines who had come to know and revere Andy Haldane and Hillbilly Jones in ways unique to men who daily faced death together added immeasurable impact to the episodes in which both officers were killed. Even six decades afterward, these men's interviews with the author were charged with raw emotion, especially those of Anderson, Burgin, Higgins, and McEnery.

Several members of Jones's family provided invaluable background information on the guitar-strumming young lieutenant at the time of his death. These included Hillbilly's younger brother, John Jones; his sister, Anna Mosher; his sister-in-law, Marlyn Jones; and his late brother, Ken Jones, author of a family history pamphlet entitled "Everything Is Lovely and the Goose Is Hanging High." Hillbilly's last letter home, written on 10/9/44, the day before his death, was printed in its entirety in the pamphlet, as was the letter to Jones's mother from Chaplain Van Thompson explaining the circumstances of his death. Each contained facts that were unavailable from any other source. Official killed-in-action records on both Haldane and Jones were supplied by the Marine Corps Historical Center.

Additional information for this chapter came from author interviews with Sarrett and Santos. Sledge's reactions to Haldane's death, as detailed here, are recounted in his *With the Old Breed at Peleliu and Okinawa.*

Descriptions of the overall campaign against enemy forces in the Pocket during this period were provided by Gayle's *Bloody Beaches,* Hallas's *The Devil's Anvil,* Hough's *The Assault on Peleliu,* McMillan's *The Old Breed,* and Ross's *Peleliu: Tragic Triumph.*

Notes

Page 275   *In the words of one officer:* This quotation appears in Hough's monograph, *The Assault on Peleliu.* The officer is not identified.

Page 278   *When K/3/5 pulled back to a rear area:* The observations concerning Lieutenant Jones's feelings and actions at this time are based on his letter of 10/9/44, author interviews with relatives and former neighbors, and printed materials provided by his family.

15. LEGION OF THE ALMOST-DAMNED

Sources

The Marines' last bitter hours of combat on Peleliu, as witnessed through the eyes of those who struggled through them and survived, were re-created through author interviews with Andrusko, Burgin, Mace, Santos, and Womack. Others interviewed by the author for this chapter included Jackson, Leyden, Miller, and Pope.

Both d'Leau's videotaped interview and Sledge's *With the Old Breed at Peleliu and Okinawa* emphasize the bone-weariness of the survivors as they boarded ships to leave Peleliu, and Andrusko's memoir, *Love and War Beneath the Southern Cross,* describes how difficult it sometimes was to distinguish the living from the dead.

Other published sources providing information on the Marines' withdrawal from action and the Army's assumption of responsibility include Hough's *The Assault on Peleliu,* Gailey's *Peleliu 1944,* McMillan's *The Old Breed,* and Ross's *Peleliu: Tragic Triumph.*

Notes

Page 300   *When Geiger got the word, he breathed a deep sigh of relief. "I'm glad it's finally over":* Quoted from Ross's *Peleliu: Tragic Triumph.*

Page 300   *The new CO, a stranger who'd assumed command:* This un-named officer, a captain recently sent out from battalion headquarters, is mentioned in Andrusko's *Love and War Beneath the Southern Cross.* In an interview with the author, Andrusko also discussed the new CO but asked that his name not be published.

16. NEXT STOP: OKINAWA

Sources

Author interviews with Burgin, Dan Lawler, Leyden, Mace, McEnery, and Womack helped make it clear how the Old Breed managed to replenish its leadership ranks, rejuvenate its veterans, and initiate new members into the brotherhood in the interval between Peleliu and its next major test at Okinawa. Sledge also discusses this transitional process in *With the Old Breed at Peleliu and Okinawa.*

A newspaper article from the Bowdoin College Archives reported that an athletic field "somewhere in the Pacific" had been named in honor of Captain Haldane. Author interviews confirmed that the field was located on Pavuvu.

Sledge's *With the Old Breed at Peleliu and Okinawa* deals extensively with K/3/5's role in the battle for Okinawa, and author interviews with Burgin and Leyden lent a final touch of drama to conclude the wartime journeys of two of the main figures in this story.

Other published sources utilized in this chapter include Gailey's *Peleliu 1944,* Hough's *The Assault on Peleliu,* McMillan's *The Old Breed,* and Ross's *Peleliu: Tragic Triumph.*

Notes

Page 319   *Unaware that the dawn of the atomic age:* These estimates of American casualties in the event of an invasion of the Japanese homeland are contained in remarks entitled "Operation Downfall: U.S. Plans and Japanese Counter-Measures" by D. M. Giangreco during a 1998 symposium at the University of Kansas.

Page 332   *"This is expected to be the costliest amphibious campaign":* Quoted from Sledge's book, *With the Old Breed at Peleliu and Okinawa.*

Page 337   *When the battle was officially declared over:* These figures are cited by Sledge in *With the Old Breed at Peleliu and Okinawa.*

EPILOGUE

Sources

Author interviews with Burgin, Hanson, Jackson, Jenkins, Leyden, Mace, Mosher, Pope, Sarrett, and Womack produced most of the information presented—and opinions expressed—in the Epilogue.

Other sources include the Bowdoin College Archives, Gailey's *Peleliu 1944,* Hoffman's article "The Truth About Peleliu," McMillan's *The Old Breed,* Morison's *The Two-Ocean War,* and Richmond's *My Father's War.*

BIBLIOGRAPHY

BOOKS

Andrusko, Edward. *Love and War Beneath the Southern Cross*. Boulder, Colorado: Edward Andrusko, 2003.

Davis, Burke. *Marine!: The Life of Chesty Puller*. Boston: Little, Brown, 1962.

Davis, Russell. *Marine at War*. New York: Little, Brown, 1961.

Deen, Braswell D., Jr. *Trial by Combat*. Atlanta: Braswell Deen, 2000.

Gailey, Harry A. *Peleliu 1944*. Annapolis, Maryland: Nautical & Aviation Publishing, 1983.

Gayle, Gordon D. *Bloody Beaches: The Marines at Peleliu*. Washington, D.C.: Naval Institute Press, 1996.

Hallas, James H. *The Devil's Anvil: The Assault on Peleliu*. Westport, Connecticut: Praeger, 1994.

Heinl, Robert D., Jr. *Soldiers of the Sea: The United States Marine Corps, 1775–1962*. Annapolis: United States Naval Institute, 1962.

Hough, Major Frank O. *The Assault on Peleliu*. Washington, D.C.: Historical Division, U.S. Marine Corps, 1950.

Howard, Clive, and Joe Whitley. *One Damned Island After Another*. Chapel Hill: University of North Carolina Press, 1946.

Hunt, George. *Coral Comes High*. New York: Harper & Brothers, 1946.

Lea, Tom. *Peleliu Landing*. El Paso, Texas: C. Herzog, 1945.

Leckie, Robert. *Helmet for My Pillow*. New York: Random House, 1957.

———. *Strong Men Armed*. New York: Random House, 1962.

McMillan, George. *The Old Breed: A History of the First Marine Division in World War II*. Washington, D.C.: Infantry Journal Press, 1949.

Morison, Samuel Eliot. *History of United States Naval Operations in World War II*, Vol. 12. Boston: Little, Brown, 1958.

———. *The Two-Ocean War*. Boston: Little, Brown, 1963.

Richmond, Peter. *My Father's War: A Son's Journey*. New York: Simon & Schuster, 1996.

Ross, Bill D. *Peleliu: Tragic Triumph: The Untold Story of the Pacific War's Forgotten Battle*. New York: Random House, 1991.

Sherrod, Robert. *The History of Marine Aviation in World War II.* Washington, D.C.: Combat Forces Press, 1952.

Sledge, E. B. *With the Old Breed at Peleliu and Okinawa.* Novato, California: Presidio, 1981.

Smith, S. E. (ed.). *The United States Marine Corps in World War II.* New York: Random House, 1969.

Steinberg, Rafael. *Island Fighting.* Morristown, New Jersey: Time-Life Books, 1978.

Toland, John. *The Rising Sun.* New York: Random House, 1970.

PERIODICALS

Alexander, Joseph H. "Rifleman Sledge." *Leatherneck,* July 2001.

Andrusko, Edward "Black Angels on Peleliu," *Old Breed News,* June 1996.

"Boy Killed Riding Atop Subway Car." *New York Daily News,* June 19, 1938.

Conkey, Don. "Quincy War Hero Comes Home; Everett Pope Talks to NQS Students." Quincy, Massachusetts, *Patriot Ledger,* October 26, 2001.

Evans, R. A. "Infantillery on Peleliu." *Marine Corps Gazette,* January 1945.

"Funeral Arranged for Marine Hero." *Baltimore Evening Sun,* October 27, 1948.

"Haldane Field Named Overseas for 'Andy.'" Portland, Maine, *Press Herald,* March 9, 1945.

Hammel, Eric. "World War II: 50 Years Ago: Peleliu." *Leatherneck,* September 1994.

Hemingway, Al. "Island Without Mercy." *World War II Magazine* (special Pacific war edition), 2003.

Hoffman, Jon T. "The Truth About Peleliu." *Naval Institute Proceedings,* November 2002.

Link, Millie. "Pacific Campaign: Memories of a WWII Marine Infantryman— James C. Anderson." *Hay River Review,* Prairie Farm, Wisconsin, March 2002.

"Maine Friends Mourn Death of Famed Bowdoin Athlete." Brunswick, Maine, *Record,* November 5, 1944.

Martin, Robert. "Toughest Yet." *Time,* October 16, 1944.

O'Leary, Jeremiah A. "Hell in the Umurbrogol." *True,* October 1945.

Rothstein, Kevin. "Quincy Native, Veteran Shares Tales of Valor." Quincy, Massachusetts, *Patriot Ledger,* October 25, 2001.

Sledge, E. B. "Peleliu: Recollections of a PFC." *Leatherneck,* September 1983.

Talbert, Sara. "Young Soldier Proved to Be War Hero." Dublin, Texas, *Citizen,* April 10, 2003.

"Toy Bowl Champions Remembered." McComb, Mississippi, *Enterprise-Journal,* December 1, 1991.

Walt, Lewis. "The Closer the Better." *Marine Corps Gazette,* September 1946.

AUTHOR INTERVIEWS

Corporal Jim Anderson, May 2003

Corporal Edward Andrusko, April 2004

Mrs. Ted Barrow, June 2003

PFC Frank Batchelor, July 2003

Corporal Don Bishop, October 2003

Mrs. Rudy Bock, March 2003

PFC Edgar Brown, September 2003

Corporal R. V. Burgin, March 2003, June 2003, February 2004

Sergeant Jack Cannel, October 2003

PFC Joe Dariano, September 2003

Corporal Braswell Deen, January 2004

PFC Fred Fox, September 2003

PFC Jesse Googe, September 2003

Corporal Henry Hahn, June 2003

Corporal Wilfred Hanson, June 2003, August 2003

Sergeant Dick Higgins, April 2003

PFC Wayne Hook, June 2003

PFC Arthur Jackson, August 2003

Pharmacist's Mate Bill Jenkins, January 2004

Gary Jones, April 2004

John (Jack) Jones, April 2004

Marlyn Jones, April 2004

PFC Dan Lawler, January 2004

PFC William J. Leyden, April 2003, August 2003, January 2004

PFC Sterling Mace, August 2003, October 2003, March 2004

PFC James Mason, October 2003

Corporal Tom Matheny, March 2003

Sergeant Jim McEnery, June 2003, August 2003

Sergeant Fred Miller, May 2003

Anna (Jones) Mosher, April 2004

Ernest and Dorothy Neeper, May 2004

Captain Everett Pope, September 2003

PFC Ray Rottinghaus, July 2003

Corporal Matthew Rousseau, August 2003

Sergeant Richard Saldivar, November 2003

PFC Vincent Santos, May 2003

PFC George Sarrett, May 2003

Lieutenant Ray Stramel, October 2003

Corporal Charles Womack, June 2003, July 2003, March 2004

OTHER SOURCES

Corporal Jim Anderson. Videotaped oral history (courtesy Jim Anderson).

Corporal R. V. Burgin. Filmed interviews (courtesy R. V. Burgin).

PFC Jay d'Leau (deceased). Filmed interview (courtesy R. V. Burgin).

"Everything Is Lovely and the Goose Is Hanging High." Commemorative historical pamphlet written by Ken Jones and published by family of Lieutenant Ed Jones, October 1982 (courtesy John Jones).

PFC Fred Fox. Oral history (courtesy National Museum of the Pacific War).

D. M. Giangreco. "Operation Downfall: U.S. Plans and Japanese Counter-Measures." Remarks on plans for U.S. invasion of Japan during symposium at University of Kansas, February 16, 1998.

Captain Andrew A. Haldane. Collected letters. Bowdoin College Archives.

PFC Arthur J. Jackson. Medal of Honor citation.

PFC Roy R. Kelly (deceased). Filmed interview (courtesy R. V. Burgin).

"Know Your Enemy! Japanese Military Caves on Peleliu." Confidential CinC-Pac-CinCPOA Bulletin 173-45, July 1945 (declassified).

PFC Dan Lawler. Oral history (courtesy Dan Lawler).

PFC William J. Leyden. Filmed interview (courtesy William J. Leyden).

PFC Sterling Mace. Oral history (courtesy Sterling Mace).

Marine Corps Historical Center. Killed-in-action records.

Captain Everett P. Pope. Medal of Honor citation.

AUTHOR'S NOTE

I never knew Corporal Rudolph K. Bock. He died before I had a chance to meet him—or even contact him by phone—yet he was instrumental in making this book a reality. It might never have been written if I hadn't stumbled across Bock's name and photograph on the Internet in late February 2003 when *Brotherhood of Heroes* was nothing more than a vague idea, and I was urgently trying to locate Peleliu veterans for exploratory interviews.

Rudy Bock was the leader of a communications team from the First Battalion, First Marine Regiment, whose assignment was to lay wire for field telephones through an area of heavy enemy fire during the first precarious hours after the Marines landed on Peleliu. He braved vicious Japanese mortar fire to get the job done, and he was awarded the Bronze Star in recognition of his "daring initiative, outstanding courage, and unwavering devotion to duty in the face of grave personal risk."

I found a newspaper article about Bock on a Web site offering information on a recent Marine reunion. The article mentioned that he lived in Overland Park, Kansas, and I quickly found a phone number for him. But when I dialed the number, Bock's still grieving wife answered and told me that he'd died a couple of months earlier. However, she gave me the names of two other Marine veterans in the area who knew her husband well, and she was pretty sure that one or both had also served at Peleliu. That's how I managed to reach Sergeant Fred Miller of Kansas City, Kansas, a field-cook-turned-rifleman, who was severely wounded shortly after the D-Day landing on the island.

"I was only on Peleliu about an hour and a half," Miller said, "but I'll tell you the guy you need to talk to. R. V. Burgin was a mortar squad leader in my company, and he was there for the whole thing. He's also the secretary of the company veterans organization, and he sends out a quarterly newsletter to all the members. Burgy can put you in touch with a lot of other Peleliu Marines."

To my amazement, Miller told me that Burgin lived less than twenty miles from my home in Dallas. I'd found the end of a thread that eventually led me to dozens of other Peleliu veterans in all corners of the country. Most talked to me graciously, informatively, and at considerable length. A few declined for reasons that I totally understand and respect.

Brotherhood of Heroes is their story. Unfortunately, Rudy Bock isn't in it, but the story really started with him.

Despite the thousands of World War II veterans who pass from this mortal scene each month, their surviving comrades are still all around us. Most are quiet, grandfatherly men who blend into the fabric of their communities, often unnoticed by younger Americans who hurry past without really seeing them.

I was stunned to learn, in the summer of 2003, that a Peleliu veteran named Ted Barrow, who served with many of those I interviewed later and who could've been an invaluable resource, had lived within four or five blocks of me for more than twenty years. But he, too, had died before I realized he was there. Each time this happens, a window to the past slams shut, never to be reopened—and it happens with distressing regularity these days.

Within the rapidly thinning ranks of our World War II combat veterans lies the essence of America's unique greatness as a nation. To lose it would damage and diminish all of us. My hope is that *Brotherhood of Heroes* can help preserve that greatness by telling the individual stories of a few of these men, thereby passing to another generation the qualities represented by millions who fought against Nazi Germany and Imperial Japan.

Along the way, of course, I've encountered unavoidable gaps and kinks in this narrative thread. Among the most daunting was a dearth of information about Lieutenant Edward A. Jones, the popular and courageous young officer who was killed in action at Peleliu.

A gifted singer and musician affectionately known to his comrades as Hillbilly, Jones was fondly remembered by every surviving member of his Company K, Third Battalion, Fifth Marines, but no one even knew for sure where he was from. One previously published source gave Jones's home state as West Virginia, but that turned out to be an error. With assistance from the Marine Corps Historical Center, I eventually learned that Jones was actually from the tiny hamlet of Whiteford, Maryland. But even then, I couldn't find anyone who remembered him or his family.

Finally, after a weekly newspaper in nearby Delta, Pennsylvania, agreed to run an article on my search, I located a half-dozen relatives and former neighbors whose collective memories enabled me to bring a long-dead hero back to life. His sister, Anna (Jones) Mosher; his brothers John and Gary Jones; his sister-in-law, Marlyn Jones; and his childhood friends, Ernest and Dorothy Neeper, were especially kind and helpful. Because of them, the often frustrating hunt for the real Hillbilly Jones ended on a successful note. I believe most readers of this book will be as glad as I am that it did.

Many people in all corners of the country helped in piecing together the story of what happened at Peleliu in September and October 1944, as viewed through the eyes of a small group of men who were there. R. V. Burgin graciously devoted countless hours to answering my questions and providing important background and contact information on other veterans. So did Fred Fox, Wilfred "Swede" Hanson, Bill Leyden, Sterling Mace, Jim McEnery, and Charles "Red" Womack.

Through Leyden, I was able to get in touch with Arthur Jackson, one of two living Peleliu Medal of Honor winners, who talked with me candidly and at length about the battle and his role in it. Vincent Santos, George Sarrett, and Fred Miller also made time for lengthy one-on-one interviews and loaned me personal papers and pictures. Jim Anderson, Don Bishop, Joe Dariano, Wayne Hook, Matt Rousseau, Ray Stramel, and others also sent me important photos and documents by mail. In all, some thirty Peleliu veterans allowed me to interview them, either in person or by phone, and each of them gave me insights and interpretations that aren't available anywhere else.

Richard Lindemann, director of special collections and archives at the Bowdoin College Library in Brunswick, Maine, and Allyson Algeo of the college's public affairs office provided a wealth of background information on Captain Andrew A. Haldane, another exemplary officer who died on Peleliu.

Haldane, who commanded one of the companies on which the book focuses, was a Bowdoin graduate and former star of the college football team. The school's archives contain letters that Haldane wrote from the South Pacific that were vital in capturing his personality and character. Also indispensable were personal recollections gained during interviews with Everett Pope, Peleliu's other surviving Medal of Honor winner and a former Bowdoin classmate of Haldane's.

Jeff Hunt, curator of the National Museum of the Pacific War in Fredericksburg, Texas, and other members of the museum staff were extremely helpful in providing Peleliu battlefield photos from the museum's extensive collection.

Words of appreciation are also in order for the authors of two outstanding memoirs written much earlier by Marines who lived through the hell of Peleliu. The late George P. Hunt's *Coral Comes High*, published in 1946, and the late Eugene B. Sledge's *With the Old Breed at Peleliu and Okinawa*, which first appeared in 1981, are classics among books of their type. They not only offered close-up personal views of parts of the broader action I describe but also provided names of still living potential interviewees.

Others who played key roles in the making of this book include my wife, Lana Henderson Sloan, who always found time to edit my rough drafts and offer thoughtful criticism; my good friend, Floyd Wood, who willingly shared his vast and varied knowledge of World War II; my tireless agent, Jim Donovan, whose enthusiasm kept me going when my own threatened to fizzle; and my patient, perceptive editor at Simon & Schuster, Roger Labrie.

My gratitude extends to a multitude of people who helped in myriad ways. If I neglected to mention you here by name, please accept my apologies.

Bill Sloan
Dallas, Texas

INDEX

About the Author

Bill Sloan is a former investigative reporter and feature writer for *The Dallas Times Herald,* where he was nominated for the Pulitzer Prize. The author of nearly a dozen books, he lives in Dallas.